Organizational Communication

ORGANIZATIONAL COMMUNICATION

Foundations, Challenges, and Misunderstandings

Fifth Edition

Daniel P. Modaff • Jennifer A. Butler

University of Wisconsin – La Crosse

Bassim Hamadeh, CEO and Publisher
Todd R. Armstrong, Publisher
Sara Watkins, Developmental Editor
Michelle Piehl, Senior Project Editor
Abbey Hastings, Production Editor
Abbie Goveia, Junior Graphic Designer
Trey Soto, Licensing Specialist
Natalie Piccotti, Director of Marketing
Kassie Graves, Vice President of Editorial
Jamie Giganti, Director of Academic Publishing

This book was previously published by Pearson Education, Inc.

cognella® | ACADEMIC PUBLISHING
3970 Sorrento Valley Blvd., Ste. 500, San Diego, CA 92121

Brief Contents

Contents

PART II   Challenges and Misunderstandings

Preface

Communication is central to the existence of the organization; it creates and recreates the structure that constitutes the organization. That structure, in turn, affects the nature and flow of communication within it. Viewing organizational communication in this way illustrates the dynamic interrelationship between communicating and organizing, as well as the complexities of the process. It should be expected, then, that things can go wrong at any point in the communication process and often do. *Misunderstandings*—which we use as an umbrella term to connote the problematic nature of interaction in organizational settings (beyond just ineffective communication between members of an organization)—seem to characterize communication in organizations.

As organizations develop, both productive and unproductive features emerge, such as layers of hierarchy, opposing goals, struggles for power, use of technology, gender and cultural differences, reward systems, and control mechanisms. These features serve to complicate the communication process to such an extent that misunderstanding is as prevalent as understanding, if not more so. We center our perspective on the concept of misunderstandings. This focus positions communication at the center of organizational life and shows how and why communication can serve to create and resolve misunderstandings of all types and in every aspect of organizational functioning. *Organizational Communication: Foundations, Challenges, and Misunderstandings* explores organizational communication from the perspective of *all* organizational members, not just management. The fifth edition provides a foundational overview of the field and intersperses the discussions with excerpts from stories elicited from organizational members at all levels in a variety of organizations.

This book is written for an introductory course in organizational communication. In writing this book, we made several assumptions: (1) students will have had some previous course in communication; (2) the purpose of this course is to familiarize students with the basic elements of the field of organizational communication; (3) students will cover methodological and philosophical orientations of organizational communication more deeply in a subsequent advanced course. Given these assumptions, we had to make choices regarding content. For example, we have not included chapters on external organizational communication (e.g., public relations) or macro-organizational communication (e.g., organizational memory, life span). Our intention is to focus on internal communication and organizing issues that are on the organizational behavior level.

The title of the book describes our twofold intentions—to introduce basic concepts and to deal with misunderstandings. In Part I, we expose students to the foundations of organizational communication. Therefore, in the early chapters, we offer extensive discussions on the foundations of the discipline. Chapter 1 introduces students to the field of organizational communication and discusses the central organizing feature of the text—*misunderstandings*. Chapter 2 lays the foundation for the field by examining the classical management theories. Chapter 3 describes the progression from the classical theories to those based more on concern for individuals. We have chosen to treat the theories of human relations and human resources together in this chapter because they are so closely linked. Chapter 4 covers systems theory, which represents a shift from material dedicated to prescriptive theories of organizational communication and management to theories that provide an analytical framework. Chapters 5 and 6 continue with additional analytical frameworks for understanding communication in organizations—organizational culture and critical theory.

In Part II, we present challenges and misunderstandings, which underscore our particular approach to the field of organizational communication. Throughout Part II, we have attempted to frame the topics traditionally covered in organizational communication textbooks in terms of misunderstandings and to illustrate the relevant issues with excerpts from the stories gathered from organizational members. Chapter 7 explores the concept of realistic recruitment. We use it as the beginning of Part II to show that organizational communication is a process that begins even before an individual becomes an official member of the organization. Chapter 8 continues with the next step of the process, detailing the socialization of organizational members. Chapter 9 explores the relationship and communication between supervisors and subordinates. Chapters 10 and 11 examine communication in other important organizational relationships—among peers and within teams, respectively. Chapter 12, the final chapter, provides an overview of communication as it relates to leadership in organizational settings.

New to This Edition

In preparation for writing the fifth edition of this book, we gathered stories from organizational members both through an electronic questionnaire and student-conducted interviews. As a result, we were able to choose from close to 100 stories to weave throughout the book as a means of breathing life into and illustrating the concepts and theories discussed. These stories continued to reveal that a common theme of organizational life can be characterized by what we broadly term *misunderstandings*.

This edition of the book offers many changes that came about as a result of several different factors. First, the realities of modern organizational life, specifically the challenges brought forth by the pandemic, have led to more organizational members engaging in remote work, work-life balancing concerns, and challenges to supervision and leadership. We address these challenges throughout many of the chapters in this new edition and provide new stories to show how these challenges are communicatively managed in day-to-day life. Second, recent research in the field of organizational communication has revealed new perspectives on organizational life. As a result, we broadened our explorations of research related to communication via social media and other communication technology in different relational contexts, such as co-workers, supervisor-subordinate, and realistic recruitment. Fourth, we incorporated feedback from peer reviewers—both past and present—as well as from our students to further refine the content. Fifth, we integrated our coverage of diverse perspectives and voices regarding communication in organizations throughout the text rather than secluding them in a separate chapter. Considering all of these factors, we would like to highlight a few of the significant changes in this edition of the textbook. We achieved the following:

- Integrated all-new stories from organizational members throughout the book

- Increased the readability of the text by including fewer statistics and news stories and focusing more on the narratives regarding the research and experiences of the organizational members who supplied stories for the book

- Removed topics or reduced the coverage of areas of the field of organizational communication that have received less attention in the past decade or are less relevant than they used to be

- Simplified the opening chapter to focus on our definition of organizational communication, the concept of misunderstandings, and the primary theory of organizational communication—the communicative constitution of organizations

- Situated the growing literature on corporate social responsibility in Chapter 4, "Systems Theory"

- Expanded the coverage of diversity and discrimination and relocated it to Chapter 6, "Critical Theory"

- Strengthened Chapter 12, "Leaders and Leadership," with a section covering global perspectives on leading and leaders

Acknowledgments

This book would not have been possible without the help of many people. First, to the many reviewers throughout this book's various editions. For this fifth edition, we particularly thank Lisa Joniak Athearn (University of Florida), Marsha L. Bayless (Stephen F. Austin State University), Lisa V. Chewning (Penn State University—Abington), Suzy D'Enbeau (Kent State University), and Jeannette Kindred (Eastern Michigan State).

We would like to thank Todd Armstrong at Cognella for giving us the opportunity to pursue a fifth edition of this textbook in the way we envisioned it and Michelle Piehl from Cognella for her tireless energy and support as we navigated the challenges of writing during a pandemic.

Dozens of students from the University of Wisconsin—La Crosse served as interviewers for this edition. To preserve the anonymity of the organizational members that they interviewed, we will not name them here, but this book would not have been possible without them, and we appreciate their hard work on our behalf. We are also grateful to the dozens of anonymous contributors of stories via the electronic questionnaire we distributed through social media and professional networks.

Finally, thank you to Ryley Butler Modaff, John Modaff, Phil Modaff, and Mark Collins for their extraordinary help and support throughout the revision process.

We hope you enjoy reading this book as much as we enjoyed writing it.

Dan Modaff
Jennifer Butler

PART I

Foundations

Introduction

LEARNING OBJECTIVES

1. List the assumptions and features of the definition of organizational communication
2. Identify constructive outcomes of misunderstandings in organizational life
3. Explain why misunderstandings occur in organizations
4. Outline the response strategies to misunderstandings
5. Examine how the four flows model attempts to explain the relationship between organization and communication

Organizations are fascinating. We make our friends and our foes in them, meet our partners in them, lose sleep over them, strive to become a part of them, and rely on them for our livelihoods. We spend our lives in them. They are not living or breathing, yet we give them life through our participation in them. We treat them as if they are people, celebrating their accomplishments and berating their missteps. But what we sometimes lose sight of is that an organization is, when it comes down to it, a collection of people communicating with one another in pursuit of a common purpose. While the purposes vary from farming, to manufacturing, to social justice, to education, at the core of each organization is communication. Without that, we do not have organizations. And because of that, organizations are complex and complicated, full of problems but laden with potential.

Consider the following situation described by TreAnne Jackson, who began her position 6 months prior as a grants administrator for a small foundation in the southwestern United States. The foundation has a very stringent workplace culture and a top-down management style, which makes working cross-functionally (as is appropriate with grants) especially difficult:

> These past 6 months have been long with many challenges. One challenge relates to the lack of communication between program officers and finance regarding grant funds and contracts. Finance never sees a grant contract or grant application, so they are not often aware of the proper use of grant funding. My job has been to bridge that relationship, which has been met with resistance and suspicion from both

directions. Finance is uncertain about my queries into financial matters (i.e., grant expenditures). They believe this is confidential information. Programs are equally suspicious about my queries into grant expenditures, as they see grant monies as discretionary, instead of restricted, funding.

The lack of transparency across the organization about how and why grant monies can be spent has fueled my suspicions that we are engaging in some form of grant fraud. I shared my concerns with my immediate supervisor when I started my position. At first, she concurred with me and shared my concern. But about a month after we discussed these issues and the need for greater transparency, she did an abrupt about-face. She accused me of acting like an investigator who was trying to expose some big secret. She told me that I was alienating colleagues with all the questions I ask about grant spending. She requested that I allow her to lead me at this organization. So, fearful of losing a much-needed job, I discontinued asking questions about grant spending and became more passive, waiting for my supervisor to lead me. About this same time, I learned that my predecessor had quit the job because of perceptions of grant fraud and that the position was filled with a grant writer who stayed only 2 weeks once learning about the grant fraud.

I would like to say that my supervisor has started leading me, but alas, that has not happened. What has happened, though, is that I have started building stronger relationships with my colleagues. COVID, working from home, and just a general desire to connect with other people have brought us together in some interesting ways. As an outcome, I have found that more colleagues have reached out to me for my grants work and have been more transparent about their projects. I can say that we are genuinely friends. Last week, I was particularly busy. I worked about 50 hours, and colleagues from all areas were reaching out to have me assist with their projects. I decided to update my supervisor on this positive turn via a Microsoft Teams message:

Me: I've been so popular this week. It feels good.

Supervisor: Is that good or bad?

Me: Good. I can see that my colleagues are really recognizing how I can be a resource for them.

In a recent check-in meeting with my supervisor, she asked me to clarify my comments about being popular at work. An important piece of context is that this is all during the civil rights movement that is unfolding due to the police murder of George Floyd in Minneapolis. I explained that I had been talking with my colleagues and that it seemed like my colleagues were seeing me as a resource.

Then my supervisor asked me, "Are you organizing your colleagues to do something?"

I responded, "About what?"

She explained that she interpreted my message as being about me seeing myself as an expert on racial matters and the civil unrest and that she was concerned I was organizing my colleagues to take some sort of action. I was confused. I replied that I was not doing so. I affirmed that many colleagues were chatting via Microsoft Teams about the civil rights movement that was unfolding, indicating that they feel sad and scared, yet hopeful. I assured her that was not something I was leading but rather that people were reaching out to one another as you would a friend—that is, to show care and concern. I then returned to my original message to her and explained that I felt the first couple of months of my employment were somewhat vexed and that it felt promising to see how I was creating relationships with my colleagues and being seen as a resource for their projects. I indicated that I was hopeful that the transparency I so strongly believed in would follow now that my relationships were stronger.

Our phone call ended, and I have not heard from her since, yet I remain confused about the dots she was connecting between my feeling as though I am making greater contributions to my colleagues' work and that of being a conspirator who is seeking to organize colleagues to take some sort of social action related to civil rights.

TreAnne's situation shows the realities of the modern workplace. Organizational culture, management style, organizational teams, distrust of new employees and other organizational departments, transparency of decision making, dissent regarding perceptions of unethical organizational practices, relational development with coworkers, remote work, online communication, impacts of sociocultural events, and a host of other issues came to bear on this organizational situation. Many perspectives could be taken to understand this situation and others like it, but none address the core issue from which the others arise—communication.

This lived example reveals the centrality of communication to life in organizations. TreAnne was hired to bridge a gap in communication between two departments in the organization—program officers and finance. When she sought to establish that communication through what she felt was diligent information seeking, she was met with distrust and suspicion. Upon communicating her concerns to her supervisor, TreAnne was eventually responded to negatively, with claims that she was overstepping her bounds and attempting to usurp her supervisor's authority to lead. TreAnne felt disconnected, confused, and left to wonder about her place in the organization.

Soon, through positive communication, TreAnne began to build relationships with her coworkers and earn their trust; she began to feel valued as an organizational member as they relied on her input regarding organizational, as well as external, sociocultural issues. When she communicated what she felt was a positive change in her situation to her supervisor via an online messaging system, she was met with more suspicion and additional claims of her engaging in harmful behavior. While communication with her coworkers has improved as has the transparency of the grant expenditure process, communication with her supervisor has halted, and she is left to wonder about what is coming next. As this situation demonstrates, communication is not only something that happens in the organization, but it also produces and reproduces the patterns of action in organizations that construct the experiences of the organizational members. Said another way, "Our organizing communication creates *organizations*—entities to whose authority we then surrender" (Nicotera, 2020, p. 3).

A communication-centered approach to the study of organizations is the basis of the field of organizational communication. It is our intention in this book to provide you with an overview of the field of organizational communication and to demonstrate the critical role communication plays in almost every aspect of organizational life. Much as a microscope can help the scientist to see the building blocks of life in a drop of blood, an intense focus on communication allows us to understand that it is the lifeblood of organized human activity.

Defining the Study and Practice of Organizational Communication

Organizational communication as a discipline seeks to help people understand the central nature of communication in all aspects of organizational functioning. The English word *organization* comes from the Greek word *organon*, which means "tool" or "instrument." Communication is both the means by which that tool or instrument (the organization) is created and sustained *and* the prime coordinating mechanism for activity designed to attain personal and organizational goals. Hence, communication and organization are intimately interrelated.

The definition of organizational communication that we propose is a slightly modified version of one developed by Jablin (1990a). According to our definition, **organizational communication** is the process of creating, exchanging, interpreting (correctly or incorrectly), and storing messages within a system of human interrelationships. Central to this definition is the concept of a message. A **message** (loosely based on Stohl & Redding, 1987) is a use of a symbol or symbols (written, spoken, or nonverbal) that the recipient interprets as having been created intentionally. The focus on symbol use becomes important as a means of differentiating the study of organizational communication from related fields, such as management and industrial psychology, and as we develop the central feature of the text—misunderstandings.

Inherent in the definition of organizational communication are several assumptions and features:

- Communication is central to the existence of the organization; it creates and recreates the structure that constitutes the organization. That structure, in turn, affects the nature and flow of communication within it.

- Organizational communication as "process" indicates its dynamic nature. The concept of process implicates the past, present, and future such that communication within an organization at a particular moment in time is dependent on prior conditions, as well as expectations for the future. For example, a particular interaction between a superior and a subordinate at a given point in time (the present) is related to their prior interactions and interactions with other superiors and subordinates (the past) and their expectations for how they will interact in the future.

- Communication involves more than the physical act of exchanging messages. Communication is an inherently complex process that also includes the energy associated with creating, exchanging, interpreting, and storing messages.

- Things can go wrong at any point in the communication process and often do. Throughout this book, we will refer to this very broadly as "misunderstandings." The concept of misunderstandings, as used here, involves more than ineffective communication between members of an organization; it is an umbrella term used to connote the problematic nature of interaction in organizational settings.

- Misunderstandings seem to characterize communication in organizations. As organizations develop, both productive and unproductive features emerge, such as layers of hierarchy, opposing goals, struggles for power, use of technology, gender and cultural differences, reward systems, and control mechanisms. These features serve to complicate the communication process to such an extent that misunderstanding is as prevalent as understanding, if not more so.

Researchers in organizational communication study the various elements associated with our definition by focusing on different organizational contexts, concepts, and relationships. Organizational communication researchers Mumby and Stohl (1996) pointed out that a common theme among all of these concepts and research activities is language: "The use of language as a symbolic means of inducing cooperation in beings that by nature respond to symbols, constitutes our disciplinary foundation . . . a concern with collective action, agency, messages, symbols, and discourse" (p. 53). How messages are sent and understood, through the use of language, forms the basis of communication study in general and organizational communication specifically. For this reason, we offer a message-centered definition of organizational communication and integrate issues of the creation, exchange, interpretation, and storage of messages throughout the text.

As students of organizational communication, you are particularly ready to meet the demands of the contemporary workplace. You are "trained to focus on the complex and collaborative nature of communicating, organizing, and knowing" (Mumby & Stohl, 1996, p. 54). These skills—communicating, organizing, and knowing—are central to effective membership in any organizational setting. As partial evidence of this, the *Job Outlook 2020* study conducted by the National Association of Colleges and Employers showed that communication-centered skills such as ability to work in a team, leadership, and written and verbal communication topped the list of important candidate qualifications. Communication skills included the ability to work in face-to-face settings, as well as in virtual environments.

In this initial chapter, we introduce issues and concepts that provide the foundation for the chapters that follow. We begin with an introduction to the central feature of this book: the concept of misunderstandings. We use the concept of misunderstanding as a lens through which we examine the concepts, theories, and practices presented throughout the text. We conclude the chapter with an overview of the communication-centered approach to understanding the relationship between communication and organizations—communicative constitution of organizations.

Misunderstandings and Organizational Life

The central idea of this book is that organizational life is inherently problematic and that communication plays a major role in the creation and resolution of this quality. As the number of people in an organization increases, the following phenomena also tend to occur:

- More levels of hierarchy *or* more work teams with more members
- Cultural, age, sex, gender, religious, political, and value differences
- Struggles for power
- Emergence of sub- and counter-organizational cultures
- Competition among peers for scarce resources
- Monitoring of employee behavior and technology use

As you can see from this much-abbreviated list, organizational life, almost by definition, is fraught with problems in human interaction.

We have chosen the term **misunderstandings** to represent the inherently problematic nature of organizational life. We consider misunderstandings to include situations in which features of organizational life (such as those just listed) serve to impinge on the efficient and effective functioning of organizational members. We chose the term *misunderstandings* because it highlights the central nature of communication.

Our use of the term *misunderstandings* is in no way meant to oversimplify the complicated nature of organizational functioning. While some organizational problems are caused by a true lack of shared meaning between organizational members because of the limits and constraints of language, even more are related to deeper organizational characteristics. Consider the following story from Nellie, a career coach at Point Pleasant University. Although on the surface it may seem to be an instance of an ineffective supervisor, the problem is much deeper and is related to many issues, including a lack of organizational socialization efforts, low organizational identification, an organizational culture that tolerates abusive communication, and insufficient interorganizational coordination.

> After relocating to a new state for my job, I was eager to start my new position as a career coach at Point Pleasant University. On my first day, I had not been contacted about onboarding, training, parking, or where my office was located on campus. Being new to the area and never having been on campus, I was concerned by the lack of communication from my supervisor. Through my own efforts, I found the office and was awkwardly greeted by someone at the front, whom I found out was my supervisor. We met in her office and talked about my first day. I was told to simply set up my office, as no training had been arranged for me aside from the HR training I had participated in earlier. I felt disappointed but wanted to continue being positive about the experience and hoped communication would be better moving forward.
>
> Within that first week, I experienced my supervisor arguing with my coworker after she had shown me around campus. My supervisor openly scolded my coworker in the hall, expressing that she shouldn't have brought me across campus and needed to get work done. I remember feeling embarrassed and uncomfortable that my supervisor would openly scold another employee in the hallway, especially when that person was just trying to make me as a new employee feel welcome and help me navigate campus.
>
> Shortly thereafter, I found out from my coworker that she had been accosted in private by my supervisor for disagreeing about how to approach marketing in the office. My coworker expressed that she felt belittled and bullied in the conversation, and she went back to her office to cry after the interaction. In group meetings with my supervisor, she would often become aggressive when team members would express different ideas from the way we were currently doing things and when team members would disagree with her point of view. It often had passive-aggressive undertones, and she would always use "well in my experience . . . " or "in the past, we've done . . . " to try and justify why she was right and to stop team members from being able to express new ideas or disagreement.

Over time, our meetings became silent environments in which we felt we couldn't speak up for fear of receiving passive-aggressive communication or judgment of our ideas. It led to decreased morale and increased communication issues within our team.

In a meeting with the new director of career services, I was asked about concerns I had with my team and the office. I expressed my concerns about my supervisor's communication style and the way it impacted the team and culture of the office. The director listened to my feedback and explained that she did not envision someone who created a negative culture and communicated in a negative way would be able to survive in the culture she hoped to establish in the office. She alluded that the person would either need to change or would be removed.

Fast-forward 6 months later, and my supervisor has just returned after a 2-month leave of absence (about which no reason was given). In our most recent team meeting, she once again expressed passive-aggressive communication regarding our team wanting to change the survey that we were using to assess our services provided to students. Our team brought up that it would be helpful to condense the survey into fewer questions with a focus on a specific goal so that we know why we're doing the assessment and to make it easier for students to take. Immediately, she got defensive and questioned why we wanted to change it and that it has been effective in the past, so it doesn't make sense to change it. The same "in the past, we've done . . . " excuse she has used over and over again. The energy on our team suddenly shifted, and everyone went quiet.

The breakdown of communication isn't only present on our team but in the entire unit. No one knows what people on the other teams do, what our goals are as a unit, how we are supposed to work toward those goals, etc. It leaves people in a state of perpetual confusion and a small group of us often discuss how challenging it is to work in this environment. Although it is not the only reason, the poor communication on my team and in the office as a whole is a large part of why I am leaving to work at a different university.

Although on the surface, Nellie's account may seem to be a "simple" case of miscommunication, the misunderstandings associated with it were much more complicated than that. An examination of the narrative shows that several issues were at play:

- There was an organizational culture that was not tolerant of change and seemed to breed separation of work tasks and relationships rather than encouraging collaboration.

- Nellie's supervisor was a micromanager who was concerned more with protecting her power base than the effective and ethical functioning of the foundation.

- Few if any efforts to socialize new employees into the organization were made, leaving organizational members to learn the ropes on their own.

- Information was not shared among interdependent work teams, making it difficult to coordinate efforts and fostering an environment of distrust.

Although these were certainly not the only issues relevant to this case, it is obvious that this misunderstanding was not merely a matter of a lack of shared meaning; it was much more complex than that. When we use the term *misunderstandings* in this book, we are referring to situations such as this one.

We propose that misunderstandings should be expected and considered to be normal. By "normal" we do not intend to imply that misunderstandings are acceptable and always manageable or without consequence. Instead, it is important to approach misunderstandings from two simultaneous orientations. At the broad level, we should enter the organization expecting there to be problems—that is a natural consequence of organizational life. On the day-to-day level, though, we will, of course, often be surprised by or disappointed when misunderstandings occur. Despite misunderstandings being normal, there could very well be negative consequences for individuals and the organization depending on their nature, extent, and handling. The hope is that misunderstandings can be managed in such a way that they lead to alternative task structures and roles, help members consider new ways of acting, or aid in creative problem solving.

Structuration theory (discussed later in this chapter) supports our claim that misunderstandings are a natural part of organizational life. The connection between structuration and misunderstandings is clearest in three ways. First, structuration theory highlights the centrality of communication and interaction in organizational life. Communication theorists and everyday practitioners know that communication is inherently messy and that as people muddle through their days using language and symbols to express their feelings and ideas, misunderstandings (linguistic, pragmatic, cultural, and otherwise) are prevalent. Acknowledging the central role of communication in the production and reproduction of organizational structures is also an acknowledgment that misunderstandings will occur. Second, if organizational members do indeed have choices (agency) in organizational life, then the possibilities of individual member's choices and actions being in sync with each other are low. This reality will necessarily lead to situations where members are at odds with one another, either philosophically or pragmatically, which causes misunderstandings. Third, as members enact their agency, they will produce unintended consequences. These unintended consequences are almost by definition misunderstandings because the consequences of their actions were neither intended nor could be controlled.

Constructive Outcomes From Misunderstandings

While the consequences of misunderstandings can certainly be problematic, there can be constructive outcomes as well, depending on how the organizational members respond. Three constructive outcomes are (1) new ways of structuring tasks and roles, (2) alternative ways of acting, and (3) creative problem solving.

First, misunderstandings can lead to *new ways of structuring tasks and roles*. In one case, we worked with a leadership team that had very clearly defined roles—each member knew what the other was supposed to do and what they were responsible for themselves. Because their roles were so clearly defined, no one would dare suggest a change in an area not specifically assigned to them. A new boss, without knowledge of these clearly defined roles, assigned tasks to this group that crossed previously defined lines of authority. At first, there was confusion and anxiety, but a fresh look at operations identified ineffective practices that the team simply did not see. A number of changes in practices occurred, and roles were redefined with more flexible boundaries. Input was encouraged from all areas rather than being discouraged as it had been before when no one wanted to step on someone else's territory.

Second, misunderstandings can also help people to consider *alternative ways of acting*. One supervisor frequently worked on electronic communication on the weekend because he traveled during the week. He had a habit of sending emails to employees late at night while he was working. He did not expect answers until the employee was in the office during the week. The employees misunderstood this practice and thought it meant they should come into the office on the weekend to do the research in order to answer the emails being sent. This caused frustration as the email traffic increased during nonworking hours. When the supervisor noticed that he was receiving emails back at unusual times, he finally mentioned to one of the employees that he had not expected an answer until later in the week. He discovered the misunderstanding and the implicit message he was sending. Two behaviors changed: the supervisor stopped sending so many messages on the weekend, and when he had to send messages, he made it clear that he did not expect an immediate answer. This improved the climate in the office and gave everyone, including the supervisor, a little more sense of down time away from the job during nights and weekends.

Finally, misunderstandings can lead to *creative problem solving*. For example, three science department supervisors misunderstood budget numbers. In this case, the supervisors misunderstood communication from the budget officer. They thought the budgetary allocation for certain chemicals was listed for the year when in fact the allocation was per quarter. They actually had more money available than they thought, but when they talked to the budget officer, they misunderstood. They thought they confirmed their worst fears: they would not have enough money to cover the cost of the chemicals they needed. Meanwhile, the budget officer thought they were simply complaining that they were not given more money. The supervisors began to examine their budget, looking for any unnecessary expenditures that they could eliminate that were less important than buying the chemicals. After careful analysis, they were able to eliminate some expenditures that, given the alternative, did not seem that important after all. They moved money from one category (visiting speakers) to another (purchase of chemicals) and were able to buy the chemicals. When they discovered their misunderstanding and realized they actually had saved money in the budget, they were able to buy a piece of equipment that they had been arguing for but were told previously there simply were no funds for it. In this case, the misunderstanding led to a creative solution for the needs of this department.

Why Misunderstandings Occur

We would also like to examine the reasons that misunderstandings occur so that organizational members can be prepared for them. We have identified three typical reasons for misunderstandings to occur in organizations: (1) conflict in values, (2) lack of information, and (3) strategic misinterpretations. We know there are many more reasons but offer these as a starting point for the discussion and invite you to add your own.

Misunderstandings may result from a *conflict in values*. Such conflict may involve (1) a disparity between individual and organizational values or (2) the suppression of a marginalized member's contributions. Misunderstandings that occur because of a disparity between individual and organizational values are not likely to be resolved easily, if at all. For example, there was a graduating college senior who was getting desperate for a job. She was very bright and motivated but was having difficulty finding a position that used her skills. A job came open with an organization in her hometown that endorsed social and religious values that were quite different from her own values; however, the position for which they wanted her was perfect. She took the job but regularly found she was uneasy with the nature of the events that she was responsible for planning. She talked to her boss, but her boss would only tell her, "That's what we do here." More conversation will not necessarily resolve this situation for the new employee.

Communication strategies can, however, help people cope with an inability to change the situation. Although communication is not likely to dramatically change a person's basic values, organizational members should recognize the fact that these differences will be present. These opportunities can also push members into creative problem-solving frameworks to contain the differences and limit their negative impact.

Misunderstandings based on a conflict of values also occur when particular "voices" are not valued within an organization. Organizational members from marginalized groups, in particular, are faced with situations in which their contributions are not given due consideration, either intentionally or unintentionally. As members of these traditionally underrepresented groups begin to occupy more and varied positions within organizations, members are confronted with the reality of interacting with people different from themselves. Some organizational cultures explicitly value the contributions of dominant groups while devaluing those of marginalized members. Other organizational cultures, although willing and open to change their deeply entrenched values to include the contributions of members from marginalized groups, might unintentionally suppress the contributions of these members by relying on standard modes of operation. Either way, problems or misunderstandings arise.

Misunderstandings may also be caused by a *lack of information.* This is a broad category that encompasses many situations. Some of the most common are (1) intentional and unintentional suppression of information to newcomers, (2) interruption of the chain of communication because of geographic separation, (3) information gaps resulting from hierarchical or functional differences, and (4) removal of information cues with the use of communication technology.

First, misunderstandings may result from intentional or unintentional suppression of information to newcomers. As we discuss in Chapter 8, when a person enters an organization for the first time or begins a new role in her present organization, she often experiences a sense of information deprivation (Miller & Jablin, 1991). This information deficit can be the result of either unintentional or intentional circumstances. At times, established members in the organization may simply forget what it was like to be a newcomer and, as a result, not remember everything a newcomer does not know but should be told. This unintentional circumstance may lead to a lack of information for the newcomer and subsequent misunderstandings. For example, we have a colleague who started work and was never told where the mailboxes were; he figured someone would tell him soon. After several days, he still did not know and at that point was afraid to ask for fear of looking dumb. In the meantime, several important documents were put in his box that needed immediate attention. Phone calls started coming in from his new boss and colleagues asking why he had not replied. Misunderstandings arose because of a lack of information caused by unintentional circumstances.

At other times, a lack of information may be the result of intentional circumstances. As we discuss in Chapter 7, organizational representatives often neglect potentially negative information and overstate positive information about a job or position when recruiting potential organizational members. As the newcomer begins work, the reality of organizational life sets in, and the newcomer senses the lack of information. For example, we know a person who was heavily recruited for a sales position. During recruitment, he was told of the wonderful people with whom he would be working, the great potential for financial gain, and the travel opportunities. The recruiter failed to tell him that he would be working 6 days a week, at least 12 hours a day. The newcomer assumed that he would be working a traditional nine-to-five, 5-day workweek and behaved in that manner for the first few days. He was eventually called into his boss's office and told that if he did not shape up, he would be fired. The newcomer was shocked to hear that he had done something wrong and quickly changed his behavior.

Although a lack of information can result from recruiting practices, it can also occur after the newcomer begins work. Organizational incumbents often test newcomers by intentionally not supplying them with the information they need or by communicating ambiguous messages (Jablin, 2001). This is often a matter of trust. Incumbents are often unwilling to share pertinent information with a person whom they do not yet trust.

Second, misunderstandings can occur when organizational members work in different physical locations. As organizations grow larger and more workers engage in remote work, not all members will be present in the same physical location. Whether separated by floors, miles, or continents, members often encounter misunderstandings because of differing communication experiences. Consider the following example told to us by Walt, a regulatory affairs manager:

> Our office space was recently moved to a new building, which had an open office seating environment—no walls, offices, or other separations to allow for the feeling of individual space. This was intended to create a more collaborative environment. But the open seating office space environment was complicated by another corporate initiative—flexible work schedules. This included allowing employees to work from home. Many employees, including me, now take advantage of that; however, this prevents leveraging any benefits that an open office space could provide, as the employees are now sitting at home completely disengaged from the face-to-face environment.

Walt's situation points to how physical separation can lead to exclusion from the important communicative activities that often happen when people are physically located together in the workplace. In Walt's open office environment, space is available for members to casually interact, and in those interactions, decisions are made, alliances formed, feelings of solidarity manifested, and information relayed. When some of the members are working remotely, however, they are not part of these spontaneous communicative interactions, and misunderstandings could emerge as a result. Interestingly, the source of misunderstanding described by Walt is also a function of a conflict of values reflected in two organizational policies that work against each other despite the good intentions of each separate policy.

Third, misunderstandings can be caused by information gaps resulting from hierarchical or functional differences. As we discuss in Chapter 9, there is often a gap in information between supervisor and subordinate caused by differing levels of responsibility and knowledge. Supervisors are often privy to the "bigger picture" in organizations because they are responsible for more aspects of organizational functioning than are the subordinates. This gap in information can lead to negative feelings because the supervisor may not recognize that the subordinate does not have access to the same information and the overall picture. This is what happened to Shannon, who works in the therapeutic recreation department of a children's hospital:

> A few weeks ago, my colleague Krista and I were approached by directors of the organization's media and communications team to be featured in a video that would promote creative ideas on what recreation activities children and their families can participate in at home due to the safer-at-home order. This was requested by the communications director in email format and was sent to our direct supervisor and our department

manager, and I was CCd. Permission was granted by both our direct supervisor, Penny, and the department manager for us to proceed. No other questions or concerns were exchanged in this email, so I responded that I would be happy and excited to participate in promoting our field and would communicate with Penny when it would be taking place. It was indicated in the email that the media team would like both myself and Krista to participate. The goal of the communications team was to create the video by the end of the week, so we scheduled it to be filmed the following day. I emailed Penny and informed her of the when, where, who, and place. After the video was broadcasted on social media and our organization's page, Penny held a meeting with Krista and me, stating that she was upset about how much detail we went into explaining the thera-peutic benefits of each activity and that it stepped on other departments' toes (such as, psychology and child life specialists). Penny shared with us how she has had to now deal with the wave of problems we created.

Shannon experienced the gap in information that exists between supervisor and subordinate and the problems that can cause when one or both parties do not rec-ognize it. In this situation, Shannon's supervisor, Penny, may have assumed that she and Krista understood what their limits should have been in the video, but she did not communicate those expectations. Shannon assumed that since her supervisor did not bring up any concerns in the email chain that she was cleared to proceed as she saw fit. These assumptions, based on differing levels of knowledge of the larger organizational picture, led to a misunderstanding.

Finally, misunderstandings may occur as information cues are removed or altered with the use of communication technology. Fran, a senior data administrator for a marketing research firm, told us the following story that illustrates this point:

Since COVID, we work from home—most of our company works from home, but we don't have the video part, so we usually just communicate through audio, so we lose a lot of facial expressions. When you're training somebody, it is important to see their face or how their facial expressions are because you can tell from that if they are understanding the content of the training or not.

Fran's story demonstrates that when communication media other than face-to-face are employed, important elements of the communication process may become muted or absent. For instance, when technologies are used that only include voice, important nonverbal and physical aspects such as eye movement, facial expressions, and gestures are absent. As a result, the participants are left to fill in the blanks, so to speak, and this lack of information may lead to misunderstandings. For Fran, she was not receiving immediate feedback from her trainees because she could not see their facial expressions. As a result, she may have made assumptions about their under-standing that could have negative consequences in the future. Even in situations where more visual cues are incorporated into the technology (e.g., video conferencing), the communication cues available are still limited and may lead to misunderstandings caused by the lack of information inherent in their use.

We have observed individuals who want to misunderstand the message purposely because it benefits them in some way—we refer to this as **strategic misinterpretation**. For instance, Talley is a 22-year-old certified nursing assistant who had been working for her organization for 2.5 years and decided she needed to quit:

> It was in November, and I told my boss that I would be working only until December 1, and she basically said, "Okay that's fine," and "We are going to miss you." So, I worked my hours every week after I told her I was going to be quitting, and I did what I was supposed to until December 1. Then I emailed her, and I said, "Let me know the exit process and how it works." She emailed me back, and she said, "Can you come into the office," and I did. When I was there, she said, "Well you didn't sign your two weeks' resignation form," and I had no idea about this resignation form or anything. And I am a full-time student and working as a bartender, and I just started other classes, so I really had no time to finish my two weeks. She said I could go unavailable for three months, which was fine, but she said after the three months, I have to come back in and work another two weeks. So, I am technically still working for them because I have not completed my last two weeks due to COVID. This is ridiculous because I told her before that I did not want to work after December 1, and she should have told me about the two weeks' notice then. It made me feel like I was being used in a sense because I know they are short on staff because not a lot of people enjoy doing this kind of work. I feel like she was using me for my hours and trapping me in this job that I did not plan on working for more than a few years.

While there are certainly many factors at play here, Talley seems to have been the victim of a strategic misinterpretation by her boss regarding the time line and process for her exiting the organization. Talley communicated her time line, asked about the exit process, and followed up appropriately. Her boss, though, seemed to have strategically misinterpreted the situation to keep Talley employed with the organization as staffing was a concern. While strategic misinterpretations do not always carry with them such heavy ethical implications, in this particular case, the strategic misinterpretation by Talley's boss surely does.

The preceding sources of misunderstandings in organizations are in no way exhaustive. We invite you to consider additional sources of misunderstandings as you read the following chapters. Our intention in this section was to illustrate the prevalence of misunderstandings in organizations and their sources.

Responding to Misunderstandings

Misunderstandings have the potential to develop into conflict, depending on the nature of the misunderstanding and the circumstances surrounding it. Just as in our personal relationships, workplace misunderstandings that develop into conflict can make employees miserable and less productive or can be the impetus for creative change. When one is enmeshed in a conflict, the possibility of creative change may seem far-fetched, and indeed, it sometimes can be impossible. However, with energy, anticipation, and communication, new ways of thinking, acting, believing, or feeling can emerge. Knowing how to respond to misunderstandings is an important part of organizational life. Misunderstandings are a natural component of organizational life and as such should be expected and planned for. The lack of an appropriate response could cause the misunderstanding to develop into conflict. In this section of the chapter, we discuss different communicative responses to misunderstandings and how those responses are related to different levels of learning.

The overarching principle for all members when it comes to responding to misunderstandings actually occurs upon entry to an organization. Organizational members should recognize that organizational life is inherently problematic and characterized by misunderstandings. It is the obligation of every organizational member to recognize misunderstandings as they occur and acknowledge their impact. If organizational members can recognize that misunderstandings will naturally occur in any organizational situation, then their occurrence will not be paralyzing. Instead, depending on the strategy used to respond to them, they may be made manageable or could possibly lead to individual and/or organizational learning.

The first strategy for addressing misunderstandings is to **contain** the problem or misunderstanding so that its negative impact is minimal. No energy is put into dealing with the emotional or pragmatic needs of those involved in the misunderstanding. When time or resources are limited, organizations may choose this strategy. In addition, if the organization does not want to draw attention to itself or the misunderstanding, it may choose this strategy because it stops the problem and then continues with status quo operations. For example, when one of our interviewee's employees was caught stealing from the cash register, he chose to contain the situation by firing the employee in question, immediately hiring a new employee, and not discussing the situation with the rest of the workers.

The second strategy is to **cope** with the communication problem or misunderstanding, which means dealing with the present situation and allowing all affected members to express their concerns and have their problems addressed. This strategy takes more time and resources to address the human resources involved in the situation. For example, when a beloved assistant pastor of a large Southern church was discovered to be addicted to drugs, and it was learned that he had been stealing from the church to support his habit, the church used the coping strategy. They relieved the assistant pastor of his duties but also paid for him to go to drug rehabilitation. The pastor took time out of a regular Sunday service to address the issue and hear the concerns and emotions of the congregation. This strategy allowed those affected to cope with their feelings regarding this very difficult situation.

The final strategy is to **construct** a new interpretation of the misunderstanding so that learning can occur; in particular, new attitudes, values, behaviors, or practices could emerge. The use of this strategy requires that the misunderstanding be addressed; that the affected organizational and environmental members are allowed to express their concerns, emotions, and ideas; and that the individuals and organization somehow change as a result of the process. For example, in 1982, seven people in the Chicago area were killed when they unknowingly ingested Tylenol Extra Strength capsules laced with cyanide. Once it became clear that the cyanide-laced capsules were the issue, the maker of Tylenol, Johnson & Johnson, immediately alerted the public throughout the nation via the media not to consume Tylenol until further notice. They also stopped production of all Tylenol products and suspended advertising. In addition, they recalled all Tylenol products from the market. If Johnson & Johnson would have stopped there, they would have engaged in the coping strategy because they addressed the problem and allowed the affected public and employees to express their concerns. However, over the next several months, Johnson & Johnson rethought their product packaging and as a result changed the way they and the industry packaged many goods. Later that year, Tylenol was back on the shelves, but this time with tamper-resistant packaging that would make attempts to alter the product evident. In response to this tragedy, Johnson & Johnson engaged in the construct strategy, which allowed the company to rebound and the consumers to have safer products.

We conceptualize these responses to misunderstandings in terms of a continuum, with contain, cope, and construct as different strategies for dealing with misunderstandings (see Figure 1.1).

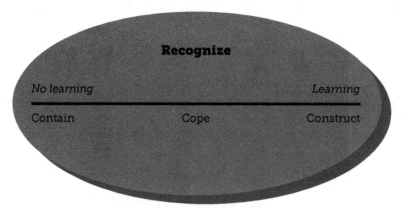

Recognize

No learning   *Learning*

Contain   Cope   Construct

FIGURE 1.1 Responses to Misunderstandings Continuum

The basic premise is that organizational members must recognize that misunderstandings can occur in any situation and that they can arise from many different catalysts (as described in an earlier section of this chapter). With recognition as a baseline practice, the remaining three practices are arranged on a continuum with *no learning* and *learning* as the two poles. The argument is that for any particular misunderstanding, one strategy may be more appropriate than the others. Associated with the particular strategy use is a certain level of learning; the least amount is learned with containment, whereas constructing allows for the most learning.

Saliency of the issue, time availability, and willingness to engage in constructive dialogue are three factors that affect the choice of practice. If one or more of the factors are limited, containment is the most likely choice. As saliency, time, and willingness to communicate increase, coping or constructing, further along the continuum, may be chosen.

One of the interviews conducted for this book provides a good example of misunderstandings that were addressed using one strategy, but when that strategy failed, the organizational members did not have the skills to employ another strategy, leading to a deteriorating situation. Abigail is a speech-language pathologist with 20 years of experience in a school district who relayed a story about their secretary and her problematic communication:

> One example is when our secretary is interacting with parents and families of the children we evaluate. There are some instances where parents have complained about the way she treats them on the telephone. She can be rude and inflexible when scheduling families to come in and see us. Another example is when she sends us test schedules, and she frequently makes mistakes, and whenever we catch a mistake and say something to her about it, she blames us in one way or another. This has been an ongoing problem for many years.
>
> We have talked to the supervisor about difficulties we've had with the secretary, and at one point, she asked us to document every problem that we had with the secretary and to share that with her. We did that probably over a 6-month period. It was a lot of work on our part to document the issues that we were having, but we were happy to do it with the idea that something would change. It didn't.
>
> The secretary continues to make errors. She will tend to get a little bit better every time our supervisor talks to her; she will maybe make a slight effort to be a little kinder or a little more thorough with her work to try to not make mistakes. I think the fact that she's been talked to so many times by our supervisor about her job performance makes her even more of a concern. She won't admit when she causes a problem or makes a mistake because she is more worried about getting caught, so she lies a lot to try to cover up her mistakes.
>
> When I need something specific, I try to send it through an email so it's in a written format so that way we have a means to track the information. That helps with just that ownership, so we know who communicated the

information and what their response was and how the follow-up communication was. Another thing that our supervisor has done to try to help the situation is to enlist other people. There is a paraprofessional who works with our team, and she is in charge of proofreading everything that our secretary does, so every schedule that is created by our secretary goes to another person to proofread for errors and that is a way that we have caught a lot of her errors and are able to fix them before they go out to our families. Another thing that's happened is another secretary is leading all of the evaluation plans so that there are not as many mistakes. So that job is actually taken away from the secretary who's making all of the errors.

How does the continuum apply to this problematic situation? First, the history of negative communication and errors from the secretary indicates that the relevant organizational members around her failed to recognize the problem early enough in her career to be able to respond to the situation. Second, Abigail and the other affected district personnel did eventually go to the secretary's supervisor in an attempt to address the problem. The response was to contain the problem through a 6-month documentation of errors in hopes that the documentation would provide evidence for a change to occur. The contain strategy did not work, however, primarily because of a lack of follow-up by the supervisor to ensure that acceptable communication behaviors were being engaged in and errors reduced. Finally, instead of moving to another strategy where the secretary may actually learn or be replaced, the supervisor opted for the contain strategy again but this time enlisting scarce district resources to fix the errors of the secretary and shift responsibilities away from her that she was deficient in. If, instead, the supervisor would have engaged in the construct strategy after the contain strategy failed, then perhaps the secretary could have learned how to improve or even shared what barriers to her success were there in the first place. The construct strategy could have been the most successful approach, but it would have taken effective communication and a commitment of resources from all parties.

As should be becoming clear, organizational life is inherently complex and often fraught with problems. Whether those problems are based on communication, organizational policies, socialization of new employees, information technology, or marginalized identities, they must be acknowledged and understood in an appropriate manner. In the final section of this chapter, we introduce a communication-centered approach to the study of organizations: the communicative constitution of organizations.

Communicative Constitution of Organizations

As you can see by the assumptions of our definition of organizational communication and our focus on misunderstandings, we believe that communication is more than just something that happens in an organization—it constitutes organizations. The communicative constitution of organizations (CCO) represents the first theory developed by the field of organizational communication. The coproduction relationship between organization and communication has its roots in structuration theory proposed by sociologist Anthony Giddens (1979) in his book *Central Problems in Social Theory*. This theory has been adopted by a variety of scholars in several different ways to create the exciting emergence of CCO. First, we will briefly overview several of the key ideas of structuration theory, and then we will discuss McPhee and Zaug's (2000) CCO four flows model.

Giddens (1979) argued that the macrolevel structure (organization) is both a medium and an outcome of microlevel social practices (interaction), something he referred to as the "**duality of structure**" (p. 5). In other words, organizational structure is not a concrete entity but is produced as people interact on a daily basis, attempting to accomplish their individual and collective purposes (structure as outcome). That structure, in turn, serves to mediate and constrain future interaction (structure as medium). **Recursivity** is the continual production and production of the structure similar to the process nature of communication.

Claiming that structure is created through individuals' daily actions assumes that to some degree individuals are **knowledgeable agents**. Being a knowledgeable agent means that individuals know that their interactions are either helping to maintain or change the existing organizational structure (Goodier & Eisenberg, 2006). Some of the activities and/or feelings are easily explained by individuals (**discursive consciousness**), whereas other experiences, behaviors, and feelings are not as easily put into words (**practical consciousness**). Because the practical consciousness is not easily talked about or even recognized by individuals, it is easiest to see its role in the organization through the regular routines that people use to get through their day.

Regardless of whether people can express in words why they participate in the activities that they do or not, individuals possess a degree of **agency**, an aspect of action that means that the individual makes choices over those actions. According to Giddens (1979), "at any point in time, the agent could have acted otherwise" (p. 56). What the individual chooses or what type of choices they have available to them is irrelevant. The fact that the individual could choose to act one way or another implies some level of agency within the structure that they are a part of creating. While individuals can control their own responses, they cannot control how others in the organization will respond or react (they have their own agency). This is referred to as an **unintended consequence**.

Structuration theory helps us understand the ways in which structure is produced and reproduced in an organization through interactions, while the CCO is a set of theories that attempt to better understand the nature of these interactions and their organizing properties (Bisel, 2010). Although scholars have advanced the CCO model in different ways, McPhee and Zaug's (2000) four flows model is the one most closely grounded in structuration theory. The premise of this model is that there are four interrelated communication processes, or flows, that constitute an organization. These flows are interactive and are carried out in multiple places at multiple times and contexts by numerous people. Some of the people engaged in the flows have formal organizational roles and speak on behalf of the organization, such as a manager or CEO. Some have informal roles and speak on behalf of the organization, such as a mentor, and some individuals may not be speaking on behalf of the organization at all, such as a disgruntled employee (McPhee, 2015). The four flows include membership negotiation, reflexive self-structuring, activity coordination, and institutional positioning.

Membership negotiation is the series of interactions that lets the employee's status emerge in relationship to the organization. While much research has focused on membership negotiation during the newcomer socialization and orientation process (these interactions assist the newcomer in understanding their role in the organization), membership negotiation continues throughout an employee's career (McPhee, 2015; McPhee & Iverson, 2009). This communication flow helps create or constitute the organization because it directly or indirectly makes reference to the organization and helps establish who "we" as an organization are and who can speak on "our" behalf.

Reflexive self-structuring is the communication flow that allows the organization to come into being because it communicates decisions, such as division of labor, rules, and policies. This flow represents the more authoritative acts and the ways that resources are distributed in the organization. Reflexive self-structuring allows organizational members to talk about the boundaries established during membership negotiation, as well as their larger organizational role (McPhee, 2015; McPhee & Iverson, 2009).

Activity coordination is those interactions that involve negotiation of task roles within the organization. Coordination could be an effort by organizational members to complete required tasks, avoid undesired tasks, solve problems, or respond to changes in the work process (McPhee, 2015; McPhee & Iverson, 2009). For example, activity coordination could be several employees who decide to clean the store at closing time, thereby leaving stocking for the morning shift. Activity coordination can create cooperation as with the closing shift employees working together to complete a task, or it can create a sense of conflict or competition, such as the morning shift being upset that they were left with empty shelves to begin the day.

The fourth flow, **institutional positioning**, involves the presentation of the organization at the macrolevel or to those outside of the organization, such as through public relations campaigns or public events. Organizations attempt to identify which external forces provide legitimacy and then what kinds of communication are necessary to appease or please them.

Each of the four flows contributes to the production and reproduction of structure by providing linkage. Membership negotiation links members and the organization, self-structuring links the organization to itself, and institutional positioning links the organization to its environment. Activity coordination enables (or constrains) the organization to adapt to new and developing situations, as well as specific work activities or problems.

Research using CCO and the four flows is mounting. One example comes from Nordbäck et al. (2017), who conducted research on companies attempting to institute flextime policies into their work environments and found the policy success was highly dependent on the company's four flows. The company that focused on activity coordination and the individual in messaging during membership negotiation was successful in implementing flexible work arrangements. However, the company that focused on rigid self-structuring (focused on the organization) produced a structure that did not support the individual using flex arrangements.

CCO represents an emerging approach to the study and understanding of the relationship between communication and organizations and is more complex and complicated than we can cover here in this introductory text (see Brummans et al., 2014, for a comprehensive review).

Summary

Organizational communication is the process of creating, exchanging, interpreting (correctly or incorrectly), and storing messages within a system of human interrelationships. The study of organizational communication helps people to understand and appreciate communication as the central process in the organization.

In this chapter, we have argued that misunderstandings are a central feature of organizational life and that certain communication behaviors and practices can assist members as they encounter them. In their daily activities, members are confronted with misunderstandings resulting from a variety of sources, including a conflict in values, a lack of information, or strategic misrepresentations. As these misunderstandings are addressed through communication, members create and recreate the organizational structure that encompasses them.

As you read the following chapters, please keep the concept of misunderstandings in mind. You should be able to visualize the types of misunderstandings that might occur in organizational relationships, processes, and outcomes and anticipate solutions to them.

As a student, no matter what your future area of expertise may be—finance, management, health care, law, medicine, engineering, or the arts—it will be important for you to understand how communication functions in an organization and how you can make it work for you. We hope that after reading this book you will have a greater understanding of all aspects of organizational life. An appreciation of the historical development of organizational communication, a more developed sense of organizational culture, and an understanding of the many human communication processes that are a part of organizational life are the desired outcomes. In addition, knowing that there are a variety of choices you can make about your own communication behavior will help you decide how to complete the tasks of your job successfully.

If you are a communication major, or more specifically an organizational communication major, others will turn to you for assistance in improving communication in the organization. You may have an official position devoted to communication, such as communication trainer, social media specialist, manager of internal communication, or work in the general area of human resources management. Or you may use your communication expertise in sales, management, administration, or project management. As a communication specialist, your goal should be to reduce misunderstandings through communication.

Classical Theories of Organizations

LEARNING OBJECTIVES

1. Analyze the pros and cons of characterizing an organization by the metaphor of a machine
2. Explain how the classical approach to reducing misunderstandings in organizations may lead to other problems
3. Examine the relevance of Taylor's elements of scientific management
4. Explain how Henri Fayol's management principles may be used to achieve his elements of management
5. Describe how Max Weber's theory of bureaucracy is based on the execution of written rules for effective organizational functioning

We imagine that you have heard a version of the quote attributed to Maya Angelou (1997), "You can't really know where you are going until you know where you have been." This is the guiding force behind our next few chapters. We don't offer the content merely as a history lesson but as a way of understanding how we got where we are in organizational life and how so much of what happened more than a century ago still affects organizations and how we communicate in them today. To that end, we begin the discussion of the study of organizational communication with a brief sketch of three theorists whose contributions represent the classical approaches to organizations. These three theories of organization emerged in the early part of the 20th century and still permeate many aspects of organizational life today.

As the Industrial Revolution changed the nature of Western civilization in the 18th and 19th centuries, it became necessary for newly emerging organizations to have efficient and effective means of managing their modes of production. Theorists turned to the two principal organizations of the time, the military and the Catholic Church, as models for modern industrial management (McGregor, 1960/1985). Strict control of workers, absolute chains of command, predictability of behavior, and unidirectional downward influence (among others) were characteristics of these two successful organizations that made their way into modern organizational theory. The resulting organizational theories are referred to here as the classical approaches to organizations and communication within them.

As you read this chapter, keep in mind the following points. First, to understand how modern organizations function and particularly the role that communication plays in effective organizing, it is vital to understand the theories that guided organizational functioning in the preceding decades. Remnants of these theories still exist to a greater or lesser extent (depending on the industry) in managerial practices today. Understanding the theoretical bases for these practices will provide you with useful information for performing successfully when you are part of an organization. Second, contemporary organizational theorists offer principles and practices that are in opposition to classical theories. Knowing the elements of classical theories will help you understand why modern organizational theorists recommend what they do. Finally, you will perhaps notice that several principles of classical theories make inherent sense. Unfortunately, these principles may never have been integrated into practice or were integrated in ways not intended by the original theorists. The information in this chapter should provide you with enough knowledge to make those distinctions.

The Metaphor of the Machine

A useful way to introduce the different organizational theories covered in the next several chapters is through metaphor. Each type of theory is based on specific assumptions about the nature of organizations, which can be expressed metaphorically. The classical approach to organizations is characterized by the metaphor of a **machine**. From this perspective, organizations are viewed as if they are machines; managerial principles, modes of operation, treatment of workers, and communication in the organization are considered in light of this metaphor.

Consider for a moment the properties of a machine. A machine is very predictable in how it will function. It rarely deviates from the norm (outside operator error) unless some part of it ceases functioning properly or stops completely. In cases where parts of the machine no longer function or function ineffectively, they are replaceable by another standard part just like it. Additionally, specific rules exist regarding the repair of the machine and the specific role that each part of the machine plays in its functioning. In other words, each part of the machine is highly specialized.

When the machine metaphor is applied to organizations, the properties just described hold true for the organization as well and guide management as it attempts to regulate behavior, including communication. If an organization is a machine, then the workers are the parts of the machine. In accordance with the properties of a machine, the workers are to behave predictably so that management and the other workers will know exactly what to expect of each member of the organization at any given moment. If a worker operates outside the boundaries of what is expected, someone who can perform the functions of the job effectively, efficiently, and predictably will replace that worker.

The machine metaphor in organizations has obvious benefits for the organization and for some workers. The resulting efficiency and predictability help create a perception of stability for everyone involved. At the same time, the machine metaphor can affect workers in ways that may not be so positive. Take for example the story of a student, Allie, whose father had worked in a factory for more than 10 years. He wore the same uniform every day, did the same work, and was discouraged from thinking for himself, as the company just wanted him to do what he was told, how he was told to do it, and nothing more. Our student recalled that her father was worn out and weakened from being treated like a part of a machine day in and day out, so much so that it took away his happiness and sense of who he really was.

Her story conveys several important points. First, treating members of the organization as if they are parts of a machine may lead to positive outcomes for the organization, but it may also have negative implications for the workers. Second, the use of a metaphor has very real effects on managers and workers. Finally, how people are treated at work may affect the worker at home and could also have implications for their families. The situation Allie described is a vivid example of how misunderstandings can be created as a result of the ways that work is structured and how workers are treated.

Minimizing Misunderstandings

By promoting the principles of specialization, standardization, and predictability in organizations, classical theorists were essentially attempting to minimize the occurrences of misunderstandings (as characterized in Chapter 1). Classical theorists hypothesized that problems in organizations occurred when tasks were not directed and workers were left relatively unregulated—that is, free to experiment with work styles and procedures and able to communicate with anyone about anything at any time. Strictly regulating how work was accomplished, who could speak to whom and when, and managing through fear are all instruments for reducing misunderstandings in classical theories.

As you will see throughout this chapter, however, attempts to regulate behavior strictly through these means created a whole new class of misunderstandings. Attempts to increase predictability by demanding that everyone follow exact rules for behavior led to workers whose creativity and intelligence were underutilized, which in turn increased their dissatisfaction, lowered motivation, and decreased commitment to the task and the organization. Regulating communication by emphasizing messages that flowed mainly in one direction—from supervisor to subordinate—minimized instances of arguments and increased efficiency but decreased communication effectiveness by generating more miscommunication and decreasing worker satisfaction.

As you read about the three different classical theories, imagine how the creators of these theories were seeking to minimize misunderstandings. At the same time, think about the new forms of misunderstandings created by these theories as **unintended consequences**. For example, consider the following story from Betsy Heart, a billing specialist whose company integrated the classical theory concept of efficiency:

> I think the biggest issue at my company is that it has become more inter-
> ested in production, getting things done faster, than actually doing quality
> work. We have an efficiency report that comes out now, and we have to
> do so many claims in an hour. People are freaking out about this because
> they are worried they are going to lose their jobs if they don't meet their
> quota. So they do these claims without necessarily doing them correctly,
> and then we wind up doing them over two or three times, which is not
> right. We need to do them right the first time, even if it takes longer. It's
> all about the money now, not necessarily the quality of the work—trying
> to get it in as fast as they can.

As you saw from the machine metaphor and will learn more about throughout this chapter, efficiency is a core principle of classical theory. What Betsy's situation demonstrates, though, is that the intentions of the theory do not always translate into practice. In her case, the company was focused on efficiency, which is sensible from a classical perspective, but they did this without providing training that would ensure quality in this efficiency-based system. Workers were left to focus not on getting the job done right but solely on getting the task done quickly out of fear that they would lose their jobs if they did not. This is a perfect example of how elements of classical theory designed to minimize misunderstandings may contribute to the occurrence of different problems.

The classical approach is represented by three theories: Frederick Taylor's *theory of scientific management,* Henri Fayol's *administrative theory,* and Max Weber's *theory of bureaucracy.* They are described in the following sections.

Taylor's Theory of Scientific Management

Frederick Taylor (1856–1915), who is considered the "father of scientific management," proposed his theory of organizations in *The Principles of Scientific Management* (1911/1998). In this work, he outlined his theory of scientific management and how managers could maximize profits for both the employer and the employee.

The main problem, according to Taylor, was getting employees to work at their maximum capacity at all times. He noticed that employees rarely worked at this level; in fact, most would expend only enough effort to work at the safest, minimum-output level. He referred to the behavior of deliberately working slowly to avoid expending more effort than deemed necessary as **systematic soldiering**. Jim Roberts, the director of public works in a local government setting, told us a story that exemplifies systematic soldiering and what can happen to workers who exceed the expected minimum-output level:

> We recently initiated a multiyear program to replace the automated meter
> reading devices in our 11,000 customer locations. To begin this pro-
> gram, we hired an additional employee who would be trained by current

employees and then work a nonregular shift in order to better accommo-date customer availability. We developed a training program that would first have him observing an experienced employee perform, then perform the work himself under supervision of his trainer, and finally be sent out on his own.

Because the program was new and because each replacement may pres-ent its own challenges, we took a conservative approach to scheduling appointments to make sure he would have plenty of time to get his work done. We also worked in breaks and his lunch period to the daily schedule. Once he was free to work on his own, he quickly set a work pace that was significantly more productive than we initially established, and he asked us to reduce the amount of time between appointments. In fact, he prepared a proposed new schedule and a report showing how much more productive he could be under his plan. Management was both impressed and pleased with his productivity (his recommended schedule would reduce the length of the program by at least 6 months). The union members, however, were less impressed. His union steward took the employee aside and told him he was making the rest of them look bad and that he should slow down. This employee's response was to go back to his supervisor with a newly revised plan, which would further increase his productivity by reducing the amount of prep time at the beginning of shift and clean up/restocking time at the end of his shift. The union never said a word to management about it; the employee was ostracized by many in the union.

As Jim's story demonstrates, systematic soldiering is a problem for organizations, and workers who attempt to perform at a higher level may face negative consequences from their coworkers despite the quality work they are doing for the organization.

Taylor offered three reasons for the prevalence of systematic soldiering. First, he said that workers believe that if each one works to his full capacity, then the number of workers who need to be employed will be reduced. Taylor argued the opposite: as each employee produces more, the price per unit of the product drops. As prices drop, demand increases, and more workers need to be employed to meet it.

The second reason for systematic soldiering, according to Taylor, is the **piecework system of remuneration**. Under the piecework system, employees are paid a sum of money for producing a certain amount during an average day. If the employer dis-covers that the worker can produce more than she is actually producing in a day, the employer raises the amount to be produced without raising the amount of pay. This adjustment would lead the fast worker to artificially lower her rate of production to that of the slowest worker in the group so that the employer would not change the rate of pay. Taylor argued that every worker knows the maximum amount the employer is willing to pay for a day's work. Given this figure, the workers artificially lower their output level so that the rate will not be changed.

The third reason for systematic soldiering, according to Taylor, is the use of rule-of-thumb methods of training employees. Taylor observed that workers learn how to do their particular tasks by observing the people around them. This would lead to the same job being done in a variety of ways, most, if not all, of which were inefficient. Taylor devoted much of his time to resolving this cause of systematic soldiering, and his theory of scientific management was the result.

Elements of Scientific Management

The theory of scientific management has four elements:

1. The scientific design of every aspect of every task

2. The careful selection and training of the best workers

3. Proper remuneration for fast and high-quality work

4. Equal division of work and responsibility between worker and manager

The first element of Taylor's theory is the *scientific design of every aspect of every task*. Believing that the rule-of-thumb method of training employees was a major contributor to systematic soldiering, he sought to eliminate it. Through the use of **time and motion studies**, the most efficient and effective means of accomplishing every aspect of every task could be determined. To conduct a time and motion study, a manager would study the exact motions of workers using a stopwatch to help determine the most efficient way of completing each task.

Taylor conducted time and motion studies using this procedure in a number of U.S. factories during the early 1900s. For example, he examined the science of shoveling at the Bethlehem Steel Company. He noticed that the 600 workers at the company were operating inefficiently and ineffectively; they were using different types of shovels, taking different sizes of shovel loads, and using different mechanics to shovel. To remedy this problem, he conducted exhaustive time and motion studies and determined that the optimal shovel load for each worker was 21 pounds (regardless of the type of material being shoveled—e.g., coal, ore, or ashes). Gathering 21 pounds per shovel load would yield the maximum productivity for each worker; 18 pounds would be too little, and 25 pounds would be too heavy and lead to fatigue. Different shovels for different types of material were developed so that 21 pounds of material would comfortably fit on each shovel. Taking 21 pounds per shovel load and using the motions and timing designated by the managers, workers were able to maximize their output and increase their pay accordingly.

The second element of scientific management is the careful selection and training of the best workers. Once the most efficient way to perform the task is determined through time and motion studies, managers must select workers who are capable of performing the task as designed and capable of producing at the maximum level. Workers are not expected to understand the science of task design, so it is the job of management to train each worker on how to perform the task. This idea reveals an important aspect about Taylor and his view of workers and managers. Taylor believed that there is an inherent difference between the two groups—managers are intelligent, and workers are and should be ignorant:

> Now one of the very first requirements for a man who is fit to handle pig iron as a regular occupation is that he shall be so stupid and so phlegmatic that he more nearly resembles in his mental make-up the ox than any other type. The man who is mentally alert and intelligent is for this very reason entirely unsuited to what would, for him, be the grinding monotony of work of this character. (1911/1998, p. 28)

Perhaps nowhere else in Taylor's writings is his view of the difference between management and workers so clear. Read from today's perspective, this passage would seem to indicate a disdain for workers, an absolute hatred of them. Writing such things in the 21st century would surely lead to dismissal from the community of scholars, rejection of the theory, and widespread outrage. At the time it was written, however, Taylor was praised for his insight and his concern with the worker. Although the preceding passage indicates that he did not have the highest regard for their mental abilities, his overall theory was designed to provide opportunities for workers to achieve greater financial rewards in a more comfortable fashion. Reading just the last sentence of the quotation shows that Taylor understood the need to challenge people mentally in the workplace. Unfortunately, he only considered those in management positions to be worthy of such challenges.

The third element of scientific management is *proper remuneration for fast and high-quality work.* Taylor argued that the workers should be able to increase their wages by 30% to 100% under the scientific management system. Given that the individual worker is motivated almost solely by wages, Taylor thought that the best way to maximize their output would be to promise them higher wages *if* they provided maximum effort. Through the scientific design of tasks, the most efficient output level is determined. If the worker meets that output level, they are rewarded with appropriate, good wages. If the worker exceeds that output level, they are rewarded with a bonus. If the worker produces under the appropriate output level, they are immediately informed of the fact and given instructions as to how to perform the task to meet the goal. If the worker cannot meet the goal after sufficient training, they are removed from that task.

The fourth element of scientific management is *equal division of work and responsibility between worker and manager.* Under old systems of management, the plan for accomplishing the task was left up to the individual worker. Under Taylor's system, the manager was responsible for planning every detail of the task for every worker, training the worker on how to perform the task, and evaluating the process and product of each worker at regular intervals. This increased role of the manager led Taylor to say that there was now an equal division of work.

Think back to the first story in this chapter from Betsy Heart, the billing specialist, and apply Taylor's principles to it. You can readily see that her organization expected fast work but failed to incorporate the other elements of the theory into their practice. The result was low-quality output and a workforce that was constrained by their fears of losing their jobs.

Scientific Management in Contemporary Organizations

Are Taylor's principles present in contemporary organizations? In some respects, absolutely. Although Taylor's less-than-appropriate language has for the most part disappeared, several of his principles still permeate many modern organizations. Assembly-line plants are prototypical examples of the scientific design of tasks. Workers (in conjunction with machines) must perform tasks in regulated ways for the system to operate efficiently and effectively. Efficiency is promoted through strict control of the task process. Many fast-food restaurants and franchised sub-sandwich shops also operate using Taylor's ideas.

Although Taylorism was designed with manual labor work as the prototypical form of work, modern applications of Taylor's principles have been used to restructure other forms of work. Advanced communication technology and computerized information systems have made it possible to structure and monitor interactions between organizational members and customers. This use of technology to monitor and restructure work to be more efficient is often referred to as **digital Taylorism** (Altass & Wiebe, 2017; Gautiè et al., 2020). In the time of Taylor, data were collected by managers and technicians in white lab coats holding stopwatches and clipboards; however, in the era of digital Taylorism, data are collected by automated computer processes but still serve to control the labor processes. "Digital Taylorism is providing parallel opportunities including standardization through automation, specialization . . . , digital surveillance systems, and databases to decrease the cost of many kinds of knowledge work presently carried out via middle class managers and professionals" (Günsel & Yamen, 2020, p. 115).

For example, the call center, which is a segment of an organization or a separate organization responsible for interactions with customers, typically in the form of customer service or technical support, is one organizational form that has been restructured according to Taylor's principles (Bain et al., 2002; Taylor & Bain, 1999). Taylor and Bain (1999) show how a typical call center employee's work unfolds:

> In all probability, work consists of an uninterrupted and endless sequence of similar conversations with customers she never meets. She has to concentrate hard on what is being said, jump from page to page on a screen, making sure that the details entered are accurate and that she has said the right things in a pleasant manner. The conversation ends and as she tidies up the loose ends there is another voice in her headset. The pressure is intense because she knows her work is being measured, her speech monitored, and it often leaves her mentally, physically, and emotionally exhausted. (p. 115)

The exhaustion that call center workers experience is in part attributable to the idea that the digitization of the work not only affects task-related behaviors such as targets for the number and length of calls to be made but also more qualitative aspects of the work experience such as building rapport with customers and expressing pride in the organization (Bain et al., 2002).

While digital Taylorism has served to increase efficiency and reduce turnover in some organizations, critics argue that digitizing scientific management has led to unnecessary surveillance and the invasion of privacy of organizational members. Amazon, for example, has been granted two patents for a wearable wristband technology that will track the location and actions of its employees as they move throughout the warehouses, alerting them with a buzz on their wrist when they have arrived at the correct location. The technology, while time-saving and helping to ensure efficiency, has led to incredible pressures on the workforce to push themselves past their personal limits (Yeginsu, 2018). Additionally, with COVID-19 moving more workers home to accomplish their work remotely, the technology that allows that freedom also serves to structure the work and monitor the workers' progress on their tasks (Blumenfeld et al., 2020). In essence, Taylorism, which once lived in the workplace, has moved home with the worker in the age of digital Taylorism.

Taylor's influence in modern organizations remains strong. The principles of scientific management have seen a resurgence given advanced monitoring technologies, and issues of efficiency, job redesign, and reengineering of work are alive and well. Obviously, either explicitly or implicitly, Frederick Taylor's principles are still affecting workers more than a century after they were introduced.

Taylor's system of scientific management is the cornerstone of classical theory. The other two classical theorists, Fayol and Weber, both refer to Taylor in their writing and consider him to be a visionary and pioneer in the management of organizations. They differed from Taylor, though, in their foci. Taylor's main focus was on the task, whereas Fayol and Weber had their sights set more broadly. We now turn to the work of Henri Fayol.

Fayol's Administrative Theory

Henri Fayol (1841–1925), a French citizen, had four careers during his lifetime. He was a mining engineer, a geologist who developed a new theory of coal-bearing strata, an industrial leader, and a philosopher of administration (Urwick & Brech, 1949). It was as a philosopher of administration that he contributed most widely to the theory and practice of organizational management.

In his book *General and Industrial Management* (published in French in 1916 and then published in English in 1949), Fayol outlined his theory of general management, which he believed could be applied to the administration of myriad industries. His concern was with the administrative apparatus (or functions of administration), and to that end, he presented his administrative theory—that is, principles and elements of management.

Principles of Management

Fayol forwarded his 14 principles of management as prescriptions for practical ways that managers should accomplish their managerial duties. Fayol was concerned with reducing or eliminating inefficiency by focusing on management and how they structured the workplace. In doing so, he was attempting to minimize misunderstandings, such as the one told to us by Daniel, a sheet metal worker, who had a coworker, Scott, who overstepped his authority and position regularly:

> Scott was supposed to be considered an equal in the workplace—not a boss, but an equal. He would think he was the boss and try to take charge and take control of a situation that was not up to him to take control over.
>
> One time, there was a job with two sheet metal workers (one was me) and one plumber, Scott. Scott came in and asked us what we were doing, and we proceeded to tell him what we were doing for our work that day. Well, he started telling us that he needed to be in charge and be kept informed about what was going on each and every day. As this was happening, our project manager, who happens to be the owner of the company, walks in behind him. As Scott was being all puffy-chested and very confrontational with us, the owner is standing behind him and all of a sudden says, "Hi!" And Scott immediately cowers down. Scott had to basically backpedal and eat his own words with what he just said to us in front of the owner. He just had no business trying to take charge of things that he wasn't supposed to be in charge of.

In this example, Scott, the plumber, created a very uncomfortable situation for himself and the rest of the crew because of a lack of attention to Fayol's principles. In particular, the example demonstrates that the following problems that Fayol was specifically interested in were at play in this misunderstanding: not adhering to the prescribed set of tasks, putting the interests of the individual over the organization, not attending to the chain of command, and not working for the spirit of the group.

Notice as you read these principles that Fayol was attempting to minimize problems before they occurred. What follows is a brief description of eight of the most long-lasting principles of management outlined by Fayol (1949):

1. **Division of work**. Each worker should have a limited set of tasks to accomplish.

2. **Unity of command**. An employee should receive orders from only one supervisor. If this principle is not upheld, "authority is undermined, discipline is in jeopardy, order disturbed, and stability threatened" (p. 24).

3. **Unity of direction**. Only one head (i.e., one manager) shall administer a group of activities having the same purpose. In other words, two managers should not have direct authority over the same set of activities.

4. **Subordination of individual interest to general interest**. The interest (e.g., demands, needs, wants, desires) of an individual employee or group of employees should not come before the interest of the entire organization.

5. **Remuneration of personnel**. Employees should be paid a fair price for their services. Interestingly, Fayol believed that remuneration could be more than just financial reward: "There is no doubt that a business will be better served in proportion as its employees are more energetic, better educated, more conscientious and more permanent" (p. 32).

6. **Centralization**. Centralization occurs when decisions are made at the top of the hierarchy rather than at lower levels (decentralization). Although centralization is often tied most directly to decision-making power, Fayol also conceptualized it as being related to the full use of the employee: "Everything which goes to increase the importance of the subordinate's role is decentralization, everything which goes to reduce it is centralization" (p. 34).

7. **Scalar chain**. The scalar chain is the traditional organizational structure that defines the "chain of superiors ranging from the ultimate authority to the lowest ranks" (p. 34). The scalar chain is the communication plan for Fayol's theory (see Figure 2.1). Communication, according to Fayol, should follow the scalar chain. If worker F needed to communicate with worker G, the communication would have to flow up the scalar chain through supervisors D, B, and A, and then back down to C, E, and, finally, G. Fayol recognized that there are times when it is necessary to communicate a message quickly. It is proper at such times to go outside the lines of authority and communicate directly across the scalar chain. The "gangplank" (represented by the dotted line from F to G in Figure 2.1), which later became known as Fayol's bridge, is what allows two people on the same hierarchical level to communicate with each other directly. The gangplank should be employed when not using it will result in a "detriment to the business" (p. 36). Additionally, if F and G need to communicate using the gangplank, they must inform their respective supervisors immediately, and the supervisors must agree that it is necessary. If either of these conditions is violated, the scalar chain must be used.

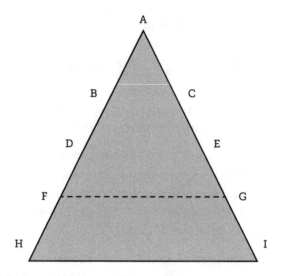

FIGURE 2.1 Scalar Chain

8. **Esprit de corps**. Fayol described the principle of esprit de corps as "union is strength" (p. 40). Fayol meant that a strong organization is one that has loyal members who will strive to keep the organization together at the cost of their personal interests.

Fayol's principles plainly tell managers how they should manage. As opposed to Taylor, who focused mainly on the elements of the task, Fayol believed that managerial practices were the key to predictability and efficiency in organizations. Examining the principles shows that Fayol had a particular interest in minimizing misunderstandings caused by communication. Unity of command, unity of direction, centralization, and the scalar chain were all mechanisms intended to simplify the communication process such that misunderstandings caused by multiple supervisors and free-flowing communication would be eliminated.

From a communication perspective, however, it is readily apparent that such mechanisms can lead to misunderstandings of many forms. The scalar chain, for example, with its emphasis on one-way communication (particularly downward), neglects the interactive nature of the phenomenon. We know communication to be a two-way process, where both participants contribute to the process of creating meaning. An example of this was told to us by Ernest, a novice employee at a limestone quarry, who encountered a boss whose tendency to speak precisely and yet without full explanation blended with his tendency to assume too much:

> Conveyors used throughout the quarry were run by huge electrical motors geared down to provide power to move tons of newly blasted and crushed rock long distances with speed and ease. The motors drove large v-belts (like the fan belt of a car but much bigger) on pulleys connected to gearboxes. Of course, those belts wore out in the dust and the constant strain. When one of these belts was about to break, Jorge, my boss, called me over

and said, "I've got a trip for you and it's important. Get out to Plainville right now and pick up one of these belts and take it down to Kenny in the hole." But what I heard was, "Go get this thing and take it down and put it on." He had not said that, but that's what I gathered.

Like a good soldier, I drove madly to Plainville, picked up the belt from a hot dusty shack, and tore back to the quarry. At this point, my mistake began to take shape. Having noted Jorge's urgency, and having seen people get to fixing things quickly in the past, I took the belt down to Kenny and he and I proceeded to try to install it. This required shutting down the conveyor. While we struggled longer than we thought we should have to install the belt, Kenny noticed over my shoulder the tiny but growing form of a man flailing his arms, his shouts like pebbles dropping on sand. As this figure grew, wending its way down the twisting gravel ramps to our position, we saw it was Jorge. He was shouting something, and it didn't matter what, we knew we were in trouble.

It seems his intention was that I should bring back the belt to HIM, to be installed at a time when shutting down the main conveyor would not shut down the heart of the operation. Kenny and I did not know this, though I might have surmised it, so I was the more responsible of the two. My intention was to please the supervisor as promptly as possible by solving the stated problem. He had said that the belt job was urgent, so I assumed that meant seeing it through to installation. After all, what good is a belt that is still in the wrapper? We were chewed out mightily for slowing even for ten seconds the main operations of the plant.

As Ernest's story demonstrates, one-way communication, though efficient in Fayol's scalar chain model, can fail when the message does not meet the needs of the receiver(s), is unclear, or it is open to multiple interpretations. In the end, the message was neither efficient nor effective.

The scalar chain also contributes to misunderstandings by minimizing the use of horizontal communication. By relegating horizontal communication to emergency situations as a means of increasing predictability and order, Fayol also removed its positive contributions to communication, such as building collegiality, increasing job and communication satisfaction, and verifying the meanings of messages communicated in other forms.

Elements of Management

Although Fayol's principles of management describe the practices in which managers should engage, his elements of management are the general objectives that management needs to accomplish (1949, p. 7). Through the effective implementation of the principles of management discussed previously, managers should be able to execute the elements of management. Here we discuss briefly the five elements of management (planning, organizing, command, coordination, and control):

1. **Planning**. This first element of management involves creating a plan of action for the future, determining the stages of the plan and the technology necessary to implement it.

2. **Organizing**. Once a plan of action is designed, managers need to provide everything necessary to carry it out, including raw materials, tools, capital, and human resources.

3. **Command**. With the plan of action in place and the necessary resources secured, managers must begin implementing the plan. To do so effectively, managers must understand the strengths and weaknesses of the personnel, eliminate incompetent workers, audit the organization regularly, and strive to maintain the principles of management as discussed in the prior section (particularly as they relate to personnel).

4. **Coordination**. The high-level manager must now work to "harmonize" (Fayol, 1949, p. 103) all the activities to facilitate organizational success. Communication (particularly information sharing) is the prime coordinating mechanism.

5. **Control**. The final element of management involves the comparison of the activities of the personnel to the plan of action; it is the evaluation component of management.

It is perhaps easiest to think of Fayol's five elements as managerial objectives and his 14 principles as tools for accomplishing those objectives. Looked at in this way, it is quite easy to see why Fayol proposed the principles that he did. The five elements are phrased in machinelike terms, with little attention paid to the humanistic side of the organization and its members. The objectives were to keep the machine functioning effectively and efficiently and to quickly replace any part or process that did not contribute to these objectives. The principles were tools for accomplishing exactly that. Downward communication, unity of command, esprit de corps, and subordination of individual interests, for example, seemed to be the best ways to allow for planning, organizing, command, coordination, and control to occur.

Fayol's administrative theory differs noticeably from the theory of scientific management advocated by Taylor. The main difference lies in their foci; Taylor focused on the task, whereas Fayol focused on management. Another difference between the two theorists is important to the study of organizational communication. Fayol appears to have slightly more respect for the worker than Taylor had, as evidenced by Fayol's proclamation that workers may indeed be motivated by more than just money, such as the opportunity for better education or more job security. Fayol also argued for equity in the treatment of workers, which should include being kind to them and helping to promote justice for them. Perhaps of most importance to the study of organizational communication is the emphasis Fayol placed on communication. Although he believed in a strict scalar chain, he did acknowledge the necessity of using horizontal communication at certain times. Although these principles seem overly stringent today, Fayol's positioning of communication as a necessary ingredient to successful management was an important step in the early 20th century.

Administrative Theory in the Modern Workplace

Fayol's elements and principles of management are still alive in modern organizations in several ways: as accepted practices in some industries, as revamped versions of the original principles or elements, or as remnants of the organization's history to which alternative practices and philosophies are being offered. Fayol's elements of management, for instance, are recognizable as the main objectives of modern managers, though today they are often expressed in more humanistic and participative terms. In other words, although the labels for the objectives themselves seem to have survived into the new century, the meaning of those objectives has changed. Consider two of the elements in this fashion. As Fayol described the element of "planning," he talked about it as a unidirectional phenomenon where the manager plans the activities, goals, and objectives of the workers. A large part of the modern manager's job is indeed planning, but now the planning is often done in conjunction with the workers in a participatory fashion.

Fayol's element of "organizing" is another example of how the objective remains in the modern workplace but its meaning has changed. Fayol argued that every high-level manager should have certain attributes and knowledge, such as intelligence, moral qualities, managerial ability, and central task competence. Modern managers must be equipped with several of these qualities but are now expected to be much more skilled in the areas of human relationships and communication. Modern managerial skills can include building positive working relationships, prioritizing tasks, decision-making, communication, and understanding the needs of stakeholders (Moss, 2018). The two lists certainly have some overlap, but they contain a few very interesting differences. Of particular note is the fact that the majority of the modern manager's skills need to be in the area of communication and relationships, whereas Fayol's managers needed technical mastery and strong personalities. These differences are illustrative of the changes that have occurred in many modern organizations—changes that attempt to move past treating organizational members as parts of a machine.

Several of Fayol's principles of management are also followed today to a degree depending on the industry and the particular organization. The U.S. military is a prime example of an organization that has continued to use these principles. Division of work, unity of command, subordination of individual interest to general interest, centralization, and the scalar chain, in particular, characterize managerial practice in all branches of the military. Other modern organizations, too, follow Fayol's principles. In particular, organizations that have grown large tend to turn to several of these principles, such as the scalar chain and centralization as a means of imposing order.

The final classical theorist discussed in this chapter is Max Weber, whose theory has several features in common with Fayol's administrative theory but is more descriptive than prescriptive. Whereas Fayol was *prescribing* objectives and tools for managers to use in the workplace, Weber set out to *describe* an ideal or pure form of organizational structure that would probably never be attained.

Weber's Theory of Bureaucracy

Max Weber (1864–1920), a German sociologist, developed a theory of organizations that, although having some of the same elements as those by Taylor and Fayol, was born more from theory than industrial experimentation. The English translation of Weber's (1947) book *The Theory of Social and Economic Organization* appeared in the United States about the same time as Fayol's *General and Industrial Management.* In it, Weber theorized about an ideal type of organizational structure, which he called a **bureaucracy**. Weber's bureaucracy was not "ideal" in the sense that it was the perfect structure for every organization, but that it was a "pure" organizational form.

For Weber, bureaucracy allows for the optimal form of authority—**rational authority**. The exercise of authority is the underlying interest for Weber:

> It is necessary, that is, that there should be a relatively high probability that the action of a definite, supposedly reliable group of persons will be primarily oriented to the execution of the supreme authority's general policy and specific commands. (1947, p. 324)

In other words, Weber believed that for organizations to function effectively and efficiently, there needed to be an assurance that the workers would respect the "right" of managers to direct their activities as dictated by organizational rules and procedures. Without this assurance, the system would be ineffective.

Based on experience, Weber posited three types of legitimate authority:

1. **Traditional authority**. Traditional authority is based on past customs and involves personal loyalty to the person in the leadership position. According to Weber, traditional authority rests "on an established belief in the sanctity of immemorial traditions and the legitimacy of the status of those exercising authority under them" (p. 328). The best example of this type of authority is royalty. Kings and queens of nations and tribes often have authority based on inheritance and tradition. Their subjects are loyal to the tradition of the throne and believe that the person occupying it deserves their loyalty, regardless of ability to lead.

2. **Charismatic authority**. Charismatic authority is based on personal trust in the character or skills of the person to whom authority is attributed. According to Weber, this form of authority rests "on devotion to the specific and exceptional sanctity, heroism or exemplary character of an individual person and of the

normative patterns or order revealed or ordained by him" (p. 328). Charismatic authority differs from traditional authority in that the former is rooted in the characteristics, attributes, or skills of the person in authority, whereas the latter is related more to loyalty based on tradition. Martin Luther King Jr., is an example of a person to whom charismatic authority was attributed.

3. **Rational authority.** Rational authority is often referred to as rational-legal authority or legal authority because it is based on the rational application of rules or laws. Weber described this form of authority as "resting on a belief in the 'legality' of patterns of normative rules and the right of those elevated to authority under such rules to issue commands" (p. 328). He preferred this form of authority to traditional or charismatic authority because it is rooted in the rational application of rules instead of personal character or loyalty to tradition. According to Weber, the probability that order (and hence organization) would be upheld using this form of authority was higher.

Tenets of Bureaucracy

The basic tenets of bureaucracy are mechanisms dedicated to preserving and enhancing rational authority. What follows are eight components of Weber's theory (the list is by no means exhaustive):

1. **Rules.** Rules are the essence of bureaucracy and the basis of rational authority. Bureaucracy is based on a system of written rules that cover all possible contingencies within an organization. The rules are both universalistic, meaning they should be applied impartially to every member of the organization, and impersonal, meaning that people are treated according to the rules. Rational authority is effective only to the extent that there is obedience to the established and agreed-upon rules and that there is a consistent rational application of those rules to all members of the organization. With a rule for every possible contingency, members of a bureaucracy are able to act predictably and consistently in any situation with which they are confronted.

2. **Specified sphere of competence.** This component of bureaucracy refers to a division of labor. Every organizational member (a) has an obligation to perform the functions specified by the division of labor and (b) should have the authority to carry out those functions.

3. **Hierarchy.** Weber, like Taylor, believed in a strict chain of command. In a hierarchy, every lower office should be under the strict control and supervision of a higher office.

4. **Specialized training.** Only those individuals who have demonstrated competence through specialized training should be part of the administrative staff, for it is

only through a thorough understanding of the functions and procedures that a rational application of the rules of the bureaucracy is possible.

5. **Workers do not own technology.** In a pure bureaucracy, no worker or member of the administration should own any nonhuman form of production used in the functioning of the organization. Ownership of the technology would lead to a form of protectionism, making a rational application of rules impossible.

6. **No entitlement to "official position" by incumbent.** No worker or member of the administration should have "title" to his or her position (as Supreme Court Justices do). If a member does have such entitlement, the tendency to act as if she is beyond the boundaries of the rules would counteract the need for a rational application of rules to all members of the bureaucracy.

7. **Everything written down.** Perhaps the second most important tenant of bureaucracy is the notion that everything should be in writing. All decisions, meeting minutes, rulings, and especially the guiding rules of the organization must be written down and accessible because they constitute the "central office" of the modern bureaucracy. Without a written record, deviation from and nonrational application of the rules is likely to occur.

8. **Maintenance of "ideal type"—bureaucracy.** One of the main functions of any bureaucracy is to maintain the proper and rational functioning of the bureaucracy itself. Without appropriate monitoring, maintenance, and updating, the bureaucracy will fail.

In summary, Weber's theory of bureaucracy is more closely related to Fayol's administrative theory than to Taylor's theory of scientific management, though differences do exist with the former. Whereas Fayol focused on management, Weber was concerned with describing the ideal structure of an organization. The cornerstone of Weber's theory is the existence of written rules, the rational application of which would ensure the promotion of legitimate authority and the effective and efficient functioning of the organization.

Bureaucracy in the Modern Workplace

The word *bureaucracy* is a common one in use today. People easily point to large organizations guided by countless rules as being "bureaucracies" (whether they really are or not) and readily supply examples of having to cut through the "bureaucratic red tape" when attempting to accomplish something. Unfortunately, the concept of a bureaucracy has been linked in modern society with inefficient, slow-moving organizations, which, ironically, is antithetical to the theory outlined by Weber.

Countless modern organizations have characteristics of bureaucracies. Many government agencies, universities, airports, and assembly-line plants, just to name a few, tend to operate according to bureaucratic principles. Even smaller organizations implement some of these procedures. For example, Gretta is an owner/operator of a small coffee shop. She was a barista for 3.5 years, transitioned to general manager for another 3 years, and then bought the business less than a year ago. She told this story in an interview for the book:

> When I first took over as owner, I wanted to be much more organized than the previous owners, so I created a handbook, and in it, I listed all the procedures and policies and how things work around here. Of course, there were certain ones highlighted so that if you don't follow them it could lead to termination with or without warning depending on how severe it was.
>
> I did once have an employee violate two of those policies, one of which was even more serious than the other. When I sat down to discuss this with the employee, they were a bit surprised that I was having this conversation and that it was so serious. They thought that since they had apologized then it was just over with. So on my end, it was a bit shocking because it was so laid out in the handbook that those were serious violations if they were to occur.
>
> I decided I was going to give them like a grace period, kind of more like a probation period kind of, instead of terminating them right away as the handbook stated should have happened. I think the problem was that we have a very relaxed work environment, and I don't like to micromanage. Since it is so relaxed, they just thought there wouldn't be any serious consequences to their violations of the handbook.

Gretta made an important error as she attempted to integrate elements of bureaucracy into her organization in an attempt to be more organized. She did not communicate to her employees that, regardless of the relaxed nature of the work environment, the handbook is central to their functioning as an organization. Mixed messages will not work in a bureaucracy, and Gretta now must expend considerable communicative energy to help her employees understand her intentions. As Taylor (2001) pointed out, in a bureaucracy, "if the rules of the organization cannot be formulated explicitly, they do not count" (p. 129). The problem with bureaucracies, then, seems to be as much in the human execution of the system as in the type of structure itself.

Summary

The Industrial Revolution brought many changes to the United States by the beginning of the 20th century. Whereas individuals and families had once been the primary producers of goods and services, large organizations were now taking over. Organizational theorists Frederick Taylor, Henri Fayol, and Max Weber were the major contributors to thought regarding the most efficient and effective means of running an organization.

Although Taylor, Fayol, and Weber differed in their approaches to organizational theory, they remain linked in that all three were attempting to enhance management's ability to predict and control the behavior of their workers. Table 2.1 summarizes the information presented in this chapter and highlights the role of communication in each theory.

TABLE 2.1 Classical Theories of Organizations

	TAYLOR	FAYOL	WEBER
Theory	Scientific management	Administrative theory	Rational-legal bureaucracy
Focus	Task	Management	Ideal organizational structure
Central feature	Scientific reasoning, empirical validation	Scalar chain	Reliance on hierarchy, rules
Role of communication	Task-structuring orders, downward, written	Task oriented, downward (horizontal when approved), written	Rule oriented, downward (grievances allowed), written

Communication was important to the classical approaches to organizations, though the extent to which the three theorists considered communication in their theories is minimal. All three theorists considered only the task function of communication (ignoring for the most part the relational and maintenance functions of communication). For Taylor, communication was the primary means by which workers were informed of how they were to perform their jobs. In Taylor's theory, communication was primarily written, generally flowed down the hierarchy, and was used to give orders. Fayol's use of communication was also task oriented, but he proposed the notion that communication may at times have to flow horizontally, instead of following the scalar chain. That, however, was to be done only in very limited circumstances. For Weber, communication was also central but was mainly limited to written rules and downward communication.

When you look at the classical approaches through the lens of misunderstandings, several things become clear. First, classical theorists certainly understood that anticipating misunderstandings was an important part of organizational life; however, they relegated this duty to managers. We suggest that *all* members of the organization approach organizational life with this mindset, not just managers. The classical theorists did not believe that workers were capable of this level of thinking. Second, classical approaches to organizational management were designed to help predict and control behavior in organizations. Although the strict hierarchies, rigid scalar chains, and rule-oriented structures helped reduce misunderstandings based on role obligations, for example, the same elements helped create misunderstandings based on mistreatment of workers, lack of information regarding an overall mission, lack of attention to human concerns, and myriad other issues. Third, communication skills necessary to execute classical management were all but absent in classical approaches to organizations. Because workers were considered to be parts of the machine, two-way, person-centered communication was unnecessary and antithetical. Finally, classical theorists would opt for the *contain* strategy on the responses to misunderstandings continuum. When a misunderstanding occurred in a classically structured organization, the organization would not be concerned with the emotional and relational needs of the organizational members but would concentrate on minimizing the impact of the misunderstanding on the general operation of the organization and seek to restore order and efficiency quickly. It is possible that some learning could occur but most likely it would be manifested in the creation of a new rule or reexamination of the design of a particular task.

Classical theories of organizations are still evident today, more than a century after they were introduced. Many manufacturing plants (particularly those whose primary technology is the assembly line), utility companies, certain factions of the local, state, and federal government, and the military are organized in this way. Even those organizations moving toward a more humanistic approach to management (discussed in Chapter 3) still have elements of these classical management theories. Understanding the origin of these elements, why they are in place, and what their benefits and limitations maybe is beneficial as you strive to function competently as a member of an organization. In the next chapter, we discuss the next wave of organizational theory designed to help alleviate some of the pressure caused by the misunderstandings fostered in classically run organizations.

Humanistic Theories of Organizations

LEARNING OBJECTIVES

1. Examine the importance given to social relationships by the human relations theories

2. Outline the misunderstandings that emerged when transitioning from classical theory to humanistic theories

3. Identify the importance of the contributions of Mary Parker Follett, the Hawthorne Studies, and Chester Barnard to the development of humanistic theories

4. Explain the differences between McGregor's Theory X and Theory Y assumptions

5. Describe how the work of Likert and Blake and Mouton advanced the development of human resources theory past human relations theory

Part of what determines your satisfaction, effectiveness, and desire to stay in an organization is the extent to which the structure of the organization meets your needs and wants. If you are someone who appreciates precision, direction, clear rules, and hierarchy, then organizations structured according to classical principles such as the ones described in Chapter 2 will work very well for you. However, if close management control is not something that you thrive under, then classically structured organizations will seem very constraining to you. Such a situation happened to Malika, who worked as a program manager in the admissions office of a local college. Her job consisted of making over 150 attempts each day to contact potential students via phone, email, text, or in-person interviews. She was required to recruit a certain number of students per quarter and make sure they made it through all steps of enrollment. She told us this story:

> I worked directly under the director of admissions, Jackie. Jackie was a good person overall, but she and I did not work well together. I have never worked in an environment where I felt so micromanaged and left without freedom to succeed. I am not a person who works well with someone who watches my every move; I need independence and to be trusted to thrive, which I am highly capable of doing.

> I remember one day Jackie called me into her office. She was concerned
> about me not reaching my goal (number of students recruited) for the
> quarter when the week before I was praised for my performance from
> the previous quarter. Rather than acknowledging my capabilities and
> supporting me, she moved my cube to right outside of her office to listen
> to my phone calls. If someone is going to do that to me, I am going to try
> less hard because I hate being micromanaged. I know I am fully capable.
> It was embarrassing having the entire office look at me when I moved
> my things from my desk and had to tell them that she needed to listen
> to my calls.

Malika clearly did not appreciate the level of control that her supervisor exerted over her, and it affected her productivity and desire to stay. In fact, she put herself on the job market soon after this incident. Malika was in an organization where close supervision and strict attention to daily productivity were the norm, but she was the kind of worker who needed a supervisor who empowered her to make her own decisions and allowed her to use the aspects of her personality and skill set that she knew could make her successful. The strain that Malika felt is, in part, analogous to the historical development of organizational theory.

As the number and types of organizations grew in the early and mid-20th century, so too did the desires of theorists and practitioners for a more *humanistic* approach to managing. The classical approaches to management that emphasized coercion, control, and punishment that had been deemed to be effective and efficient were beginning to be questioned. Classical approaches, particularly Taylorism, were starting to be cast as having high "supervision cost, lack of flexibility, loss of creativity, central information processing overload, unattractive work on the shop floor, a class with democratic values and bureaucratization" (Pruijt, 2000, p. 447). Competing management theories emerged that were based on very different philosophical orientations regarding the relationship between work and workers.

Human relations theory and human resources theory were developed to promote the concerns of the individual worker in an atmosphere that was mainly focused on production. Human relations theory appeared first, soon followed by human resources theory, which attempted to remedy some of the philosophical and practical issues related to human relations. This chapter discusses the origins and the major theorists associated with both human relations and human resources theories.

There is no widely accepted metaphor for the organization in the humanistic approach as there is for the classical approach (i.e., the machine). Authors have employed metaphors for the organization from the humanistic approach such as *organic, family,* or *identity,* but none of these have the level of endorsement that accompanies the classical machine metaphor. Instead of attempting to develop a new metaphor for the organization from the humanistic approach, we offer a metaphor for the *relationship* between management and workers—the suggestion box. The relationship between managers and workers in the humanistic approaches is perhaps the biggest change from classical theory. Managers are asked to solicit and value the opinions of workers, to understand their needs, likes, and dislikes, and how the organization can be improved. Based on this, we feel the suggestion box metaphor captures that relationship. The suggestion box is a way for managers to connect with employees and solicit their feedback, and employees have the opportunity to provide their input. We will use the metaphor of the suggestion box to explain how the various humanistic approaches to organizations have worked and not worked in practice.

Human Relations Theory

As we begin the discussion of human relations theory, consider the following story from one of the interviews conducted for this book with George, who was a manager for a railroad. His story is a modern illustration of the situation that led to the development of the human relations approach to organizations.

> I was working as a member of a railroad development team that included a director, four other managers, and a staff assistant. We were charged with developing an advanced railroad electronics system, using cutting-edge technology, including the global positioning system and data communications to take dispatching of trains to a higher level of efficiency.
>
> We all knew we were just a few weeks from having everything solved, but the ultimate question was asked by our director. Simply, he asked the question, "Does anyone here have any reason why we shouldn't turn the system on and test our progress?" There were a few of the sideway glances going on around the table of 25 or so attendees when someone finally spoke up, but that person didn't get the opportunity to express their concern. Instead, our director began a swearing rant and criticism directed at that person, as well as members of both teams. Taking out all the expletives, the rant essentially said, "You guys have been messing around with this system for three years and we're going to turn it on." To which the recipient of the rant responded, without swearing: "Well, if you already had your mind made up, why did you ask the question? And if you don't want to hear bad news, don't ask questions thinking you're only going to get the answers you want to hear."

George's story demonstrates the feelings that arise in some workers when they are confronted with organizational practices based on classical theory. As you may recall from Chapter 2, to maintain predictability and control, classically run organizations concentrate the decision-making power at the top of the hierarchy, minimize input from lower level employees, and rely on science and rules to guide behavior. By doing so, a whole new class of problems is created.

George's story shows that in some classically run organizations, workers tend to feel as if they do not have any control over their work situation, that management does not care about their opinions, and that their feelings and ideas are unimportant. Betsy, a financial aid office worker, described this last point well:

> So we have an open-door policy at work, which is good, but I don't believe the bosses are always listening to what we have to say. I know some things can't be changed. I realize that, but I think they should try to work on some of them.

George and Betsy would have been much more satisfied in an organization guided by the principles of human relations theory.

Misunderstandings and the Emergence of the Worker

Human relations theory is characterized by a shift in emphasis from task to worker. Human relations theorists argued that the individual worker was being tapped only for their physical contributions, leaving their creative, cognitive, and emotional aspects unattended. The theories suggested by this movement put a greater emphasis on communication, cooperation, participation, and celebration of the worker. They emphasized "choosing to use human skills instead of trying to incorporate these into information systems" (Pruijt, 2000, p. 447).

This shift of emphasis from the task to the worker can be understood in light of misunderstandings. The previous chapter noted that classical theories recommended strict organizational structures and regulated communication as a means of increasing predictability and decreasing misunderstandings. However, as the stories of George and Betsy illustrate, those attempts created a whole new class of misunderstandings that served to reduce the effectiveness and satisfaction of the workers. Lower level workers felt as if their creativity, initiative, and experience were not being used in a system that relied primarily on one-way, downward, and rule-based communication. Therefore, the very system designed to reduce misunderstandings actually served to produce misunderstandings in other forms.

Human relations theory is based on a slightly more dyadic (two-way) conceptualization of communication. Human relations theorists argued that social relationships are at the heart of organizational behavior and to promote effectiveness, managers must promote the social well-being of the workers. The prime mechanism for doing so is communication that flows in all directions in the organization. Workers should be allowed to voice their opinions, complaints, suggestions, and feelings; the result should be a reduction in misunderstandings, as well as increased satisfaction and production.

Just as classical theory created misunderstandings in an attempt to reduce them, so did human relations theory. As you read, keep the concept of misunderstandings in mind and think of what new forms of misunderstandings may have arisen. In this section, we begin with a brief introduction to Mary Parker Follett, whose critiques of the assumptions of classical theorists laid the foundation for humanistic approaches to management. Next, we discuss two precursors to human relations theory that introduce an emphasis on relationships and communication: the Hawthorne Studies and the work of Chester Barnard. This section concludes with a summary of the major work on human relations theory, Douglas McGregor's Theory X and Theory Y.

Questioning Classical Assumptions: Mary Parker Follett

The approaches to managing workers and work forwarded by the classical theorists, particularly Fayol and Taylor, had a stronghold in organizations by the early decades of the 1900s. Their arguments for objective, fact-based structuring of tasks and administration were welcomed as organizations that previously struggled with organizing their growing labor force welcomed the seemingly no-nonsense approach to productivity and efficiency. Mary Parker Follett (1868–1933), however, was an early critic of classical theorists, and though her work has been largely overlooked in the history of management, her arguments were well-reasoned and forcefully presented (Parker, 1984). As a result, we join others in crediting Follett with bolstering the move away from classical theories by questioning assumptions upon which those theories were based.

Follett, after her education at Radcliffe and subsequent study in Paris, returned to the United States and worked with the poor and otherwise disadvantaged, founding centers for community development where the underserved could receive vocational guidance (Parker, 1984). This work seems to have informed her perspective on organizational life, particularly leading her to take issue with the "experts" who relied purely on "facts" to run their organizations and manage their workers. She had disdain for the theorists who seemed to think so little of the workforce when she summarized their position this way: "For the people, it is assumed, will gladly agree to become automata when we show them all the things—nice, solid, objective *things*—they can have by abandoning their own experience in favor of a superior race of men called experts" (1924/2013, p. 3). In other words, Follet attempted to show us that classical theorists thought so little of workers in that they would gladly give up their individuality in the name of the god terms of *objective* and *experts*. Follet seemed to be calling Taylor to task directly on this point of surrendering individuality when she wrote, "The automatic result of scientific investigation is overcoming of difference. This view both fails to see the importance of diversity, and also ignores the fact that the accumulation of information does not overcome diversity" (1924/2013, p. 5).

Follett laid the groundwork for the human relations movement that then gained a foothold as a result of the Hawthorne Studies, which you will read about next. Before we summarize those important studies, though, we want to emphasize that Follet deeply understood the value of the individual and the value of diverse approaches to work and organizing. She based this value on her conviction that objectivity was a farce because any behavior is deeply connected to the behavior of others, which then affects future behavior for all involved. Follet argued, "*While* I am behaving, the environment is changing because of my behaving, and my behavior is a response to the new situation which I, in part, have created" (1924/ 2013, pp. 63–64). She believed that theorists who only view objective reality are missing the social dimensions that create and recreate that reality, which is then changed by their behavior within it. And it is from this point of contention with classical theorists that we introduce the Hawthorne Studies.

The Beginning of the Human Relations Movement: The Hawthorne Studies

From 1924 to 1932, a series of industrial studies was conducted at the Hawthorne Works of the Western Electric Company in Chicago (Roethlisberger & Dickson, 1939). The **Hawthorne Studies**, as they have become known, eventually led to the development of the human relations school of management, most closely associated with Elton Mayo of Harvard University (Landsberger, 1958).

Officers of the Hawthorne Works conducted the first of the Hawthorne Studies in 1924. The officers (who were essentially following Taylor's scientific management principles) were interested in the "relation of quality and quantity of illumination to efficiency in industry" (Roethlisberger & Dickson, 1939, p. 14). The results of the illumination studies surprised the investigators and served as the impetus for a series of three studies (conducted between 1927 and 1932) by Elton Mayo, in conjunction with F. J. Roethlisberger (also from Harvard) and William Dickson, from Western Electric. The methods used and conclusions drawn from the Hawthorne Studies have been subject to much criticism, but their impact on the theory and practice of management cannot be discounted.

The Illumination Study began in November 1924 and was designed to test the effect of lighting intensity on worker productivity. The prediction of the researchers (following Taylor's principles) was that a certain level of illumination would lead to an optimum level of worker output. To find this level of illumination, the researchers segregated two groups of workers into two separate rooms of equal illumination and measured their output. In one room, the light remained relatively constant (this was the experimental control room). In the other room, the light was increased and decreased. After each change in illumination level, worker output was measured. In both the control room and the test room, productivity increased; there was no significant difference in the production rates of the control group (relatively constant level of illumination) and the test group until the illumination for the test group dropped to a point where they could hardly see. Despite the apparent "failure" of the Illumination Study to determine the appropriate level of illumination for optimum output, the researchers found value in the results. The general conclusion was that more investigation into the influence of human relations on work behavior was necessary. The results of the Illumination Study led to the next study, this time headed by Mayo and his Harvard University research team.

The Relay Assembly Test Room Study was conducted with a smaller group (five experienced female workers who were willing and cooperative) in a separate room, away from the regular shop floor. The task the five women were to complete was the assembly of telephone relays (consisting of putting together 35 small parts and assembling them with four machine screws). The number of hours per day and the number of days per week worked were changed throughout the course of the study, as were the number and duration of rest pauses, the method of remuneration, and the extent to which informal talk between the workers was allowed or encouraged. Each worker's output was measured regularly, and the workers' comments and suggestions were shared with an observer. The results of this study were similar to the results of the Illumination Study. In general, production and satisfaction tended to increase regardless of the changes made in workday length and rest pauses. The research team posited five possible explanations for these results but eventually concluded that the workers' increased output and increased satisfaction were related to changes in supervisory practices (Roethlisberger & Dickson, 1939). The investigators were beginning to believe that human interrelationships (particularly between worker and supervisor) could be an important contributing factor when considering worker productivity.

The Relay Assembly Test Room Study indicated a connection between supervisory practices and employee morale. The Interviewing Program was designed to gather data regarding this possible connection. The Interviewing Program began in September 1928, and when they were finished, a total of 21,126 employees had taken part. The actual results of the interviews were perhaps less important than the process itself. As a by-product of having the opportunity to provide feedback on their personal work situation, many workers indicated a more positive feeling toward the company and a better mental attitude. Although some employees could not see the benefit of the Interviewing Program, Roethlisberger and Dickson indicated that many of them welcomed the chance to talk about their feelings and ideas. The interviews provided them with an opportunity to participate in the effort to improve the workplace. The results of the Interviewing Program led the researchers to the concluding study in the series.

The data from the Interviewing Program indicated that social groups might exercise very strong control over the production of individual work behavior on the shop floor. The primary concern of the research team and company officers was the possibility that there might be a form of informal leadership operating to restrict employee output. The Bank Wiring Room Observation Study was conducted because the research team wanted to see for themselves how the social control they had heard about in the interviews actually manifested itself on the shop floor. For this study, the researchers put 14 bank wiremen in a separate room and had them complete their individual tasks. They were not informed of the nature of the study, and the researcher present in the room acted like a disinterested spectator. The investigators concluded, based on observations and output data, that each worker was artificially restricting his output; output was lower than the company-established target. As Roethlisberger and Dickson related, "This standard was not imposed upon them, but apparently had been formulated by the workmen themselves" (1939, p. 445). Informally developed group norms were present in the work group that operated to restrict individual worker output. From the Bank Wiring Room Observation Study, it became clear that an *informal organization* that serves to constrain individual employees' behavior is present within the formal organizational structure.

Implications of the Hawthorne Studies

The Hawthorne Studies had several implications for management theory. First, the Illumination Study led to the notion that the mere practice of observing people's behavior tends to alter their behavior (a phenomenon that has come to be known as the **Hawthorne effect**). Management theorists translated this conclusion into a principle for supervisors: Pay attention to your workers to increase their satisfaction and productivity.

Second, the Relay Assembly Test Room Study changed the way human interrelationships were viewed. As a result of these studies, the relationships among workers and between workers and their supervisors were believed to be very powerful. Whereas classical theory treated these relationships only according to task requirements and in a unidirectional form, the resulting theory began to view them more personally. This set of studies also demonstrated that this new relationship form would increase the amount and quality of worker participation in decision-making.

Third, the Interviewing Program demonstrated for the first time the powerful influence of **upward communication**. The fact that workers were asked for their opinions and told that they mattered was enough to increase their positive attitudes toward the company.

Fourth, the Bank Wiring Room Study led future theorists to account for the existence of **informal communication**. Classical theories did not acknowledge the usefulness of communication other than that which occurred formally (e.g., supervisor to subordinate). In fact, as you may remember, great pains were taken to ensure that horizontal and upward communication were minimized at all costs.

Although these implications may not seem newsworthy today, it is important to remember that at the time of these studies, little was known about the powerful nature of social relations in the workplace. The Hawthorne Studies represented a major turning point in the development of management theory and practice, moving managers more toward the interpersonal aspects of organizing.

The extent to which the Hawthorne Studies affected the trajectory of management theory cannot be denied. As Sonnenfeld (1983) remarked, "Given such unusual breadth of validity and significance, one must question just whose interest is truly served by continuing this tired historical debate" (p. 908). The processes and results of these studies led not only researchers at Hawthorne to reconsider the underlying principles of classical theory, but now other theorists were also beginning to propose competing theories based on vastly different views of human nature. In the next section, we discuss the contribution of Chester Barnard to the development of the human relations approach.

The Emergence of Communication: Chester Barnard

Chester Barnard, an executive with American Telephone and Telegraph Company for more than 40 years, can be considered a bridge between classical and human relations theories (Kreps, 1990). Barnard's (1938) book, *The Functions of the Executive*, is an executive's analysis of organizational life, written because Barnard found that previous writings on the subject neither mirrored his experience as an executive nor demonstrated an understanding of the leadership practices of successful organizational executives with whom he interacted. His experience also led him to disagree with Max Weber's philosophy of organization with its focus on economic interests over human behavior.

Although some of Barnard's ideas are rooted in classical theory (e.g., he prescribed strict lines of communication), he spends much of his time arguing for a more person-centered system of organization that recognizes the potential of every worker and the centrality of communication to the organizing process. Based on these ideas, Barnard can be considered an important link between classical theory and human relations theory and an important person in the development of the field of organizational communication.

The Functions of the Executive covers a variety of topics related to industrial life. Here we discuss four issues most relevant to the field of organizational communication: (1) formal versus informal organization, (2) communication, (3) authority, and (4) zone of indifference.

Formal Versus Informal Organization

Barnard recognized the existence of an informal organization and how it differs from a formal organization. **Formal organization** is a system of activities that are coordinated consciously by two or more people. The people must be able to communicate with each other, be willing to contribute to the collaborative action, and work together for a common purpose. The **informal organization**, by contrast, is based on myriad interactions that take place throughout an organization's history. The informal organization has the following characteristics: (1) it is indefinite; (2) it is structureless; (3) there are no definite subdivisions of personnel.

The informal organization differs from the formal organization in two main ways. First, the formal organization is a definite, structured entity, whereas the informal organization is not bound by structure or function. Second, the concept of a common purpose is not present in the definition of an informal organization as it is with a formal organization. This is not to say, though, that the informal organization does not have definite effects. According to Barnard, the informal organization allows for the construction of social norms, customs, and ideals. The informal organization also makes it possible for the formal organization to come to fruition. Barnard believed that most executives were unaware of the existence of the informal organization and its relationship to the formal organization. According to him, the informal organization must be recognized and understood so that the formal organization may operate effectively. One of the keys to successful organization for Barnard is the concept of cooperation.

Communication

Communication is critical to cooperation, though Barnard understood it is a complex human process. He considered communication to be both the most likely reason for the success of cooperation and the reason for its failure. Given this, he argued that the primary function of the organizational executive is to serve as a channel for communication. To aid the executive in serving this function, Barnard outlined a system of communication. He argued for some classical orientations to communication, such as following appropriate channels of communication, and keeping the distance in the communication chain as short as possible. He also distanced himself from classical approaches when he suggested that executives be skilled in communication in addition to their formal task competencies.

Barnard's system of communication is an interesting mix of classical theory and something more humanistic. As opposed to classical theorists, Barnard seemed to understand the centrality of communication to the functioning of the organization and the manager's job. But his understanding of communication is still quite limited. His system appears to be aimed directly at reducing misunderstandings, but it lacks in the areas of relationship formation and maintenance, which are the essence of organizational life. Although communication is central to cooperation for Barnard, a cursory review of the system of communication just outlined reveals it to be tied to the concept of authority.

Authority

Authority is associated with securing cooperation from organizational members and is intimately tied with communication. As Barnard described it, authority is an inter-relationship among at least three elements: the originator of the communication, the communication itself, and the receiver.

Barnard privileged authority based on position over authority based on an individual (much as the classical theorists did). **Authority of position** is authority ascribed to a communication based on the fact that it originates from a superior position in the organizational structure, regardless of the relative ability of the person occupying the position. **Authority of leadership** is authority ascribed to a communication based on the knowledge and ability of the person communicating the message, regardless of the position they occupy. Combining authority of position with authority of leadership creates a situation where those receiving the communication will tend to obey a given order with little question.

Zone of Indifference

The final concept we will discuss from Barnard integrates communication, authority, and human behavior. According to Barnard, if you were to line up all the possible orders for action that could be given, some would be clearly unacceptable (outside the boundaries of what the individual anticipated was necessary as a member of the organization) and would not be followed. Other orders would be either mildly unacceptable or mildly acceptable and might or might not be followed. The remaining orders would be acceptable and would be followed. The **zone of indifference** marks the boundaries of what that person will consider doing without question, based on expectations developed on entering the organization.

The best interest of the executive is to broaden the zone of indifference for each worker, such that orders for action are carried out with little questioning of authority or appropriateness. The zone of indifference narrows or broadens depending on the extent to which the perceived benefits of following the order outweigh the costs.

As is evident from Figure 3.1, though, a large portion of orders for action may fall outside a worker's zone of indifference.

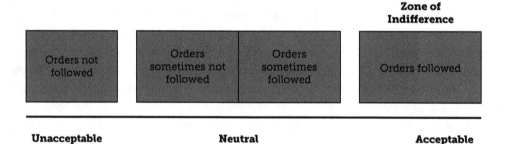

FIGURE 3.1 Zone of Indifference

How, then, do organizational executives induce workers to follow such orders? Barnard posited that an executive who has authority based on both formal position and personal knowledge can create a situation in which organizational members will follow orders they might not otherwise have obeyed.

Although authority of position is an element of the formal organization, authority of leadership is more a property of the informal organization and arises through interaction. It is for this reason that Barnard can be considered an organizational communication theorist. The principles discussed here, drawn from *The Functions of the Executive*, represent an important contribution to the development of a theory of organizations based on communication.

In conjunction with Mary Parker Follet, Barnard's work represents an important link between classical theory and human relations theory because he began to draw attention away from formal organizational structures and toward such things as communication, cooperation, and the informal organization. His work introduced important concepts that were then integrated by other theorists in the human relations movement. In the next section, we discuss the prime example of a human relations theory that developed based on the work of Mayo, Roethlisberger, Dickson, Barnard, and others.

Theory X and Theory Y: Douglas McGregor

Douglas McGregor (1906–1964), a Sloan Professor of Management at Massachusetts Institute of Technology, articulated the basic principles of human relations theory.

In *The Human Side of Enterprise* (1960/1985), he argued that to understand human behavior, one must discover the theoretical assumptions on which behavior is based. Of particular interest to him was the behavior of managers toward workers. McGregor believed that managers are guided in their treatment of workers by beliefs about how the workers collectively think, act, and feel.

McGregor understood that managers wanted to accomplish two interrelated objectives with regard to workers: (1) predict and control their behavior and (2) tap their unrealized potential. The problem for him was that existing managerial theory, classical theory in particular, was inadequate in this regard. The theoretical assumptions of classical theory are unable to assist managers in accomplishing these objectives. Most importantly, McGregor believed that classical theorists' assumptions about human behavior were incorrect. It is this issue, misguided or wrong assumptions of classical theory, to which McGregor turned his attention in *The Human Side of Enterprise.*

He took the most exception to the assumption that authority is the central form of ensuring organizational control. Overreliance on authority as a means of control meant that other, perhaps more productive, forms of control were ignored, particularly those that acknowledge and foster the individual skills and abilities of the worker. McGregor argued that if a manager is seeking collaboration, authority is a crutch.

Because McGregor rejected the basic assumptions of classical theory, he put forward a competing theory of management based on vastly different assumptions—assumptions that he argued were more firmly rooted in the reality of human nature. He termed classical theory and its assumptions *Theory X* and human relations theory and its assumptions *Theory Y.*

Theory X

To begin our discussion of Theory X, consider another story from Ernest, the novice limestone quarry worker from whom we heard in Chapter 2:

> Part of my job was to drive a tanker truck around the quarry to fuel up various stationary pieces of equipment. All of the operators driving mobile rigs would sidle up to a refueling tank placed outside of the shop. Keeping this tank full was important so vehicles running up to refill would not be slowed in their operations.
>
> One day, I had just filled many tanks, ending with the aforementioned one, and had parked the fuel truck in its spot next to the shop and main diesel pump station. Having completed my fueling duties, I returned to the interior of the shop to see what other duties were needing attention. Jorge was standing out back, visible through the long shop and out the huge sliding doors. I noticed he was inspecting the fuel tank I had recently finished filling, and a piece of equipment was nearby, I assumed in need of a fill. He slammed his arms to his sides and half ran into the building. He pointed at me and ordered me to come outside.

Jorge: "I thought I told you all of the tanks need filling! Why is this one empty? I just tried to fill up the cherry picker and now time is wasted because you did not fill this tank!"

Me: "But I did fill it."

Jorge: "It's empty! I just tried to pump from it. Nothing! It's empty!"

With each repetition, he waved a raised index finger chest high toward me. Not touching, but aggressively close. He was, like many bullies, so tense that he appeared to be muscular, and his eyes were naturally wild, even more so at this moment.

Jorge: "Fill the tank!!!" he roared, storming off to spread love and sunshine elsewhere.

I then did the one thing his rage had not allowed him to consider after finding the pump hose dry and the ON lever useless: I opened the filler door atop the tank and peered in. Full. Jorge had not seen that the fill hose had twisted into a kink along its considerable length. He jumped to the conclusion that the moron college boy had screwed up again. He was so certain as to the problem's cause that he ceased further inquiry that would have proven he was wrong.

Ernest's story is a perfect way to introduce Theory X. Jorge assumed that Ernest was lazy, incompetent, and needed to be reprimanded at every turn. Ernest, however, had eagerly done his job effectively but could not overcome the assumptions that his boss had regarding him. Ernest was, to say the least, demoralized.

Theory X, or classical theory, consists of three assumptions that managers hold regarding workers. First, humans inherently do not like work and will avoid it if possible. Second, because of this, humans need to be coerced, threatened with punishment, and controlled to get them to do work on behalf of the organization. Third, above all, the average human avoids responsibility, would rather be directed, but would prefer to avoid responsibility. These assumptions represent well how the limestone quarry boss, Jorge, viewed Ernest.

Based on these assumptions, managers naturally treat workers with little respect, motivate them mainly through punishment and financial reward, and spend the majority of their time monitoring and coercing them into behaving appropriately. McGregor disagreed with these assumptions and the resulting practices, arguing that they did little to explain the breadth and depth of human behavior in organizations. In other words, although McGregor understood that managers could coerce and control people into working, it is against their nature to be treated in this way. What is needed is a theory of management that more soundly resonates with human nature.

Theory Y

McGregor argued that while management was becoming more concerned with the human aspects of organizational life, managers' basic assumptions about human nature had not changed; they were still firmly rooted in Theory X. In contrast to Theory X, McGregor proposed **Theory Y** and its competing assumptions about human nature (1960/1985, pp. 47–48), which are as follows:

1. The expenditure of physical and mental effort in work is as natural as play or rest.

2. External control and the threat of punishment are not the only means for bringing about effort toward objectives. Man [*sic*] will exercise self-direction and self-control in the service of objectives to which he is committed.

3. Commitment to objectives is a function of the rewards associated with their achievement.

4. The average human being learns, under proper conditions, not only to accept but to seek responsibility.

5. The capacity to exercise a relatively high degree of imagination, ingenuity, and creativity in the solution of organizational problems is widely, not narrowly, distributed in the population.

6. Under the conditions of modern industrial life, the intellectual potentialities of the average human being are only partially utilized.

The assumptions of Theory Y are vastly different from those of Theory X and paint a more positive picture of human nature. When managers operate from the assumptions of Theory X, the potential ways in which they can interact with their employees is limited. If they operate from the assumptions of Theory Y, though, the range of possibilities for new managerial practices expands.

Perhaps the greatest implication of Theory Y rests in the matter of control. If work is as natural as play or rest and the average human seeks responsibility, then most people are inherently more creative and driven than Theory X would lead one to believe. How do managers control their behavior so that they achieve quality production? For McGregor, the answer was commitment to objectives. If workers could be committed to the organizational and task objectives, they would naturally respond with high-level production. It was important, he noted, that commitment to objectives would come not from punishment or financial reward (necessarily) but from the premise that the individual's goals are best achieved by the success of the organization, which is a principle McGregor termed integration. Commitment, then, is the key to control and production.

Although the assumptions of Theory Y are attractive in principle, what does Theory Y look like in practice? McGregor suggested the Scanlon Plan, a philosophy of management based on the assumptions of Theory Y, as a prototypical example. The Scanlon

Plan (named for its creator, Joseph Scanlon) has two central features: (1) cost-reduction sharing and (2) effective participation.

A few words about the first feature may be useful for the present discussion. The Scanlon Plan advocates cost-reduction sharing for organizational members. As organizational members contribute to the overall performance of the organization, they should be rewarded financially (in addition to the personal satisfaction they are already receiving from increased participation) when the organization increases its profitability.

More important to the study of organizational communication is the second feature of the Scanlon Plan—effective participation. Effective participation is a formal means of providing opportunities to every member of the organization to contribute ideas for improving organizational effectiveness. Effective participation is based on the Theory Y assumption that workers are generally underutilized:

> Even the repetitive worker at the bottom of the hierarchy is potentially more than a pair of hands. He is a human resource. His know-how and ingenuity, properly utilized, may make a far greater difference to the success of the enterprise than any improvement in his physical effort, although of course his effort is not unimportant. Moreover, he achieves recognition and other important social and ego satisfactions from this utilization of his capacities. (1960/1985pp. 113–114)

Although participation seems to be the key to member satisfaction and productivity, as well as overall organizational effectiveness, McGregor warned that it must be implemented appropriately. Groups of managers, consultants, and academics have divergent views regarding participation. Some believe it to be the magic formula for every organizational problem, whereas others see it as a form of managerial relinquishment that wastes time and undermines the manager's power. Those who understand participation, however, know how to use it successfully. They recognize that it is useful but that it is not the solution to every problem. This group would never use participation in a manipulative way. McGregor aligned with the latter group and argued for a sincere but realistic implementation and vision of what effective participation could produce for an organization.

What the adoption of Theory Y assumptions and practices means for an organization and its members is very complicated. Perhaps the most important change that occurs is that there is a concern for relationships in the organization. As the need to increase commitment increases, so does the need to develop strong, communication-based relationships among organizational members, particularly between the supervisor and the subordinate. Supervisors must have genuine concern for the attitudes, needs, and potential contributions of their subordinates and must recognize the interdependent nature of their relationships. Cahn (1971) stated this point simply by saying, "embracing this philosophy does not remove the fact that one does not easily solve the problems of people working with people" (p. 23). As managers work with the people they supervise, they must do so not only with the philosophical orientation of Theory Y but also with communication skills that support that philosophy. According to Sager

(2008), the "profile of the Theory Y superior, characterized by supportiveness, non-verbal expressiveness, a relaxed demeanor, and communicative behavior that leaves a lasting and presumably positive impression, could be described as 'warm'" (p. 309).

Human relations theory, originating from the Hawthorne Studies and perhaps best exemplified by McGregor's Theory Y, attempted to reverse the treatment of workers as it occurred under classical theory. Although human relations theorists posited new ways of managing organizations, organizational practitioners were less enthusiastic about the full-scale implementation of the participative management principles. In the next section, we discuss the emergence of human resources theory as a remedy to the misapplications of and misunderstandings caused by human relations theory.

Human Resources Theory

Managers and workers of the time (and today) often found it difficult to adopt the principles of human relations theory. The following story from one of our interviews illustrates the problems that occur when making the transition from classical theory to human relations theory. Julian is a production operator for an organization that supplies ingredients to other food manufacturing organizations:

> When I first started, there seemed to be a lack of trust between the supervisors and the employees. I remember when I started, they had all the employees take a survey that the company needed everyone to take to see what the organization could improve on. However, the response rate from the employees was low. What I noticed is that the employees did not trust the supervisors in what they were saying—that the survey was there to help them rather than to get people in trouble. A lot of people did not take the survey, though, as they were just not able to trust what they were being told. That's when the higher-ups got involved and questioned why employees weren't taking the survey. Having worked there for 6 months now, I noticed that a lot of the complaints my coworkers have are ignored by the supervisors. They might not take it seriously or leave the complaint unattended. I assumed that it was a part of the culture and how they communicated.

Julian's story illustrates what happens when classically trained supervisors are compelled to change their ways by their bosses, to care more about their workers, and seek their input. In this case, the culture of the organization and years of being inculcated with the traditional ways of doing things did not allow for the implementation of more participative management, and the workers did not trust the supervisors' intentions. What sounded good in principle was not feasible in practice.

This, too, was the fate of human relations theory. Managers, trained according to traditional principles, were instructed to start "caring" for their workers and to allow them to participate in the decision-making process. In many cases, managers were not equipped with the new skills or the supporting organizational structure or culture to make this rather dramatic change. As reported in a July 22, 1973, edition of the *Daytona Beach Sunday News Journal*, a union representative at the time went so far as to call the new managerial approaches "a stop watch in sheep's clothing" (Fialka, 1973, p. 7E) because the managers used caring as another means of control.

Miles (1965) argued that the key element of human relations theory, participation, was used only to make workers *feel* as if they were a part of the organizational decision-making processes:

> Participation, in this model, is a lubricant which oils away resistance to formal authority . . . . In sum, the human relations approach does not bring out the fact that participation may be useful for its own sake. The possibility that subordinates will, in fact, bring to light points which the manager may have overlooked, if considered at all, tends to be mentioned only in passing . . . . The ultimate goal sought in both the traditional and the human relations model is compliance with managerial authority. (pp. 149–150)

Julian's story comes to mind at this point. Workers in his organization were being asked for their participation in improving the organization, but based on years of their suggestions being ignored, they had no reason to trust that their supervisors all of a sudden cared for them and their opinions.

This situation also returns us to the notion of misunderstandings. As mentioned earlier in the chapter, elements of human relations theory served to reduce the misunderstandings created under a classical management system, but new forms developed. In particular, misunderstandings arose when workers were told they were important but were not treated as such. This contradiction led to suspicion on the part of the workers and unwillingness to trust management. Our metaphor of the suggestion box is useful here to understand what happened with the relationship between management and workers in human relations theory. Think of the problems that occurred in practice with human relations theory as a suggestion box being installed, but it does not have a bottom and there is a garbage can below it. Suggestions may be put in, but they are not seen or attended to; instead, they are readily discarded. Workers quickly distrust the process after learning that their suggestions are solicited but not truly appreciated. This is what happened to Julian and his coworkers.

Misunderstandings also occurred because managers lacked the communication skills necessary to interact with workers on a humane level. Managers knew how to communicate using fear, orders, threats, and one-way communication but were seemingly lost when they were supposed to show concern for their workers, solicit their input, and engage them personally. The good intentions of the theory led to a whole host of misunderstandings.

Given the apparent failure of human relations to improve the general state of affairs for workers in organizations, Miles proposed the theory of human resources as an alternative. Human resources theory differs from human relations theory in three main ways. First, human resources theory assumes that all people (not just managers) are "reservoirs of untapped resources" (1965, p. 150). Given this assumption, it is the obligation of the manager to tap these resources, whether they are physical or creative.

Second, human relations theory (as practiced) often led to managers retaining decision-making power for all but the most routine decisions. Human resources theory prescribes that many decisions can be made more effectively and efficiently by those workers who are most directly involved with their consequences. That is what Kumiko, the pig farm manager, was advocating. Miles argued, "The more important the decision, the greater is [the manager's] *obligation* to encourage ideas and suggestions from his subordinates" (1965, p. 152). In other words, participation in decision-making and actual decision-making power cannot be relegated to either false or perfunctory status. Returning to the metaphor of the suggestion box, human resources theory installed the bottom to the suggestion box that human relations removed. As a result, workers not only provide input, but their input is collected, viewed, and incorporated.

Finally, Miles suggested that the greatest difference between human relations and human resources is the relationship between employee satisfaction and performance. In human relations theory, increased satisfaction is a direct result of increased participation in the decision-making process. The eventual outcome of increased satisfaction in this model is greater compliance with authority. Human resources, by contrast, suggests that satisfaction is not necessarily a direct result of participation but is instead a derivative of the improved decision-making and self-control that results from effective, genuine participation. With this gain, the cycle feeds itself again, and improved satisfaction and morale contribute to improved decision-making and control.

In essence, the human resources theory of satisfaction and morale says that workers are not satisfied with merely being given a voice in the decision-making process; far too often their voice is not heard. Instead, increased satisfaction is related to the improved decision-making and self-control that occurs because of participation that is genuinely solicited and heard.

Interestingly, Miles noted that most managers in his day subscribed to the human relations model for their workers, but when it came time to being viewed by their own superiors, they subscribed to the human resources model. In the next section, we discuss two prevalent human resources theories: those of Rensis Likert and Robert Blake and Jane Mouton.

Four Systems of Management: Rensis Likert

In his book *New Patterns of Management*, Rensis Likert (1961) proposed a theory of management that exemplifies the basic tenets of human resources theory outlined by Miles. Likert maintained that a new system of management was necessary because of the changes occurring in U.S. society at the time. As a result of increased education, Likert argued, people are less likely to accept direct orders and close supervision. Society, in general, was promoting greater freedom and individual initiative.

He suggested a series of four management systems that range from a more classically oriented system to one based on human resources theory (see Table 3.1).

TABLE 3.1 Summary of Likert's Systems of Management

	SYSTEM I	SYSTEM II	SYSTEM III	SYSTEM IV
Type	Exploitative, authoritative	Benevolent, authoritative	Consultative	Participative
Basis for motivation	Fear, threats, reward	Potential of both reward and punishment	Rewards and some punishment	Economic and participation
Level for decision-making	Top	Top for policy, constrained at lower levels	Top for general decision, specific decisions at low	Spread throughout
Communication	Downward	Downward with limited upward	Downward, upward with some constraints	Free-flowing

Adapted from: Rensis Likert, *New Patterns of Management.* McGraw-Hill, 1961.

The four systems appear to be separate, but Likert regarded them as blending into one another, making a "continuum with many different patterns" (1961, p. 234). He focused on management systems for his theory because he believed management to be critical to all organizational activities and outcomes. According to Likert, high-producing departments and organizations tend toward System IV, or the participative system, whereas low-producing units favor System I, the exploitative authoritative system.

The first system of management, the **exploitative authoritative system**, is rooted in classical theory. In this system, managers tend to motivate their workers through fear, threats, punishment, and occasional reward. Decision-making under this system occurs at the top of the organizational hierarchy, and the decision-makers are rarely aware of problems at lower levels of the organization. Goal setting takes the form of orders being issued from the top. Communication in an exploitative authoritative management system is mainly downward. Subordinates tend to be very suspicious of their superiors and rarely initiate any communication upward. Under this system, relevant outcomes such as satisfaction and productivity are not very positive.

The second of Likert's systems of management, the **benevolent authoritative system**, is only a bit less controlling than the exploitative authoritative system. Motivation under the benevolent authoritative system is based partially on rewards and partially on the potential for punishment. The decision-making arena is expanded a bit. Policy decisions are made at the top of the hierarchy. Lower levels are granted some decision-making power but within a framework prescribed by upper management. Communication in the benevolent authoritative system is mostly downward, though there is a limited amount of upward communication. Upward communication, however, tends to be distorted to avoid the communication of bad news. Relevant outcomes are only slightly more positive than under the exploitative authoritative system. Employees tend to be dissatisfied to moderately satisfied. Productivity is fair to good, and turnover and absenteeism remain moderately high.

The **consultative system** of management is perhaps most closely aligned with the way human relations theory is traditionally practiced (as outlined by Miles). Workers are motivated through rewards, occasional punishment, and limited involvement in decision-making and goal setting. Communication in the consultative management system flows both up and down the hierarchy, though upward communication is not as free-flowing as downward. The increase in communication tends to create an atmosphere where employees are cooperative, and their relationships are generally positive. Competition with peers and condescension toward subordinates still exists but at a much lower level than in the benevolent authoritative system. Satisfaction, productivity, and turnover all improve in the consultative system.

Likert argued for the **participative system** of management as the most effective form. This system underscores the basic elements of human resources theory: genuine participation in decision-making and goal setting, free-flowing communication, full use of every worker's skills and creative energy, and a high level of responsibility and account-ability for the goals of the organization. Decision-making occurs widely throughout the organization, and management is well aware of the problems that occur at the lower levels. Organizational goals are fully accepted by members because in all situations, except for emergencies, goals are determined through group participation. Communication in a participative management system is critical to its success. Communication flows in all directions and can be initiated at any level within the organization. Subordinates have the opportunity to question communication from superiors. As stated earlier, Likert asserted that productivity is at its highest level under the participative system. Satisfaction tends to be relatively high; production is excellent; turnover and absenteeism are low.

Likert's participative system of management addresses Miles's concerns about the genuine versus surface use of participation in organizations subscribing to the human relations approach. Another problem associated with the human relations approach was the notion that the theory attended too much to the needs of the workers, to the disadvantage of advancing the task of the organization. Blake and Mouton's Managerial Grid® is another human resources theory that was designed to alleviate this difficulty with human relations theory. We now turn to an abbreviated discussion of this work.

Blake and Mouton's Managerial Grid

Robert Blake and Jane Mouton (1964), in their book *The Managerial Grid: Key Orientations for Achieving Production through People*, proposed a human resources theory of management that stresses the interrelationship between production and people. Management's main purpose, according to Blake and Mouton, is to promote a culture in the organization that allows for high production at the same time that employees are fostered in their professional and personal development.

As a framework for promoting such a culture, Blake and Mouton recommended the Managerial Grid (later termed the Leadership Grid; see Figure 3.2).

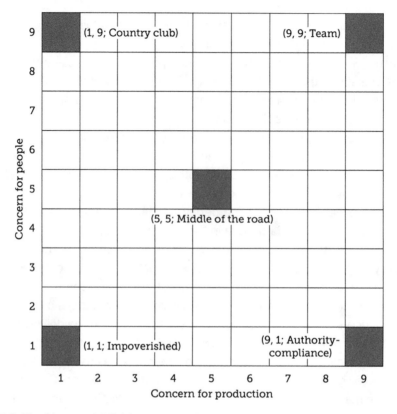

FIGURE 3.2 The Managerial Grid

Adapted from: Robert R. Blake and Jane S. Mouton, *The Managerial Grid III.*
Copyright © 1978 by Gulf Publishing Co.

The Managerial Grid provides managers with a useful way of diagnosing their personal orientation toward people and production within the organization; it can be used at all levels of the organizational hierarchy.

Much like McGregor, Blake and Mouton argued that the assumptions managers hold affect their behavior and managerial style. But Blake and Mouton differ from McGregor in what those assumptions concern. Whereas McGregor focused attention mainly on a manager's assumptions about human nature, Blake and Mouton argued that it is important to uncover a manager's assumptions about concern for people and concern for production. Concern for people involves the "productive unit" (p. 7) of the organization and can involve a number of things:

- Concern for the degree of personal commitment to one's job
- Trust-based rather than obedience-based accountability
- Self-esteem of the individual
- Interpersonal relationships with coworkers

Concern for production is the "emphasis supervision places on production," or the basic tasks of the organization (p. 7) and involves the use of people and technology to accomplish organizational tasks. "Concern for" in these cases does not refer to issues of quantity or even quality but instead indicates the degree to which the manager has consideration for these matters. In other words, to what extent do the manager's basic attitudes toward people and production (and their interrelationships) affect actual supervisory behavior?

Blake and Mouton offer an extensive survey that attempts to measure a manager's concern for people and production. The results of the survey are compiled, and the individual manager is assigned a value on the Managerial Grid that indicates his managerial style related to these two concerns. Five points on the Grid have been assigned descriptive titles and will be discussed later. It is important to realize that the points on the Grid do not represent personality traits of the manager, but instead indicate a specific orientation toward production and people. This distinction is important because, they argue, a manager (based on the situation) has the ability to acquire skills and hence change their managerial style.

In view of the similarities between Blake and Mouton's styles to Likert's four systems of management, this section will provide a snapshot of the styles rather than an extensive discussion. The **authority-compliance management style** is rooted in classical theory, in which there is high concern for production and low concern for people. This manager feels a contradiction between meeting the production needs of the organization and the needs of the workers. To accomplish production, the manager minimizes attention to feelings and attitudes. Communication in the authority-compliance management style is unidirectional, downward through the hierarchy.

The **country club management style** puts concern for people above concern for production; employees are "valuable in their own right" (p. 57). This manager avoids direct pressure to perform with the hope of gaining acceptance from the workers. The manager tends to lead by example rather than goad employees into working hard for the organization. Communication under this management style is heightened, with particular emphasis on the informal communication systems of the organization, such as the "grapevine" (gossip).

The **impoverished management style** can be characterized as being laissez-faire— that is, hiring workers for particular jobs and then leaving them alone to do their work. The manager is not concerned with the well-being of the workers and exercises no power, opting instead merely to pass down orders that come from higher levels. The impoverished-style manager uses the communication system minimally.

The **middle-of-the-road management style**, indicated by a medium concern for both people and production, is best characterized as a compromise or balance-seeking position. The manager uses the carrot-and-stick approach to supervision, prodding the workers when necessary to increase their production but also offering adequate social and personal rewards to maintain adequate worker satisfaction. Communication in this approach can also be characterized by balance. Formal and informal communication systems are used equally.

The **team management style** is the prototypical human resources approach to management and is the one Blake and Mouton advocated. It is characterized by a high concern for people and a high concern for production with no inherent conflict between them. The intent of the team style is to "promote the conditions that integrate creativity, high productivity, and high morale through concerted team action" (p. 142). It may seem on the surface that the team and middle-of-the-road orientations are very similar in that both are concerned for people and production. The essential difference between the two approaches is an important one. The team style does not seek a compromise between people and production (thereby reducing the eventual effectiveness of both). Instead, it seeks the highest level of production through a commitment to the creativity, skill, and energy of the workers. The goals of the organization and the goals of the individual can be achieved simultaneously if the satisfaction of one leads to the satisfaction of the other (or if they correlate with each other).

The team orientation promotes self-direction and self-control through genuine participation in planning, decision-making, and goal setting. It differs significantly from the fear-of-punishment system present in the authority-compliance style. The theory is that organizational members attempt to reach maximum production when they have a stake in the process and the outcome. To accomplish this goal, communication must flow in all directions and must be "authentic and candid" (p. 150).

Particularly interesting about this approach is its position regarding misunderstandings, one that we advocate in a different form in Chapter 1:

> Mistakes occur because of misunderstandings, not because of deliberate intent … .
> Mistakes frequently can be traced to misunderstandings, assumptions based on faulty information and facts or differences in expectations between a boss and a subordinate. [T]he aim here is to discover the cause of the problem, not just to identify and punish the person associated with its occurrence. Through problem identification, critique and follow-up action, the work situation becomes a learning situation, par excellence. (Blake and Mouton, 1964, pp. 148–149)

The team style recognizes the natural existence of misunderstandings in organizations and proposes the notion that they should be used as learning situations for all involved. This perspective on misunderstandings demonstrates a significant move forward in organizational theory and practice, one that is more humanistic in nature and grounded in the realities of human communication.

Summary

The middle of the 20th century saw a flurry of activity regarding organizational management theory. With the Hawthorne Studies pointing to the need to focus on the relational aspects of management and organizational behavior, emerging theories emphasized the worker over the task. Mary Parker Follet, Chester Barnard, and Douglas McGregor offered perspectives or theories of management and organizations that replaced ideas of strict control and authority with improved social relations, cooperation, communication, and informal organization. The human relations movement sought to improve organizational life by reversing the attitudes of managers toward workers. Workers were no longer to be considered lazy, deceitful, and in need of coercion but energetic, creative, underutilized, and eager to participate in decision-making at all levels.

Human resources theory (as exemplified by Likert's systems of management and Blake and Mouton's Leadership Grid) was developed to remedy the problems associated with the misapplications or misguided applications of human relations theory in organizations. Theorists realized that participative management strategies were not being used appropriately; workers were being told overtly that they were important but were not being treated accordingly. Human resources theory emphasized genuine participation in organizational processes and advanced the idea that both production and personal satisfaction could be maximized if they were interrelated. Table 3.2 summarizes the information presented in this chapter and highlights the role of communication in each theory.

TABLE 3.2 Humanistic Theories of Organizations

	HUMAN RELATIONS	HUMAN RESOURCES	HUMAN RESOURCES
Theorist	McGregor	Likert	Blake and Mouton
Theory	Theory Y	Systems of management	Managerial Grid
Focus	Worker (as perceived by managers)	Management	Management
Central feature	Workers are inherently creative and underutilized	Participative system of management	Team managerial style
Role of communication	Relationship oriented, focus on upward	Task and relationship oriented, flows in all directions	Task and relationship oriented, flows in all directions

Viewing humanistic theories through the lens of the misunderstandings yields multiple perspectives. Looking at human relations theory this way shows that organizations were beginning to anticipate misunderstandings. The misunderstandings that were attended to were revolving primarily around the individual worker and were less about the task itself. Attention was beginning to be paid to the communication skills of managers and workers. The cope strategy from the responses to misunderstandings continuum was perhaps favored above other strategies, as managers were to be concerned primarily with the emotional and social needs of their employees. When evaluating human resources theory, both task and social bases for misunderstandings were beginning to be anticipated. The aspects of social interaction that were developed in human relations theory were retained, and organizational members at all levels were able to implement the most appropriate of the three strategies of the responses to misunderstandings continuum (i.e., contain, cope, and construct) based on the particular situation.

LEARNING OBJECTIVES

1. Explain how the systems perspective attempts to address misunderstandings within organizations
2. Explain how Ludwig von Bertalanffy's principles draw similarities between living organisms and organized human activity
3. Identify the characteristics of organizational systems theory
4. Analyze conflict with respect to interactions that occur in organizations
5. Describe how corporate social responsibility is practiced by organizations in relation to their environments

I n Chapters 2 and 3, we discussed various classical and humanistic theories of organizations, each of which proposed principles or prescriptions for organizational structure or managerial practice. Each theory contained fairly specific elements or characteristics that could be implemented in day-to-day practice, either at the interpersonal or organizational level, depending on the theory.

In this chapter, we present a theory that has less to do with prescribing organizational behavior or structure and more with providing an analytical framework or perspective for viewing an organization in general. Systems theory is considered by Kurtyka (2005) to be "one of the main intellectual movements of the twentieth century. It arose in response to overspecialization in the sciences as a way to find a more integrated view of knowledge and the world." Systems theory and its derivatives provide new and varied lenses for analyzing and understanding organizations and the behavior within them. As Poole (2014) asserted, "The appeal of systems theory for organizational communication research lies in its potential to represent the complexity of organizations and organizational communication in a rigorous yet manageable fashion" (p. 50). Management practices have emerged from these theories and will be discussed where appropriate. We begin this chapter with a discussion of the systems framework and then outline the perspective of an organization as a system. We conclude by using systems theory concepts to explore the concept of corporate social responsibility.

Misunderstandings and the Organization as a System

When organizational life is viewed from a systems theory perspective, new areas for potential misunderstandings come into focus. Consider the following story told to us by Fran, a senior data administrator for a marketing research company:

> Part of our team right now is offshored in India, and they usually work in the office. With the COVID-19, though, and everybody having to work from home, the team members in India don't have the capabilities to work from home.

> So, a week ago Monday, we had scheduled online training to take place and none of the team members in India showed up. We had no idea where they were. That's because they shut down India, and the people couldn't go into the office, and they were scrambling to get laptops. They had to find laptops and get them set up at home so that they could work. Some of them were on like a bus and trying to do the training through their phone, so it was crazy. Communication was bad because they didn't have the equipment they needed. So in the middle of a training session, all of a sudden, they couldn't hear us, or we couldn't hear them, or they couldn't see our screen. So that's been very challenging. For some reason, they did not communicate to us what was happening ahead of time so that we could react, or reschedule the training, or have additional resources to complete the work.

> The outcome was our project plan was delayed, which is a negative. And the rest of the team had to work longer hours to meet the deadlines. And we're still working on them getting the connection they need from their homes.

The situation Fran described is complex. From a classical theory perspective, one would probably approach it by examining the training needs to maintain optimal productivity and cost-efficiency. Rules would be instituted for how and when to request information from technical support, and appropriate responses would be scripted to ensure uniformity and predictability. From a human resources perspective, one would explore the impact of interpersonal relationships and loyalty on productivity. Management would have to be instructed to assist current organizational members with managing professional relationships and ensuring that everyone is trained appropriately with regard to both task and relational communication competencies.

The approach from a systems theory perspective would be a bit different. Systems theory, as you will discover in this chapter, demands that a broader picture be drawn of the situation, a picture that includes the environment within which the organization exists and how changes in the environment affect the organization. A systems approach also looks at the interconnections between the different parts of the organization to determine how well it is functioning.

What does systems theory have to offer the study of misunderstandings? Several things. First, a systems approach demands that we broaden our perspective of organizational life. In this example, we have a global team tied together through technology. The classical approach would look at this as a case of a broken machine—the failure of one part (the team members in India) to communicate the problem they were having with technology. However, a systems approach would dictate that we look at the factors in the environment, in this case cultural values, that may have made it untenable for the team members in India to be explicit about the technology problem they were experiencing. Second, as COVID-19 spread in India, the team members there were forced to work from their homes where they did not have the appropriate technology. A systems perspective on the situation would have had the team anticipating this situation and being prepared with a contingency plan for the team members in India and the United States to continue their work. Third, failure to be prepared with contingencies meant that the team members in India were left to panic, perhaps about losing their jobs, and potentially expose themselves to the coronavirus as they sought any avenue possible to maintain a virtual connection to the U.S. team for their training session.

Clearly, then, the systems approach broadens the lens through which we view organizational behavior, particularly misunderstandings. Systems theory reminds organizational members to view interconnections within the organization and between the organization and the environment as possible sources of misunderstandings. Keep Fran's situation in mind as you read this chapter and think about how you would analyze it using the concepts and approaches you encounter.

Systems Framework

The movement from classical theory to human relations and human resources theories marked the recognition of the role the individual plays in organizational functioning. The focus on workers and their interrelationships, however, was myopic according to some theorists, who argued that a more comprehensive view of organizations was necessary, one that situated the organization within its relevant environment. Organizational theorists turned to general systems theory for guidance, particularly to the work of the biologist Ludwig von Bertalanffy.

Systems theory replaces the "machine" metaphor of classical theory with the metaphor of an "organism." Viewed as an **organism**, an organization is a living entity in an environment that can provide it with energy and to which it can return an output. The organism is surrounded by a permeable boundary (much like skin or cell walls) that allows for the exchange of inputs and outputs with the environment. These organisms must be structured so that they can efficiently and effectively turn inputs into outputs and adapt to changes in the environment. If inputs are restricted or the internal processes of the organism are not functioning properly, the organism begins to deteriorate.

Although systems theory itself is not a theory of management, such as those offered by classical, human relations, and human resources theorists, it does provide us with a new way of conceptualizing organizations and studying them. According to Poole (1997), systems theory can be very useful for the field of organizational communication. Poole outlined four "promises" of systems theory (1997, p. 49):

1. **It is designed to deal with complexity.** The complexity comes from a model with many interdependent elements and an understanding of the multiple levels of associations (e.g., organization with a group, organization with the environment, individual with the organization). For evidence of the number and types of interdependencies, recall the complexities of the situation Fran described earlier in the chapter.

2. **It attempts to do so with precision.** Despite the complexities, systems theory seeks to specify relationships between elements and levels. To understand how the organization functions, it must be determined exactly how the parts interrelate.

3. **It takes a holistic view.** Systems theory forces us to look outside the organizational or departmental boundaries to see the bigger picture of how all aspects are interrelated. Fran's situation is a perfect example because interpersonal relationships, virtual communication practices, and team-based structure affected the functioning of the organization and the ability of its members to operate safely and effectively.

4. **It is a theory of emergents.** Systems theory demonstrates how actions and outcomes at the collective (department or organization) level emerge from the actions and interactions of the individuals who make up the collective. In this way, systems theory combines individual-level behavior with broader organizational- and environmental-level issues, a perspective unique to this point in the discussion of organizational theories.

As you can see, systems theory offers significant insight into the realm of communication in organizations. In the next section, we discuss several basic principles of general systems theory proffered by von Bertalanffy and outline the characteristics of organizational systems theory.

Principles of General Systems Theory

Ludwig von Bertalanffy (1968), in his landmark book *General System Theory*, proposed that the laws that govern biological open systems (living organisms) could be applied to systems of any form (such as an organization). The leap from organisms as systems to organizations as systems is not that large, as von Bertalanffy argued that organisms are organized and that we consider things such as crystals or molecules to be organizations. If organizations are systems, then what are the universal principles applicable to both living organisms and organized human activity? Several principles from von Bertalanffy's theory are relevant for our purposes, and we discuss them next.

Open-Systems Theory Principles

A **system** is "a set of elements standing in inter-relations" (von Bertalanffy, 1968, p. 55). This is a rather simple explanation of a rather complex concept, but it is sufficient for beginning our discussion. Perhaps the most important aspect of this definition is the notion that the parts that make up the system (which can be referred to as **subsystems**) are **interrelated**; the existence and proper functioning of one part are dependent on the existence and proper functioning of the other parts. If we consider the human body to be a system, then it is defined by its subsystems (e.g., the respiratory system, nervous system, reproductive system) and their interrelationships. The relative "health" of the overall system is determined by the extent to which the subsystems coordinate their functions effectively and efficiently. The same holds true for an organization when conceptualized as a system. The interrelated parts (e.g., marketing, engineering, sales, and accounting) must function well together for the overall strength of the organizational system to be maintained. If they do not, negative consequences can occur. For example, consider the story told to us by Walt, a manager at a food company:

> I am responsible for ensuring a labeling update is completely capturing the bioengineered status of our retail food product. I am currently stalled with the project and have been dealing with roadblock after roadblock. This has included a senior leadership team that has not been engaged with the project. While they are accountable, they are being pulled in too many directions to give my project the time it deserves. Unfortunately, without senior leaders aligning on this project we can't get budget dollars allocated to the activities. We also can't get workers assigned to the project.

> There are six other functional areas that have to be involved. Their response to my requests for engagement include, "I'm too busy," "my boss isn't authorizing my time on this," and "we'll get to it." The rollout is also complicated by the fact that the federal agencies responsible for developing the regulatory model have not provided the industry key information, including fermentation and enzyme implications, as well as a testing protocol sufficient to assess the DNA status of the product. This will also involve a supplier survey process that will inevitably involve slow responses and the identification of questions or concerns that are not known at the moment.

> It is expected that at some point in the process, our private label partners that we pack for are going to call and insist that their packaging is updated "now." Without the surveys back, we run the risk of making labeling decisions that ultimately would not be supported by the suppliers. The deadline for the labeling project is about 2 years away. That seems like a long time;

however, it will go by quickly given the hundreds of finished product SKUs involved, the thousands of ingredients that must be reviewed, the time required to coordinate the six functional areas, and the normal time required to execute a single labeling change.

Walt's story demonstrates how the parts of a system are interrelated, and the efficient and effective functioning of one part of the system is dependent on the other parts. In this case, key interdependent parts were not coordinating or participating in the project, and as a result, the project is bound to stall and key partners will be left to wonder why the company is not fulfilling its obligations.

But the news of general systems theory is that biological systems do not exist in a vacuum; they are situated within an environment. To capture this notion, von Bertalanffy argued that biological systems are open systems. **Open systems** are those that attempt to maintain a balance as they import and export material to and from the environment. **Closed systems** are those that have no exchange of material with the environment. The environment, often referred to as the **relevant environment** by organizational systems theorists, consists of those entities outside the system that are relevant to the survival of the system. Returning to our example of the human body, the system (body) constantly adapts to changes in the environment. When nourishment is diminished, for instance, the body slows down its metabolism to conserve energy and use what energy it has stored up more efficiently. Or when the external temperature decreases to an uncomfortable level, the body often goes into involuntary shakes to produce heat. The body, as a system, does not remain unchanged in the face of changing environmental conditions; it self-regulates in an attempt to function effectively and efficiently and promote its own survival.

Systems should be considered open in nature because they have permeable boundaries. A **boundary** is that part of the system that separates it from its environment. A boundary is **permeable** in that it is capable of having material pass through it, to and from the environment.

The concept of openness is particularly useful in the study of organizations. Past theories of organizations (particularly Weber's theory of bureaucracy) virtually ignored the fact that organizations exist within an environment. Viewing the organization as an open system, however, demands that the organizational theorist understands the complex interactions the system has with its environment *in addition to* the means by which the subsystems of the organization import and export material to and from the environment. This point is made very clear in Walt's example of the food company project. Walt's job was to understand the organization's environment and respond appropriately to the needs of his clients so that, in turn, the organization could handle the demand for services.

One further point about openness in organizational systems theory is necessary. The permeable nature of a system's boundaries is often under the control of the organization itself. At certain times, the system can restrict the amount and type of material imported and exported, whereas at other times, it can maximize these efforts. In other words, the system has some ability to regulate permeability. This notion is referred to as **relative openness**. We will discuss this concept in more depth later in the chapter.

In a closed system (where material neither enters nor exits), the tendency is for the system to become disorganized. This essential property of organized systems is referred to as **entropy**. Left unchecked, entropy will continue to increase until the system weakens and eventually ceases to exist. To combat these effects, systems seek to enhance **negative entropy** (also termed negentropy), or a state of survival and growth.

To foster negative entropy, the parts of the system must function well together. When the subsystems work in conjunction with one another, they produce extra energy or **synergy**. The synergy produced allows for an attractive feature of systems known as **nonsummativity** or the principle that the whole or total is greater than the sum of the individual parts. In other words, when operating efficiently and effectively, the subsystems working together are able to produce more than if they were working alone and their outputs were added together.

One final principle from von Bertalanffy is important because it differentiates potential management strategies based in systems theory from those based in classical theory. Classical theory is characterized by the "one best way" to do every job. From a closed-system point of view, this makes sense because conditions rarely change, the "best way" to accomplish the task can be established and performed every time. But if a system is considered open, there will inevitably be changes in the system making the "one best way" quite unlikely. The concept of equifinality illuminates this situation. **Equifinality** indicates that "the same final state may be reached from different initial conditions and in different ways" (1968, p. 40). In other words, if the desired final state for a biological organism is to secure enough food to stay alive, it can do so by eating a variety of harmless food gathered in a variety of ways. It does not have to eat the same thing garnered in the same fashion. The same lesson holds true for organizations. Organizations have the capacity to reach the same final state (e.g., product or service) in a variety of ways; the "one best way" does not have to guide organizational functioning and in many instances may be counterproductive.

Now that we have introduced some of the basic elements of systems as presented by von Bertalanffy and offered some initial implications of them for organizational theory, we move on to the characteristics of systems theory applied to organizations based on the work of later scholars.

Characteristics of Organizations as Systems

Daniel Katz and Robert Kahn (1978) in their book *The Social Psychology of Organizations* put forward a theory of organizations based on systems constructs, although the impetus for the book is rooted in the work of Rensis Likert. Their work signals a shift away from the psychological, interpersonal-relationship bases of human resources theory toward what they argue is a more comprehensive view of organizational reality.

Katz and Kahn advocated systems theory as a way to approach organizations because it is able to encapsulate both micro- and macroconcepts (human relationships and organization-environment relationships, respectively), something that human relations theory and human resources theory (both micro-oriented theories) were unable to do.

This theory differs from psychology-based theories of organizations in that the central focus is less the thoughts and behaviors of organizational leadership and more the input–processing–output relationship the system has with its environment. To this end, Katz and Kahn offered a theory of organizations built on systems characteristics derived from the work of von Bertalanffy and others. What follows are selected characteristics of organizational systems theory that are most relevant to the study of organizational communication.

Input–Throughput–Output

When an organization is viewed as an open system, the emphasis shifts from managerial behavior to the relationship between the system and its environment. This relationship is characterized by three interrelated processes: input, throughput, and output, which form the basic model of systems functioning. The model is simple. An open system imports some form of energy or material through its boundaries from the environment. Once inside the system, **throughput** occurs where the parts of the system (or subsystems) transform the material or energy in some fashion. Finally, the system returns some product to the environment; that product is termed the **output**. Because the input undergoes some form of change when processed by the subsystems, the systems model is often referred to as the **transformation model** (Kreps, 1990).

Any organization can be examined using the transformation model. For example, Harley-Davidson, a major motorcycle manufacturer, must import a variety of materials and energy from its relevant environment. Inputs for Harley-Davidson include things such as steel, rubber, wire, aluminum, electricity, gas, bank loans, customer demand, and information on competitors. Once the inputs enter the system, the subsystems must coordinate their efforts such that the material and energy are transformed into an appropriate output, in this case motorcycles.

The transformation model provides a wider angle lens through which we can view organizational behavior and functioning. From this perspective, it is impossible to consider the internal functioning of the system without considering the relationship of the system to its relevant environment. What systems theory teaches us is the need to coordinate internal functioning with changes in the environment. It is through the process of feedback that this coordination happens.

Feedback and Dynamic Homeostasis

System inputs carry with them information that is useful in both regulating the relative openness of the system itself and coordinating the efforts of the subsystems. This information is often referred to as **feedback** and can take two primary forms. **Positive feedback** is information that alerts the subsystems to move from status quo behavior to a specified state of behavior. For example, if Tesla's salespeople double the sales of their latest electric car, the manufacturing division will need to move from its normal state of behavior to one that allows it to produce twice as many cars. **Negative feedback** is information that indicates to the subsystems that they should return to the status quo. Returning to our example, if Tesla's salespeople were unable to secure the same number of sales during the next sales period, the manufacturing division would need to stop producing at the doubled rate and return to its normal level of production.

Feedback is necessary to promote a balance of inputs and outputs between the subsystems and between the system and the environment. The balance, in turn, is important to help stave off entropy (or to promote negative entropy). **Dynamic homeostasis** represents a balance of energy exchange. An imbalance would lead to an excess or debit of energy or material, causing the system undue strain, thereby enhancing the potential for entropy.

Equivocality and Requisite Variety

Karl Weick (1979), a well-known organizational psychologist, offered a systems approach to organizational behavior in his influential book, *The Social Psychology of Organizing.* He contended that any input into a system carries with it some level of uncertainty, ambiguity, or what he referred to as **equivocality**. Whether the input is raw material, energy, customer orders or complaints, or federal legislation, it will carry with it the potential for several different outcomes. To deal with this fact, Weick argued that the main function of organizing is to reduce equivocality to a manageable level.

Dealing with equivocality is not a simple matter. Weick proposed that the concept of requisite variety be employed when attempting to manage equivocal information inputs. **Requisite variety** is the notion that complex inputs must be addressed with complex processes, and vice versa. In other words, the old adage applies: "There are no simple answers to difficult problems." If a simple process is applied to a complex input, the chances are high that only a portion of the input will be attended to, leaving the remainder unaddressed and potentially damaging the system and its components. The implication of requisite variety is that "systems adapt to their environments by becoming similar to them in terms of structure" (Poole, 2014, p. 53).

Role of Communication

In systems theory, communication acts as a "system binder" (Almaney, 1974). Communication binds the parts of the system together and binds the system to the environment. To say this in a different way, the role of communication in systems theory is twofold. First, communication mechanisms must be in place for the organizational system to exchange relevant information with its environment. This is referred to as an **adaptive mechanism** (Almaney, 1974). People who perform this function are often referred to as **boundary spanners** because they move information across the boundaries of the organization. Boundary spanners have contact with the relevant environment through the course of their jobs. Individuals who work in such areas as sales, customer service, advertising, social media, and public relations are typical boundary spanners and should be considered important communication links with the environment. Robert's, from the opening story of this chapter, is an excellent example of a boundary spanner. His role as branch manager has him constantly interacting with customers and potential customers. As he interacts with them, he gathers information to bring back into the system and communicates information from the system to the environment. In addition to boundary spanners, media outlets also serve as an important communication link between the system and the environment. Online news sources, Twitter, Facebook, industry publications, broadcast media outlets, and traditional print media serve as important sources of receiving and distributing information.

The second role of communication in systems theory is to provide for the flow of information among the subsystems. This role of communication is also known as a **maintenance function** (Almaney, 1974). To maintain homeostasis (balance of inputs and outputs), the subsystems need to coordinate their inputs and outputs; this is a matter of information exchange. Meetings, memos, retreats, enterprise social media, and texting are all examples of the mechanisms used to provide for the necessary communication among subsystems. Given their interdependent nature, subsystems are reliant on efficient and effective communication to promote homeostasis and negative entropy.

Systems, Subsystems, and Supersystems

As discussed earlier, a system is a set of interrelated elements. In light of the transformation model, a system can be considered to be a set of interrelated parts that turns inputs into outputs through processing. The interrelated parts of the system that do the processing are the subsystems. Every system is part of a larger system, or **supersystem**, which consists of other systems in the relevant environment important to the survival of the focal system.

Whether an organized unit is considered a system, subsystem, or supersystem to some extent depends on the level of analysis. Consider university life for a moment. If the university is the focal system, then the different colleges in the university would be subsystems; the supersystem could be the conference to which the focal system belongs (e.g., Big 12, Pac-12, MAC). If the College of Business is the focal system, then the subsystems may be the different departments within the college (e.g., marketing, finance, and management). The supersystem would be the university. Finally, the marketing department itself may be the focal system, making the College of Business the supersystem and the professors, staff, and students within marketing the subsystems.

Without effective and efficient coordination among the subsystems, the system will eventually become strained and die. This is not to say, however, that the different elements in a system are tightly linked, are highly responsive to one another, and have indistinguishable identities. It may be that systems (or subsystems or supersystems) could instead be loosely coupled (Orton & Weick, 1990; Weick, 1976). Loosely coupled systems contain elements that "are responsive, *but* that each also preserves its own identity and some evidence of its physical or logical separateness" (Weick, 1976, p. 3). This way of thinking about relationships between systems, subsystems, and supersystems is important because it provides a more realistic picture of the nature of structural and interpersonal relations in organizations. Without it, there may be a tendency to expect very logical, rational, and seamless connections between organizational elements. For example, one might expect that in a city fire department the fire chief and deputy fire chief, whose offices are right next to each other, would be tightly connected and willingly supporting the same mission. However, in reality, although these two officers are connected and responsive to each other's changing situations, they still retain their own identities and may pursue goals or objectives that are divergent or even competing. These two elements of the system would be considered to be loosely coupled.

Boundaries

With all this talk about systems, subsystems, and supersystems, not to mention the systems' relevant environment, the question becomes: How do you know where one stops and the other begins? As mentioned earlier in this chapter, the concept of boundaries is designed to make this a bit clearer. In social systems, however, a boundary is not a distinguishable entity as it is in physical systems. The boundary of the human body, for example, is the skin, but in social systems, there is no such tangible feature that marks the end of one level from the beginning of another. Yet organizational members are quite readily able to distinguish system and subsystem boundaries and may be implicitly or explicitly involved in their construction and definition (Poole, 2014).

Becker (1997) offered four types of boundaries that may help provide a bit more meaning to the term as it relates to social systems (p. 133). A physical boundary is the most concrete and can be something such as a security system that prevents unauthorized personnel from entering the actual organizational location. A linguistic boundary involves the use of jargon, or specialized language, to separate members from nonmembers. Systemic boundaries are rules that regulate how members interact or how they interact with nonmembers. For example, organizational members may be allowed to address one another by first names but are required to address all outsiders using last names and titles. Finally, psychological boundaries are stereotypes, prejudices, or biases that members hold toward others and serve to restrict communication. For example, members of a sales department may believe that the members of the manufacturing division are not as "refined" as they are, and as a result, they treat them with contempt.

Thus different systems and subsystems can be distinguished in ways that do not involve concrete physical boundaries. It is important for organizational members to recognize the existence of the different boundary types, particularly those that may be causing unintended misunderstandings. Linguistic boundaries may cause computer customers, for example, not to understand what computer technicians and salespeople are telling them. Psychological boundaries may lead to barriers among parts of an organizational system that truly need to interact with one another for the overall success of the organization.

Systems Theory and Conflict

The systems perspective points us to the fact that as subsystems and systems interact, there will be conflict. **Conflict** is the "competition between interdependent parties who perceive that they have incompatible needs, goals, desires, or ideas" (Van Slyke, 1999, p. 5). As mentioned earlier in this chapter, the systems concept of "interdependent parties" means that two parts of the system (e.g., people, teams, departments) have some connection to each other and depend on each other in some way to accomplish tasks. If the parties were completely independent, with no connection to each other, there would be no impetus for conflict to develop. When two people work together, one might have a stronger need to finish a task on time than the other or one person's goal might be to use the task to establish ties to another project, whereas the other person only wants to complete the immediate task. These different goals can eventually pit the two people against each other. Putnam and Poole (1987) have defined conflict as "the interaction of interdependent people who perceive opposition of goals, aims, and values, and who see the other party as potentially interfering with the realization of these goals" (p. 552).

Interaction is central to these definitions. Social interaction is the way conflict is identified and framed. Until individuals discuss the issues in the conflict, it remains a conflict only in a person's mind. In conflict, individuals know that they oppose each other and have different goals. This situation is different from misunderstandings, which of course can lead to conflict. Misunderstandings occur when there are differences or uncertainty or ambiguity about values, goals, or courses of action. Instances in which people who are communicating do not share meaning would be misunderstandings. Conflict is when they are in direct opposition to each other.

Consider the following situation, described to us by one of our interviewees, George, who was a new manager of a railroad. Think about the definitions and components of conflict as you read it:

> Over the many years of operation, until I arrived, there were habits and behaviors that developed between the workforce and management that became normal ways of doing business. A lot of these behaviors and habits should be considered bad habits. Over time, the habit of late starts and early quits became normal, although recognized by supervisors as not right they were in a tough position to try and change because they participated in the same practices when they were mechanics and operators.
>
> By union agreement, employees were to report to the job site in advance to allow them to change into their work clothes and be ready to go to work at the start of their shift. They were also to work until the end of their shift prior to changing back into their civilian clothes. Over time, employees

and management got into the bad habits of arriving at the job site at the start of the shift, changing into their work clothes, and then reporting for duty. Likewise, the same was true at the end of the shift—employees would start changing into their civilian clothes up to half an hour prior to the end of their shift. Again, this practice was not in compliance with the rules in place.

Enter me—the guy from the outside, the same guy who is going to make this place run better. After watching this practice for a few days, I knew we as a company were paying people for unproductivity. I decided it was time to make a change, and I went about making that change, but I didn't fully understand my audience. I instructed the supervisors working for me to lead each shift briefing by stating that the late starts and early quits had to stop and those not complying would be docked pay accordingly. Well, everything hit the fan. I immediately had slowdowns and sabotage on my hands and went about remedial steps to correct the unrest while still sticking to the union agreement.

I started off with personally holding shift briefings, making some progress, and having some setbacks. It was during this time that I really began to understand my audience. My audience was roughly the same age as I was at the time, 38 years old, most of them working at the transloading facility since they got out of high school, most of them were hired because their father worked there. The thing I felt was the biggest obstacle to overcome was this: these employees realized that more than likely their whole working career was going to be spent doing the same thing every day for the rest of their working life. I knew someday I would be leaving this facility, but they were going to be stuck there.

I was told in so many words they were going to do things to me, and I wouldn't even know it. I took that comment in and knew I could not let that threat to me go idle—I walked over to the person making the threat, looked him in the eye, and told him simply, "You know, you're talking about playing hardball and that's a game I never lose; do you have any other comments?" A hush came over the room, and things got more civil.

My audience was very strong in large groups, and I realized that the large group setting became a feeding frenzy for the alpha workers trying to dominate and intimidate during the conversations. I quickly understood that I would be doing more personal briefings and doing those briefings with smaller manageable groups and actually saving time by doing such, avoiding all the show of force.

We as a facility got over the hardship of making the change to no early quits and late starts, and it became a normal work practice. I also realized that I had to change the attitude of my management staff; they needed to take more ownership, and I had to give them the ownership. The same was true for our shift workers—I gave them more ownership. I learned that communicating changes is generally going to be difficult.

As you can see, George, his supervisors, and the railroad workers are interdependent parties. Things were going well for a few days as George took in the situation, but when he started to make changes to long-standing organizational practices, conflict quickly emerged. George and the workers had opposing goals, desires, and ideas, and that opposition quickly escalated into threats and intimidation. The conflict was not as simple as a difference in personalities but was deeply rooted in history, work-norms, distrust, and negative perceptions of the other.

Conflict, similar to an interaction, can be viewed as an emergent process (Felstiner et al., 1980–1981). Conflict, in this emergent view, is *subjective* because it is interpreted and evaluated by individuals who may not show their feelings about the conflict in their behaviors. It is *unstable* because continued interactions will influence and change an individual's reaction to the perceived conflict. It is *reactive* because individuals will continue to respond to these new interactional developments. Finally, given the unstable and reactive nature of conflict, parties may and will avoid closure because new claims continue to surface (Kusztal, 2002). Thankfully, in the previous story, George realized that continuing with his strong-arm approach to communication with the workers would only serve to escalate the conflict, and after changing communication approaches and empowering his supervisors and workers, the conflict de-escalated, and the changes became the new norm.

Conflict may be either substantive or affective. **Substantive conflict** occurs when organizational members disagree on task or content issues. **Affective conflict** deals with inconsistencies within interpersonal relationships. This form of conflict occurs when organizational members realize that their feelings and emotions regarding one or more issues are incompatible (Rahim, 2001). In the case of the railroad example, both substantive and affective conflict were at play. George and the workers disagreed on the task (the practice of early quits and late starts), which is substantive conflict. They also were engaged in affective conflict as George introduced the changes; the workers found George's personality and style incompatible with their approach to life in the organization.

From a systems perspective, three types of conflict can occur within an organization: interpersonal, intragroup, and intergroup (Rahim, 2001). **Interpersonal conflict** refers to conflict that occurs between two or more people that may or may not have to do with organizational tasks or task-related feelings. Interpersonal conflict is similar to conflict that would occur in relationships outside the organization. Intragroup conflict, sometimes referred to as *intradepartmental conflict*, occurs among members of a group, often between subgroups that have interdependence in terms of goals, tasks, and procedures. This type of conflict can occur when individuals within a group disagree on how best to solve a problem or approach a task, and the group divides into sides because of this disagreement. Intergroup conflict, or interdepartmental conflict, occurs when two or more units or groups within an organization disagree over a specific task, behavior, or procedure. A well-known example of intergroup conflict is conflict that occurs between labor and management, much like what happened in George's situation.

Several factors contribute to the likelihood that conflict will occur (Rahim, 2001). First, the likelihood of conflict increases when individuals are required to engage in a behavior that is inconsistent with their needs or interests. Conflicts regarding overtime or not being granted leave for family events are examples of this factor. Second, the likelihood of conflict increases when individuals are forced to compete for scarce resources that they either desire personally or need to successfully do their job. One example of this would be a preferred customer list in a telemarketing firm; conflict could occur when one individual or group of individuals has access to such a list, whereas another individual or group of individuals is forced to rely on randomly generated lists of potential customers. Third, organizational conflict is more likely when an individual possesses attitudes, values, skills, or goals that are exclusive of another party's. One example might be a manager who holds racially or sexually discriminatory attitudes toward other organizational members. Finally, the likelihood of organizational conflict is increased when parties who are interdependent have at least partially exclusive behavioral preferences regarding joint activities. If one sales agent likes to conduct business over dinner and drinks in the evening, whereas another sales agent likes to maintain traditional working hours and does not believe in the use of alcohol, the potential for conflict based on behavioral preferences greatly increases, particularly if the two agents are teamed together.

The organizational response to conflict is to either resolve or manage it. The difference between the two is not merely word choice (Rahim, 2001). **Conflict resolution** involves reduction, elimination, or termination of conflict. Alternative dispute resolution is usually aimed at conflict resolution. It may include negotiation, bargaining, mediation, or arbitration. If the situation is deemed detrimental or serious enough, resolution may be necessary for both individuals and the organization. Examples of such situations would be *ad hominem* attacks (attacking the person instead of the idea), threatening comments, or discriminatory remarks. Reduction strategies include changing the context of the conflict, altering the issues in the dispute, or removing or relocating one of the individuals involved in the conflict (Shell, 2003).

Sometimes, though, as previously discussed, conflict can generate positive outcomes for both individuals and organizations. In such situations, conflict management may be the desirable course of action. **Conflict management** involves implementing strategies to decrease the negative effects of conflict and creating an environment in which conflict can enhance the learning and effectiveness of individuals and the organization (Rahim, 2001). The organizational socialization process may include teaching new members how to deal with conflict constructively and presenting conflict-management styles that work best in a variety of situations. For conflict-management strategies to be successful, they should satisfy the following three criteria: (1) contribute to organizational learning and long-term effectiveness (discussed at the end of this chapter), (2) satisfy social needs, and (3) fulfill moral and ethical needs of members (Rahim et al., 1992).

Alternatives are available to the basic forms of conflict management and resolution mentioned previously: bargaining and negotiation—as well as forms that require a third party—mediation and arbitration. Putnam and Poole (1987) defined **bargaining** as "a unique form of conflict management in that participants negotiate mutually shared rules and then cooperate within these rules to gain a competitive advantage over their opponent" (p. 563). This is different from other conflict-management approaches in that there is an exchange of proposals in an attempt to reach a joint settlement. Bargaining and negotiation, from this perspective, are interchangeable and are both aimed at settling disputes over the distribution of scarce resources, contractual relationships, and policy.

Mumby and Stohl (1996) described the **negotiation** process in organizations as a deliberative process in which the participants create knowledge about their situation. They view the goal of negotiation as

> no longer exclusively getting an effective settlement, but also as the redefinition of the problem, a perceptual change in the elements of the problem, and a new appreciation of the socio/historical context of the dispute. From the perspective of organizational communication, communication-as-negotiation has a transformative power that transcends notions of technical and instrumental rationality. (p. 62)

This perspective on negotiation in the organization views the participants as engaged in the process of themselves defining the conflict and its environment. The two themes of rationality and effectiveness help define many aspects of organizational life.

Mediation and arbitration are forms of alternative dispute resolution that involve third parties. Research has indicated that successful managers spend more time mediating conflict than unsuccessful managers (Luthans et al., 1985). **Mediation** involves balancing power between disputing individuals, full participation of the individuals involved in the conflict, flattened lines of communication that allow all voices to be heard, and a democratic decision-making process (Wiseman & Poitras, 2002). The mediator has no decision-making authority but guides the disputing parties through a process of reaching an acceptable outcome for both. Although the mediation process is designed to have a neutral third party, this poses an inherent dilemma for managers. Recognizing the struggle to navigate between hierarchal power distribution and the power balance needed for successful conflict mediation, many organizations are offering or requiring managers to attend mediation workshops and training sessions.

Arbitrators, however, often have legal authority to make decisions for conflicting parties when a decision cannot be reached in other ways. Arbitrators make formal binding decisions based on evidence collected during initial negotiating processes (Putnam & Poole, 1987).

In the next section, we discuss one of the first extensions of systems theory into management practice—contingency theory.

Contingency Theory

The first applications of systems concepts to organizations are now referred to under the umbrella term **contingency theory**. Contingency theory posits the notion that there is no one best way to structure and manage organizations. Instead, structure and management are contingent on the nature of the environment in which the organization is situated. This approach extends to communication in the organization as well; contingency theory "argues for finding the best communication structure under a given set of environmental circumstances" (Barnett, 1997, p. 21). In the interest of space, we will briefly discuss only two of the better-known contingency theories (see Woodward, 1965 for another contingency theory not covered here).

Burns and Stalker (1968) provided a contingency theory based on environmental stability in their book *The Management of Innovation*. There they described how they set out to study workers in a factory, but that "was never realized, because it soon became evident that the social structure of the factory interlocked with, and often mirrored, that of the small isolated town in which it was situated" (p. 1). What followed was a theory that showed how organizational systems should vary based on the level of stability in the environment.

Through their research in a variety of organizations, Burns and Stalker noticed that there were two different types of management systems: mechanistic and organic. **Mechanistic systems** are appropriate for a stable environment, where there is little change, or the change is predictable. They are characterized by specialization, centralization, clearly defined roles, and vertical communication (particularly downward instructions). **Organic systems** are required in changing environments with unstable conditions. Such systems have several characteristics. First, specialized tasks are performed in light of interdependence with other specialized tasks. Second, jobs and tasks are continually redefined through interaction among organizational members. Third, communication is both horizontal and vertical and tends to be in the form of consultation rather than orders. Finally, information is a commodity used in decision-making, where "the limits of feasible action are set more widely" (p. 11). Mechanistic and organic systems represent two ends of a continuum, not two parts of a dichotomy.

Although there are many more details and nuances to this theory, the essence is that an organizational system and management practices are intimately related to the environment within which the system is situated. Stable environments provide for mechanistic systems, whereas unstable environments demand an organic system capable of adapting quickly to the novelties of the shifting environment.

In their book *Developing Organizations: Diagnosis and Action*, Lawrence and Lorsch (1969) offered another contingency theory similar to the one offered by Burns and Stalker. Whereas Burns and Stalker focused on the stability of the environment,

Lawrence and Lorsch pointed to environmental uncertainty as the key issue. They began with the premise that more attention had been paid to improving internal relations in organizations than to exploring and improving the organization's relationship with the environment. This focus, they contended, was at least partly due to the fact that it is easier to attach blame or cause to an internal organizational member (e.g., a corporate leader) than to an external entity. It is also quite difficult to gather information about boundary spanning because the information sources are outside the control of the organization.

Lawrence and Lorsch theorized that the organization would have to match certain characteristics with the demands and nature of the environment. In particular, they postulated that an environment could be characterized along a certainty-uncertainty continuum. Environments that were fairly stable or certain would require less and less complex information for the organization than would environments that were more uncertain (changing).

The focus of this theory then was on information flow. Organizations that have a stable environment can operate more easily from predetermined rules; any changes in the environment can be handled through the hierarchy because time is not a critical factor. It follows that the managerial style should be primarily task oriented. In essence, this is a centralized organizational structure.

Organizations in a more uncertain, changing environment must have more complex systems for adapting to the information gathered from that environment. To increase contact with the environment, they should use a decentralized structure. Rules would be too constricting, so free-flowing communication is necessary. Given this situation, strong interpersonal relationships are needed, as is a person-centered managerial style.

Both contingency theories covered here posit a direct relationship between the internal structure of the organization and the type of environment in which it is situated. Burns and Stalker started with the notion that it is the stability of the environment that is important, whereas Lawrence and Lorsch, developing that thesis, focused on the level of uncertainty present in the environment. Both theories treated organizations as systems, inextricably tied to their environment, which must attend to the changes (or lack thereof) in the environment to survive. Contingency theory is widely used to guide and understand management practices in a variety of fields, including accounting (Granlund & Lukka, 2017), marketing (Williams et al., 2016), and human resources (Yu et al., 2020).

Now that you have a broad understanding of systems theory and how it applies to organizations, we want to conclude this chapter by applying the concepts you have learned to a popular topic in organizational life—corporate social responsibility.

Corporate Social Responsibility

When you evaluate your employment opportunities, you could be more interested in being part of an organization that has a sense of social responsibility than you are in the size of your paycheck (Donia, 2021). You can usually research an organization's philosophy and practices in this area by searching for their corporate social responsibility (or CSR) statement on their website. Many organizations have these statements now, as organizations have increasingly become more cognizant of their obligations to social and environmental responsibilities past what the law or basic expectations might dictate (McWilliams et al., 2019). **Corporate social responsibility**, while conceived of differently depending on the discipline, is defined for our purposes as "context-specific organizational actions and policies that take into account stakeholders' expectations and the triple bottom line of economic, social, and environmental performance" (Aguinis & Glavas, 2012, p. 933). CSR is an interesting organizational concept to examine through the lens of systems theory because it involves the interrelationships between the system, subsystems, and the environment. Before we examine CSR through using systems theory concepts, though, let's dig a bit more into the concept.

What do CSR policies and practices look like? The following are summaries of four organizations' CSR policies and practices as outlined on the CSR pages of their websites:

Coca-Cola Company:
- Prioritize sustainability goals
- Offer 500+ brands, including reduced sugar and smaller packages
- Accomplish the goal to collect and recycle a bottle for every one sold and to have packaging be 100% recyclable
- Try to improve safe and clean drinking water in communities that need it most
- Attempt to reduce carbon emission by 25% by 2030 based on 2015 baseline

McDonald's:
- Attempt to reduce, reuse, and recycle
- Use low energy LED light bulbs
- Provide waterless urinals and other energy-saving equipment
- Recycle cooking oil into biodiesel for the McDonald's fleet of trucks

Lego:
- Children: employees volunteer to support children in communities where the needs are highest
- Environment: phase out single use plastic in boxes by 2025
- People: develop a diverse and inclusive workforce and ensure suppliers and partners share the commitment to minimize environmental impact

TOMS:

- Give away a pair of shoes for every pair sold—for every $3 they make, give away $1 to causes such as the following:

  - COVID-19 Global Giving Fund

  - Organizations that work toward physical safety, mental health, equal opportunity

As you can see from these examples, organizations develop philosophies and practices that connect them to social and environmental causes. Some organizations focus on reducing their environmental impact, others on helping consumers make healthier choices, while still others contribute financial and human resources to much-needed community programs.

Why do organizations engage in CSR? Dhanesh (2015) argued that there are two primary drivers of organizations' incorporation of CSR into their missions: moral and strategic. When organizations engage in CSR because they believe it is the right thing to do, this is referred to as a *moral* driver. When organizations engage in CSR because the organization itself will benefit from market appreciation of their efforts, this is referred to as a *strategic* driver. For example, Dhanesh found that in India, a primary driver for CSR was a moral imperative, or the desire by organizational founders (typically wealthy individuals) to give back to those in poverty. Another driver was an economic imperative that could improve the stability and longevity of the organization and improve relationships with organizational members. The competing drivers of organizational CSR policies may lead consumers to not trust the intentions of the organization (Kim & Ley, 2011) and employees to view their own participation in them as involuntary (O'Connor et al., 2016).

You can think about CSR as having three domains or overlapping dimensions: economic, legal, and ethical (Schwartz & Carroll, 2003). The *economic* domain involves organizational activities that are designed to directly or indirectly impact the financial position of the company. The *legal* domain involves the expectations by society that the organization complies with the legal obligations, avoids litigation, and even anticipates potential changes to relevant legislation. Finally, the *ethical* domain includes the expectations of stakeholders (external and internal) that the organization live up to societal ethical standards.

Numerous studies have found that a company's CSR record will affect an organization's ability to recruit and retain qualified employees (Chesloff, 2010; Greening & Turban, 2000). Murray (2008) found that one third of the respondents felt that working for a caring and responsible employer was more important than the salary that they earned, and nearly one half would turn away from an employer with a negative CSR history. Once employees are in the organization, the CSR policies and practices can affect their retention as well. For example, the 2017 Deloitte Volunteerism Impact study found that when a company creates a culture of volunteerism, this may serve to increase morale, brand perception, and the overall workplace atmosphere (Deloitte, 2021), all of which are important to employee retention.

With that brief overview of CSR, we can now look at it through the lens of systems theory. When you think about it, when an organization (system) engages in CSR, it is because they recognize that their relevant environment consists of more than just suppliers, customers, and competitors. When a system engages in CSR it is situating itself in connection with the relevant environment in ways that are not solely dictated by the inputs and outputs needed to keep the organization financially viable. In the case of Tom's, for example, the system's output to the environment is not only in terms of shoes for consumers to buy and waste from the manufacturing process but also a financial and human resource infusion into disadvantaged communities and their programs.

One overlooked piece when it comes to organizations' CSR practices, though, is that the parts of the system (i.e., the members) are the ones who need to enact the policies and practices. Organizations may put together teams of members to volunteer in disadvantaged communities, for example, and those teams need to work well together to create the synergy needed to accomplish the goals of the policies. The existence of a CSR policy is not enough; the subsystems must be empowered both financially, emotionally, and physically to put the policies into practice while at the same time ensuring that the critical functions of the system are still being accomplished (i.e., their jobs). Otherwise, entropy will progress, and the organization will fail to survive.

Summary

In this chapter, we have offered an overview of the framework of viewing organizations that is different from those presented in prior chapters. Systems theory is not the typical prescriptive management theory, such as the theories of classical management or human relations. Instead, systems theory principles were adopted from the natural sciences in an attempt to widen the lens through which we examine and understand organizational behavior (see Table 4.1 for a summary of key points).

This chapter presented the various elements of systems theory, the way those elements have been adapted by organizational theorists, how systems theory informs organizational conflict, and a tour through the initial and more recent practical applications of systems theory. The chapter concluded with an application of systems concepts to the concept of CSR.

Given the extent to which we have integrated systems and learning concepts in our own perspectives of organizational communication, we obviously believe that there is merit in this approach to organizational life. It is shortsighted to believe that organizations are separate from their environment, that organizational teams or subsystems can operate in isolation from one another, or that the same misunderstandings and problems can continue to occur without eventually causing fatal damage to the system.

TABLE 4.1 Systems Theory

FOCUS	IMPORTANT CONCEPTS	ROLES OF COMMUNICATION	SELECTED THEORIES
Interconnections between the organization (system), its parts (subsystems), and the environment	Interdependence Boundaries Entropy Synergy Nonsummativity Feedback Equifinality Requisite variety Transformation model	Coordinate the subsystems Exchange relevant information with the environment	Contingency theory Corporate social responsibility

The systems perspective does have its shortcomings, however. In particular, when the systems perspective has been used to analyze organizational life or inform organizational practice, it has sometimes reduced organizational members to the status of "parts" of the system. This was the same situation that occurred in classical theory. Classical theorists, however, seemed to purposefully dehumanize the workers, but that mentality is not inherent to the systems approach. As it has been implemented, however, theorists and practitioners have at times focused more on the rational relationships between the subsystems and systems and overlooked the fact that those "parts" are human beings.

CHAPTER 5 Organizational Culture

LEARNING OBJECTIVES

1. Describe how misunderstandings arise as a result of the organizational culture
2. Explain the centrality of communication to the definition of organizational culture
3. Explain the central elements of organizational culture
4. Identify how the distinct perspectives of the variable and root metaphor try to understand organizational culture
5. Describe Edgar Schein's three levels of culture

We know many of you work multiple jobs to pay for college. Sometimes, these organizations just feel different, even when they are the same type of organization. For example, you may be a server for two restaurants. One of them has a very relaxed atmosphere where you call your supervisors by their first name, there is not a strict uniform code, you treat each other more like family members than coworkers, and value customer satisfaction above profit. In the other restaurant, you must refer to supervisors by their title and last name (e.g., Ms. Prescott), have very strict rules against personalizing your uniform, are not encouraged to be chatty with your coworkers, and emphasize profit first and customer experience second. While both organizations are successful, you live them very differently, and the behavior in one is not acceptable or understandable in the other. The organizational theories we have covered so far do not help fully explain what you are experiencing, but in this chapter, we offer a perspective that will.

To introduce this perspective, we need to take a quick look at history. In the 1980s, the United States was experiencing intense competition from Japan in many industries, particularly the automotive and electronics industries. Japanese products and services were outselling and outperforming those from the United States, which led practitioners to ask why. Concurrently, organizational theorists began to reconsider the basic assumptions of traditional management theories and found that they were unable to adequately explain the behavior and practices occurring in modern organizations. Both issues led to interest in the concept of organizational culture. Organizational practitioners examined their values and rituals and attempted to change them to meet the demands of the new marketplace. Organizational theorists embraced the concept because it provided a philosophical shift from traditional, highly rational theories to one that was more fluid and capable of explaining behavior that seemed to be irrational, yet deeply rooted.

In this chapter, we discuss organizational culture theory as it has developed and gained prominence since the 1980s. We begin with a discussion of the roots of organizational culture and then examine misunderstandings from this perspective. Next, we define organizational culture and explain the assumptions of the definition. This is followed by an organizing scheme for the elements of organizational culture and a discussion of two perspectives on organizational culture. The chapter concludes with an illustration of Schein's model of organizational culture.

Roots of Organizational Culture

Scholars have been studying culture since the end of the 18th century (Sackmann, 1991), but in the 1970s and 1980s, organizational theorists turned to such studies to help explain the behavior they were observing in organizations. Traditional explanations of organizational behavior (classical theories and humanistic theories) were too limiting in scope; they were unable to explain satisfactorily all forms of behavior *within* organizations and certainly were not able to account for vast differences *among* organizations. The logical, rational explanations offered by classical and humanistic theories were no longer sufficient for many scholars, who were beginning to believe that unspoken (seemingly nonrational) norms, values, and beliefs of organizational members may guide their behavior on a day-to-day basis.

The concept of culture is derived from the field of anthropology. Anthropologists study groups of people (such as tribes and nations) and attempt to understand their culture. To do so, they immerse themselves in all aspects of the group's life, examining (and where possible, living) their customs, rituals, rites, language, dress, food, values, beliefs, and attitudes. Through an in-depth examination of these (and many more) dimensions of culture, anthropologists can provide a rich description of the people, including *how* they tend to behave and *why* they behave as they do.

The word *culture* is used regularly in conversation when describing groups of people or geographic regions. For example, you hear people talk about Appalachian culture, Native American culture, Hispanic culture, the culture of the inner city, African American culture, Western culture, and so on. When the term is used in this way, it is meant to encapsulate the dress, language, customs, prescribed behavior, values, and so on for a certain group of people. The culture of a group is a description of how members of that group live and make sense of their world together.

Perhaps most important, a culture provides a lens through which its members interpret, interact with, and make sense of reality (Louis, 1980). Consider the following story from Brent, a pharmacy supervisor:

The two newer technicians have worked at a pharmacy previously, so they did have pharmacy experience. This helped a lot of things that could have been communication issues because they were already somewhat familiar with the position and weren't coming fresh into it. But because they had been trained at a different pharmacy and were used to doing things a different way at the other pharmacy, sometimes they would do some tasks the way that the other pharmacy did it. This was partially because they were go-getters and didn't need to be led all of the time, which was great that they didn't, but that ended up creating communication issues because nothing was asked, and they just went about doing it as they saw best based on their pharmacy. It ended up that we needed to discuss it later that things are done a different way in our pharmacy for good reasons.

You see, they worked for a larger chain and because of that, they are not as customer oriented. So, it was a matter of getting them on board by making sure the customer is greeted immediately and answering the phones immediately. In a lot of the larger chains, you go in like a machine almost and you do what you're supposed to do. The culture within ours, because our pharmacy is not as convenient as some of the larger chains, the place where we really have to excel is customer service. So, yes that is an area that because they came from a different healthcare organization that had to be trained and discussed.

Brent's story demonstrates how viewing organizational life through an organizational culture lens can help make sense of an otherwise nonrational set of behaviors. To an outsider, this situation could seem quite troublesome and perplexing. Why would a supervisor have a problem if their workers are doing their jobs effectively? Why would the new pharmacists be called in to see the supervisor for taking initiative? Why would the supervisor want the pharmacists to slow down and take more time with each customer, even though that was not very efficient? From an organizational culture perspective, these seemingly nonrational behaviors make sense to the organizational members and serve to reiterate and reproduce the culture of the organization.

As a member of a culture, you may have become enculturated with the values and assumptions of the group. As you go through your daily life, those values and assumptions help you to make sense of what is going on around you. They provide you with meanings for routine events so that you do not have to be cognitively involved in every aspect of your life. Although culture does not *determine* how you will think and behave in every situation, it may help explain patterns of behavior and thought that characterize you and the group with which you are associated. These ideas regarding organizational culture led Alvesson (2002) to argue,

[T]he culture dimension is central in all aspects of organizational life. Even in those organizations where cultural issues receive little explicit attention, how people in a company think, feel, value, and act are guided by ideas, meanings and beliefs of a cultural (socially shared) nature. Whether managers think that the culture is too soft or too complicated to bother about or whether there is no unique corporate culture does not reduce the significance of culture. (p. 1)

Researchers and practitioners interested in organizational culture believe that organizations have the same characteristics as societies and therefore can be understood through a cultural lens. The interests of researchers and practitioners are similar but have notable differences. Researchers, for example, attempt to develop a deep understanding of the elements and nature of organizational culture, how it is determined, and connections between culture and key variables such as power, authority, control, and identification (among others). Practitioners, on the other hand, tend to be interested in how organizational culture can be managed and how it can be changed as key conditions, such as competition, products, and leadership change (Jung et al., 2009).

The utility of the cultural perspective for both researchers and practitioners should not decline anytime soon. As Keyton (2005) noted,

> [I]nterest in organizational culture exists and continues to be stimulated because organizational culture is both changeable and complex, as it emerges from the interactions of organizational members. Moreover, as new organizational structures appear (for example, a workforce of virtually connected employees), they continue to challenge our understanding of organizational culture. (p. 2)

In addition, from our perspective in this book, the cultural lens also provides a new way of looking at misunderstandings in organizations, one that focuses less on systemic and structural issues and more on the values, behaviors, and assumptions of members.

Misunderstandings and Organizational Culture

Perhaps one of the most intriguing aspects of anthropological research is how it has shown that groups of people, who are essentially the same biologically and physically, develop cultures that are so vastly different. As a result, differences in behaviors, values, and assumptions, not to mention language, dress, and appropriate social behavior are far-ranging. These variations are often the cause of major and minor misunderstandings as the groups come into contact with one another. Israel and Palestine, African Americans and Caucasians, Native Americans and government bureaucrats, environmentalists and land developers, and Christians and atheists are but a few well-known examples of groups with different cultures that seem to clash on a daily basis in the modern world. Bridging the differences between them often seems like trying to bridge the Great Divide.

Consider the realm of organizations instead of anthropology, and for "environmentalists and land developers" substitute Starbucks and Dunkin' or Nike and Birkenstock.

These paired organizations, although in the same industry, are known to have vastly different cultures that espouse different values, have different assumptions about how to treat employees and customers, and have even developed different specialized languages to facilitate their day-to-day operations. Birkenstock and Dunkin' are two organizations that have positioned themselves as being "different" from their competition (i.e., Nike and Starbucks, respectively). The differences are not only reflected in business practices, products, and services but also in their cultures. These organizations embody different core values, attitudes, and beliefs that make them appear quite distinct from each other.

But the value of the organizational culture perspective is not in illustrating the misunderstandings that occur *between* organizations because of cultural differences, although that can be enlightening. The true value of this perspective is the insight it provides into the basic underpinnings of organizational behavior *within* an organization. The organizational culture perspective sheds light on why things are happening in organizations that seem to have no logical explanation (recall Brent's story from earlier in this chapter). As you read this chapter, you will discover that these same issues serve as the basis for many misunderstandings in organizations.

Misunderstandings based in organizational culture issues take many forms, and as you read this chapter, you will quickly recognize the breadth of this reality. They are readily apparent, for example, when a newcomer enters an organization and has not yet learned its culture. The newcomer struggles to understand the language that is used, the relationships that people have and how they may differ based on their level in the hierarchy or function, the appropriate ways to act in meetings, how late to stay at the end of the workday, or even their obligations to attend social events, among many other things. Consider this brief story told to us by Dave, a professor:

> As a newish faculty member at an Appalachian regional university, I was part of a culture where every action is measured by its potential effect on the achievement of tenure. Put simply, one said "yes" to nearly any request in order to establish and maintain good standing with the people who would someday vote on one's tenure and thus one's future well-being. So, when a veteran psychology professor (not my home department) who lived down the street from me called asking if I had any musical equipment and would I join him and his colleagues for a jam, I said "yes" with overt enthusiasm.
>
> I went to his house that evening, toting amplifiers and instruments as requested, and noted a houseful of people who looked about as uncomfortable as one could expect outside of a courthouse. This was not the casual, relaxed atmosphere of the usual jam I'd grown accustomed to in other states and places where the musicians set up, goofed around some with snatches of patterns and songs, and would soon launch into something we all knew or that was simple enough to play. All of a sudden, the

host, who was also the department chair of psychology, produced a stack of binders and passed them around to players and pals. Binders? Turns out, the tradition in "jams" run by this person (who could be voting on my tenure) required songbooks that he had created. Everyone present was given one, whether they were a musician or not. The jam lost all of its appeal for me, and I wondered how I could get out with my job intact. The whole jam mentality and feel were ruined, but the odd thing was that everyone there (but me) dutifully opened their binders, ready to "jam."

Dave's story illustrates several issues related to organizational culture and misunderstandings. The most important is that the culture Dave found himself in seemed to dictate the need to say "yes" to participating in events and activities that may not be part of the actual job just to help ensure a positive tenure vote. His story also illustrates how different words (in this case, "jam") can mean very different things in different organizational cultures.

As stated earlier, organizational culture provides meaning for routine organizational events, thereby reducing the amount of cognitive processing and energy members need to expend throughout the day. Although culture can be beneficial, it may also be the root of misunderstandings. Organizational culture provides a certain way of viewing reality that may have proven to be successful in the past, but that same culture may hinder the organization from progress in the future. In a marketplace characterized as fast paced, multidimensional, and evolutionary, it is likely that deeply entrenched values could make change and adaptation difficult. This likelihood holds true both on the organizational level regarding such things as market strategy and customer relations and on the individual level in terms of how individual workers approach organizational problems.

As we will discuss later in this chapter, organizations consist of many subcultures. Subcultures may be based on proximity, function, level in the hierarchy, or a variety of other possibilities. Subcultures differ slightly from one another with regard to the cultural elements discussed to this point. As a result, as members from these different subcultures interact on a daily basis in the organization, they may encounter misunderstandings based on differing values, practices, and meanings for events and language. It is common to hear people on the account executive side of an advertising agency, for example, say that they "just don't understand those people in the creative department." These subcultures, although part of the same organization, often seem worlds apart.

A last general area of misunderstandings as related to organizational culture involves the merging of organizations. Mergers have always been a part of organizational life, but now with increased communication technology and practical intercontinental travel, mergers between international companies are becoming more common. Whenever organizations merge, misunderstandings caused by the clash of cultures are inevitable. When the organizations are based in different societal cultures, however, the difficulties are increased. For example, Cheng and Seeger (2012) reported on the difficulties that occurred because of the organizational culture differences between two international organizations that merged—BenQ, a Taiwanese-based company, and Siemens, a German organization.

> Siemens is considered the archetype of German engineering prowess. Its long-standing tradition of labor harmony and powerful worker's councils is highly resistant to this type of change. BenQ . . . is known for its fast, flexible, innovative and enterprising spirit, reflected in the company's visionary name—Bring Enjoyment and Quality to life. Organizationally, BenQ's corporate culture was informal and less structured, whereas Siemens was more formal and more structured. (p. 122)

When energy is not devoted to the cultural aspects of organizational mergers, misunderstandings abound.

There are certainly many more areas in which misunderstandings are related to organizational culture. As you read this chapter, continue to think of ways in which the issues discussed may shed light on organizational misunderstandings. In the next section, we discuss our communication-based definition of organizational culture.

Defining Organizational Culture

You have probably heard the saying, "You cannot step in the same river twice." But why not? The location is the same, the landmarks are all there, and you may have even stepped in your own footprints if the river is shallow enough to see them. The reason is because the movement of the river brings different water, carrying different living and nonliving things down the river changing it ever so slightly as each new element is introduced and older elements move on or are somehow altered by time and forces of energy. That is how you should think of organizational culture. The organization's culture is rooted in history, much as the location of a river is; however, the culture is not static, just as a river is not, because people are constantly communicating and joining and leaving the organization. As they communicate and interact, the culture is dynamic but still guiding how people behave in it, much as the flowing water is guided by the riverbanks and riverbed but makes changes in them at the same time.

Therefore, we offer a definition of organizational culture that emphasizes communication and history (see Conrad, 1990 for more on these connections). **Organizational culture** is a communicatively constructed, historically based system of assumptions, values, and interpretive frameworks that guide and constrain organizational members as they perform their organizational roles and confront the challenges of their environment.

Let's dig a little deeper into some of the parts of the definition. Perhaps the most important part to understand is that cultures are communicative constructions. They do not exist separate from organizational members; cultures are created, sustained, and influenced by and through human interaction. In telling stories, writing memos, having meetings, conducting rites and rituals, and through other communicative actions, members develop and articulate (to themselves, as well as to other members and nonmembers) the central values of the culture.

At the same time, the culture of the organization influences the communication of its members. Organizational members communicate based on the values and interpretive frameworks of the culture, thereby legitimizing the use of specialized language, appropriate media for communication, and the conventions of who talks to whom about what. In other words, the relationship between communication and organizational culture is reciprocal; communication influences organizational culture, and organizational culture influences communication (see Figure 5.1).

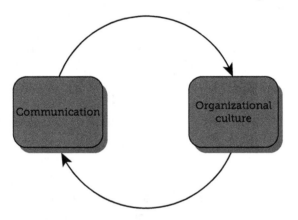

FIGURE 5.1 Relationship Between Communication and Organizational Culture

Figure 5.1 and the preceding discussion should not be interpreted as advocating a direct causal relationship between organizational culture and human behavior. Although organizational culture certainly may *influence* human behavior in organizations, it does not *cause* members to act predictably in every situation. Because individuals are, by nature, unique and have freedom of choice, human behavior will always be unpredictable. Nevertheless, organizational culture provides frameworks for what is acceptable and expected; it is the members' choice to behave within that framework.

A different way to think of it is that organizational culture is intangible. Organizational culture is a construction formed through human interaction, but it is not concrete at its core. Organizational culture, as described previously, consists of values, assumptions, norms, and frameworks for understanding, none of which are tangible objects. Organizational culture is often confused with the tangible objects or observable activities that occur within an organization. The dress code of an organization, the stories that are told in it, the daily rituals, and ceremonial rites are all elements of organizational culture that serve to create, maintain, change, and reflect it, but they are not in and of themselves the organization's culture.

Another important part of the definition is that organizational cultures are historical. "[Cultures] emerge and develop over time, adapting to changes in their membership, functions, problems, and purposes" (Conrad, 1990, p. 17). Organizational cultures are rooted in the history of events and actions (particularly the communicative actions) as they have unfolded in and around the organization.

The definition assumes that organizational culture involves something that is shared. When we say that organizational culture involves a *system of assumptions, values, and interpretive frameworks*, we are saying that the members of the culture share common ways of understanding and interpreting organizational phenomena. This statement does not mean that all members of the culture think the same way, believe the same things, or act in the same way. It simply means that an organizational culture provides its members with ways to understand and interpret events, but the extent to which a member is enculturated with them is a matter of socialization (see Chapter 8) and individual differences.

A final part of the definition that needs attention is that organizational culture affects human behavior. This is perhaps the most important, though it may not seem so. Organizational culture is not merely another way of attempting to run organizations more profitably; it is a construction of human interaction that affects and is affected by the behavior of all members of the organization. Organizational culture provides frameworks (or logics) for interpreting organizational events as the members experience them on a day-to-day basis, particularly as they figure out how to perform their organizational roles and how to make sense of any changes happening in their relevant environment. If we are to understand how and why organizational members behave as they do, we must understand the organizational culture that guides and constrains them.

In the next section, we take a closer look at the elements of organizational culture that are subsumed by this definition.

Elements of Organizational Culture

Given the complexity and richness of organizational culture, it is no surprise that researchers have identified more than 100 dimensions or elements of the construct (Jung et al., 2009). The elements themselves do not constitute organizational culture, but organizational culture is produced and reproduced as the elements are enacted through time by the members. Think of it as a musical performance. For a musical performance to occur, there are countless elements that go into it: band members, instruments, rehearsal time and space, training, sound equipment, sound engineers, songs, an audience, money, electricity, and a performance venue, not to mention the actual physical performances of the musicians themselves. The individual elements are not the performance; it is the combination of these elements over time that leads to the performance. The performance is also not a static event that is experienced the same by every person involved. Instead, the performance unfolds, and each person involved experiences something different. It is the same for organizational culture. The elements of organizational culture that we discuss next should not be confused with organizational culture itself; instead, think of organizational culture as a performance that brings to bear these elements over time and is experienced differently for each person in the organization.

One of the more useful ways of explaining the elements of organizational culture was offered by Driskill (2018) in his book, *Organizational Culture in Action.* What follows is an outline of the major elements of organizational culture informed in part by the work of Driskill.

Values

Values are a group's common beliefs and preferences for what they want to be priorities. The values of the organizational culture serve to distinguish the organization's culture from other cultures and provide a sense of identity to its members (Hoelscher et al., 2016). For example, the stories, legends, and artifacts that are shared in the organization often serve to reinforce or reflect the values of the culture. In turn, as the organization seeks to modify the values of the organization, the elements too will have to change.

It is important to realize that there is a difference between espoused values and lived values. Espoused values are those values that are articulated publicly by the management of the organization (and perhaps even the other members) but are not actually practiced on a day-to-day basis. For a value to be foundational to an organization's culture, it should be a lived value—one that is actually practiced by the members of the organization and reflected in the other elements of the culture. Consider the following story from Elena, who is the director of a diversity and inclusion department at a university:

> When requesting administrative support for a new initiative to offer racial equity and social justice professional development to employees (free of charge), I created a draft email describing the opportunity and asked for that to be distributed. The administrative leader did indeed send out an email, but it included none of the original text. Instead of encouraging employees to participate, many employees indicated that they felt discouraged from applying. The distributed email included language like, "Discuss the possibility with your supervisor to determine whether it is feasible as a component of your role," even though we claim that equity and inclusion are campus-wide values and everyone's responsibility. The email went on to say, "If you are academic or university staff, work with your supervisor to determine the appropriate level of work and/or personal time to be used in order to be involved in this experience," even though professional development is typically an on-the-clock opportunity for most of us. Apparently, when it relates to anti-racism work, we need to take vacation to engage in that . . . at least, that's how some people received the message.

Elena's story illustrates the difference between espoused values and lived values. In her situation, Elena's university espoused the value of diversity and social justice, but when it came to the enactment of that value, there was no true support from the administration.

Symbolic Elements

Symbolic elements are those elements in the culture that stand for or represent cultural values. Although it can be argued that all elements in the culture are important and represent meaning, symbolic elements are set aside because they are basic communicative forms on which the other elements rest. Four symbolic elements we would like to cover are symbols, stories, language, and metaphors.

Symbols are the physical representations of the organization's culture. Examples of symbols in this context are such things as logos, mascots, newsletters, websites, physical spaces (e.g., building architecture, parking spaces, or green space), speeches given by important organizational members, and even certain organizational members themselves who have come to symbolize the culture over time. These symbols serve as more formal representations of the organizational culture to the members and the relevant environment. Just as with values, symbols have different meanings for different people and can have espoused, as well as lived, meanings. Although the organization may attempt to invoke certain meanings with particular symbols, how people interpret the symbols cannot be prescribed.

Stories can serve to symbolize values in an organization's culture. Stories about key organizational members such as founders or CEOs, turning points in the organization's history, and defining actions (appropriate or inappropriate) of organizational members are told and retold by organizational members as a way of reifying the values and socializing newcomers. Stories that are told over and over provide clues as to the values of the culture.

Language/nonverbal, the third symbolic element, includes the specialized language, nonvocal body movement, terms and vocabulary, and other verbal and nonverbal aspects of organizational life that serve to communicate the culture to its members. Being fluent in the language and nonverbal communication activities of an organization is an indication of membership and serves to distinguish members from nonmembers and old-timers from newcomers. Think of the first time you stepped foot on your school's campus. Chances are you heard people using terms, phrases, and acronyms that just did not make sense to you. This language is deeply embedded in the culture of the organization, and as you fumbled your way through the first few months as a newcomer, you began to learn and use the language appropriately. As you became more fluent with the language and nonverbal actions, you slowly began to move from an outsider to an insider.

Metaphor is the final symbolic element forwarded by Driskill. A metaphor allows the communicator to explain an unknown idea by comparing it to something that is known. Metaphors are used to help communicate how organizational members are to act toward one another, clients and customers, competitors, and other members of the relevant environment. They also guide and constrain organizational members as they confront the realities of their everyday workplace. There are, as with the other elements, espoused metaphors, as well as lived metaphors. The management of an organization may say that the organization is like a family, but the realities of day-to-day life do not follow that metaphor; the espoused metaphor is not a lived metaphor.

Let's explore that well-worn organizational metaphor of "family." When members of the organization refer to the organization as a family, then they are to treat other organizational members as family members, worthy of the respect, care, and concern that is often reserved for kin. Organizational members have a general sense of being "at home" while at work, and they are actively involved in the personal, as well as professional, lives of other organizational members. However, as stated earlier, metaphors do not only guide behaviors or organizational members, but they constrain them as well. In the example of the family metaphor, as a way of keeping the peace, organizational members may be constrained from engaging in conflict. This conflict avoidance could lead to negative feelings, stress, burnout, and a reduction in creative problem-solving.

Role Elements

Another category of elements of organizational culture is role elements. The two primary role elements identified by Driskill are heroes and outlaws. Although many other roles are identified in the organizational culture literature, these two are perhaps the most readily identifiable. More than one person can fill a role (i.e., there can be more than one hero or one outlaw), and it is possible that the same person can fill both roles depending on the perspective of the organizational members. For example, at the national level, it is equally easy to find people in the culture who will consider the sitting president to be a hero, whereas others consider him or her to fill the role of outlaw. In organizations, as in national cultures, perceptions of members are social constructions that vary based on individuals.

Heroes represent or embody the values of the organizational culture. Sometimes the hero is the founder, such as Fred Smith from Federal Express, Sam Walton from Walmart, or Clara Barton from the American Red Cross. Other times, the hero is a well-known figure (either currently in the organization or from the organization's history) who is well connected to or revered by most organizational members and embodies the values of the culture. Universities, for example, often have figures who "bleed" the colors of the school and whom most members respect as the person that best reflects the values of the institution. These heroes may not be formal leaders and may not be formally recognized as heroes by the organization but serve to remind the members and the relevant environment of the values of the culture.

Outlaws, on the other hand, are people who represent values or ideals that are counter to the espoused values of the organization, yet their presence in the culture serves to cultivate the espoused values for the other members. Although it may at first be difficult to understand how an outlaw is valuable to the cultivation of values in an organization, think of the number of children's stories that have a villain of one kind or another. This character is present in the story to personify the opposite of what should be done or believed or is there as a foil for the heroes of the tale to conquer. The existence of outlaws in organizational cultures can serve to remind organizational members and the relevant environment of the values by showing the superiority of the preferred values.

Another reason that outlaws are useful is because they may offer an alternative way of approaching organizational life that, although counter to the values of the organization, could stimulate critical thinking. As discussed earlier, values are the foundation of organizational cultures, and as such, they both guide and constrain organizational members. Values help organizational members know how to think, act, and feel in the situations in which they find themselves. At the same time, the value system can limit how the organizational members interpret the situations in which they find themselves and consequently restrict how they handle those situations. The presence of an outlaw in the culture can act as the proverbial devil's advocate that can help loosen the constraints of the value system.

Interactive Cultural Elements

Interactive cultural elements are named such because they can only be observed in interactions between organizational members. The three interactive cultural elements are rituals, informal cultural rules, and organizational style.

Rituals are social actions "in which a group's values and identity are publicly demonstrated or enacted in a stylized manner, within the context of a specific occasion or event" (Islam & Zyphur, 2009, p. 116). Driskill listed a variety of interactions that constitute rituals, including organizational practices and procedures, informal office gatherings, coffee room talk, and award ceremonies.

How do rituals contribute to organizational culture? Much as with the other cultural elements, cultural values are often reflected in the informal, planned, and unplanned interactions in the organization. As the members go about doing their daily lives and taking part in these rituals, they are creating and recreating the culture by adhering to (or perhaps attempting to change) the values. For example, at one university with which we are familiar, it was a daily ritual that the older faculty members in a particular department would go to have coffee together. Going to coffee was an important time for them to socialize, tell stories, and be "collegial." However, those who did not choose to go to coffee regularly (or at all) were often considered to be poor departmental citizens and not team players. What the older faculty members did not realize was that the younger faculty members purposefully did not attend these daily coffee sessions because they wanted to create a new value system—one that put a premium on the time they were on campus because their off-campus time was often spent conducting research, preparing for class, or caring for their families.

Informal cultural rules are prescriptions for what kind of behavior is required, discouraged, permitted, and preferred or not preferred in the organization. This cultural element is referred to as "informal" because there is generally nothing written regarding these rules or norms. Instead, organizational members come to understand them over time, through interactions with others, or through violating the rule or norm themselves without even knowing it. Once the violation has occurred, the member tends to sense that he has done something wrong or is told directly by another member. There are more of these informal cultural rules in organizations than could ever be mentioned here, but some of the most prominent include the informal dress code; length of coffee breaks; cafeteria seating; orientation to time; how people address coworkers, bosses, and subordinates; appropriate time to leave work; and afterwork socializing. The following story is from one of our colleagues, and it is a perfect example of an informal cultural rule:

> When I became president of Hanover College I started on July 1. Therefore, I had been on campus for 2 months before the first day of classes. On the Friday before Monday's first classes, I was talking with one of my cabinet members who said, "I really dread Monday because I'll have to wear a tie to work." I said, "Why do you have to wear a tie?" He replied, "You mean I don't have to?" I said I certainly didn't care if he had a tie on or not as long as he looked professional. On Monday, he was the only man sitting around the conference table without a tie on. When one of his colleagues attempted to chide him about it, he said, "Well, the president said I didn't have to." That's how I found out that for 20 years men had been required to wear a suit and tie on the first day of class, and women could not wear pants. This rule was so old I am surprised that no one challenged it. From that day forward, there was no longer an informal dress code for administrators on campus. In fact, I frequently encourage them to wear college gear. I received thank-yous from across the campus from administrators, some of whom were young and thought they were going to have to buy a suit for the start of the school year. This norm wasn't written down, but everyone was following it. I stumbled upon it accidentally and changed it because I felt that no one should be forced to wear formal attire unless there was a formal occasion.

As often happens, it is through the experiences of a newcomer that the informal cultural rules come to light.

Organizational communication style, the final interactive cultural element, involves the organizationally preferred channels for communicating. The three most common channels that translate into a particular style are written, oral, and electronic. Talia, a graphic designer for a beauty salon, provided a vivid example of a culture that has an electronic organizational communication style:

I think communication would be the most common problem because all our project management is done online. We use a specific platform online to organize all of the projects we do for the whole year. Because everything is online, everyone is getting email notifications from everyone about current projects. Designers are responsible for multiple projects, so, it can get messy to the point where people are missing emails. For example, a manager misses an email, and now I'm waiting for that manager to approve something because everything needs to be done online and documented. So, my part can't be done until they okay it. It might be a day or two that I don't get any answer, so I have to go back and ask them again and then they'll reply. So, I guess it's communication digitally, but I guess since everything's online it's a lot of notifications you must go through too. You get a notification for everything that you are a part of and there's multiple projects being worked on simultaneously. So, if you're a manager, you're going to get the most notifications.

I'm pretty sure other people feel the same way. I think the designers would agree on it the most. I'm in a position where we can't go onto the next step until someone approves it. All of our work is done for someone and that someone needs to approve it for us to pass it on to the next person.

I wouldn't ask them personally; it's done digitally. Our desks are in the same room, but sometimes people are busy with other things, so really all you can do is go back into the project and make a comment, like "Hey is this approved yet?" So, it is like you have to remind them to do their part pretty much.

Talia's story shows the effects of the organizational communication style on the culture. In her situation, the electronic style affects how people interact with one another, how they are given orders by their bosses, how their bosses approve their work, and how it affects the overall climate of the organization. Talia went on to talk about the benefits of this type of style but did also make it clear that many misunderstandings arise because of the lack of face-to-face interaction.

Context Elements

The final category of elements is context elements. The two elements in this category show how organizational cultures are shaped by aspects that may be outside the direct control of the current organizational members. The two primary elements in this category are history and place.

History is knowledge of the evolution of the organization, including information about the founders and the purposes behind the founding. Understanding an organization's history and the story of the founder is often considered a valuable resource for current members and may be used as an indicator of the extent to which a particular member is connected to the culture. Walmart, for example, spends considerable time and energy educating its members regarding the founder (Sam Walton) and the history of the organization, despite the tremendous changes that Walmart has experienced in the past few decades. Walmart considers the history of the organization and the story of Sam Walton to be valuable pieces of information for the members because the values of the culture are deeply entrenched in those stories.

Place refers to the environment in which an organization is situated, such as the local area, the state, country, or global contexts. This final element is often overlooked by organizational practitioners but plays a key role in understanding the development and maintenance of organizational culture. This systems theory perspective reminds us that what happens in the organizational culture is connected to the relevant environment. National and industry cultures are often shown to affect the development of organizational culture, but it is also important to understand how local/community culture can affect it as well. Place can also refer to the physical layout of the organization itself, such that the physical environment can affect the culture of the organization. For example, Zerella et al. (2017) showed that an open-office design can be related to a more collaborative culture.

In the next section, we offer two ways of viewing organizational culture as a phenomenon—culture as variable versus culture as root metaphor.

Two Perspectives on Organizational Culture

Smircich (1983) provided useful terminology for explaining two competing perspectives on organizational culture: (1) culture as variable and (2) culture as root metaphor. The two perspectives are fairly separate and distinct belief systems regarding the nature of organizational culture.

Culture as Variable

From the **culture-as-variable perspective**, organizational culture is something the organization *has* (Smircich, 1983). Organizational culture is a by-product of organizational activities; as organizations produce goods and services, they also produce cultural artifacts, such as stories, rites and rituals, and heroes. Organizational culture, from this perspective, is likened to other influential elements in the organization, such as the organizational structure, the performance appraisal system, or the formal organizational policies.

Consider the term *variable* for a moment. A variable, in research terms, is something that does or can be changed. From the culture-as-variable perspective, then, culture is something that is considered changeable, particularly by the management of the organization. Because culture resides mainly in the artifacts, behaviors, and practices of the organization, it follows that it can be manipulated and changed relatively quickly and for the better by those with the power to do so (Curran, 2005). Those who subscribe to this perspective treat culture as a management tool to enhance organizational effectiveness and productivity.

Two successful popular press books from the 1980s typify the culture-as-variable perspective: *In Search of Excellence* by Tom Peters and Robert Waterman (1982) and *Corporate Cultures: The Rites and Rituals of Corporate Life* by Terrence Deal and Allen Kennedy (1982). These two books were bestsellers and influenced much of the managerial thinking about organizational culture in the decade that followed. The authors prescribed methods for creating ideal organizational cultures.

Peters and Waterman argued that excellent companies (those that continually respond to changes in their environment) tend to have similar cultures guided by a limited set of shared values (or themes). The authors attempted to convince managers that the "soft side" of organizations (shared values), once thought to be beyond the scope of management, could and should be managed. In essence, they consider organizational culture to be a "tool" for enhancing organizational effectiveness. With the appropriate awareness, managers can develop the "skill" to use the tool to improve their organization's productivity and performance.

Deal and Kennedy argued that effective, high-performing organizations have *strong cultures* or "powerful lever[s] for guiding behavior" (Deal & Kennedy, 1982, p. 15). They described four key components to a strong culture, of which the first three were discussed in the previous section: values, heroes, rites and rituals, and cultural network. The *cultural network* consists of the informal communication network in the organization and is the primary carrier of cultural information between management and workers. Stories, myths, legends, jokes, and gossip all carry culturally relevant information and serve to promote the values of the organization (Deal & Kennedy, 1982).

Corporate Cultures and *In Search of Excellence* are prototypical examples of the culture-as-variable perspective. Although these popular books were on the reading list of most corporate managers in the early 1980s, many critics were less enthusiastic. They gave three main criticisms of the perspective embodied in these two books. First, they stated that the idea that certain cultural values or beliefs are "strong" and will lead to "strong" or "excellent" organizations is shortsighted. Several of the attributes discussed by Peters and Waterman (such as "autonomy and entrepreneurship" and "productivity through people") are viable principles worthy of emulation, but to prescribe these attributes as the key attributes for every organizational culture ignores both the unique nature of the organization's situation and the true essence of culture as a construct. Second, they maintained that although values certainly represent the core of organizational culture, they are equal to more than business strategy and managerial goals. Third, they declared that culture is not simply a tool, skill, or lever to be used by management to improve organizational productivity. Culture is a complex, communicative phenomenon, rooted in the history of the organization's events. The culture-as-root-metaphor perspective acknowledges these aspects of culture.

Culture as Root Metaphor

The **culture-as-root-metaphor perspective** treats culture as something the organization *is.* This perspective "promotes a view of organizations as expressive forms, manifestations of human consciousness" (Smircich, 1983, p. 347), as opposed to treating the organization as a material entity, such as a machine or organism. Treating the organization in this way yields a complexity and human nature that is missing when an organization is considered to be a material entity.

Whereas the culture-as-variable perspective considers culture to be a managerial tool, and rituals, stories, legends, gossip, and other symbols as "culture itself," the root-metaphor perspective treats culture as the process of sense-making created and sustained through communication and interaction. Rituals, stories, and so on are very important to this perspective, but they are considered "generative processes that yield and shape meanings and ... are fundamental to the very existence of organization" (p. 353).

The root-metaphor perspective on organizational culture is more difficult to delineate than the variable approach, which is one reason why many organizational practitioners have not embraced it. It does not offer any quick-fix tools or methods for managers, nor does it offer generalizable knowledge useful for every organization. What it does do is provide a deep understanding of the way members of a particular organization make sense of the world around them.

Consider the label *root metaphor* for a moment. When we say that something is a root metaphor, we mean that it is more than just a way of using one concept to help us understand another. Instead, we mean that it is the *essence* of that concept, that the two constructs are essentially inseparable. In other words, the essence of an organization is culture from this perspective (see Smith & Eisenberg, 1987 for an extended discussion). One cannot consider the organization without considering culture, for the organization *is* a culture. The root-metaphor perspective is composed of many dimensions; three are described next.

The first is that organizational culture is complex. Schein (1985) put forward the notion that "culture is a *deep* phenomenon ... *complex* and difficult to understand" (p. 5). Contrary to the culture-as-variable perspective, the root-metaphor perspective treats organizational culture as a multilevel construction with surface and deep levels. The surface level of culture consists of fairly tangible and concrete elements, such as rites, rituals, ceremonies, architecture, clothing, decorations, logos, slogans, stories, and language use. The culture-as-variable perspective often considers culture only at this surface level; if a leader can change the surface level, then he has changed the culture. However, that perspective often overlooks the deeper levels of organizational culture.

Below the surface-level manifestations of organizational culture are its basic elements. As stated in the previous section, values, beliefs, attitudes, sense-making logics, and basic assumptions are the essence of organizational culture. They reside not in the surface-level artifacts but in the minds and bodies of individuals and groups. Some researchers argue that this is why organizational culture is such a powerful force; its connection to the deep-seated emotional needs of the organizational members makes it so (Pizer & Härtel, 2005).

Researchers who espouse the root-metaphor perspective often begin their examinations of organizational culture by studying one or many surface-level forms in an attempt to help them understand the deep levels. For example, Smith and Stewart (2011) advocated examining organizational rituals in part because the rituals communicate important organizational values. Di Domenico and Phillips (2009) observed 22 formal dinners at Oxbridge colleges and demonstrated how the dinners served to reaffirm social structure, order, and interaction. Boje (1991) recorded and analyzed stories told during executive meetings, training sessions, and hallway conversations.

It is important to remember that an organization's culture cannot be understood by examining one or a few surface-level forms of culture in isolation. Researchers using the root-metaphor perspective integrate their observations of surface-level forms with in-depth interviews, long-term observation, and any other available forms of data they can gather before they attempt to describe an organization's culture. This process takes a tremendous amount of time and energy, but the result is often an understanding of not only the surface but also the deep nature of organizational culture (Martin, 2002). As Rafaeli and Worline (2000) suggested, "To understand the cultural system of an organization is to understand the reactions, interpretations, and actions of organizational members, as well as how those actions, thoughts, and feelings are shaped by the collectivity" (p. 72).

The second dimension of the root-metaphor approach is that organizational culture is a communicative construction. From the root-metaphor perspective, organizational culture is not something that is dictated by the management of the organization (as some in the variable camp would argue); it is, instead, constructed and reconstructed as members of the organization interact together and confront their environment. This perspective assumes that organizational culture is a sociohistorical construction (Deetz, 1982). In other words, organizational culture is created and recreated as people interact (communicate) over time.

In attempting to explain the concept of culture, Geertz likened culture to a web. Pacanowsky and O'Donnell-Trujillo (1990) articulated Geertz's metaphor, which connects culture and communication:

> [T]he web not only exists, it is spun. It is spun when people go about the business of construing their world as sensible—that is, when they communicate. When they talk, write a play, sing, dance, fake an illness, they are communicating, and they are constructing their culture. The web is the residue of the communication process. (p. 147)

The metaphor of a web is an interesting choice in that webs represent strength, life, and cohesion, but they are also things that need constant maintenance, vary to meet the conditions, and are the direct result of the energy supplied by those who spin and inhabit them. By using the web metaphor, Pacanowsky and O'Donnell-Trujillo argued for the centrality of communication to culture; the two, in fact, cannot be separated (see Keyton, 2014, for a discussion of the connection between communication and culture).

The third dimension of the root-metaphor perspective is that organizational culture consists of subcultures and countercultures. The culture-as-variable perspective proposes the idea that there is one overarching culture shared by all members of the organization. The root-metaphor perspective acknowledges that although many members may share certain organizational values, organizational culture is not monolithic; instead, it is appropriate to consider that the culture of an organization may consist (naturally) of subcultures and countercultures.

Although a **subculture** may diverge only minimally from the values and practices of the organizational culture, a counterculture may develop that is in opposition to the accepted culture. As Trice and Beyer defined it, a **counterculture** is a subculture "whose basic understandings question and oppose the overall culture in some way" (1993, p. 244). Countercultures may develop as a result of corporate mergers, disgruntled employees, or highly differential group missions. Although countercultures certainly have the potential to be destructive to organizational cohesiveness, they may also be productive. Countercultures, by nature, oppose the values of the dominant culture. If values and assumptions go unchecked in any organization for too long, they may become so deeply entrenched that change, even change necessary for survival, becomes difficult if not improbable.

The variable and root-metaphor perspectives are not the only ways to characterize the research and thinking about organizational culture. For example, Martin (1992) offered three perspectives on organizational culture that differ in the extent to which there is one core culture in an organization and the extent to which culture is a stable entity. More recently, Eisenberg and Riley (2001) put forward seven theoretical frameworks regarding organizational culture, each with a different philosophical starting point, and Keyton (2014) articulated several ways in which organizational culture and communication are connected. Given the variety of ways in which culture has been approached, it should be no surprise that it is difficult to find agreement on how to define the concept. In the next section, we discuss existing definitions of organizational culture and offer our own working definition.

In the final section of the discussion of organizational culture, we offer one model of organizational culture from the vast literature on the subject, that of Edgar Schein. It offers a multilevel perspective on culture that acknowledges both its surface and its deep aspects.

Schein's Model of Organizational Culture

In his book *Organizational Culture and Leadership*, Edgar Schein (1985) outlined a model of organizational culture that articulates three interrelated levels of culture: (1) artifacts and creations, (2) values, and (3) basic assumptions. Although they are conceptually distinct, it is important to understand how they are related to one another.

Level 1: Artifacts and Creations

The first level of Schein's model of organizational culture, **artifacts and creations**, consists of the tangible, physical, or hearable things in the environment of the organization. Schein argued that despite the fact that this level is the most "visible," its elements are quite difficult to decipher.

Researchers often begin their study of an organization's culture by familiarizing themselves with its artifacts. Much as anthropologists study the artifacts of a tribe to understand how they live; organizational culture researchers examine the physical creations (whether they be tangible objects or communicative events) to help them understand the culture. For example, as mentioned earlier, Trice and Beyer (1984) examined rites and ceremonials. They argue that certain rites, such as training programs, seminars, and holiday parties, may be reflections or manifestations of the values of the organization. Barley (1983), in an analysis of the culture of the funeral home industry, studied the physical artifacts of the funeral home, the behaviors associated with removal of the body from a home after a death, and the practices associated with preparation of the corpse for disposal. Barley found that these physical manifestations were important in creating a sense of "normalcy" and "naturalness" for the loved ones of the deceased.

Although artifacts and creations are observable elements of organizational culture, they should not be confused with the culture itself. Schein argued that it is important to understand the connection of the artifacts of the first level to the values of the second level.

Level 2: Values

Schein defined values as an individual's or group's "sense of what 'ought' to be, as distinct from what is" (1985, p. 15). As individuals come together to form a collective (e.g., work group, research team, organization), they are soon confronted with the need to have a common basis for operating together. Schein argued that someone in the group, typically the leader or the founder, has particular thoughts and feelings (or convictions) about the nature of reality and will articulate ideas about the problems the group faces on the basis of those convictions. If the actions proposed by that person are adequate in addressing the problems, the convictions that underlie those actions may evolve into preferences of how situations should be handled in the future. In other words, the convictions of one or a few become useful enough and strong enough to become a basis for what "ought to be" in the future. Members of the culture are often aware of and can articulate the values of the organization, but they do not always recognize the extent to which they are present in the conduct of their actions on a day-to-day basis.

What is the relationship between level 1 and level 2? Values are inherently intangible, cognitive constructions, but many are expressly articulated or codified by the organizational members. In this way, the values may be "visible" in artifacts, behaviors, and creations. At other times, however, organizational members (particularly leaders) may articulate a value that contradicts the artifacts and behaviors of level 1. In this case, the value may not be a "real" value at all, but simply an "espoused value" or a "fantasy value."

Two examples will help with this distinction. In Company A, leadership says that there is a value of "equality" in the organization. An examination of the artifacts of the organization reveals the following: parking spaces are not assigned, office space is equally distributed, and furnishings are similar, anyone can speak freely at an office meeting, and pay raises are based purely on performance. For Company A, it would appear as if the articulated value of "equality" is congruent with the artifacts of the organization.

In Company B, the organization articulates a value of "equality," but an examination of the artifacts reveals something different. Pay raises are often based on nepotism and personal associations, corporate officers have the best parking spaces, and office space and furnishings are highly differentiated between management and workers. In this case, the espoused value of "equality" does not reconcile with the artifacts of the organization. The lesson is an important one: Just because a value is articulated by the leadership of an organization does not mean that it is a "real" value of the culture.

Level 3: Basic Assumptions

Basic assumptions represent the essence of culture for Schein. He argued that once a solution to a problem has shown itself to work time and time again, it becomes "taken for granted." That being so, members holding the basic assumptions find behavior that deviates from them to be incomprehensible.

Schein put forward five basic assumptions around which organizational cultures may form and the questions that arise from them (adapted from Schein, 1985, p. 86):

1. **Humanity's relationship to nature.** At the organizational level, do the key members view the relationship of the organization to its environment as one of dominance, submission, harmonizing, finding an appropriate niche, or what?

2. **The nature of reality and truth.** Linguistic and behavioral rules that define what is real and what is not, what is a "fact," how truth is ultimately to be determined, and whether truth is "revealed" or "discovered"—basic concepts of time and space.

3. **The nature of human nature.** What does it mean to be "human," and what attributes are considered intrinsic or ultimate? Is human nature good, evil, or neutral? Are human beings perfectible or not?

4. **The nature of human activity.** What is the "right" thing for human beings to do on the basis of the preceding assumptions about reality, the environment, and human nature: to be active, passive, self-developmental, fatalistic, or what? What is work, and what is play?

5. **The nature of human relationships.** What is considered to be the "right" way for people to relate to each other, to distribute power and love? Is life cooperative or competitive, individualistic, group collaborative, or communal, based on traditional lineal authority, law, charisma, or what?

As you can see, basic assumptions involve the deepest levels of culture and often pose very difficult questions. Cultures, though, over time and through interaction develop "theories-in-use," as Schein calls them, which are reflected in values and guide behavior. Without assumptions, organizational groups lack guiding principles or baselines to which they can refer for making sense of organizational reality.

Schein's model offers a useful means for both the researcher and the organizational member to comprehend the culture of an organization. It is a tool for digging into the deep layers of organizational culture so that one does not mistake surface elements for the heart of the culture.

Summary

In this chapter, we provided an overview of the roots of organizational culture and showed how organizational culture serves to create, as well as uncover, misunderstandings. We discussed our definition of organizational culture, which highlights the centrality of communication and history to the development of culture. We then covered one classification scheme of the elements of organizational culture, which was followed by a discussion of the two perspectives, culture as variable and culture as root metaphor. The two perspectives differ in regard to the depth of culture, the role of communication, and whether culture can and should be changed. Table 5.1 outlines the differences between the variable and root-metaphor perspectives. Finally, Schein's model presented one means of examining organizational culture.

TABLE 5.1 Comparison of Variable Versus Root-Metaphor Perspectives

ISSUE	VARIABLE	ROOT METAPHOR
Nature of culture	Something the organization "has," a tool, skill, or lever	Something the organization "is," expressive form
Role of communication	Inform workforce of values	Create, sustain, and influence culture
Culture change	Through management directive and intervention	Through natural evolution, all members influence culture

Looking at organizational culture through the lens of misunderstandings yields a complicated picture. As discussed earlier in this chapter, one of the strengths of the organizational culture approach is the focus on different types of misunderstandings that could occur in organizations. Organizational culture broadens the perspective of organizational members and facilitates the process of recognizing how misunderstandings can arise that were otherwise left uncovered from other organizational perspectives. As we came to understand that behavior in organizations is rarely rational, yet often considered normal for organizational members, we also came to understand that norms, values, philosophies, assumptions, symbols, language, and so on are all areas of potential misunderstanding.

In the next chapter, we offer a discussion of critical organizational theory. Critical perspectives reject the notion that organizations are value-free sites, as prior theories have implicitly or explicitly advocated. Instead, organizations are viewed as sites of struggle between management and workers, resulting in domination and oppression of the powerless by the powerful.

Critical Theory

LEARNING OBJECTIVES

1. Illustrate the role of organizational practice where the interest of one group becomes a site of managerial domination
2. Describe how critical theorists center issues of diversity and discrimination in their perspectives on organizing
3. Identify the interrelationships between power, ideology, hegemony, and concertive control
4. Describe how critical theory views communication technology in organizations
5. Describe how organizational democracy and feminist organizational communication theory are related to critical theory

In the 1970s, Americans started to experience a form of societal conscious-ness-raising with regard to the oppressive atmosphere in organizations for workers, particularly women and minorities. Both theorists and practitioners of all types (including corporate and government leaders) began to discuss the inequities and oppressive circumstances present in the workplace. Organizations started examining their hiring practices, treatment of employees, and promotion standards in light of the disparity between members of the majority and the minority. Also, organizational theorists with roots in the work of Karl Marx turned their attention to the structure of organizational life to show how accepted management practices and "agreed-upon" values were serving to advance the interests of management while restricting those of the workers.

Critical theory, which is based on the work of Karl Marx, was integrated into the study of organizations in the 1970s (Alvesson & Deetz, 1996; Mumby, 2014). As a field of inquiry, critical theory has its roots in the Institute for Social Research in Frankfurt (now commonly known as the Frankfurt School), founded in the 1920s (Foss et al., 1985). The Frankfurt School philosophy was twofold. First, knowledge in society is not objective; it is indelibly tied to the participants and tainted by their interests and the power structure. Second, the plight of the theorist is to involve themselves in the inner workings of society, reveal the contradictions associated with the imbalance of power, and provide a critique that will allow for the reversal of those conditions in the future (Foss et al., 1985).

Organizational communication scholars operating from a critical theory standpoint attempt to reveal how social and technological structures within organizations serve to oppress workers. Moreover, researchers attempt to educate workers about these oppressive forces and provide means for workers' emancipation. For critical theorists, insight (such as that provided by systems theory or organizational culture) into organizational functioning and problems is insufficient (Deetz, 1982); researchers must also engage in consciousness-raising among members (Redding & Tompkins, 1988).

Critical theorists view an organization as a **site of domination** where the interests of the dominant group (typically owners and management) are elevated above the interests of subordinate groups (typically the workers). Consider the following brief example from Malika:

> There was a time that I had some very personal things going on in my life, which I shared with my team. I ended my 9-month engagement to my fiancée. My entire team knew about my struggles and my work to go to therapy for help. When I attempted to take one personal day for my mental health, Jackie, my boss, turned me down. She knew I was struggling but valued meeting numbers more than the sanity of those who were helping her get to those goals.

What Malika is describing is a lived example of how the interests of management can dominate the interests of the workers, even to the extent that the mental health of the worker in this case was in jeopardy.

Mumby (2014) argued that a central tenet of the critical perspective is that power is concentrated with the owners and managers of capital who also get to mediate between capitalists and workers rather than that power being evenly distributed. In the following summary of situations faced by Walt with his organization during the first year of the pandemic, we see the power of management play out:

> Company Says: Safety is our number one priority.
>
> Employee Says: "So why are you asking me to work during COVID-19?"
>
> Company Does: Provides hazard pay.
>
> Company Says: Safety is our number one priority.
>
> Employee Says: "I'm not getting enough training on workplace ergonomics."
>
> Company Does: Provides a training on workplace ergonomics . . . once. And makes sure their liability premium is paid . . . every year.

Walt's quick but powerful summary illustrates how management can wield power, making it seem as if employee concerns are being attended to, but in reality, they are only being provided surface treatment. The framework Mumby described is substantially different from prior theories (e.g., classical theory or systems theory), which offered no critique of the negative and harmful results of their prescriptions. Aktouf (1992) articulated this exact point when he wrote, "For almost a century, functional-consensus theories have been masking the welter of conflicts and contradictions undermining both the discipline and practice of management" (p. 410). In other words, theories such as those found in classical theory and human relations and human resources movements often propose visions of management that are far more clear-cut and value-free than reality shows them to be.

Traditional organizational structures that rely on bureaucratic procedures, centralized decision-making, and hierarchical control favor the interests of those in management, while the interests of the workers are subordinated. Managers are able to frame the interests of the workers in relation to their own interests (Mumby, 1988). For example, management may offer a somewhat lucrative commission plan for its sales force that, on the surface, appears to reward hard work. On further critique, though, the commission plan may lead to an overwhelming pressure on the sales force to work longer hours, travel more frequently, and subsequently ignore their personal and family lives in favor of increasing profits for the organization. In other words, a practice that appears to be in the interest of one group (workers) is, in actuality, a form of domination and control serving the interests of the dominant group (management).

Diversity and Discrimination

Perhaps one of the most dramatic changes in organizations over the past few decades has been diversification of the workplace. **Diversity** refers to a variety of personal and societal bases of identity including but not limited to age, country of origin, ethnicity, gender, mental or physical ability, political affiliation, race, religion, sexuality, socio-economic status, and veteran status. While organizations are certainly more diverse, critical theorists would question if they have become more inclusive. According to the Society for Human Resource Management, inclusion means the achievement of a work environment where all employees are treated fairly and respectfully, have equal access to opportunities and resources, and can contribute their ideas fully to the organization's success.

While many statistics are available to look at individual variables of identity in the workplace, they do not do justice to truly representing who individuals are. To fully represent one's identity, critical theorists advocate examining identity using an intersectional lens. **Intersectionality** refers to the points where multiple aspects of a person's identity intersect, cross, or overlap (Crenshaw, 1991). Take for instance pay inequality. It is frequently cited that women make on average 81 cents for every dollar that a man makes. When you look at pay through an intersectional lens (gender and race overlapping), you can get a very different set of numbers according to Payscale (2019). Hispanics and Latinas, on average, earn 75 cents, while Black men make 87 cents for every dollar that a White man makes. These differences, among many others, illustrate that while organizations are experiencing higher levels of representation of minorities in management and other positions, inequalities persist.

Although federal laws (e.g., Civil Rights Act of 1964, Equal Pay Act of 1963, Family Medical Leave Act) exist to address many forms of discrimination, companies are still left to develop policies and attempt to create an organizational culture that is accepting of and open to differences. In this section, we will look at some of the forms of discrimination that occur in organizations.

Discrimination

Discrimination in organizations can take many forms and have many outcomes. The terminology that has emerged through the study of discrimination in organizations helps to make sense of the myriad forms and outcomes.

The term **glass ceiling**, thought to have first been used in a May 24, 1986, *Wall Street Journal* article by Carol Hymowitz and Timothy Schellhardt, was defined later by Daily and Dalton (1999) as a metaphorical barrier that prevents minorities from advancing in an organization. The glass ceiling is an artificial and invisible barrier that prevents upward job opportunities based on misconceptions, beliefs, and stereotypes. Another way to think about it is that the glass ceiling is an invisible but real form of job segregation (Fernandez & Campero, 2017). Consider this story from Larkin, which shows how the glass ceiling plays out daily for her as she struggles to compete in her new organization because of her gender:

> You know, something that I don't really talk about is the amount of men that work with me. I'm literally the only female software developer at our company. I obviously didn't expect to walk into a tech company full of female employees, but I also didn't expect to be the only one on my team. I think that because I am a female, I am a minority who is discriminated against. Although this may not occur outright, I think people do discriminate unknowingly.
>
> For example, as a new employee who happens to be female, I am the lowest in the food chain and the least respected, in my opinion. If I am in a conference meeting with five different men, let's just say if I wasn't there it wouldn't make a difference. I try to include myself, but I'm always ignored and talked over. Oh, and two male members on my team have already received promotions. Oh, and I often feel like I have such a small voice when I'm in meetings with my team or other people in our organization. It's sad in a way. It does make me uncomfortable, and I definitely shouldn't ever feel like that at my place of employment. I don't know. I am obviously as smart as everyone else. I got the position for a reason, so it definitely has to do with some sort of gender bias.
>
> I would say that communication plays an effect when I am the only woman. I feel like all the male software developers have closer friendships than I

do with them. So, there may be a lack of communication between them and me, and there may just be communication that is hostile, fake or even unwanted. It just seems like they would rather talk among each other rather than with me, and that's fine. Some people get along better with others. However, I know that it is not just because they get along better with each other. It does definitely have to deal with some sort of gender bias. This just makes communication harder with my coworkers.

It's more of a problem that I keep to myself because I don't want anyone to feel hurt by the situation. If I had to say that there was a specific outcome, I think that maybe I would just say it's me realizing the gender bias among us and just accepting it. I definitely could speak up if I wanted to, and I should be able to, I just don't know if I should, you know? I'm new to the company; I'm young; I'm a female. There are a lot of factors that wouldn't help me in this situation.

Larkin very much feels the limits placed on her because of her gender identity through the exclusion from informal communication networks, muting of her voice during formal interactions, and being passed over for promotion while those (male) team members around her are promoted.

Researchers and activists have explored the **concrete ceiling**, referring to the unique challenges faced by women and minorities of color. This metaphor may be more representative of the difficulties by women of color because concrete is denser, not as easy to see through or shatter, and more accurately represents the additional cultural biases, stereotypes, and double standards that Black women face as they negotiate organizational life (Barnes, 2017; Moore & Jones, 2001). Researchers have also considered the bamboo ceiling and the adobe ceiling to take into consideration the unique challenges faced by Asian American women and Hispanic women. Regardless of the metaphor, however, it is important to remember that these are discrete, invisible barriers that are difficult to prove but have a real impact on the lives of organizational members. These barriers are not obvious; there are no flashing signs indicating that certain employees are not welcome or formal company policies that discourage the promotion of minorities (Hesse-Biber & Carter, 2005).

Five factors have been used to explain why women and other minority groups have had such difficulty breaking through these barriers. These factors include stereotypes, discrimination, mentoring and networking availability, funding availability, and family challenges.

First, stereotypes, overgeneralized perceptions applied to an entire group of people, keep the playing field uneven (Boselovic, 2006; Bible & Hill, 2007). One example is that women *take care*, while men *take charge*. Unfortunately, this stereotype is reinforced by statistics that show that even in professional fields such as medicine, women are found in more caring positions, such as nursing, pediatrics, or family medicine, while men are in more high-power positions such as surgery or specialized fields. When

discrimination, which is defined as treatment or action based upon a stereotype, is invisible or ingrained into cultural practice, it becomes difficult to overcome.

Brief and often subtle forms of discrimination are known as microaggressions. A **microaggression** communicates a negative or derogatory message to an individual who occupies a minority status (Constantine et al., 2008). Microaggressions can be verbal, behavioral, or even environmental elements that in some way belittle someone. Often these microaggressions are manifested by other employees who do not recognize the discriminatory origins or implications of their actions and may, in fact, become defensive if confronted (Nadal, 2008; Sue, 2010). Resnick and Galupo (2019) found that heteronormative assumptions meant that often employees didn't realize that they were marginalizing their LGBT colleagues—for example, asking an LGBT colleague for an opinion to represent an entire category of people. While the colleague doing the asking did not understand it was an inappropriate question, neither did the colleague being asked fully understand the implications of the question beyond it being uncomfortable. Nothing, therefore, was addressed, and the situation could repeat itself in the future.

Research indicates that there are three types of microaggressions (Sue et al., 2007). A **microassault** is the use of explicit and intended verbal or nonverbal behaviors, such as *"Go back where you came from."* **Microinsults** are frequently unconscious verbal or nonverbal communication that is insensitive or demeaning about a person's heritage or identity. One example is implying that someone speaks a particular language based on perceptions about their country of origin. **Microinvalidations** can also be unconscious communicative acts that exclude or negate the experiences of an individual of an oppressed group. An example of a mircoinvalidation is a student complaining that another student always blames everything on his or her race. Microinsults and microinvalidations may be more subtle than microassaults, which can make them even more challenging to confront in the organizational environment.

The third explanation often cited for difficulties in breaking through artificial organizational barriers has to do with mentoring and networking opportunities. Mentoring and networking opportunities increase one's exposure and likelihood of promotions. Although it is considered a joke in business circles, many deals are still made on the golf course and other venues where women and other minority groups are not readily invited to join. In-depth mentoring and networking significantly increase your chances of being considered for and eventually promoted as well as the potential for client referrals or even hearing about an upcoming opening within the organization. For example, consider the following from Diane, one of a few female lawyers in a large law practice:

> One late afternoon, I was up on the seventh floor of our building, and I walked by a room that is usually locked, but the door was open a bit, and I could hear people laughing and joking behind it. When I opened the door, I saw several of the other lawyers, all-male, sitting around, drinking alcohol, and having a great time. I walked in and said, "What is this room?

I didn't even know it was here." One of the male lawyers said with a smirk on his face, "Oh, that's because only the kings have keys."

In this law firm, a boy's club was alive and well. Aside from the personal interactions that were occurring in this private room, chances are high that premium client accounts were awarded and advancement opportunities and openings discussed. Not being a part of this particular network would hurt anyone who was excluded. Although this example has a literal locked room, in many instances, the private networks are not as obvious, and the "doors" are more figurative than literal.

The final factor in an individual's inability to break through discrimination barriers involves funding. Although women make up the fastest-growing segment of entrepreneurship, they receive significantly less funding to do so. In fact, women receive only 3% of the available venture capital funds in the United States (Hassan et al., 2020) You might find interesting a study that Boselovic (2006) conducted. Prospective investors were given the chance to invest in one of two companies. The companies were of equal caliber and promised similar short-term and long-term results. The only difference in the companies was that one was male-owned and one was female-owned. Overwhelmingly, investors choose to invest in the male-owned business, for no other reason than gender. Similarly, companies with Black CEOs only receive 1% of the available venture capital funds (Lang & Van Lee, 2020). Of course, this is further complicated when factors such as race, ethnicity, and sexuality are figured into the equation, demonstrating the importance of intersectionality when discussing diversity or discrimination within an organization.

Gender Identity

As you have undoubtedly discussed in many other classes and was alluded to in the previous sections, society has many gendered expectations for workers (Britton, 2004; Padavic & Reskin, 2002; Schilt & Connell, 2007). When individuals do not conform to those expectations, they may be subjected to various forms of workplace discrimination. The National Center for Transgender Equality found that 97% of respondents in their survey had experienced some form of maltreatment or discrimination in the workplace (Thoroughgood et al., 2017). These experiences include negative hiring practices (e.g., not receiving a promotion or being fired), being verbally ridiculed (e.g., being outed, called names, referred to by former gender pronoun or name), feeling forced to behave in a traditionally gendered manner, or denied access to an appropriate bathroom (Brewster et al., 2014; Thoroughgood et al., 2017).

Transgender is an umbrella term used to describe a wide spectrum of individuals whose gender identity or gender expression differs from the sex they were assigned at birth (Brewster et al., 2014). Although this spectrum covers a wide variety of individuals, several terms are useful to remember. First, remember sex refers to the biological classification of individuals as male or female, whereas **gender** is a culturally defined set of behavioral, cultural, psychological, or social traits that society has associated with a particular sex. There is no biological basis for gender, and standards for what is considered feminine or masculine will vary from one culture to the next. **Gender identity** is one's psychological, or deeply felt, sense of gender and may or may not align with one's sex. For example, *cisgender* is when one's assigned sex and felt gender identity match, whereas that might not be the case for someone who is transgender. **Gender expression** is an individual's choices with regard to how they express themselves using gendered behaviors and appearance (Sawyer & Thoroughgood, 2017). When an individual's gender identity is inconsistent with their assigned sex, they may choose gender transition. **Gender transition** is a continuum of options that allow an individual to modify how they present, or express, their gender identity. While gender transition is often associated with surgery, individuals can also modify their gender expression by changing their appearance with clothing or hair modifications; social adjustments, such as name changes; or hormone therapy (Brewster et al., 2014).

According to the Human Rights Campaign (2020), 83% of Fortune 500 companies do have policies prohibiting gender discrimination based on gender identity. Gender transition is a unique process for each individual, and while no road map exists, what is clear from the research previously discussed is that organizations are often ill-equipped to support transgender employees. Management and human resource departments frequently do not know what steps they need to take when an employee announces their transition. By attempting to use policies that they have adapted from other organizations without first assessing the strength of the policy or having any knowledge of how to implement the policy, management and human resource departments often don't know what steps to take when an employee is transitioning (Elias et al., 2018). Research looking at factors that mitigated perceptions of discrimination found that external supports, such as clear formal organizational policies and supportive coworkers, were the most effective factors for diminishing perceptions of transgender discrimination (Ruggs et al., 2015). The researchers theorized that these external supports lowered perceptions of discrimination by sending the message that discrimination was not tolerated in the organization.

Concepts: Power, Ideology, Hegemony, and Concertive Control

Management in organizations is based on the control of resources, workers, and/or consumers (Alvesson & Deetz, 1996). Control is created and maintained in a variety of ways: through the outright, explicit exercise of power; through the unknowing adoption of a dominant group's values and beliefs (hegemony); or through adherence to a work team's socially constructed norms (concertive control). In the following section, we provide an overview of these concepts that are central to critical theory.

Power

Classical writers from Aristotle to Hobbes to Machiavelli have offered conceptualizations of *power*. Modern theories of power have their roots in Marx, Weber, and Parsons

(Hickson et al., 1981). Weber's definition of power as "the possibility of imposing one's will upon the behavior of other persons" (1947, p. 323) is visible in the conceptualizations of power presented in the current review. Research on power has progressed from conceptualizing it as intrinsically tied to moments of decision-making and overt conflict (Dahl, 1957), to finding traces of power in other times that could include overt or latent conflict or both (Bachrach & Baratz, 1970; Lukes, 1974).

Dahl (1957) advanced a behavioral theory of power that has become known as the one-dimensional view of power. His definition reads as follows: A has power over B to the extent that A can get B to do something B would not otherwise do. Central to this view is the exercise of power. This approach to power is focused on identifying observable, decision-making behavior that, in turn, involves conflict: "Conflict, according to that view, is assumed to be crucial in providing an experimental test of power attributions: without it the exercise of power will, it seems to be thought, fail to show up" (Lukes, 1974, p. 14). Researchers from this perspective monitor overt conflicts, observe members' positions on important issues, and detail the outcomes of the conflicts (Conrad, 1983, p. 175). This conceptualization of power concentrates on behavior in decision-making situations where conflict is present.

Bachrach and Baratz (1970), in their book *Power and Poverty*, responded to Dahl's one-dimensional view of power with a two-dimensional view of power. They criticized Dahl for his focus on overt decision-making. They argued that a theory of power must consider both decision-making and non-decision-making, where the latter is a decision that results in the suppression of a latent challenge to the values or interests of the decision-maker. Even though Bachrach and Baratz added nondecision to power, they remained connected with Dahl on the crucial factor of conflict: If there is no conflict, then the presumption is that there is consensus. The two-dimensional view of power, while focusing on conflict and decision-making, emphasizes that power may be present when conflict is covert (i.e., behind the scenes or hidden) as well as overt (out in the open).

Lukes (1974) praised Bachrach and Baratz for the criticisms of Dahl but argued that their two-dimensional view of power was still inadequate. In response, Lukes offered a three-dimensional view of power, which focuses on three main issues: (1) decision-making and control over the political decision (not necessarily through decisions), (2) issues and potential issues, and (3) observable (overt or covert) and latent conflict. Latent conflict is a "contradiction between the interests of those exercising power and the 'real interests' of those they exclude" (pp. 24–25). This view of power introduces the idea that power may be present in situations where there is no conflict on the surface and at times other than when decisions are being made. From this perspective, power has both a surface and a deep structure (Conrad, 1983; Frost, 1987). The *surface structure* is a dimension of power that guides and constrains employees during overt open negotiations and decision-making (Conrad, 1983). The *deep structure*, on the other hand, is a dimension of power that is hidden within larger organizational or cultural structures and influences employee decisions about who and what to fight.

Similarly, Mumby (2000) posited that the two levels of concern with power in critical theory involve individual and social group relationships and the interests and values on which knowledge claims are made.

Ideology and Hegemony

Although critical theorists are certainly interested in the exercise of power in all forms and at all levels, they are particularly interested in the ways in which power or control manifests itself implicitly. Therefore, they often attend to latent conflicts and the deep structure dimension of power. According to Mumby (1987), the cultural approach to organizations (from the previous chapter) does not get at the "deep structure process through which certain organizational realities come to hold sway over competing world views" (p. 113). To explain this concept, we need to begin with a discussion of ideology. **Ideology** refers to the "integrated set of values, ideals, and understandings about a particular part of social reality that justifies certain commitment and actions" (Alvesson, 1993, p. 8). According to Gibson and Papa (2000), ideology represents social reality by telling organizational members what is good, what is normal, and what acceptable behavior within the organization is.

Four functions of ideology have been identified in the literature and articulated by Mumby (1987). The first three of these functions are based on the work of Giddens (1979, pp. 193–196), whose theory of structuration you read about in Chapter 1. Here is a brief summary of the four functions of ideology:

1. **The representation of sectional interests as universal** (Mumby, 1987, p. 118). This function of ideology has the interests of management made to seem as if they are representative of all the members' interests. This allows the dominant group (management) to define key terms and structure processes in a way that enacts the cooperation of everyone because those actions are purported to be in everyone's best interests.

2. **The denial or transmutation of contradictions** (pp. 118–119). In a political system where democracy is the norm and individuals have the right to cast a vote in their own best interest, this function of ideology shows how perceptions of that right change as members enter the organization. In the organization, members give up their one person-one vote right, which then allows a group of a few (management) to make decisions that affect everyone.

3. **The naturalization of the present through reification** (pp. 118–119). This function of ideology shows how reality, which is socially constructed, is made to seem objective and unchangeable. The "objective" reality, propagated by the dominant group, is naturally in the dominant group's interests. For example, Mumby uses the example of the hierarchy in organizations. Hierarchy is a socially constructed concept, but it is made to seem to be objective or just the way things have to be. The existence of the hierarchy benefits those decision-makers located at the top of the hierarchy.

4. **Ideology as a means of control** (p. 119). Mumby added this function to connect ideology with control and show that organizational members actively participate in these control processes. He argued that ideology functions as control through active consent rather than passive acceptance.

In this final function, Mumby connected the concepts of ideology, power, and control and began to articulate the important concept of **hegemony**:

> Hegemony does not refer simply to the domination of one group by another, but indicates the process by which one group actively supports the goals and aspirations of another, dominant group, even though those goals may not be in the subordinate group's best interest. (Mumby, 1988, p. 55)

The key to the concept of hegemony is the idea that the subordinated group actively supports the interests of the dominant group, often unknowingly, which results in oppression. The subordinated group is actively participating in the maintenance of the dominant group's ideology.

For example, consider a midsize steel manufacturing company that purports to uphold the organizational value of "family." In this organization, the metaphor of family is used regularly in newsletters, meetings, and informal conversations in and out of the workplace to describe the relationship between organizational members at all hierarchical levels. Most members seem satisfied with their work life and often talk about making sacrifices for their organizational family; they work late, pick up the slack for other "family members" who are having trouble, and generally feel a sense of dedication to the organization.

A critical theorist, after extensive research in the organization, may consider this situation to be an example of hegemony. The use of the family metaphor may be considered a way for management to create a situation in which the workers actively support organizational interests while working against their own. Despite the fact that many workers may feel comforted by the family metaphor and the atmosphere created by it, they are subtly being forced to work harder, keep longer hours, and sacrifice their own family lives for their organizational "family." The metaphor is representative of the behaviors and attitudes, in other words, the ideology, that management desires workers to hold. What seems on the surface to serve the interests of the workers in actuality serves the interests of management and may even be oppressive to the workers.

Concertive Control

As some organizations made the move to more participative, decentralized, self-managing work-team structures, as discussed in Chapter 3, managers feared that they would lose the explicit control built into the traditional structures (e.g., bureaucracy and scientific management). Recent research, however, has shown how a form of member-based control is present that is often considered to be stricter than that in traditional structures (Barker, 1998; Hawkins, 2013; Larson & Tompkins, 2005; Papa et al., 1997; Wright & Barker, 2000). Tompkins and Cheney (1985) termed this form of control **concertive control**. Concertive control is based on adherence to socially constructed norms and values developed by organizational members themselves as they attempt to structure their environment.

When an organization adopts a truly participative system, which usually encompasses the notion of self-managing work teams, organizational members are responsible for structuring the work environment and processes, tasks once assigned to managers in traditional structures and in which workers had little participation. As workers engage in the structuring process, they reach "a negotiated consensus on how to shape their behavior according to a set of core values" (Barker, 1998, p. 130). The consensus to adhere to these values and the pressure to adhere to them is strong because the workers themselves develop them.

In some situations, management establishes a set of core values for the organization but does not provide direct control mechanisms or structured activities for achieving organizational goals. Barker (1998) conducted research in a manufacturing organization where the structure was changed from a traditional one to that of self-managing work teams. As the change occurred, the head of the organization articulated a set of core values he wished to guide the organization in the future. Workers were trained to perform in self-managing work teams and were cross-trained on all necessary organizational tasks. Barker found that workers exerted control over one another as they developed norms for behavior that were congruent with the stated core values. If a team member violated a norm, the other team members immediately confronted the team member. Each member strictly adhered to the norms to avoid facing the disappointment of other team members. Many workers reported this form of control, concertive control, to be stricter than what they experienced under the traditional structure.

Although concertive control can result from socially constructed norms based on an overall vision provided by management, it can also occur when the members themselves initially develop the values and norms. Papa et al. (1997) described this form of concertive control in their research on the Grameen Bank in Bangladesh. The Grameen Bank organizes loans for micro-enterprise endeavors in the poorest regions of the country. Despite not requiring collateral at the time of the loan, the bank has a 99% loan recovery rate. Papa et al. found that concertive control, based in part on high levels of identification, was operating in this organization. In motivational programs that all field workers and low-level managers attended, a "team" metaphor was proposed. The mutual development of this guiding metaphor resulted in the value of laboring together and constant peer pressure to maintain the high loan recovery rate. As the workers strove to help their team members, they often sacrificed their personal lives. Of importance, it was the workers themselves, not management, who provided the pressure to recover the loans. Additional evidence of the strength of the effects of concertive control came from Hawkins (2013) in an ethnographic study of two self-directed work teams. The research demonstrated how team members' actions and language were regulated by concertive control, but the control reestablished gender and social hierarchy norms that served as discrimination against the female team members.

Concertive control in the team environment can have positive and negative consequences. According to Wright and Barker (2000), the positive consequences of concertive control can include role clarity, guidance for team members, and increased discipline within the team. However, if the control mechanisms are either too strict or too loose, negative consequences can occur. If the system is too constraining, then innovation will be restricted, which will result in lower motivation and dissatisfaction. If the system is too loose, team members will not have enough guidance or role clarity to adequately meet the team or individual goals.

In this section, we have discussed a core feature of critical theory—how control manifests itself in a variety of forms, which in turn may serve to oppress workers. Next, we will look at communication technology use and monitoring from a critical perspective, and then we will conclude.

A Critical Approach to Communication Technology

At the heart of critical theory is a concern with the organization as a site of domination and how power is used and abused in the organizational setting. The role that communication technology plays in supporting management interests over workers' interests and how technology can be used in the maintenance of hegemony are prime concerns of critical organizational theorists. Perhaps because communication technology has been purported to flatten organizational structures and increase worker empowerment, critical theorists have been particularly attentive to how workers may actually be oppressed by management because of it. As with other organizational phenomena, a critical theorist would argue that communication technology is rarely "interest-free," and its use(s) should be scrutinized for instances of oppression. For example, consider the following story shared by Caleb who works in the corporate headquarters for a national distribution company.

> In my office, we have been utilizing a WebEx platform for several years. It hasn't been perfect. Periodically, there are connectivity issues and there is some technical knowledge one has to learn for it to be effective. For example, you have to learn how to share a screen, how to allow someone to share their screen, how to connect audio through the computer versus the phone, and managing multiple monitors at a time. And people want to avoid calling the help desk at all costs because they can be rude, unhelpful, and demeaning. Many times, their fix is just a temporary Band-aid, and the problem just shows up again anyway.
>
> My supervisor recently introduced a new platform—Microsoft Teams. It was rolled out with absolutely no training and no introduction whatsoever. The icon just suddenly showed up on my desktop. I have expressed on several occasions that I prefer using the old systems because at least we know the problems, and on most days, that system is functional, even if it is irritating. Introducing a brand-new system presents all kinds of new

challenges. I can't tell my supervisor to use the old system. The new system, apparently, works better for her, although I don't understand why or how it is better because she hasn't explained that. At the end of the day, I just have to follow her direction and use the system when she schedules her meetings. I still have to use the old system for my meetings because no one else in any other department uses this new system.

Although computer information systems have disbursed power across organizations because of increased access to information and the removal of hierarchical communication barriers, an alternate reading from a critical perspective shows a less-positive side. Gephart (2002) provides us with an initial critical reading of this situation:

> [C]omputerization of the workplace has complex influences on structure and primarily reinforces *status quo* organizational structure, whether it is decentralized or centralized. Implementation and operational strategies for CISs typically are decided by power elites and these strategies influence structure more than technology itself.

In other words, the technology used in an organization is decided on by management, and they will only allow the development and implementation of technology that does not interrupt their power base. In this way, management's interests are promoted, and workers' interests are restricted.

Another application of critical theory to communication technology in organizations is how the technology affects workers' professional and personal lives. Technology has enabled more people greater flexibility with regard to when and where they do their work, which to some people seems like employee empowerment. However, a critical theory perspective would question whose interests are being served and how workers are being oppressed. A Gallup Poll found that 59% of respondents routinely check their email outside of normal business hours (Newport, 2017). This, according to some researchers, has contributed to a growing e-device addiction due to telepressure (Belkin et al., 2020). **Telepressure** is when employees have a preoccupation and urge to frequently check and quickly respond to work-related messages after their normal working hours (Becker et al., 2019; Belkin et al., 2020; Hu et al., 2019). Telepressure often results from *organizational expectations for email monitoring* (OEEM) and negatively impacts an employee's rest and recovery time (Santuzzi & Barber, 2018). Telepressure due to OEEMs has been associated with employee turnover intentions, negative impacts on work-life balancing, sleep disruptions, and e-anxiety. While it may first appear as empowerment and liberation, it may actually be an instrument of hegemony as workers answer emails in the middle of the night or revise a document during their child's soccer tournament.

In addition to exploring oppressive circumstances caused by organizational technology in general, the critical perspective also shows how current trends in organizational technology policies may also be oppressive to workers. For example, a recent survey by Syntonic found that 87% of companies relied on employees to provide their own electronic devices for work. This is known as a **bring your own device (BYOD)** policy that requires employees to bring their personal devices into the workplace to serve as their organizational devices. Organizations employing a BYOD policy cite employee personal comfort with the device, increased satisfaction, and lower learning curves as benefits to the policy. The critical perspective, however, reveals that buying into these benefits serves to oppress the workers in several ways. First, the workers are expected to purchase their own technology for organizational purposes, thereby creating potentially disadvantageous financial situations for the employees; BYOD policies generate on average $350 revenue per employee each year for tech industries. Second, these BYOD policies are often very specific about the fact that all contents of the personal device are subject to investigation if deemed necessary. Finally, the BYOD policy continues to strengthen the technological chain, or electronic tethering, that binds the employee to the workplace, thereby making it nearly impossible to separate work and nonwork lives (Belkin et al., 2020).

The Case of Monitoring Employees' Technology Use

As more work in organizations is being done with the assistance of communication technology, organizations have begun to monitor how employees actually use that technology. Electronic performance monitoring (EPM) can range from surveillance cameras and telephone or email monitoring to wearable technology (Tomczak et al., 2018). Passive monitoring is monitoring that happens after the fact, such as someone reviewing archived emails, while active monitoring is monitoring that is happening in the moment, such as real-time locations (GPS), keystrokes, telephone calls, data received through network connections, or time away from desk, among other things (Fairweather, 1999; Tomczak et al., 2018). As more technology is available in organizations, there is also a higher likelihood that function creep will occur. **Function creep** is when technologies are used to gather data, either purposefully or not, outside of their original purpose (Stark et al., 2020). A CCTV might have been installed to deter criminal activity or prevent employee slacking but could now be used to monitor employee conversations. Or software used to map the most efficient route could be used to track employee movements to see if extra restroom or snack breaks are taken on the clock.

According to one Jobvite (2018) survey, when individuals search for jobs, they rely heavily on social media. While 77% of individuals indicated that they used the professional networking site LinkedIn to search for job openings, 63% stated that they relied on Facebook. As companies use social media to recruit, they also use these same sites for informal screening and selection tools (Hurrell et al., 2017). In fact, a Careerbuilder. com (2018) survey of 2,000 employers found that employers who use social media to screen potential employees were looking at both images and content of posts for provocative or inappropriate pictures, negative talk about previous employers, anything that would indicate drug or alcohol use/abuse, poor online communication skills, or derogatory comments made toward protected groups (Ruggs et al., 2016). This social media screening did not impact all potential employees the same way, which is what catches the interest of critical theorists. Racial and ethnic minorities as well as younger individuals with less work experience are more likely to use Facebook for their job search, while more experienced individuals are likely to rely on LinkedIn. The information on Facebook or Instagram is more likely to be casual and contain more personal pictures than that on LinkedIn. Recruiters can then engage a stereotyped lens to make sense of slang, typos, personal narratives, etc., to make decisions about whom to hire and not (Ruggs et al., 2016). Employers may continue to monitor social media use after hiring, looking for suspected illegal activity, defamation of supervisors or the organization, or behavior the company deems inappropriate (Drouin et al., 2015).

Why do companies monitor their employees in these ways? First, companies may be *financially* motivated. What employees are doing while they are on the clock can have an impact on the company's profit and overall efficiency (Fairweather, 1999; Fink, 2014). For example, an employee's keystrokes on a computer keyboard can be monitored to determine how much work is being conducted during the day or browsers can be monitored to see what apps are actually used each workweek. Furthermore, the resources individuals use can have an impact on an organization's bandwidth and email capacity. Second, a company may be motivated by *liability* prevention. Employers may be concerned about the dissemination of inappropriate material or confidential or protected material, or they may monitor the work environment for dangerous behaviors, such as violence or drug or alcohol use. Third, companies may have *reputational* motivations. The ways that employees represent themselves while in uniform or online may be perceived as representing the company (Fink, 2014). Fairweather (1999) also found that companies often feel that because they own the technology network, they have the right to monitor activity that occurs on that network and track down any misuse that occurs.

The primary tension from a critical perspective surrounding the issue of electronic monitoring is that although organizations certainly have the right to monitor what their employees are doing, the employees themselves feel that they also have a certain right to privacy in the workplace (Snyder & Cornetto, 2009). EPM has been demonstrated to result in feelings of unfairness, decreased job satisfaction and organizational commitment, lower task performance and productivity, and greater levels of stress (Alder & Tompkins, 1997; Toczak et al., 2018). Take for instance Anteby and Chan's (2018) research on Transportation Security Administration (TSA) workers. They found that when TSA workers were being monitored, they worked harder to avoid monitoring, which in turn led to increased monitoring. From a critical perspective, the managerial desire for control being exercised through electronic monitoring is being fulfilled at the expense of the workers. The critical theorist would ask: Is invasion of privacy coupled with negative health effects justification for such practices?

Research has also shown that the extent to which employees find the monitoring justifiable or acceptable is related to the socialization messages received from the organization upon entering the organization (Allen et al., 2007). Employees are also more likely to view passive monitoring more favorably than active monitoring because passive reflects the monitoring of an artifact of behavior, whereas active monitoring is the actual monitoring of in-progress behaviors. A critical theory reading of this research is that justification for electronic monitoring that occurs during newcomer socialization is an attempt to get members to believe the monitoring is not personal and to buy into practices that are not in their best interests but instead serve management's interests. The socialization stage of the assimilation process is one filled with vulnerability for the new employee, and messages received during this period are more likely to be ingested rather than questioned as the worker struggles to learn the job, organization, culture, and prove themself to their coworkers.

Critical organizational communication theorists attempt to uncover the communication practices, whether interpersonal, team-based, or organization-wide, that promote an unhealthy imbalance in organizations. In the final section of this chapter, we discuss some of the issues and challenges raised by critical theory that any member of the workforce will benefit from understanding.

Critical Theory: Unearthing the Taken for Granted

We realize that the critical framework may be a bit difficult to grasp and the implications of the core concepts and research seemingly unrelated to the other theorists covered so far in this book. But, as with systems theory and organizational culture, critical theory is another way of understanding behavior in organizations that can help make sense of why people behave and feel the way they do. It can also educate them on how to improve their organizational situations. We close this chapter with two examples of how critical theory is used both to unearth taken-for-granted assumptions that lead to oppression and to offer solutions for change.

Workplace Democracy: Creating a More "Human(e)" Workplace

Perhaps the greatest contribution the critical framework has to offer is that the oppressive reality of organizational life does not have to continue. Critical organizational theorists are dedicated to uncovering oppressive structural, technological, and communicative practices in organizations that most people accept as a natural part of work life. The reality is that the oppression and oppressive circumstances exist often as a by-product of the manner in which organizations have classically been run. Workers tend to believe that this is just the nature of the beast; they must sacrifice themselves and their interests so that the organization may run according to plan. As Popsecu Ljungholm (2017) argued, "For numerous individuals, working activity is a starting place of maltreatment that destabilizes the human spirit. Furthermore, work experience and incentives may be tremendously biased among employees of distinct race, gender, and separate merit" (p. 112).

Critical theorists are interested in showing that oppression is not an inherent part of organizational life, that there are perhaps more "human" or "humane" ways to structure it (Aktouf, 1992; Cheney, 1995; Collins, 1998). Of particular note is George

Cheney's research and writing on "democracy" in the workplace (Cheney, 1995; see also Deetz, 1992; Hoffman, 2002; Russell, 1997). Cheney suggested that democracy, the political cornerstone of the United States, seldom extends to the workplace. He envisions a workplace that embraces the principles of democracy held so reverently at the political level. Workplace democracy may be characterized as follows:

> [A] system of governance which truly values individual goals and feelings (e.g., equitable remuneration, the pursuit of enriching work and the right to express oneself) as well as typically organizational objectives (e.g., effectiveness and efficiency, reflectively conceived), which actively fosters the connection between those two sets of concerns by encouraging individual contributions to import-ant organizational choices, and which allows for the ongoing modification of the organization's activities and policies by the group. (Cheney, 1995, p. 170)

According to Cheney, the process of promoting workplace democracy involves the encouragement of (1) self-reflection, (2) collective development, and (3) individual opportunity. Democracy in the workplace should lead to organizational situations where oppressive circumstances are less likely to take hold. As organizational mem-bers are afforded an absolute voice in organizational processes and both individual and team-oriented reflection are encouraged, the likelihood of oppression will be minimized. Employee voice is a critical component of organizational democracy, so much so that the phrase Collaborative VOICE has been suggested as a heuristic for how to enact it (MacDonald Milam & Guarriello Heath, 2014, p. 382). The components of the heuristic are (V)isible decision processes, (O)wnership of political power, (I) nformation balanced with deliberation, (C)ontestation allowing for dissent and diverse viewpoints, and (E)xpression should be limited, while discussion is increased. Sobering (2019) demonstrated that voice can actually be facilitated through rumors, a form of informal communication often thought to be destructive in organizations. Rumors can work with formal communication systems as a way to demand accountability and protect against unabated power.

Studies of organizational democracies in practice demonstrate the benefits of this type of organizational structure for members as well as the broader public. One study examining workplace democracy in a non-governmental organization (NGO) in Bangladesh found that women's empowerment, equality, and across-the-board internal decision-making helped not only employees but also the NGO achieve its goals (Han & Garg, 2018). King and Griffin (2019) argued that nonprofit organizations could be *schools for democracy* in the broader public sphere but also should operate democratically for the sake of the organization and its members.

One final point about organizational democracy is that sometimes organizational members and leaders equate organizational democracy with an element of democ-racy: participation. Critics of the implantation of organizational democracy argue that sometimes a cookie-cutter approach to creating an organizational democracy is put in place that does not allow for the transformative outcomes to occur. "There is clearly no 'silver bullet' for or practice of organizational democracy that maximally satisfies everyone's values, expectations, and ambitions. Nevertheless, participatory forms of organizational democracy are not equivalent to those that significantly transform the dominant shape of capitalism's real abstractions" (Bean et al., 2013, p. 268). This is an excellent reminder that organizational democracies are inherently rooted in the critical tradition and must have liberation from oppressive organizational structures as the overarching goal.

Critical theory offers you, as future organizational members and workers, both a means of identifying elements of constraint and oppression in your organization and prescriptions for improving the situation. Another area in which critical theorists offer insight for organizational members is the situation of women in organizations.

Feminist Organizational Communication Theorizing

Feminist organizational theory is a form of critical theory that is dedicated to examining the oppressive circumstances experienced by women in the workplace. Although there are many forms of feminism, all share the common assumption that the workplace is dominated by male-oriented social structures and that this situation can and must be changed (Calas & Smircich, 1996). Feminist theorizing raises our collective conscious-ness regarding the unequal treatment and oppressive circumstances women face in the workplace, attempts to uncover the assumptions on which those circumstances are based, and offers a variety of means by which the oppression can be alleviated.

As an example of the type of circumstances just described, consider the situation described by Marla, a woman attorney with a large law firm. One of your authors was contacted by the law firm to do consulting work with Marla on her courtroom communication. The partners in the law firm felt that she needed communication training to help her with her opening and closing arguments in court. After an hour-long session in which Marla had done her presentations, it was obvious that she was an excellent speaker. When she was told that she really was accomplished, Marla broke down and said, "I knew it. I knew it. Those guys up there just don't like me because I'm a woman." Digging deep into her memory (as well as the organizational chart), she recalled many more instances where men were the ones in power situations in the organization and that women were rarely, if ever, treated equally. Because of the male-dominated structures in this organization, Marla would have a very difficult time advancing professionally or even receiving treatment equal to that of the male attorneys.

Different feminist perspectives offer different reasons for and solutions to the problems individuals face in the workplace. **Liberal feminists** believe that within patriarchal structures, people are differentiated based on sex. Exclusion from laws and policies allow oppression to occur; to resolve this oppression, liberal feminists advocate working within the existing structure to gain equal opportunities and pro-mote an equal valuing for equal work done by all men and women (Buzzanell, 2020). **Radical feminists** believe that changing the existing structure would be too difficult because the ideologies that have maintained it for so long are so deeply ingrained.

Instead, radical feminists argue alternative forms of organizing around feminist ideals are necessary to resolve inequalities (Ashcraft, 2014). **Cultural feminists** believe that men and women have different values and assumptions. Oppression is a result of men's values and assumptions being used as the benchmark in organizations and women being evaluated by those standards (Keyton, 2017; McDonald, 2015). Standpoint feminists, on the other hand, look at the ways that women and other marginalized groups have knowledge about their social world and the organization based on their specific social location and nondominant group status. Standpoint feminists emphasize the ways that standpoints, or collective experiences of marginalization, can be used as the basis for organizational resistance or dissent. **Postmodern feminists**, on the other hand, believe that gender is a communicative and social construction (Keyton, 2017). These feminisms, and the myriad of other forms, allow organizational communication scholars to explore gender and issues of class, race, nationality, and sexuality from a critical lens.

Feminist organization theory has drawn significant attention to the association between rationality and masculinity (Ferguson, 1984; Kanter, 1977; Morgan, 1997). Martin (2000) argued that masculinity is at the heart of many seemingly neutral topics, such as the Hawthorne Studies, Weber's bureaucracy, bounded rationality and emotionality, and prevailing institutional and managerial theory. Historically, rationality has been linked with reason, logic, and objective judgment (stereotypically masculine qualities), whereas subjectivity, intuition, and emotions have been associated with more feminine qualities (Ross-Smith & Kornberger, 2004). Feminists vary on their stances, though, on these issues depending on the framework from which they are operating. Let's consider the example of Weber's bureaucracy.

Liberal feminists argue that bureaucracy can be in line with feminist principles. The principles behind bureaucracy are such as to prevent favoritism and discrimination and ensure that individuals are treated consistently and equitably in all interactions. Liberal feminists argue that bureaucracy only becomes problematic when the individuals enacting it rely on sexist or gendered practices. This liberal feminist critique embodies their tradition of maintaining organizational structure while modifying individual practices and behaviors that occur within the structure.

Radical feminists, however, might argue that Weber's bureaucracy highlights, enforces, and normalizes conditions of subordination, dependence, and powerlessness. Acker (1990) extends this position by arguing that bureaucracies privilege men's status in society and reproduce gender inequality in the workplace. This critique is in line with radical feminist thought that seeks to question dominant organizational forms and expose their gendered bases (e.g., Calas & Smircich, 1996; Mayer, 1995; Natalie et al., 1994).

Organizational communication scholars operating from a feminist perspective are seeking to show the centrality of language and interaction to the circumstances women face in the gendered workplace (Buzzanell, 1994). Through this research, members of organizations are able to understand how their communicative actions and interactions contribute to either the perpetuation or the reversal of the current oppressive situation. Armed with this knowledge, they can seek to change their behavior, affect the behavior of others, and help promote a more equitable and equal workplace for the sexes.

Scholars have also spent time debating the notion of feminist organizing. Morgan (1994) identified several characteristics that typically define feminist organizing. These characteristics include frequent self-disclosure and collective discussions of feelings. Members may experience higher levels of identification with the organization, as well as increased commitment to the organization's mission and values. Feminist organizing may also include a degree of bounded emotionality. **Bounded emotionality** refers to bringing elements of nurturance, caring, community, supportiveness, and interrelatedness into the workforce, although for task effectiveness, the emotionality is bound by feeling rules that emphasize individual and relational needs alongside organizational limits (Ashcraft, 2000).

The feminist framework one assumes greatly influences what one views as feminist organizing. Communication scholars argue that feminist organizations may be conceptualized as "alternative discourse communities that develop counter-discourses of gender, power, and organizing amid cultural and material constraints" (Ashcraft, 2000, p. 352). This definition enables us to conceptualize organizations as sites where workers, through their interactions, continually negotiate and renegotiate organizational structure. The emphasis is on action and the decisions that organizational members make in their daily interactions. This perspective focuses on the interplay between feminist theory and daily practice (e.g., Hatch, 1997; Putnam, 1986; Trethewey, 1999). Importantly, modern feminist organizational communication researchers are beginning to engage the notion of intersectionality (Ashcraft, 2014).

Summary

To review, critical theory, which is based on Marxist philosophy, assumes that traditionally organized activity inherently places the interests of the dominant group over those of the subordinate group. This chapter forwarded the notion of the organization as a site of domination; described and illustrated the principles of diversity and discrimination, power, ideology, hegemony, and concertive control; outlined a critical analysis of technology use in organizations, particularly as used for employee monitoring; and concluded with two extensions of critical theory that demonstrate how the theory can be embodied in different ways to unearth taken-for-granted assumptions about organizational life.

Critical theory has never enjoyed the popular (pragmatic) success that organizational culture theory has. The most evident of the many reasons is that it asks organizations to examine their own structures and behaviors to reveal instances of domination and oppression. Table 6.1 summarizes the key concepts and extensions of critical theory.

TABLE 6.1 Critical Theory

FOCUS	IMPORTANT CONCEPTS	EXTENSION OF CRITICAL THEORY
Interconnections between communication, power, and organizing	Site of domination	Organizational democracy
	Diversity and discrimination	Feminist organizational theory
	Power	
	Ideology	
	Hegemony	
	Control	
	Concertive control	

Most organizational representatives are unwilling to make themselves this vulnerable to disapproval. But critical theorists have enjoyed some success; their work has influenced the mindsets of various workers and policy makers throughout the country and the world. Although the work of critical theorists may not yet have been translated directly into theories of practical management, the situations faced by women and minorities in the workplace have been brought out of the shadows, and society has been made aware of the oppressive circumstances fostered in many modern organizations. Viewing the critical approach to organizations through the framework of misunderstandings yields some interesting conclusions. First, the framework demands that the researcher and practitioner start from the assumption that organizational life is inherently problematic. Although the framework does not point the user in any particular direction, it does start with the assumption that organizational members need to be vigilant. Critical theory starts with the same orientation, although the nature of the problems from this perspective is rooted in management oppression of the workers. The concept of misunderstandings alerts organizational members to the fact that problems are natural and should be anticipated; it does not, however, assume (as the critical approach does) that the organization *is* a site of domination.

The critical perspective is also compatible with the misunderstandings framework in that it alerts organizational members to the different types of misunderstandings that most likely will occur in organizations, such as value differences, power imbalances, and inequity. Critical theorists also search for such things in the deep structure of the organization.

Importantly, critical theorists are interested in representing the voices and interests of organizational members *other than* management. From the critical perspective, these voices have been far too loud through the history of organizations, and as a result, organizational structures of all sorts have been created with their best interests in mind. The misunderstandings framework, although not dismissive of managerial interests, does represent the interests of *all* organizational members and provides a lens through which to view organizational life that will serve the interests of workers and management alike.

PART II

Challenges and Misunderstandings

Realistic Recruitment

LEARNING OBJECTIVES

1. Outline the negative consequences when job applicants or organizations misrepresent themselves

2. Recount the human and financial costs when organizations misrepresent themselves during recruitment

3. Outline the formal and informal practices adopted by organizations to address applicant misrepresentations

4. Examine how realistic recruitment attempts to address the issues of applicant misrepresentation

5. Recognize how realistic recruitment anticipates and addresses misunderstandings before they occur

The study of organizational behavior, particularly communication, does not begin when the new employee begins work. Understanding the process of how organizational members are recruited and selected (or *not* selected) is important. The communication during this time by both the applicant and the employer affects vital individual and organizational outcomes if and when the applicant becomes a member of the organization.

The hiring process is a stressful time for both the applicant and the employer. The applicant is attempting to find the best position that matches his or her needs and wants, as well as abilities. The employer is searching for the best employee who matches the requirements of the position as well as the intangible aspects of the organization, such as the culture of the workplace. The desire for both parties to find the "best" often results in each exaggerating strengths and positive qualities, while downplaying negative or weaker ones.

Applicants might intentionally invent or exaggerate their skills to meet the demands of a particular job. At the same time, employers might intentionally mislead applicants on important factors, such as working conditions and hours, in an attempt to recruit the best employees. Although this situation could seem like the status quo for the employment process, such behavior can have negative short- and long-term consequences for both the individual and the organization. Consider the following stories, the first of which is a recounting of a story told by Amari, a student, in class:

> I applied for this job where one of the requirements was to be skilled in Microsoft Office. I said I was and honestly thought I was. What I didn't really think about was that Office is more than just Word and PowerPoint.
>
> During my first week, my boss sent me a pile of electronic invoices and told me to create an Excel database from them and generate a report on the company's sales from the past year. Well, I was completely lost and did my best to learn Excel through YouTube videos as fast as I could. I wish I could say that I faked my way through it, but I didn't. The report I turned in to my boss (two days later than they wanted) was nothing like what they expected. They knew right then that I had no clue what I was doing with Excel. I wound up looking for a new job right away because I wasn't going to last very long there after that.

Now consider the situation described by Steve, who was hired as a marketing intern for a collegiate-level baseball team that played during the summer in preparation for possible advancement to the major leagues:

> In the interview process, they definitely said that there was going to be some ballpark work and other general tasks, but they did make it sound like it was going to be more heavily focused on actual marketing activities. So I thought they didn't exactly state the reality of the position requirements very well. They emphasized marketing a lot in the interview process, but then in reality, it was a lot less of that. I also expected more of a typical workweek number of hours.
>
> I wound up doing a lot of the day-to-day activities needed to run a ballpark. Obviously, this isn't even minor league scale, but there is a lot of upkeep that needs to be taken so the fans have a good experience as soon as they walk in. For example, making sure all of the banner signs are up and in the correct places and looking good and not torn or weathered. Some other things would be painting tables and other areas like that, sweeping the grandstands when volunteers weren't available, and then also getting the kids' zone ready for the game day, which was a lot of inflatables and prizes. We actually worked a lot of hours. Over the course of a week, we logged 80 or more hours just because every day was a game day. There were probably two days a week where they didn't have a baseball game, and so on those game days, we would arrive between 9 or 10 a.m. and then not leave until 10 or 11 at night once the game had ended and everything was put away. We weren't paid hourly; we only received a stipend for our work.

As you can see, providing information that is exaggerated or false can lead to negative consequences for both the organization and the individual. In this chapter, we discuss the recruitment and selection process from the perspectives of both the individual and the organization. We contrast the traditional recruitment process with a process called realistic recruitment.

When Applicants and Organizations Misrepresent Themselves

If most organizations and applicants engage in misleading communication during the recruitment process, what is the harm? In fact, if most applicants exaggerate their skills and abilities, won't people who do not do so be at a disadvantage? If most organizations provide only positive or misleading information about the job and organization, won't the ones that do not engage in such practices lose the most qualified employees to the organizations that do?

The concerns cited are short-term concerns. In the long run, exchanging realistic, truthful information during the recruitment and selection process will benefit both the individual and the organization, affecting important outcomes, such as job satisfaction, organizational commitment, job performance, and turnover. Let's begin with a discussion of the problem by focusing on the applicant.

Misrepresentation by the Applicant

The lure of exaggerating one's qualifications, skills, work history, and so on is strong when searching for a job. Applicants often believe, especially during times when the job market is tight, that the only way they will get their foot in the door of a good company is to "stretch the truth" on their resume and during the interview, making themselves more attractive to the potential employer. This type of behavior is found not only with entry-level job seekers. We were told the following story about an applicant for a vice president position in an information technology firm:

> My old boss, the VP retired, and I was on the committee to pick his replacement. The guy we picked was really nice when we interviewed. He was really helpful, and he talked about how he kept his own calendar, and he did his own email, and how he was so tech savvy, and all these things. He didn't just have the degree; he knew all these things. He also talked about how he didn't want to make any changes; he wanted to see how things ran first. Then he got here, and he didn't keep his own calendar; he could barely turn a computer on and off, and he automatically started changing things. He thought we were overstaffed, and so everybody was worried about losing their job. So, it really changed the atmosphere a lot.

Although the VP candidate did not misrepresent his qualifications in his written material, he certainly misled the search committee in his interview, which led to his hiring. As you can see from the story, the people he misled were left with a lot of distress for the workers once the reality was discovered.

Whether at the entry-level or senior management level, some job seekers provide misleading information during the hiring process. Lying on a resume is a common form of misleading. Resume fraud, perhaps better termed *misrepresentation*, takes many forms, including overstating qualifications, providing altered or nonexistent academic credentials, offering phony references, misreporting previous work history, and a variety of other exaggerations and lies. Lui (2020) reported the results of a Checkster survey that found that 78% of job applications did or would misrepresent themselves in some way to get hired. The primary areas of misrepresentation included claiming skill mastery (such as Excel or foreign language), inaccurate reporting of length of prior employment, overstatement of GPA, not actually completing degree requirements from a prestigious university, among others.

When the applicant misrepresents themself and is subsequently hired by the organization, any number of problems can develop. If the misrepresentation was in the area of skills and qualifications, the newcomer might not be able to perform the duties of the job to the extent necessary (if at all), as happened to Amari, the student in our earlier example who did not know how to use Microsoft Excel. Alternatively, if the misrepresentation concerned the type of organizational culture the applicant preferred, the newcomer could find themself in a situation where their values, attitudes, and communication style are not in sync with the reality of the organization. The potential consequences of applicant misrepresentation can be represented as a logical chain of events (see Figures 7.1 and 7.2).

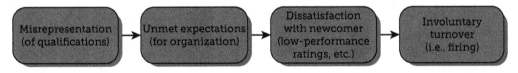

FIGURE 7.1 Applicant Misrepresents Qualifications

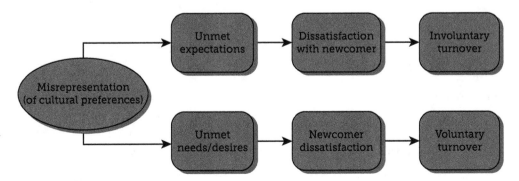

FIGURE 7.2 Applicant Misrepresents Cultural Preferences

Figure 7.1 represents a proposed chain of events when an applicant misrepresents their qualifications. When the applicant is hired based on misrepresented qualifications, they must confront the reality of the job requirements. Chances are if the misrepresentation was great enough, the newcomer will be unable to perform the duties as the organization expects. Dissatisfaction on the part of the organization with the newcomer's performance will ensue, resulting in low performance evaluations. If performance does not increase to an expected, satisfactory level, the newcomer might be fired.

Figure 7.2 illustrates what could happen when an applicant misrepresents their cultural preferences (shorthand here for attitudes, values, beliefs, communication style, etc.). The top line follows the chain of events from the organization's perspective. When the applicant misrepresents their cultural preferences and is subsequently hired partly on the basis of these preferences, they will ultimately have to perform within the constraints of that organization's culture. If there are significant discrepancies between the newcomer's attitudes, values, beliefs, and communication style and the culture of the organization, the other members of the organization will become dissatisfied with the newcomer for not fitting into the culture. If this dissatisfaction is strong enough, the newcomer might be fired for reasons of incompatibility.

The bottom line of Figure 7.2 illustrates the possible chain of events from the individual's perspective. In this situation, when the newcomer enters the organization and finds that their attitudes, values, beliefs, and communication style differ from the organizational culture, they will experience unmet needs and desires. When these needs go unresolved, dissatisfaction tends to follow. Given the availability of other employment opportunities, the newcomer might leave voluntarily.

Misrepresentation by the Organization

Just as applicants might misrepresent themselves in an attempt to secure the best job opportunities, organizations might also misrepresent the nature of the job and the organization to attract the most qualified employees, as the baseball team did in Steve's story. Wanous (1992) referred to this practice of "selling" the organization to the potential employee as **traditional recruitment**. According to Wanous (1992, p. 41), traditional recruitment involves two actions:

- Positive characteristics, rather than those things insiders find dissatisfying about the organization, are communicated to outsiders.

- Those features that are advertised may be distorted to make them seem even more positive.

In other words, traditional recruitment involves painting a picture of organizational reality that includes only information that can be construed as attractive. Any information (regarding details of the job or aspects of the organizational culture) that might seem unattractive to a potential employee is not communicated.

When the organization engages in traditional recruitment, any applicant hired might experience difficulty. Upon entering the organization, the newcomer will confront a reality that could be substantially different from the one portrayed during the recruiting process. As a result, a logical chain of events might ensue, as detailed in Figure 7.3.

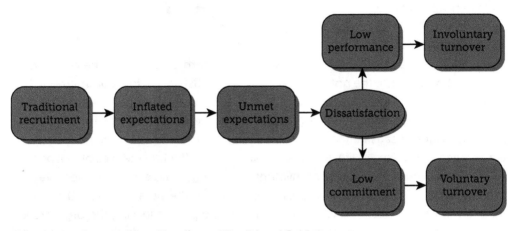

FIGURE 7.3 Potential Ramifications of Traditional Recruitment

When an applicant is subjected to traditional recruitment methods, they will have "inflated expectations," or expectations of the organization and job that are hyper-positive, based on inaccurate and overly positive information. When the newcomer encounters reality, these inflated expectations will not match that reality, resulting in "unmet expectations" or expectations that have not been fulfilled. When expectations are unmet, job dissatisfaction tends to follow.

At this point, the potential chain of events splits into two directions. These directions should not be considered mutually exclusive because events in one could be related to events in the other. One direction (the upper line in Figure 7.3) involves unmet expectations of the requirements of the job. Wanous (1992) noted that a mismatch regarding actual job requirements and the newcomer's expectations of them can result in lower job performance and eventual involuntary turnover.

The other direction (the lower line in Figure 7.3) involves unmet expectations of the characteristics of the organizational culture. Wanous proposed that this mismatch between the individuals and the culture can create unmet expectations, which can result in lower organizational commitment and eventual voluntary turnover.

You might be asking yourself, "So what? So what if the newcomer is dissatisfied? So what if there is turnover, voluntary or otherwise; can't the organization just hire someone else? Can't the newcomer just find another job? What does it matter?" In the next section, we address the potential costs, human and financial, of the traditional method of recruitment.

The Costs of Traditional Recruiting

Recruitment methods that lead to a high rate of turnover are expensive in both human and financial terms.

The Human Factor

When applicants and organizations misrepresent themselves during the recruitment and selection process, the potential exists for low satisfaction, low commitment, low performance, and increased turnover. What begins as an attempt to secure the best job or hire the best employee can result in negative consequences for the people involved. Issues of satisfaction, commitment, and turnover are not merely organizational outcomes devoid of life; they are human factors affecting the lives of real people.

Turnover, whether voluntary or involuntary, is a dramatic event. People's lives are often greatly changed, and the stress and difficulty of the situation affect the lives of their family and friends. This is true not only for the person leaving the organization but also for those with whom that person has worked; relationships have been formed (positive or otherwise), energy has been invested, and time has been spent. Even if turnover does not occur, satisfaction and commitment can be affected negatively. The possible impact on important characteristics such as self-esteem and self-efficacy should be of concern at a human level.

Traditional recruitment practices (by both the individual and the organization) need to be examined from an ethical perspective (Buckley et al., 1997). Kreps (1990, pp. 250–251) forwarded three principles to evaluate ethics of organizational communication that are useful here:

1. Organization members should not intentionally deceive one another.

2. Organization members' communication should not purposely harm any other organization member or members of the organization's relevant environment.

3. Organization members should be treated justly.

Traditional recruitment methods (from the organizational perspective) can be evaluated according to these principles.

First, do traditional recruitment methods intentionally deceive applicants? In some cases, the answer must be yes. In Steve's experience at the ballpark, he was led to believe that his position would entail marketing activities within a typical 40-hour workweek, but the reality is that the majority of his work was maintenance and customer service, and he often worked up to 80 hours per week. Organizations often intentionally misrepresent the reality of the job or the organization in an attempt to attract a potentially productive employee. The question becomes, to what extent was the deception *intentional*? Given the ambiguous nature of language and reality, one person's opinion of organizational reality can be quite different from another person's opinion. That being so, in some instances, the situation is simply a matter of differing opinions of reality. But in other instances, organizational members intentionally deceive the applicant in an attempt to lure him or her into the organization. This behavior is ethically suspect.

Second, do traditional recruitment methods harm the applicant or other members of the organization? As stated earlier, such methods can harm both the applicant and current organizational members. When a newcomer experiences unmet expectations, low satisfaction, and perhaps even turnover, harm has indeed been inflicted.

Third, do traditional recruitment practices allow for just treatment of the applicant? Some might argue that the only way to "win" in the "recruitment game" is for each party to make itself as attractive as possible to the other party because the nature of the game is so competitive. From this perspective, any practices that help either party "win" the game are justified; the means justify the ends.

But is this really true? Can you, as an applicant, only obtain a great job in a strong organization if you misrepresent yourself to one degree or another? Can you, as an employer, only attract the best applicants if you misrepresent your organization by exaggerating or inventing positive aspects and downplaying or not informing the applicants about the relevant negative aspects?

In light of these three principles, traditional recruitment practices can be considered ethically suspect; nevertheless, for some people, human costs are not enough to justify a change in behavior. In the next section, we discuss the financial factor involved in traditional recruitment.

The Financial Factor

In addition to the human costs associated with the potential outcomes of traditional recruitment practices, there are financial. The dollar amount attributed to hiring a new employee is referred to as **cost-per-hire (CPH)**. In a report of research conducted by the Society for Human Resource Management (SHRM, 2017), the average CPH in the United States was $4,425. To hire an executive, the CPH average was $14,936.

Perhaps even more revealing is another metric used by human resource managers to measure the financial impact of turnover. **Turnover cost** refers to the amount of money that can be attributed to losing one employee and replacing that employee with another. In 2019, SHRM reported that the cost of turnover involves the following types of costs (Agovino, 2019):

- *Soft costs* account for 67% of the turnover cost and include such things as reduced productivity, lost knowledge, and interview time.

- *Hard costs* are 33% of the turnover cost and include costs for temporary workers, background checks, recruiting, and drug screens.

As you can see, turnover is costly for organizations. An incredible amount of time, energy, and money are invested in the process of hiring a new employee. When turnover occurs, particularly with a new employee, the organization suffers financially. In the next section, we offer an alternative to traditional recruitment practices, which might help reduce instances and costs of unmet expectations, low job satisfaction, and turnover.

Addressing the Problem of Applicant Misrepresentation

Before we turn our attention to the focus of this chapter, realistic recruitment, we would like to offer a brief discussion of what some organizations are doing to combat the problem of applicant misrepresentation discussed earlier in this chapter. Organizations are using a combination of formal and informal practices to attempt to minimize the impact of applicant misrepresentation in the hiring process.

First, Mizell and Gips (2020) report results from SHRM that 96.1% of companies conduct some form of pre-employment background screening on potential employees. Organizations also conduct background checks that seek to verify things such as employment history, education, work eligibility, criminal records, and possibly test for drugs and scrutinize social media (Kolmar, 2020).

A second formal procedure that organizations are using is with regard to how they identify potential job candidates. Many organizations have moved away from advertising their open positions in print (e.g., newspaper, professional association newsletter) and moved to electronic job search websites, such as ZipRecruiter and Monster, and posting on social media sites, particularly LinkedIn. Others have opted for several additional alternatives, including hiring from within, taking referrals from current organizational members, and recruiting through trusted formal and informal contacts. Organizations going this route have found that they are able to reduce the amount of applicant misrepresentation they experience, as well as their employment search costs.

Finally, a growing trend among companies is to use informal Internet technology searches to scrutinize potential employees. Employers are "trolling" social networking sites such as LinkedIn, Twitter, Facebook, and Instagram, and they are using Internet search engines to gather information on their job applicants. A Harris Poll done on behalf of CareerBuilder in 2018 showed that 70% of employers use social media as a way to research applicants and that 57% of employers did not hire an applicant based on content found during their social media searches. The percentage of employers actually using social networking sites in this way may actually be higher than reported, though, given the legal considerations involved in such uses.

It is clear that organizations are attempting to minimize the impact of applicant misrepresentation in different ways. Some organizations have also recognized that their own recruitment practices have contributed to their hiring and retention difficulties, and they are attempting to remedy these problems as well. It is to this issue that we turn our attention next.

Addressing the Problem of Traditional Recruitment: Realistic Recruitment

One way to address the problems caused by traditional recruitment practices is for the organization to engage in realistic recruitment practices. The genesis of the theory of realistic recruitment can be attributed to Weitz (1956), but modern research and practice regarding the topic is based mostly on the work of John Wanous (see Baur et al., 2014 for a history of realistic job preview research).

Wanous (1992), in his book *Organizational Entry: Recruitment, Selection, Orientation, and Socialization of Newcomers*, outlined the pitfalls of traditional recruitment practices and introduces the reader to the theory of realistic recruitment. According to Wanous, **realistic recruitment** "presents outsiders with *all pertinent* information *without distortion*" (p. 43). Realistic recruitment is designed to increase job satisfaction, thereby decreasing unnecessary turnover caused by unmet expectations.

Central to realistic recruitment is the creation and use of a realistic job preview (RJP). An RJP is any attempt by the organization to provide an accurate (both positive and negative) view of the relevant aspects of the job and the organization. The RJP should serve to lower the newcomer's initial expectations and provide a better match with reality, thereby decreasing the possibility of unmet expectations. This decrease, in turn, should lead to positive levels of job satisfaction and strong job performance and the eventual lowering of unnecessary turnover. Figure 7.4 illustrates the logical chain of events attributed to the use of an RJP.

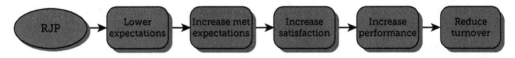

FIGURE 7.4 RJP Chain of Events

In the story of Steve and his "marketing" internship with the collegiate summer baseball team, we can see how an RJP might have affected the situation. His organization's misrepresentation of the marketing internship caused his expectations to be significantly different from reality. As he encountered the job as it really was, he became dissatisfied and told us later in the interview that he considered leaving. His organization would probably benefit by portraying the job more realistically so that newcomers' expectations would be more in line with reality. Many people are attracted to marketing positions because they match their needs and personalities. If the baseball organization would have been more realistic about the nature of the position and hours expected each week, then the interns they did bring on board would potentially be more satisfied and productive.

RJPs serve a **signaling function**, which means that the RJP signals or calls attention to important organizational characteristics and realities for the applicant. The RJP does this in two related ways (Earnest et al., 2011). First, is *instrumental* signaling, which is where the RJP provides signals regarding unknown information about the work that leads to the creation of expectations about the work that may be more in line with reality. The other way is *symbolic*, which means the RJP could signal more intangible things of interest about the organization, such as organizational honesty and overall concern for employees. Think of instrumental signaling as pointing to more noticeable or verifiable aspects of the organization and job (such as the amount of travel required or the possibilities of pay raises) and symbolic signaling as a two-step process where the RJP conveys information which in turn leads the applicant to infer certain things about the organization and the employees.

How RJPs Work

How do RJPs work? Two theories explain how an RJP accomplishes what it is intended to accomplish: self-selection and vaccination (Phillips, 1998). From the self-selection perspective, RJPs function by providing the applicant an opportunity to self-select out of the recruitment process on the basis of a mismatch of needs and/or abilities. The remaining applicant pool should consist of people who think there is a good match between their needs and abilities and the demands of the job and the organizational culture. Self-selection works only if the RJP is given very early in the recruitment process and if the information provided is realistic.

From the vaccination perspective, RJPs act just as a medical vaccination does. A medical vaccination introduces a weak dose of a disease (or the virus that causes it) into the body to give the immune system the opportunity to build up resistance to the disease and prevent an onset of it in the future. Similarly, an RJP can provide an opportunity for applicants to develop coping mechanisms for negative aspects of organizational life. If the vaccination effect is what truly occurs, then self-selection is rendered unnecessary.

Phillips (1998), based on a review of RJP research, contended that RJPs may function more as a result of vaccination than self-selection. She argued this because RJP research shows that attrition from the recruitment process is either slightly negatively related or unrelated to the use of RJPs. In other words, one would expect that if an RJP were given early in the recruitment process, a significant number of applicants would self-select out of the process, leaving a smaller applicant pool (attrition). Her review, however, shows that RJPs do not significantly reduce the number of applicants. Therefore, self-selection most likely does not adequately explain why RJPs function as they do; the most viable explanation for Phillips is vaccination.

It is possible, though, that RJPs given at the very beginning of the recruitment process might serve a self-selection function. RJPs can take the form of job advertisements or informal word of mouth and can serve to preclude a person from ever becoming a formal applicant. When an RJP functions in this way, self-selection is the most reasonable explanation. Present research cannot account for people who self-select out at this point in the recruitment process because they were never formal applicants. For this reason, self-selection should not be dismissed as an explanatory mechanism for how RJPs function.

A third reason for how RJPs work has emerged more recently and is receiving attention in the literature. RJPs may work because they create an "air of honesty" (Shibly, 2019), which then leads to a series of positive outcomes. From the air of honesty perspective, if the RJP recipient senses that the organization is being honest with them, this could lead to a greater sense of commitment by the recipient, which could increase positive feelings about the organization and reduce turnover if the applicant is hired.

Regardless of how RJPs work, two issues are important when constructing and implementing RJPs: medium of communication and time of administration. We discuss each in the following sections.

The Medium of the RJP

An RJP is typically constructed after a thorough analysis of the job and organization is performed. An analysis is conducted following the gathering of information regarding the specifics of the job, including working conditions, hours, opportunity for advancement, managerial style, job freedom, pay and benefits, and organizational values. These data are often gathered via observation of work procedures; surveys of workers, managers, and customers; and interviews with members at all levels of the organization.

The content of RJPs should be based on the information gathered and then constructed with five attributes in mind (Breaugh & Billings, 1988). *Accuracy* is the degree to which the RJP reflects reality. The accuracy of the information that is presented will affect the psychology of the RJP process. *Specificity* involves the extent to which the RJP contains specific details rather than generic information. Obviously, no RJP can tell the entire story of every aspect of the job and organization, but the choices that are made for what to include and what not to include will affect the usefulness of the RJP. *Breadth* is the idea that the RJP should include more than just the relevant aspects of the job, but it should also include relevant and realistic information about the organization. *Credibility* means that the RJP should be perceived as believable by the recipient. Credibility is a complicated attribute as it involves the other attributes as well as the production characteristics of the RJP itself, such as the inclusion of music in a video or the use of scripted material versus candid shots of everyday life in the organization. Finally, *importance* means that information in the RJP needs to not be common knowledge or already known by the applicant for the RJP to be effective.

Once the data are collected and synthesized and the RJP is constructed with the five attributes being considered, the organization must decide on the appropriate medium or media for presenting the RJP. Typically, RJPs have been presented using video, written, or verbal media. Table 7.1 illustrates the three broad categories of media available, as well as the different manifestations of each, the potential sources from which the RJPs could originate, and the outcomes related to each medium as demonstrated through research (Phillips, 1998).

TABLE 7.1 RJP Media

	VIDEO	WRITTEN	VERBAL
Manifestations	Organizationally sponsored social media or website video, organizational orientation, job orientation, training video	Job advertisement, website textual content, aptitude test, informational pamphlet, handbook, training manual	Conversation with insiders, employment interview, on-site visit, prehire orientation, posthire orientation
Source	Actors versus incumbents, managers versus workers	Human resources management	Insiders, interviewers, human resources, supervisors/coworkers
Related outcomes	Strongest positive relationship with performance	Least effective of the three forms	Greatest reduction in both types of turnover, only medium with positive relationship to job satisfaction

Before we move to the specific media available for administering the RJPs, it is important to discuss how Internet technology has impacted RJPs. While research is limited but growing in this area, there are a few key points to remember. First, information communication about an organization that is intended to be realistic is judged differently depending on where that information is found on the Internet. For example, Kaur and Dubey (2020) showed that information that is located on *organization-independent sources* (such as LinkedIn or Glassdoor) is considered to be more credible than information located on *organization-dependent sources* (such as the company Web site). Second, if the job ads or RJPs are posted on organization-dependent sources but are then linked to organization-independent sources (such as Glassdoor), then they are perceived as more credible than if they were not linked to those external sources.

Video

Video is one medium available for administering an RJP. RJPs using this medium have traditionally taken the form of job and organizational orientation videos and training videos, but more recently, organizations are streaming video RJPs on their organizational websites and social media sites. Given the fact that potential employees use company websites and social media sites as sources for company information, organizations have begun to use these outlets to distribute video RJPs. Organizations such as Transportation Security Administration, Comcast, and Alliance for Child Welfare Excellence stream RJP videos, which discuss the skills and mindset necessary to succeed in different positions and in the organizations. They also discuss the benefits, as well as the challenges, of the positions.

Video RJPs have several advantages. First, they are consistent. The organization can be confident that each time the video is played, the same message will be sent to the audience in the same way. Second, video RJPs are multimedia, reflecting the prevalence of multimedia messages in today's society. Professionally created, video RJPs communicate a message using sight, sound, and music—a multimedia presentation that may be necessary to capture the attention of today's workforce. Research has shown that job seekers are more drawn to audiovisual than to plan text because they can get a better sense of the organizational culture and can see and hear the testimonials of employees, giving them a better sense of their accuracy because they can see the employees' nonverbal behaviors (Banerjee & Gupta, 2019). Unfortunately, RJPs that are unprofessional or of poor quality can have the opposite effect.

However, video RJPs also have several disadvantages. First, professional video production is expensive and can be time-consuming. Second, video RJPs can quickly become dated. Organizations and jobs change quickly in today's world; what might have been true yesterday about a particular position can change tomorrow. Third, video RJPs are not interactive. Indeed, they are often considered a form of persuasive communication (Phillips, 1998) and as such can be understood from that perspective. We know, from the body of work in persuasion, that people are more willing to be persuaded when they are actively involved in the process. Video, although it engages many senses, is limited in its interactive capacity.

When producing video RJPs, the organization must decide whom they will use in the video as the source of information. Should the people be actors or real organizational members? Should they be managers? Coworkers? A combination of managers and coworkers? Research has yet to explore adequately the answers to these questions but has shown that if videos do not give a full picture of the organization and the job, then they are not as effective (Kaur & Dubey, 2020). We had one of our interviewees for this book look at the RJP posted on her company's website. This is what April, an employee of a manufacturing company, had to say after watching the video:

1. *One of the employees on the video smiles all the time. I have never seen that person smile in our hallways.*

2. *There is lively, upbeat, and playful music through the entire video. There isn't lively, upbeat, and playful music played during the workday.*

3. *An employee in the video says, "Everyone is willing to help." The use of the word "everyone" is generous and is not representative of any larger team. Many people may be willing to help, but not everyone. This type of message has both conscious and unconscious impacts on the recruits.*

4. *Another employee said, "I love everyone I work with!" Uhm … no.*

5. *And another employee said, "I get to make a difference beyond my job." The reality of this statement is that the "job" becomes the things that they do that, yesterday, were beyond the scope of the job. This is a great example of communicating job creep (or doing more for the same amount of money and job title) but describing it as making a difference beyond the scope of the job.*

6. *The caption beneath the video highlights our company "values." Interestingly, though, this is not how our values are communicated internally. So there isn't consistency between messages to potential employees and external stakeholders and the messages being communicated to the existing members.*

Clearly, April's organization was making an attempt to provide a picture of organizational life to applicants; however, as she demonstrated, from her experience, the messages in the video were far from realistic and as a result, they will wind up hurting the organization and the applicants in the long run, as expectations will undoubtedly be unmet when the applicant gets hired and joins the organization. For a video RJP to be effective, it must truly be realistic and not just a marketing tool.

Video RJPs have been shown to have the strongest positive relationship with job performance (Phillips, 1998). In other words, the studies that have been conducted to this point have shown that video RJPs have the strongest connection to increased job performance. If increasing job performance is the outcome of interest for an organization, then a video RJP appears to be the most reliable medium. Recent research has shown even more innovative uses of video RJPs to promote outcomes other than performance. For example, Ridgway O'Brien and Hebl (2015) argued that video RJPs can be used to manage expectations with regard to work-family balance in academic jobs.

Written

RJPs may also be written. These are perhaps the most typical and take several forms, including job advertisements, aptitude tests, informational pamphlets, handbooks, and training manuals. Written RJPs have several advantages. First, just as with video RJPs, written RJPs are consistent. Second, they are relatively inexpensive to produce in comparison to video RJPs. Considering that handbooks and training manuals are common in most organizations, incorporating realistic job information in the preexisting texts can be done with little additional expense. Finally, written RJPs are slightly less difficult to change as conditions within the organization change. A set of addenda can be added to handbooks, job posting ads can be changed, or informational pamphlets can be updated to reflect the current organizational climate. All of these changes can happen—that is, if the organization recognizes the need to change the material and puts the appropriate resources in place to do so. Sometimes, though, this is not the case, as Bethany, a human resources employee, described:

> As the human resources representative, I was responsible for facilitating the posting of positions and supported the manager who requested the hire with interviews and candidate assessments. The job description was absolutely key, as it outlined the key responsibilities and established guard rails for other legal and corporate administration topics: Equal Employment Opportunity considerations, pay structures, bonus payments, reporting structures, career advancement, etc. The reality, though, was that job descriptions were routinely out of date, at times being 10 years old and having significant errors in the job descriptions. As the hiring manager, I did my best to try and update the job descriptions.
>
> The challenges were the manager who would supervise the new employee not knowing what the job was, the manager being too busy to give me

their time, the manager not having the sophistication to document the job in an orderly and structured manner, and frequent job duty changes that weren't managed pursuant to the overall corporate compensation and job structure strategy.

New employees would see me in the hall, and we would discuss their first few weeks in the job, and often they would describe differences and unexpected "asks" from their manager. This gap in expectation versus reality was a known variable, but the time and energy it would take to fix it was simply not available, or not created, or not discussed. No one was necessarily malicious or acting with ill intent. It just seemed that anything HR related was given very little priority.

Written RJPs, particularly those related to job descriptions and job postings, can be easier to change than video RJPs, but there could be a whole host of reasons, such as the ones described by Bethany, for why they would not be changed. The lack of change to keep up with the reality of the position could turn a beneficial tool into one that could work against the interests of the organization and the applicants.

Written RJPs also have several disadvantages. First, newcomers are presented with so much written information that they might not pay as strict attention to it as they might because of information overload. Second, as with video RJPs, written RJPs are not interactive and are even less engaging than video, which is multimedia.

When constructing a written RJP, the organization is faced with many questions of presentation. For example, in what style is the RJP to be written? Should an informational pamphlet be written in a narrative style, or should it be written in a detached, third-person style? Should the RJP be written by the human resources department or by management? Should it contain quotes from organizational members? Is a four-color, glossy publication necessary, or would a traditional black-and-white piece be satisfactory?

Written RJPs have been shown to be the least effective of the three forms of RJPs and to be altogether unrelated to job performance. Perhaps because of the disadvantages mentioned, they appear to be the least productive form, although they are probably the most prevalent because of their lower production cost.

Verbal

Spoken words are the final medium available for RJPs. Verbal RJPs have many manifestations, including conversations with insiders, employment interviews, on-site visits, prehire orientations, posthire orientations, and even discussions with competitors and former employees of the organization (although these last two are more informal RJPs). Verbal RJPs have several advantages. First, given that RJPs are a form of persuasive communication, a verbal medium is perhaps the most appropriate for enhancing the persuasive appeal of the message. If the person giving the RJP is a credible source, the verbal RJP has the potential to be very effective. Second, verbal RJPs are virtually cost-free. Although on-site visits and orientation sessions certainly have costs associated with them, the cost of answering a question honestly or offering a bit of realistic information verbally is negligible when compared to printing a pamphlet or producing a video.

Nevertheless, verbal RJPs have disadvantages as well. First, it is difficult to control the content of impromptu verbal RJPs. When an applicant asks a question of a line worker during an on-site visit, the organization has little control over what that person will say. The honesty expressed during that interchange can be very helpful to the applicant, but the organization has no way of tracking the information. Second, given the first disadvantage, it is very difficult to ensure consistency among verbal RJPs. When an applicant speaks with several different people during a typical application process, she will most likely be given different information about the same topic. The applicant is then left to judge the information based on the perceived credibility of the source.

The organization must decide who will meet the potential newcomer because each of these people will be a potential contributor of verbal RJPs. Coworkers, employment interviewers, human resources managers, supervisors, and other organizational insiders are all viable candidates for offering verbal RJPs. Two very important considerations for the organization when considering verbal RJPs, then, are source credibility and consistency of messages. Consistency of messages is hard to ensure, especially when there are multiple people with whom the job candidate interacts or interviews. Consider the following example from Jerry, a human resources manager:

> I saw firsthand time and time again varying culture and job expectation statements from different people on the same interview team. These differences are of value when they are representative of an individual perspective but can be destructive when the interviewers are attempting to step outside "themselves" and capture objective day-to-day realities experienced by all.
>
> For example, a department may be decentralized, offering an informal structure. OK, that may be the fact. One person may say that the department offers the flexibility of autonomous decision-making—that is their perspective. Another person may say that the department requires strong thinkers able to develop and defend their actions. Both may be signs of a decentralized structure, but in the interview process, individual perspective begins to cloud the reality of the job and the day-to-day activities.
>
> The team should sit down and discuss how the department will be realistically presented with the employee so that individual perspective is restrained. In fact, that particular job will have its own idiosyncrasies, and it will have a supervisor that manages the decentralization their own way. These are the ways that we move past individual bias in perspective to a more objective and reality-based description that will allow the recruit to make an informed decision.

The situation that Jerry described is a complicated communication situation. Everyone has different perspectives on organizational life and those differences (or even similarities) are expressed using different language. Those language differences can be very confusing to a job applicant, and they are left to wonder who is giving them the realistic picture.

Verbal RJPs have been shown to be associated with the greatest reduction in both voluntary and involuntary turnover (as compared with written and video RJPs). Verbal RJPs are also the only kind with a positive relationship to job satisfaction. Research has shown that of all three media, spoken words are the most successful in reducing turnover and are the only medium whose use seems to increase the job satisfaction of the applicant.

Time of Administration of the RJP

In addition to deciding the optimal form of an RJP, an organization must determine the best time to administer it. An RJP can be administered during any of the following points in the hiring process:

- When the applicant first makes contact about the job opening
- After the job offer has been made but before the job is accepted
- After the newcomer starts the job

The research related to the time of administration is complicated, but several issues are relevant. First, some researchers argue that RJPs administered after the newcomer starts the job are not RJPs at all. Because RJPs given after hiring do not allow for the opportunity to self-select out of the process, they should be considered efforts at "realistic socialization" rather than realistic job previews (Phillips, 1998). We agree. Although realistic information is useful at any point in the process, by definition, information given after the newcomer starts the job is not an RJP.

Second, Phillips's (1998) research has shown that RJPs presented before the job offer is accepted have stronger relationships with important outcome variables, such as job performance. Therefore, it would seem most appropriate for the organization to invest time and resources into producing and administering RJPs early in the recruitment process, before the job offer is accepted (Chehade & El Hajjar, 2016; Griffeth & Hom, 2001). Although many organizations do not wish to expend time or money on applicants who will not become members, the research and arguments presented here indicate that the cost of turnover could be greater down the line if RJPs are not given at this stage.

Realistic Recruitment and Misunderstandings

The practice of realistic recruitment is well suited to be understood through the framework of misunderstandings. As we have shown throughout this chapter, traditional recruitment practices can contribute to unmet expectations, dissatisfaction, and turn-over. Realistic recruitment is an attempt to treat recruits in a more ethical manner, with the hope that expectations will come close to matching reality, and as a result, satisfaction, performance, and job retention will be increased. In other words, real-istic recruitment is an attempt to anticipate and address misunderstandings before they occur.

Recall that misunderstandings are a central feature of organizational life and can occur for a variety of reasons, including conflict in values and lack of information. These two causes of misunderstandings are especially relevant to the recruitment process in that potential employees need realistic information about the job and the organization, including its values, if they are to make an informed decision about their "fit." Throughout this chapter, we have included many examples of situations where a lack of information or misleading information led to misunderstandings for both the applicant and the organization. Here is one final example, from Larz, a human resources manager, who demonstrates this point perfectly:

> I was the HR manager recruiting for a marketing manager position. I knew the manager who would supervise the position we were hiring for; he was a director. The director was a seasoned veteran in his position and had plenty to offer with regard to experience and knowledge, but he was known to be impatient and intolerant of views not aligned with his own. He had been coached several times by human resources to try and improve his behavior, at times functioning as a poor supervisor and at times bordering on violating company anti-harassment/bullying policy.
>
> During the interview process, I failed to disclose to the recruits the nega-tive side of the director. Instead, I was implicitly seeking out a personality type that I thought would be a good fit for the position. There was, in fact, an interview occurring of which the recruit was not aware. I was looking for someone with thick skin, demonstrated aptitude with working in confrontational situations, and someone that had a good track record of staying in a role or a company for extended periods of time. I knew that the director would not show these negative qualities during the interview, so I would get these negative qualities in the open, sometimes, by describ-ing the company culture as fast-paced and requiring someone tolerant of communication styles that might be brash or short. This presented ethical issues that I never resolved.
>
> The particular hiring situation I'm thinking about resulted in a hire that did not enjoy the reporting structure and ended up transferring to a dif-ferent role, with a different supervisor. The consequence was another vacancy and another round of interviews. The recruiting I did was less than ideal and resulted in less than ideal reporting structures. I try not to be too hard on myself, though, because these shortcomings were

connected to other causes: a large number of vacancies, an incredibly large number of applicants for each opening, a lack of skilled applicants, and an inadequate amount of resources and time dedicated to training and continuous improvement.

You can see much of what we discussed in this chapter play out in the story from Larz. An interviewer was constrained by limited resources, few skilled applicants, and not enough time to conduct an effective search, so he resorted to more traditional recruitment practices and did not provide a realistic picture of the organizational environment. The applicant was hired but was dissatisfied as a result of the mismatch between expectations and reality and wound up transferring positions, leading to more staffing problems and the need to expend more time and resources on yet another job search. Unfortunately, according to Larz, the company did not learn much from this experience and continued with the same practices that created the misunderstandings he described.

Just as important as anticipating misunderstandings are the strategies for responding to them, which provide a variety of ways to handle misunderstandings when they do occur. The *construct strategy* is perhaps most relevant to the move from traditional recruitment to realistic recruitment. If an organization used the framework of misunderstandings, it would recognize that misunderstandings were occurring as a result of their traditional recruiting practices. Implementing the construct strategy would provide an opportunity for the organization to learn from the misunderstandings of the past, discover where and how misleading information was being communicated, and engage in more realistic recruitment. The construct strategy encourages the move from problem to solution and is particularly useful during the recruiting process.

Summary

Recruitment is a vital component of organizational behavior. The information exchanged (or not exchanged) during this process can affect important factors, such as applicant satisfaction, job performance, and turnover. Although historically both the applicant and the organization have tended to misrepresent themselves during this process, it seems more beneficial to both in the long run to engage in realistic, honest communication. The potential benefits of realistic recruitment (by both parties) include met expectations, increased job satisfaction, increased performance, and reduced turnover.

Realistic recruitment, although not the cure-all for dissatisfaction, poor performance, and turnover, is important in the communicative organization. With the fluctuations in the job market and economy that are commonplace in the United States, both applicants and organizations will feel pressure to misrepresent themselves. In a slow economy, applicants may think they have to make themselves appear more qualified than they really are if they are to secure a place in a tight job market. During times of economic boom, when organizations are vying for qualified workers, managers may try to lure applicants in with overly positive portrayals of the organization and position. We hope that both applicants and organizations remember that in the long run, exaggerating important information will potentially lead to negative consequences for everyone involved.

Socialization of New Members

LEARNING OBJECTIVES

1. Evaluate the need for communication strategies in organizations to reduce employee misunderstandings
2. Describe the different phases of organizational assimilation for employees
3. Identify the six pairs of socialization tactics to assimilate new employees
4. Describe how emotions and emotional labor are relevant to organizational socialization
5. Explain the communicative activities associated with work-life balancing

When a new employee enters the organization, they try hard to become established as a helpful, cooperative employee. Depending on the training they received (or did not receive), they will go about doing their jobs in ways that seem best for the organization or at least best for them. Sometimes this works, but other times it does not because the new employee's behavior does not meet expectations, even though those expectations may never have been clearly or explicitly stated. Felicia works as an assistant director of a student-centered office in a regional university. She described a problem in her office that is related to expectations, but she realized that the expectations had never been stated, and it is everyone's responsibility to improve the situation:

> New student office workers will email us at 2 a.m. and say, "Will you look at this?" And then we will get another email at 8 a.m. being like, "Well why haven't you looked at this?!" And all I can think is, wow, I was sleeping. But then I realize that we as office managers do the same thing. We send an email at noon, and if we don't get a response by 2 p.m., we are in their face asking why they haven't responded. We forget that we need to be role models.

> For people going into any workplace, I think it is smart to ask about expectations. Ask what expectations are for that workplace that might be different from other workplaces or contexts they have been in and

what expectations are really important for that specific workplace. Then, pay attention. Pay attention to the verbal and nonverbal communication, and if you don't understand, ask.

Leaders need to recognize that maybe it's not a professionalism issue but maybe a change in the way people are used to doing things based on other contexts. Maybe we all need to take a look at it and see what we can do to help everyone know what our expectations are. So we are now doing that twice a month; we are talking about one particular aspect of our office duties and our expectations regarding professionalism.

Felicia's story shows us how easy it is for new organizational members to rely on the behaviors they exhibit in another context when they enter a workplace and for existing organizational members to forget what new organizational members do not already know. It is a clash between uncertainty and unstated expectations, and it really can only best be addressed through communication from both parties. Felicia recognized this and began to have regular discussions with everyone about expectations regarding different aspects of the organization. She also realized that she and the other members of the organization could have been contributing to the newcomers' inappropriate behavior by serving as role models for that unacceptable behavior. According to our definition, which we introduced in Chapter 1, *misunderstandings* involve more than ineffective communication between members of an organization. It is an umbrella term used to connote the problematic nature of interaction in organizational settings. We identified three possibilities for creating misunderstandings: (1) conflict in values, (2) lack of information, and (3) strategic misinterpretations. In this case, the cause of the misunderstanding was a lack of information and Felicia responded to that misunderstanding with a *construct* strategy, which will allow for greater learning for everyone in the organization.

Newcomers regularly are confronted with situations that are characterized by uncertainty and ambiguity in many areas, including formal job duties, formal and informal role requirements, communication norms, status differences, and myriad cultural constructs. Given this situation, the organization and the individual expend energy to address these issues. The organization attempts to *socialize* the individual into the culture of the organization and to the requirements of their position and role. At the same time, the newcomer attempts to influence the organizational situation by bringing to bear their own personal characteristics, values, beliefs, skills, and attitudes as they conduct their daily activities.

In this chapter, we focus mainly on the efforts of the organization to socialize the newcomer, relegating discussions of how the newcomer attempts to influence the organization to future chapters. Also, although socialization attempts are relevant throughout a member's time with an organization (especially at boundary passages, such as promotion and transfer), we devote the majority of this chapter to the socialization of newcomers, moving through the stages of the organizational assimilation model and the communicative activities that occur within them.

Misunderstandings and the Need for Information

Misunderstandings are always relevant to organizational life, but the organization and newcomer are particularly aware of them when a newcomer enters an organization. Organizations spend much time and energy attempting to reduce misunderstandings for the newcomer through orientation sessions, task training, assigning a mentor, and informal communication with existing organizational members. Newcomers, recognizing that they have much to learn, engage in information-seeking and information-giving behaviors with their colleagues. Naturally, though, all the information needs of the newcomer cannot be anticipated or met, and misunderstandings because of a lack of information or misinterpretation of information occur.

A new employee generally receives more information about initial job tasks than about the organization's culture. Information that comes from the top of the organization down to the lowest level employee contains directions about how to accomplish a job or task, as well as a sense of the values and culture of the organization (see Hafen, 2004, for the role gossip plays in this process). Information about tasks is usually specific and narrowly defined. Cultural information is vague or sometimes implied, yet it is cultural information that affects the way people are able to integrate and use the information about tasks. In other words, the values or principles of the organization and the kind of supportive or nonsupportive environment in which people exist will have a direct bearing on an individual's ability to understand the task and its importance. For example, in some organizations, collaborative work is valued and rewarded, whereas in other organizations, only individual effort is recognized.

Unfortunately, organizations spend less time communicating their cultures, mission, and values than they do explaining the details of the task, thereby increasing the possibility of misunderstandings related to violations of cultural norms. Time pressure is often the reason cited for this (Gomez, 2009). Meiners (2004) concluded that if a newcomer needs to be integrated into the flow of work quickly and the supervisor has limited time because of other obligations, it may limit their interactions to "critical" matters, which tend to involve task information. But why do the new employees not speak up and ask questions? Remember, new employees are often trying hard to make a good impression and unfortunately think that asking a question may make them appear as if they are incompetent or complaining. Consequently, new employees attempt to fill in the gaps in their knowledge base. They are called on to perform tasks immediately that require a great deal more information, and yet it is impossible to give a new person all the information needed from the beginning. We cannot remember everything someone might need to know to perform the job well. So, the new employee makes assumptions.

One of the major functions of communication is the reduction of uncertainty. Communication researchers have known for a long time that the most difficult situation to respond to is an uncertain one. If a person always ignores you, you develop coping strategies to handle the feelings of rejection. What really throws you off balance is when that same person suddenly starts talking to you in a kind way. You do not have a set of strategies with which to respond. Therefore, the more information newcomers can collect about individuals and the organization and its mission, the more uncertainty is reduced.

Weick (1979), in his classic text *The Social Psychology of Organizing*, asserted that the more equivocal (uncertain) the message, the more the recipient needs help from others to understand it: "Organizations have developed as social systems for resolving equivocality and increasing the certainty of life. Organizations are established to undertake many of the more difficult tasks human beings face" (p. 111). Communication strategies help increase certainty. When the situation presented has little equivocality, organizational members can depend on rules to guide their behavior. As equivocality increases, they will need more communication to respond to it. If these rules have been written from a majority view of the world, then minority employees will have a difficult time understanding and following them.

Being "different" from the dominant group in the workplace creates additional barriers to being successful. Those differences may be the result of race, gender, age, religion, ethnicity, disability, sexual orientation, or language. During the assimilation process, new employees may begin to feel they must "sell out" their own values to adopt the values of the organization. Blank and Slipp (2000) identified three guidelines for consideration in "buying in" instead of "selling out" (p. 105). They suggest there are ways to become assimilated into the organizational culture without giving up your own identity. These guidelines will help you determine which you are attempting to do:

- Your fundamental value system is the final arbiter of "right." If your values—which you learned as a child, tested as an adolescent, and solidified as an adult—are in direct violation of or in contradiction with the organization's values, and you discard your values, you could be in danger of "selling out."

- If you know yourself—that is, have validated your talents, skills, and abilities—and perform a function or accept a position well beneath your talents, you could be in danger of "selling out."

- If you accept, without question, the culture of an organization that flaunts its discrimination against or disrespect for your culture, you could be in danger of "selling out."

This issue is a very personal matter. The organization is trying to help new employees assimilate into the organization, and you must decide if that assimilation is asking you to give up too much of your culture. Several options are available. First, you may decide that you will not be accepted no matter what you do and therefore you seek employment elsewhere. Another is to remain in the organization but dramatically change your style. A third is to adopt the organization's values and politics. Finally, you can adapt to the organization's culture while maintaining your own sense of identity. You go as far as you can to fit in without giving up your core values and political views. This last choice implies mutual accommodation between yourself and the organization. The type and structure of the organization you find yourself in and the structure of that organization will determine how much flexibility you have to make these changes.

According to Chapter 2, classical organizations spend a great deal of time figuring out how to be precise in their actions—thus the reason for time-and-motion studies and bureaucratic rules. They tend to rely heavily on policies and procedure manuals, thinking that if it is all written down, certainly a new employee need only turn to the appropriate page in the manual to find the answer to any question. The quantity of information shared, however, does not necessarily indicate its quality. Employees, no matter how much information might be shared, can still be disappointed with their knowledge about the company. It is the kind of information that is shared, and the context in which it is shared, that makes it meaningful. Often, employees feel there is no legitimate way for them to provide feedback about working conditions or concerns about tasks they are being asked to perform.

Organizational Assimilation

A useful context for a discussion of organizational socialization is provided by the concept of organizational assimilation put forward by Jablin (2001). Jablin defined **organizational assimilation** as "the process by which an individual becomes integrated into the culture of an organization" (2001, p. 755); in other words, how well the new member adapts to norms of behavior and adopts new attitudes valued by the organization. Organizational assimilation can be broken down into two parts: socialization (what the organization does) and individualization or personalization (what the individual does; Kramer, 2010). For example, the organization may plan an orientation session for new employees in which rules and regulations are discussed; however, the employee may learn a great deal about what is expected of her from informal conversations she has over coffee with her colleagues.

Bullis and Stout (2000) posited three assumptions on which the concept of assimilation is based. First, as evident in the description by Jablin, "individuals as well as organizations are active agents" (p. 51). Assimilation is a dual process in which organizations and individuals influence one another. Often, *assimilation* is used as a synonym for *socialization*, but this is an incorrect use of the term. Socialization is but one half of the assimilation process; individualization efforts by the newcomer must also be considered when discussing assimilation. Second, "organizations are bounded entities" (p. 49). Bullis and Stout argued that as we adopt the language of "outsiders" and "insiders," we "assume that organizations have boundaries through which individuals cross" (p. 49). Research, then, which likens the organization to a machine, organism, or culture, has been concerned with articulating the processes that lead to a "successful" boundary crossing. The third assumption regarding assimilation is that it occurs in phases: "A relationship develops over time, in stages, between the organization and individual" (p. 49). The stages typically consist of *anticipatory socialization, encounter,* and *metamorphosis* (Jablin, 2001). The assimilation model also includes organizational exit, though we will not be covering that in this chapter (see Benedict, 2020, for a review of that stage of assimilation).

Anticipatory Socialization

Anticipatory socialization is the first phase of assimilation. During this phase, newcomers form expectations regarding particular occupations and what it would be like to be a member of a particular organization. Anticipatory socialization typically takes two forms: (1) vocational anticipatory socialization and (2) organizational anticipatory socialization. **Vocational anticipatory socialization** includes the information gathered during childhood and adolescence from a variety of sources, including parents, peers and friends, teachers/school, media, and part-time jobs (Aley & Levine, 2020; Jablin, 1987, 2001; Vangelisti, 1988). Such information may affect both occupational choice and expectations for organizational behavior, including communication. This is the information that enables a person to form impressions of what it would be like to be a teacher, a lawyer, or an artist. It is all the general impressions that have been formed over the years through exposure to mass media and social media, as well as attitudes expressed by those in a person's immediate environment.

Recent research has explored the five sources of vocational anticipatory socialization and forwarded some interesting results. For example, parents have been found to be the most influential source of career information for young adults. If the young adult knows their career aspirations, then they spend most of their talk time about future careers with their parents; however, if they do not know their aspirations, then they spend their talk time about the subject with other influencers. When young adults do seek information from influencers outside of their parents, they tend to seek it from people who identify as the same gender as they do (Aley & Levine, 2020). The role of part-time jobs in the vocational anticipatory socialization process has also been explored and has demonstrated that these experiences do have socialization benefits. Most notably, part-time jobs provide the young adult with a greater sense of self-efficacy in that task skills and professional norms are learned from their experiences (Sandor Herrygers & Bieland, 2017).

It is important to note that some researchers prefer the term role anticipatory socialization, as the term "vocational" privileges paid positions, minimizing the importance of unpaid labor (Kramer, 2010). One perfect example of communication that could be considered as role anticipatory socialization is that which happens during participation in sports. Dailey et al. (2020) studied Special Olympics participants and found that participation in sports prepares individuals for general skills, such as teamwork and time management. It also provided participants with the level of confidence necessary to enter the world of work.

Organizational anticipatory socialization includes the information intentionally and unintentionally gathered as the job seeker interacts with potential employing organizations. This information serves to socialize job seekers even before they become members of a particular organization. Information can come from a variety of sources, including organizational literature (e.g., social media, websites, formal job postings, annual reports, company brochures) and interpersonal interactions, such as job interviews, company visits, and interactions with incumbents.

In addition to the aforementioned sources of information and the information covered in the prior chapter regarding realistic recruitment strategies, recent research has explored the role of internships in the organizational anticipatory socialization process (Dailey, 2016). In her research, Dailey found that interns may perhaps have an interesting advantage in learning about the organization over full-time organizational newcomers. Interns and organizations are involved in a mutual persuasive exchange, each trying to convince the other of a fit for possible long-term employment. During this time, the intern may actually have access to information provided by the organization that even full-fledged newcomers do not have. In fact, Dailey argued that if an intern is subsequently hired as a full-time organizational member, they perhaps should not be considered "new" as they may feel like full-fledged members rather than an organizational newcomer.

Organizational Encounter

The encounter phase, also known as the entry phase, of the assimilation process occurs when "the newcomer confronts the reality of his or her organizational role" (Jablin, 1987, p. 694). Although the individual is a formal member of the organization at this point, they have yet to gain the status of "insider" because they have not been socialized by the organization nor have they been given the opportunity to individualize role requirements.

Jablin (2001), in reviewing the research on communication processes during this phase, indicated that information is shared between the individual and the organization in a variety of ways: formal orientation programs, socialization strategies (discussed in the next section of this chapter), training programs, formal mentoring, informal mentoring, and so on. We can also add to this list the information that is communicated via communication technology, such as social media, websites, document sharing, video streaming, instant messaging, texting, and other electronic sources. Gossip has also been shown to have potential socialization benefits as new members may not only learn about the culture of the organization but engaging in gossip can also foster a sense of inclusion between the newcomer and the existing members (Ribarsky & Hammonds, 2019). Prior relevant experience also can help the newcomer learn their roles better as role expectations may be clearer to them than for those newcomers with no prior relevant experience (Kowtha, 2018).

Regardless of the channel used, organizational encounter is characterized by information giving to the newcomer, as well as information seeking by the newcomer. Information giving and information seeking are particularly interesting behaviors because they involve active attempts by the newcomer to affect her organizational situation. We begin with information giving from the organization to the newcomer, which takes the primary form of *organizational socialization*.

Organizational Socialization Processes

Organizational socialization represents the efforts of the organization in the assimilation process. Van Maanen and Schein (1979) defined **organizational socialization** as "the process by which an individual acquires the social knowledge and skills necessary to assume an organizational role" (p. 211). Bullis (1993) extended this notion and suggested that socialization is a "process through which newcomers become organizational members" (p. 10). Socialization processes are considered important to other relevant issues, such as "newcomer acculturation, employee attitudes and behaviors, and the shaping of newcomers' identities" (p. 10). Organizational socialization, then, is the organization's attempt to transform an organizational newcomer into a full-fledged member by instilling into the person the organization's norms, values, and beliefs, as well as the formal and informal role requirements associated with the person's position.

The socialization process applies primarily to new members because their needs for cultural adaptation are most salient, but it also serves as a means of support and renewal for an existing value system and longer term employees. In fact, this process occurs at every level of the organization and at each change the employee makes throughout her career. As the organization changes, the socialization process continues for all its members (Kramer, 2010; Kramer & Miller, 2014).

Van Maanen and Schein (1979) suggested that the socialization process is critical to the survival of the organization. Existing organizational members must teach newcomers the breadth and depth of the organizational world, including not only the job duties but also how people interact with one another, the cultural norms, and expected behaviors. As new members are "tested" in this setting for their skills and degree of commitment to the organization and the work, they can receive a number of benefits. Van Maanen and Schein pointed out these benefits. Once having passed these tests, these new members are granted inclusionary rights, which then permit them to be privy to information in the organization that they did not previously have access to and to understand how organizational members communicate with one another in ways that outsiders or newcomers would not understand. In short, the socialization process allows new members more and more access to the internal workings of the organization.

As indicated in Chapter 7, organizations expend significant resources on recruiting, hiring, and training new employees. Consequently, they have a considerable interest in ensuring that newcomers perform their roles in the intended manner and understand and adapt to the organization's culture. A sizable amount of research has been conducted investigating socialization processes and their effects (see Allen et al., 2017) for a review of this research). "Socialization tactics have been linked to adjustment outcomes, such as role clarity and self-efficacy, which in turn influence outcomes such as organizational commitment, turnover intentions, job performance, and job satisfaction" (Former & Timmerman, 2009, p. 246).

Much of the research on socialization processes has stemmed from work conducted by Van Maanen and Schein, who argued that an organization has a variety of processes available for socializing newcomers and that these processes have different potential effects. The authors were particularly concerned with the effect socialization may have on newcomers' response to their roles, which they defined as having three components: (1) a "content or knowledge base," which involves the range of possible solutions to problems that are encountered on a daily basis in the role; (2) a "strategic base," "which suggests the ground rules for the choosing of particular solutions" (p. 227); and (3) an "explicit and implicit mission, purpose, or mandate," which involves the relationship of the particular role to the overall mission of the organization. Also important is the notion of a role boundary, which "refers to whatever delineates the perimeter—and thereby the scope—of a role" (Ashforth et al., 2000, p. 474). Van Maanen and Schein's work on socialization tactics has been praised for capturing the communicative process of socialization, so next, we pay particular attention to their work (Gomez, 2009).

Van Maanen and Schein (1979) contended that how an organization socializes its newcomers will affect the manner in which the newcomer approaches their role. The authors refer to this connection as the newcomer's response to socialization. A newcomer could accept the role as it is presented, without questioning the status quo, which is considered a **custodial response**. Another response possibility is an **innovative response**, in which the newcomer makes substantive changes to the knowledge base or strategy associated with the role or redefines the purpose of role functions (i.e., the mission). In either case, the socialization tactics that the organization employs should affect the response, either custodial or innovative. If the employee assumes the custodial response to socialization, on the one hand, the organization will lose those skills and special abilities that the new employee may have brought to the position and the organization. On the other hand, the newcomer should not ignore the role that the organization expects to be filled.

To complete their argument, Van Maanen and Schein (1979) offered six pairs of socialization tactics that organizations could employ. They are presented as oppositional pairs. The list of tactics is not considered by the researchers to be exhaustive or mutually exclusive. The pairs of socialization tactics are collective versus individual, formal versus informal, sequential versus random, fixed versus variable, serial versus disjunctive, and investiture versus divestiture.

Collective socialization involves putting a group of recruits through a common set of experiences together. Peer pressure serves to "promote and intensify the demands of the socializing agents" (p. 233). Military boot camps are an excellent example of this type of socialization. In the corporate world, many large organizations conduct group training where new recruits are put together at an off-site location to learn the task and the organization's cultural requirements. This tactic is often used when the organization wants to build a collective sense of reality. **Individual socialization** occurs when recruits are brought into the organization in relative isolation from one another and put through a unique set of experiences. Examples would be apprenticeship programs, trainee assignments, and on-the-job training. The views of those socialized individually are likely to be far less homogeneous than the views of those socialized collectively.

Formal socialization occurs when newcomers are segregated, in one form or another, from regular organizational members. This tactic is used "in organizations where specific preparation for new status is involved and where it is deemed important that a newcomer learn the 'correct' attitudes, values, and protocol associated with the new role" (p. 237). Segregation can involve actual physical separation from normal daily procedures, or it could involve designating the individual as a "newcomer" in some way, such as with special uniforms or badges. Police departments, for example, often segregate newcomers from incumbents by having the recruit wear a different uniform from that of a full-fledged officer. **Informal socialization** processes do not segregate the newcomer in any special way or distinguish the newcomer's role specifically but instead use informal, laissez-faire socialization for recruits. It is important to realize that because the newcomer is not distinguished from other organizational members, the mistakes that person makes are "real" mistakes. When a recruit is segregated from other organizational members and thereby designated a "newcomer," mistakes are expected and more easily excused.

Sequential socialization is the degree to which the organization specifies a certain set of steps to be completed to advance to the target role. Professional training programs such as medical school require a series of steps that the aspiring doctor must complete before being allowed to practice. **Random socialization** "occurs when the sequence of steps leading to the target role is unknown, ambiguous, or continually changing" (p. 241). In this situation, the newcomer must provide their own sense of logic to the information provided about reaching the target role. In some extreme circumstances, the newcomer is personally responsible for creating the steps. A potential consequence of random socialization is that the newcomer is exposed to a variety of viewpoints within the organization as they attempt to negotiate their way through the process of establishing and clarifying the necessary steps.

When an organization uses **fixed socialization**, it provides the newcomer with a precise timetable for when to expect progression to the target role. For example, many organizations tell newcomers that they should expect a probationary period (e.g., 6 months or a year) when they begin employment, after which they can expect an increase in pay, benefits, and job duties. **Variable socialization** processes provide no real cues to the newcomer as to when to expect movement to the target role. Van Maanen and Schein argued that different people may progress at different rates, making it very difficult to predict when a particular boundary passage may occur.

If an organization uses **serial socialization**, it uses an experienced organizational member, who occupies a similar role to the one the newcomer will occupy, to help "groom" the newcomer (p. 247). An experienced member serves as a role model or perhaps a mentor for the newcomer. However, when an organization uses **disjunctive socialization** processes, no role models are available or provided for the newcomer. In this situation, the newcomer is left alone to discover the ins and outs of the position.

Disjunctive socialization may occur, for example, when the organization has undergone a major restructuring. Often, restructuring is accompanied by a "housecleaning" of sorts, and new personnel are brought in to occupy open positions.

Finally, the **investiture socialization** tactic affirms the personal characteristics and identity that the newcomer brings to the organization. In essence, the organization is saying, "We like you the way you are." Investiture socialization attempts to make the transition to the new organization as comfortable as possible for the new employee. By welcoming the individual and everything they have to offer, the stress accompanying the transition should be reduced. **Divestiture socialization**, however, seeks to deny and strip away certain personal characteristics of a newcomer. Boot camp is the prototypical example of divestiture socialization. In the military, the organization is attempting to increase predictability and standardization; one way to do that is to strip away individuality and rebuild the members in a particular way.

Van Maanen and Schein's argument is that the type of socialization processes employed will affect the response of newcomers to their roles. A custodial response to socialization is when the newcomer performs the role requirements exactly as they are prescribed; in doing so, they maintain the status quo. Alternatively, an innovative response to socialization has the newcomer expanding the way a role is performed or even the content of the role itself. This type of response helps create change in the organization, at least in the areas connected to the role. Reviews of the extant research conducted on this topic (see Saks & Ashforth, 1997; Jablin, 2001; Kramer, 2010; Kramer & Miller, 2014) indicate that the socialization tactics are linked with responses. Table 8.1 summarizes the tactics, as well as the associated responses:

TABLE 8.1 Socialization Tactics and Responses

SOCIALIZATION TACTIC	BRIEF DESCRIPTION	CONNECTED RESPONSE
Collective	Socialized as part of a group	Custodial
Individual	Socialized alone	Innovative
Formal	Segregated from existing members	Custodial
Informal	Not distinguished as a newcomer	Innovative
Sequential	Steps to target role known	Custodial
Random	Steps to target role unknown	Innovative
Fixed	Time to target role known	Custodial
Variable	Time to target role unknown	Innovative
Serial	Mentor provided	Custodial
Disjunctive	No mentor provided	Innovative
Investiture	Personal characteristics celebrated	*unknown*
Divestiture	Personal characteristics stripped away	*unknown*

Jablin (2001) maintained that research has not been consistent in correlating the investiture-divestiture pair with a particular response.

It is important to recognize two main points in the previous discussion of socialization tactics and responses. First, this view of socialization represents a *one-way* view that minimizes the interactive nature of the communication aspects of these tactics and processes. In fact, scant research has been conducted on the communication that takes place as these socialization tactics are enacted (Kramer & Miller, 2014). Second, the relationships between the tactics and responses presented should in no way be construed as *causal*. In other words, the use of certain socialization tactics will not guarantee a certain type of response. Given the ability of human beings to exercise choice and the fact that each person is unique, there will never be a direct causal relationship that applies to every case.

Information Seeking by the Newcomer

Whether doing so actively or passively, the organizational newcomer spends much of their time during organizational encounter seeking information about their role, their coworkers, their supervisor, and the culture of the organization. Miller and Jablin (1991) identified seven general information-seeking tactics used by newcomers during the encounter phase of assimilation:

- **Overt questioning** is asking for information in a direct manner.

- **Indirect questioning** is getting another person to respond to hints and non-interrogative questions.

- **Third-party questioning** is asking someone other than the primary information source.

- **Testing** is breaking a rule and then monitoring the target person's response for information.

- **Disguising conversations** use jokes and self-disclosure to ease information from a source without being obvious.

- **Observation** is watching another's action to model that behavior.

- **Surveillance** is reflecting retrospectively on conversations and activities to determine the information needed.

Miller (1996) later determined that the use of any of these tactics depended on the level of uncertainty experienced by the newcomer and the social costs incurred from seeking the information. For example, a person asking questions might be seen as bothersome or lacking in the necessary job knowledge. Testing might be dangerous because breaking a rule to seek information could easily be seen as being insubordinate. The tactics used also varied according to the source of the information (coworker vs. boss), as well as the type of information requested (job instructions, job performance, and how others feel about the newcomer).

Metamorphosis

The final stage, **metamorphosis**, is when the new employee actually begins to change some of their behaviors and expectations to meet the standards of the new environment and begins to alter the requirements of their role to match their needs, desires, and skills. It is at this point that the newcomer makes the transition to an organizational insider. Perhaps this new organization expects people to come to work early and stay late. Without saying anything, the new employee quickly learns that they are the only one going home at five. It is also during this stage that the new employee may attempt to put their stamp on the organization, create an individual identity within the organization, stake out their territory, or obligate the organization to adapt to the new member's values in some other way. For example, college graduates are eager to put what they have learned to work and to help their new organization benefit from what they have learned in school. Older employees may resent this "newcomer" trying to show them how to do something they have been doing for years. Working out this tension is part of the metamorphosis process.

So much occurs for the organizational member as they move from the encounter stage where they are a newcomer to the metamorphosis stage where they begin to be accepted as a full-fledged member of the organization. In the remainder of the chapter, we discuss several key concepts that are important at any stage of organizational life but seem particularly relevant as the member begins to deepen their commitment and connection to the organization and vice versa—*organizational identification, emotions and emotional labor*, and *work-life balancing*.

Organizational Identification

As organizational members transition from being newcomers to being accepted as full-fledged members, many seek to connect more deeply with the organization and their coworkers than they experienced early in their tenure. What they are seeking is termed **organizational identification**, and it is something in which both the individual and the organization have a stake. The term is adopted from the writing of rhetorician Kenneth Burke and positioned in the discipline most notably by George Cheney and Phillip Tompkins. Burke (1950) believed that the hierarchies present in society naturally divide humans from one another, an idea which seemed particularly relevant to Cheney and Tompkins in the context of organizations. Creating and sustaining a sense of organizational identification is more difficult now than ever as organizations have less loyalty to their workers, and workers have multiple sources of identification to negotiate (Scott & Stephens, 2009).

Organizational identification involves an individual's sense of membership in and connection with an organization. Bullis and Bach (1989) described it in the following way: "Individuals identify with their collectives . . . to the extent that they feel similar to other members, they feel a sense of belonging, and they consider themselves to be members" (p. 275). A variety of sources of identification are available for an organizational member, including intraorganizational sources, such as the organization as a whole, a work team, a department, a union, a lunch group, a supervisor, and extraorganizational sources, such as family, customers, influential public figures, and the media. According to Morgan et al. (2004), "Sources then become places both to draw from and to extend forward attachments to certain groups or organizations" (p. 363). Social media is an interesting context for where intra- and extraorganizational sources of identification intermingle. There is some evidence, for example, that when organizational members are connected on Facebook and then are naturally exposed to each other's outside interests, identification could strengthen with the organization (Bartels et al., 2019).

Organizational identification is not quite as straightforward as we once thought. For example, the realities of the modern workplace have called into question the desire of organizational members to want to have a high level of organizational identification, and at the same time, organizations have questioned the viability of attempting to promote identification with all its workers (Cheney et al., 2014). As the workplace becomes more unstable, the nature and extent of organizational identification fluctuates (Bartels et al., 2009; Millward et al., 2007). For example, organizational members may find themselves in a situation where their company is in turbulence. It is possible that some members of this organization may not want to identify with it any longer. Pepper and Larson (2006) referred to this as **disidentification**, which is "a purposely chosen, negotiated response by organizational members facing significant change and upheaval in their actual work lives" (p. 64). Importantly, disidentification is not synonymous with low identification; it is instead a purposeful fostering by the worker of separateness, disconnection, and emotional and social exclusion from the organization. In addition to disidentification, researchers have developed other terms to describe various states of identification, including "*dei*dentification, *ambivalent* identification, *under*identification, *schizo*identification, and dual identities" (Kramer & Miller, 2014, p. 707). Clearly, identification is a complicated concept.

Organizational identification is difficult to measure or predict. Scott and Stephens (2009) argued that organizational identification is more "fleeting" than it might otherwise be considered in research and practice. Organizational identification will fluctuate based on the activities the person is engaged in, as well as the persons with whom she is interacting. So, for example, a salesperson spending time interacting with other salespeople at a professional conference may experience greater identification with external targets than organizational identification at that point in time. As you can tell, organizational identification has been construed as both a process and a product (Scott et al., 1998). Organizational identification as a *process* encapsulates the notion that people act so as to identify with a certain aspect(s) of their organization. In this manner, organizational identification is fluid, changing, and intimately related to the process of communication (Gossett, 2002). As a *product*, organizational identification is seen as a result of socialization efforts by the organization.

Despite its complex nature, organizational identification has been correlated with several relevant organizational outcomes, including motivation, job satisfaction, job performance, decision making, role orientation and conflict, employee interaction, and length of service, among others (Cheney, 1983, p. 342). High organizational identification has been correlated with increased satisfaction and decreased turnover, whereas low organizational identification is related to communicative isolation, negative attitudes toward the organization, and inappropriate organizational behavior (Gossett, 2002). In addition to individual-level outcomes, organizational members with high organizational identification have been shown to communicatively defend their organizations' wrongdoings (Ploeger & Bisel, 2013).

Emotions in Organizational Settings

When considering all the different things that organizational members must learn to be successful at a job, one of the last things people often consider is what is expected emotionally. According to Rafaeli and Sutton (1989), it is important to know the rules for emotional management to understand organizational culture. Appropriate emotional management will help an individual develop relationships, and it can increase an individual's chances of achieving career success (Staw et al., 1994; Waldron, 2000). Consider the following story of Dani, an in-home daycare provider:

> Her first child arrived at 5:30 each morning, and the last child leaves around 6:30 in the evening. No matter how she is feeling or what she has on her mind, caregivers expect that she answers the door with a smile and greets them and their child enthusiastically. Some days, some of the children are challenging, and like any other job, she looks forward to the end of the workday. But even the last parent of the day expects her to engage in small talk and to be as upbeat as she was when they dropped off their child hours ago. Sometimes they even sit down and expect her to listen to the details of their day and show concern over what they have gone through. They don't seem to care that she still has her own children or personal work to do. Dani knows that if she ever displays frustration, anger, or relief that the parents might choose to take their children to another provider. Parents rarely think that Dani is doing this work to provide for her own family; instead, they focus on how much they must love their children, and sometimes they even get jealous about how much time she spends with their kids.

The U.S. economy has become increasingly service based; in 2020, 80 percent of employees worked to provide services rather than products or goods (statista.com). Quality of customer service is directly related to the quality of interaction between an employee and a customer. Given the growth of service-based jobs and the importance of perceived quality customer satisfaction, there is an increased need for organizations to prescribe appropriate emotional responses in employee-client interactions.

Emotional labor is the management of one's emotions to induce a desired reaction or response in another individual. Hochschild (1983) developed this concept after investigating the ways in which flight attendants and bill collectors managed their own emotions in order to achieve the organization's goals. Emotional labor involves managing not only one's own feelings but also the emotions of others to create an organizationally deemed appropriate response from both the employee and the client. We can see emotional labor in Dani's story. She must manage her emotional displays in such a way that parents leave each day feeling a particular way. The appropriate emotions for both Lisa and her clients are dictated by the organization's desired response from the client, which is for the parents to leave happy (and continue to bring their children back in order for the company to financially succeed.).

Emotional labor requires attention to emotional requirements (display rules) and the efforts to meet these requirements (emotional regulation). **Emotion regulation**, the efforts to increase, maintain, or decrease one or more components of an emotion, is often accomplished through surface acting or deep acting (Grandey & Sayre, 2019; Gross, 1999). **Surface acting** involves the external state of emotion or public display of emotions. Hochschild (1983) discussed surface acting as body language, while Grandey and Sayre (2019) described it as behavioral modulation that is done reactively. Surface acting might include amplification or suppression. *Amplification* is the initiating or enhancing of public displays of emotion whereas *suppression* consists of reducing or eliminating public displays of emotions (Cote, 2005). For example, a waitress might use surface acting to amplify their enthusiasm over a customer's birthday or a bill collector might use surface acting to suppress their job over a promotion while talking to a client.

Deep acting, on the other hand, is an emotional display that stems from an internal state or the use of cognitive strategies to proactively adapt how one is feeling (Grandey & Sayre, 2019). In deep acting, the "display is a natural result of working on feeling; the actor does not try to seem happy or sad but rather expresses spontaneously a real feeling that has been self-induced" (Hochschild, 1983, p. 35). In other words, in deep acting, employees draw on emotional memories to produce the desired emotion or emotional display. Emotional memories alone, however, are not enough to produce these emotional displays; individuals must make themselves believe they are reliving that particular experience. The emotion is genuine, but its origin is somewhere other than the employee's immediate context. Think of a time that you had to role-play; maybe the character needed to be portrayed as very angry. You were not *feeling* angry, but you needed to *display* the appropriate emotional display to play the character. If you thought of a time that you were sincerely angry and used those memories to "get into character," then you have experienced deep acting.

Research has found that when employees are hired because they have traits that closely align with the organization's emotional display expectations, they are more likely to use surface acting with less effort but deep acting more frequently (Chi & Grandey, 2016). The research has been much less consistent in regard to whether surface acting or deep acting produces the best customer service outcomes assuming that the employee is skilled at surface acting and does depend on the nature of the employee-client relationship (Christoforou & Ashforth, 2015; Grandey et al., 2017; Wang & Groth, 2014).

Emotional labor can be an intense process and researchers have linked it with health concerns, exhaustion, stress, and burnout (Jeung et al., 2018). Hochschild (1983) identified that emotional labor can lead to *overidentification*, where an employee can no longer distinguish between personalized interactions and everyday work encounters, or *separation* in that employees try to compensate for overidentification by creating an emotional separation from the work that they are doing. Other workers might compensate for emotional labor by *estranging* themselves from all levels of acting. If overidentification means that employees are too much a part of the job, then estrangement means that employees are emotionally present in too little of the job. Therefore, the goal for employees cannot be to totally mask feelings but to find a balance that meets their own needs, as well as organizational needs.

By this point, you may be overwhelmed by the prospect of burnout, job stress, and the other negative factors associated with emotional labor given the prevalence of service-oriented jobs in the United States. Morris and Feldman (1996) conceptualized emotional labor in terms beyond just emotional management. The dimensions they identified include frequency of appropriate emotional display, attentiveness to required display rules, variety of emotions required to be displayed, and emotional dissonance. The first dimension, *frequency of appropriate emotional display*, simply refers to the number of interactions and emotional displays between service providers and their clients. The second dimension, *attentiveness to required display rules*, refers to the intensity or attention that the display rules require of the employee. For example, brief emotional interactions are more likely to be scripted (e.g., please, thank you, a smile) and require less emotional intensity than more extended interactions (e.g., helping a client make burial arrangements).

The third dimension of emotional labor is the *variety of emotion required to be expressed*. Morris and Feldman (1996) argue that the greater the variety of emotions to be displayed, the more emotional labor that is involved for the employee. For example, some jobs require that the employee constantly switches between "positive emotions to build enthusiasm, negative emotions to support discipline, and neutrality of emotions to demonstrate fairness and professionalism" (p. 991). A job requiring such emotional variety requires more planning, skill, and, at times, intensity.

The final dimension in emotional labor for Morris and Feldman is *emotional dissonance*. Emotional dissonance is conflict between the emotions an individual genuinely feels and those they are required to display within the organization. The more conflict an employee feels between felt and displayed feelings, the more intense the emotional labor process is going to be. These dimensions demonstrate that not all service-intensive jobs are going to be emotionally problematic for their employees, nor are all individuals going to feel those demands the same way.

It is also important to draw a distinction between emotional labor and emotion work. Emotion work is the display of genuine or authentic emotions at work, such as that work done by health-care or human service workers. The difference between emotion work and emotional labor has largely been focused on authenticity, although stress and burnout are possible with both types of work. Because emotional work involves less acting, the stress derives from the pain of overinvolvement rather than dissonance (Keyton, 2017).

Research has indicated that emotional labor can be harmful for employees. Hochschild (1983) argued that emotional labor can lead to emotional alienation, while Van Maanen and Kunda (1989) found that emotional labor increases physical illness, burnout, and emotional numbness. Noe's (1995) research on emergency medical technicians expanded this argument by concluding that emotional labor can also cause problems in an employee's personal relationships outside of work. Other negative consequences that have been associated with emotional labor include burnout (Wharton, 1999) and depression, cynicism, and role alienation (Ashforth & Humphrey, 1993; Fineman, 1993).

Although many examples exist that demonstrate the negative effects of emotional labor, several researchers have argued that emotional labor can actually enhance the work experience. Conrad and Witte (1994) argued that there are possible health benefits to displaying positive emotions at work, even when those emotions are not genuine. Others have argued that emotional labor has a performative nature and can be enjoyable, as can be the experience of positively influencing a client's emotional state during the interaction. Shuler and Sypher (2000) conducted research on 9-1-1 operators and found that although emotional labor is trying, employees often find ways to positively manage the emotional labor, such as through humor or storytelling. In fact, some individuals may even be drawn to jobs that require emotional challenges because they enjoy the thrill of the challenge.

Organizations can also take steps to alleviate emotional labor demands. Christoforou and Ashforth (2015) found that emotional labor costs can be lessened when management allows employees autonomy to respond to their environment rather than mandating scripts that must be followed. Another study of hospital staff workers found that when employees have a supportive environment where they can express negative feelings and distress with coworkers over interactions that they have had with difficult patients, they are less likely to experience job stress and burnout (Grandey et al., 2012).

Finally, it is important to realize that the socialization process plays an important role in the ways that employees perceive and respond to emotional labor demands. The selection process has been identified in research as the "primary mechanism [for] ensuring that members would be able [to] adequately enact preferred emotion management strategies" (Scott & Myers, 2005, p. 77). Job candidates are often subjected to personality and psychological tests in addition to formal and informal job interviews. Scenarios are often presented during job interviews to gauge how the employee might respond to a given situation. The socialization process continues after an employee is hired through both formal and informal interactions. Employees will often be subjected to repeated exposure to emotionally intense stimuli (i.e., bank tellers may watch films recreating robberies and then be expected to respond to them; flight attendants will practice emergency evacuation procedures) to condition them to the organization-ally deemed appropriate response. Numerous organizations will use simulations and role-playing activities to socialize employees on the appropriate emotional displays to a variety of employee-client interactions.

Work-Life Balancing

As you begin to explore the concept of work-life balancing, read the following sce-narios and ask yourself what do they have in common?

> Kylie, 25, desperately needs to have a root canal after damaging one of her teeth while playing volleyball over the weekend. She works full time and has dental insurance, but the dentist's office is only open during the hours that she is scheduled to work.

> Chris, 31, is a single father whose child is on the autism spectrum. Chris's son needs to see a developmental pediatrician, a speech therapist, and an occupational therapist several times a month. He has worked full time for his company for 5 years and has good insurance, but he needs to attend his son's myriad appointments on a weekly basis.

> Lyle, 56, is the primary caretaker for her mother. As her mother ages, she experiences more medical problems, including visual impairment to the point where she can no longer drive herself to appointments. Lyle's mother also has difficulty remembering all of the doctor's directions, so Lyle needs to attend the appointments to help her mother keep all of the information straight.

In each situation, the individual is a loyal and productive full-time organizational member; at the same time, each has personal responsibilities that require them to be someplace during their regular working day to fulfill these responsibilities. In Kylie's case, her absence is unplanned and infrequent. Chris is faced with the need for weekly absences, but they are planned well in advance of the workweek beginning, whereas Lyle's absences are often unpredictable and of an emergency nature. While we have been discussing many of the challenges individuals may face within an organization as they try to negotiate their professional identities, individuals also need to negotiate how they will balance their personal lives outside of work with an organization's needs.

When work and life roles clash, negative effects on an organization can include turnover and lower job satisfaction rates. For the individual, this conflict can reduce organizational identification, commitment, and morale and increase the likelihood of stress, depression, physical manifestations such as ulcers, or substance abuse (Frone, 2000; Frone et al., 1997; Grzywacz & Bass, 2003). This conflict can also reduce overall satisfaction with life and personal relationships (Heilmann et al., 2009; Judge et al., 2006).

When the term work-life balance first appeared in research literature, it was rarely defined, with the assumption being that it was self-explanatory. Later, studies considered balance to be those times when there was little to no conflict or negative spillover in either one's work or personal life (Greenhaus & Allen, 2011). More recent organizational studies have focused on work-life balance as the degree of effectiveness and satisfaction that an employee has both at work and in their personal life, as well as how consistent that balance is with their values and priorities (Greenhaus & Allen, 2011). Balance often needs to be talked about as a particular point in time, as well as an ideal that may or may not be achievable (Adkins & Premeaux, 2019). This is why many researchers prefer the term *balancing* when discussing work and life because balance implies a static process that can be achieved and maintained, while balancing requires an ongoing commitment and effort (Comer & Stites-Doe, 2006).

Work-life balance policies can be described as *enabling* or *enclosing* policies (Bourdeau et al., 2019). Enabling policies are those policies that give employees greater freedom over when and where they work. Examples of enabling policies include leave policies, such as the Family Medical Leave Act or sick leave and tele- or flex work. These policies give individuals more time away from work. Enclosing policies, on the other hand, are policies such as on-site childcare or gyms that promote greater availability and longer hours on the actual work premises. Enclosing policies provide benefits or services that employees would typically need to seek outside of work hours and spaces.

Regardless of the definition used, most organizational communication research has focused on workplace accommodations for working parents. However, there are studies that examine the challenges individuals face as they try to balance caretaking roles for parents or grandparents or their own health management in the case of a chronic illness. The most commonly discussed accommodations include on-site dependent care, telecommuting, and flexible scheduling. Accommodation policies, though, have not eliminated the struggle that individuals feel when attempting to balance work and family. For example, in one study, mothers working from home reported higher levels of conflict and fatigue than their male counterparts (Kim et al., 2019).

These struggles can be understood in terms of where they cause conflict or unbalance: in the work domain or the personal domain. Greenhaus and Beutell (1985) defined these two types of conflict as work-to-home conflict and home-to-work conflict. **Work-to-home conflict** occurs when participation in work interferes with home roles or activities. Working late and missing a child's school conference or traveling out of town for work the night of your wedding anniversary are examples of work-to-home conflict. Work activities caused conflict or stress in your personal life because you could not fulfill your obligations or participate in meaningful personal activities. **Home-to-work conflict** occurs when an employee's home activities and commitments interfere with work responsibilities. Examples could include missing an important presentation at work because of a doctor's appointment for an elderly parent or not being able to stay late because of lack of childcare.

Telework (working from locations other than a principal office one or more days per week) is the most commonly presented solution for individuals trying to balance work and life. From an organizational perspective, telework can be a cost-saving option. From an individual perspective, for someone caring for an ill spouse, small child, or managing a chronic condition, the benefits seem obvious—you can work around your schedule and balance all of your role demands. The research shows a much more complicated picture though. Working from home increases an employee's flexibility to schedule around their other life demands, which can lower work-to-home conflict, but at the same time, working from home blurs work-home boundaries (Versey, 2015). Using home space for work activities can lead to increased working hours or an inability to mentally turn off work, which can also increase work-to-home conflict (Delanoeije et al., 2019). At the same time, individuals often choose to work from home because they have responsibilities that demand their attention, or they take on more responsibilities because they are working from home, which increases the likelihood of home-to-work conflict (Delanoeije et al., 2019).

When looking at work-life segmentation, it is important to distinguish between an individual's preferences and their actual behaviors (Allen et al., 2014; Rothbard & Ollier-Malaterre, 2015). An individual might believe that it is best practice to use evenings and weekends for relaxation and personal time but in practice check email or engage in other work activities. Organizational culture may encourage integration or segmentation practices that differ from an individual's preferences. An organization's work-life culture includes perceptions about time demands, consequences of using work-life policies and programs, and perceived managerial support (Thompson et al., 1999). Perceptions about an organization's work-life culture are gathered during the socialization process based on formal policies, actual practices, and expectations. Consider the informal message that receiving an email from your supervisor after hours sends; do they expect you to read and respond to the message after hours? Do they expect you to be working after hours? Like other learned roles and behaviors, employees often adapt their work-life behaviors to manage boundaries according to the perceived organizational culture. Research has found that employees are less able to detach from work when they perceive a high culture or expectation of integration with work and home (Foucreault et al., 2016).

As with other socialization processes, much learning comes from watching other organizational members and how they respond to a variety of situations. Kirby and Krone (2002) examined working parents' decision to use a variety of family-friendly organizational policies and found that coworkers exert a great deal of influence over whether an individual chooses to use a policy. Individuals will often choose to ignore an existing policy because they fear how their coworkers will perceive them if they do use it. Another study found that informal company signals, such as a manager not making use of available policies, could also create a workplace environment that limits accommodation usage (Feeney & Stritch, 2019). Consequently, the existence of such policies may do little to alleviate the work-family balance for a significant number of individuals.

However, not all research focuses on the negative or conflictual nature of work-life balancing. The **work-family enrichment** model suggests that the experiences and resources that individuals gain in one role (employment) will improve the quality of life that they experience in their other roles, such as being a friend or family member (Greenhaus & Powell, 2006). Resources shared between roles include skills and perspectives; psychological and physical resources; social capital, such as networks; flexibility; and material resources. For example, if you are the primary caregiver for your sibling with special needs, you might learn patience that can, in turn, translate into patience with coworkers or clients. An employee might learn multitasking skills that may contribute to them becoming a more organized, less stressed caregiver to a teenager with a hectic social calendar. In other words, dual roles can be mutually reinforcing and increase satisfaction with roles at both home and work.

One's experiences and perceptions of one's work-life balancing are dependent on a number of individual and situational characteristics. These factors include personality and degree of neuroticism (Bruck & Allen, 2003), an individual's level of perfectionism (Mitchelson, 2009), and their job and family demands (Delanoeije et al., 2019). Methot and LePine (2016) also argued that individuals have different segmentation preferences on how much they prefer to protect work from home (work protection preference) or protect home from work intrusions (home-work preference). The experience of balancing is going to be very different from one individual to the next depending on their individual wants and needs.

The metamorphosis stage of the assimilation process is a communicatively complex one. As members move from being newcomers to becoming accepted as full-fledged members, they must constantly communicatively manage who they are in relation to how they want to connect to the organization and its members, the emotional expectations of the position, and the emotional work that goes into balancing work and life relationships, opportunities, and obligations.

Summary

When newcomers enter an organization, they are in definite need of information about the job, the organization, the other members, and the culture. Organizations attempt to provide information during this time, and individuals attempt to supply information about themselves, but not all needs can be anticipated, and misunderstandings often arise. Organizations and individuals engage in formal and informal communicative behavior to attempt to reduce those misunderstandings, yet they still arise.

In this chapter, we introduced the concept of organizational assimilation and described its two parts: socialization and individualization or personalization. The phases of organizational assimilation include anticipatory socialization (consisting of vocational anticipatory socialization and organizational anticipatory socialization), organizational encounter (with particular attention to the information-seeking tactics employed by newcomers), and metamorphosis, which is when the newcomer transforms into a full-fledged organizational member and loses their newcomer status. We paid particular attention to three areas that must be communicatively managed by organizational members: (1) organizational identification, (2) emotions and emotional labor, and (3) work-life balancing. We also discussed the important concept of organizational identification, and showed how it is far more complicated than originally described in the early research on the concept.

The organizational assimilation process combines the interrelated concerns of the socialization goals of the organization and the individualization goals of the worker. Throughout this process, which begins before the worker joins the organization and continues to the end of employment, the organization adapts to the new worker, and the new worker adapts to the job and cultural demands of the new organization. Organizations and individuals need to work together to balance the needs of the individual and the needs of the organization in a way that is productive and healthy for both parties. The success of this enterprise is closely tied to the energy and effectiveness of the assimilation process.

Supervisor–Subordinate Communication

LEARNING OBJECTIVES

1. Recall the importance of the supervisor–subordinate relationship in an organization
2. Analyze the gaps in understanding and communication in a supervisor–subordinate relationship
3. Outline the characteristics of higher- and lower-quality leader-member exchange relationships
4. Explain the relevance of trust, feedback, upward influence, and upward dissent to the supervisor–subordinate relationship
5. Describe the use of different communication technologies relevant to the supervisor–subordinate relationship

Perhaps no relationship in the workplace is as important as the one between a supervisor and a subordinate—the boss and the worker. The success of both parties, as well as the success of the organization, is dependent on an effective and efficient relationship between these two people. As important as this relationship is, it is often fraught with problems, particularly misunderstandings.

Differences are inherent in the supervisor–subordinate relationship; the differences are based on status, hierarchical level, power, access to resources, age, sex, gender, experience, technical expertise, ethnicity, commitment to the organization, ethical perspectives, values, and so on. Whatever the basis, supervisors and subordinates readily express a feeling of separation caused by these differences.

To demonstrate the often contentious nature of the supervisor–subordinate relationship, we offer three brief segments from interviews conducted for this textbook. We begin with LaKiah:

> I have had a very bad boss in the past. He had absolutely no idea what he was doing, and I had to take it upon myself to learn and train myself. He was an ineffective leader because he had no skill when it came to the job he was supposed to do. He was supposed to train us; however, he did not know any of the material, which set us up for failure. His

behavior resulted in him not having the job for a long period of time, but
I left before he was fired because I could not stand having him as a boss.

Second, we have Jim, a director of public works, who was in charge of a supervisor attempting to cover up very dangerous decisions he made that endangered his subordinates' safety:

> On one weekend, there were three water main breaks requiring repair, and it was cold out. The following week, an employee who was on two of the repairs privately reported to me that the supervisor on the jobs did not require the employees to install the shoring (safety walls to protect the workers) before entering the excavation. The equipment was on-site, he reported, but not used. I told the employee I would look into it, and he asked me to keep his name out of any investigation. After I began a quiet investigation, the supervisor became aware and spoke with other employees who had been on the digs and instructed them to lie to me if they were asked if shoring was used. As I moved through interviews with all employees involved, it became apparent that shoring was not used. It also was apparent that several of the employees were very hesitant about speaking with me and revealing the truth out of fear of retribution from the supervisor.

Finally is this situation described by Harold:

> Luckily, I have only had one tyrant for a boss. I was teaching as an instructor at a private college and was the youngest member of the faculty. She would communicate bluntly, abruptly, and with dictatorial tone and content in private company. But when we might be walking down the hall past her dean's office, she would slip her arm into mine, smile broadly, and chat as if discussing important matters of mutual delight. A complete farce. Other annoying habits included observing instructors on the way in and calling to their offices with critiques of clothing and hair (wrong type, too long, etc.). Eventually, she was dismissed, but the hours on end it took to document her antics were wasted hours that could have been better devoted toward the educational mission.

As is obvious from these stories, relations between supervisors and subordinates often are fragile; both parties must exert energy (particularly communicative energy) to construct and maintain a productive (if not minimally adequate) relationship.

In this chapter, we discuss various aspects of the supervisor–subordinate relationship. We begin with a general overview of the relationship and then move to a discussion of misunderstandings in this context. Following that, we discuss a prevalent theory regarding the relationship, leader–member exchange theory. Next, we explore several relevant communication activities in this important dyad. We conclude the chapter with a discussion of several communication technologies and how they each address and create misunderstandings.

As you read this chapter and learn about supervisor–subordinate communication, please keep the following story from Brent in mind:

> So about a year ago, I got a new supervisor. I am a pharmacy supervisor, but he is the manager of pharmacy operations. Multiple pharmacy supervisors report to him. He came to the organization from a different organization that is in the same healthcare field. He was the manager of operations with another organization, so he did have experience as a manager but no experience as a manager in our organization directly. As an organization, each pharmacy is expected to do certain tasks that our reviews are based on, and they are based on providing the best quality of care we can to our patients. This includes things like providing immunizations, doing medication reviews to see if there are any issues or problems with our patients, and then there are other things included, such as budget and minimizing overtime. It is overall about the patients' health but also for the business to run efficiently and profitably.
>
> When he came on as my supervisor, my pharmacy was not hitting a lot of our goals. We had a very young, new staff. One had only been on for 6 months and another was just over a year. So a lot of these target numbers that we were supposed to be achieving, we were not reaching. This is because they were still learning the basics of their jobs within the pharmacy. I had monthly meetings with my new supervisor discussing these numbers and what we needed to do. After a couple of months of working on improving these numbers, I was pulled into a meeting with him and was told that I was on probation. So basically, I was on a review because we weren't meeting our numbers in two specific areas. If we did not improve in these areas, my job could be in jeopardy.
>
> When we were discussing these 20 different areas, we agreed that almost all of them needed to be improved on. We were working on all of these areas, but during the meetings, he never specified which ones he really wanted us to focus on and because of that, the two areas that he picked were not areas we were focused on, even though we were improving. That lack of communication and not being more specific caused my position to be in jeopardy.

As you can tell from this story, the supervisor–subordinate relationship is a complicated one. For reasons that will become clearer as the chapter unfolds, Brent found his job in jeopardy for what seems to be a lack of communication from his supervisor. As you read, apply the concepts already covered to help shed light on what occurred.

Nature and Importance of the Supervisor–Subordinate Relationship

Jablin (1979) defined supervisor–subordinate communication as "those exchanges of information and influence between organizational members at least one of whom has formal (as defined by official organizational sources) authority to direct and evaluate the activities of other organizational members" (p. 1,202). As we discuss supervisor–subordinate communication throughout this chapter and the remainder of the text, keep in mind that it is not necessarily limited to relationships that are distinguished by only one level in the hierarchy. Supervisor–subordinate relationships exist, as defined by Jablin, whenever one person has formal authority to regulate the behavior of another.

Exchanges of information and influence characterize the relationship between supervisors and subordinates. Historically, we have thought of supervisors as providing information to subordinates about their job duties, instructions for performing their jobs, rationale for performing them as directed, an orientation to organizational practices and procedures, and giving them feedback about the subordinate's job performance. We tended to think of the subordinate as providing information to their supervisor about themselves, their coworkers, what is working and what is not, and ideas for innovation (Katz & Kahn, 1978).

While these historically rooted lists definitely provide valuable insight into the current nature of communication between supervisors and subordinates, two points should be noted. First, the lists might be interpreted as saying that the supervisor tends to communicate only task-related information to the subordinate, whereas the subordinate communicates both task-related and personal information to the supervisor. As we will show in this chapter, both parties can share both kinds of information during their communication, but the extent to which they do so depends on the type of relationship they have established. Second, the communications are framed as information sharing, to the exclusion of information seeking or collaboration. Again, we will demonstrate in this chapter that, depending on the relationship type, supervisors and subordinates often engage in communicative behavior other than information sharing. Whatever form it might take, Jablin estimated, based on prior research, that "supervisors spend one-third to two-thirds of their time communicating with subordinates" (1990b, p. 177).

A critical role of communication is the maintenance of an acceptable relationship between the subordinate and the supervisor (Waldron, 1991). For an organizational newcomer, this relationship is particularly crucial for four reasons (Jablin, 1982; Nifadkar, 2020):

1. The supervisor may serve as a role model for the subordinate, sometimes through indirect observation (vicarious learning) by the subordinate.

2. The supervisor has the formal power to reward and punish the subordinate.

3. The supervisor mediates the formal downward communication flow to the subordinate.

4. The supervisor may develop a personal relationship with the subordinate.

From our perspective, maintaining an acceptable relationship with a subordinate is crucial for the supervisor for the following additional reasons:

1. The subordinate serves as an important channel of informal communication to the supervisor from other subordinates regarding both task-related and personal issues.

2. The subordinate's satisfaction with the relationship may have a direct impact on the supervisor's satisfaction with the relationship, as well as on the subordinate's overall job satisfaction.

3. The supervisor's performance is eventually dependent on the performance of the subordinate, which may be directly or indirectly tied to the quality of the supervisor–subordinate relationship.

As you can see, this critical relationship becomes complicated quite easily. Think back to Brent's story of the situation at the pharmacy as recounted in the prior section. Brent and his supervisor need each other to be successful, but either the lack of communication by Brent's supervisor or the inability of Brent to communicate appropriate information back to his supervisor has led to a situation where Brent's job (and perhaps his supervisor's) is in jeopardy. In the next section, we explore the idea that the relationship is often mired in misunderstandings.

The Prevalence of Misunderstandings in the Supervisor–Subordinate Relationship

Research regarding the supervisor–subordinate relationship has demonstrated that supervisors and subordinates often have vastly different perceptions of and meanings for important behavioral and organizational activities. In 1962, Tompkins coined the term **semantic-information distance** to represent this idea (Jablin, 1990b). Semantic-information distance is the "gap in information and understanding that exists between supervisor and subordinate on specified issues" (Dansereau & Markham, 1987). Semantic-information distance is also known as perceptual incongruence. However termed, this phenomenon has the ability to stunt the growth of the supervisor–subordinate relationship and seriously hinder organizational effectiveness (Jablin, 1979, 1984; Therkelsen & Fiebich, 2003).

Perceptual incongruence can occur in a variety of issues relevant to the supervisor–subordinate relationship. Jablin (1984) reported that supervisors have an inaccurate view of their subordinates' satisfaction with their jobs and the organization. More recent research has shown that managers often overestimate their own levels of effectiveness as related to the perceptions of their supervisees, and as that perceptual incongruence increases, the satisfaction of the employees with their organization decreases (Song & Meier, 2020). Schnake et al. (1990) found that there was perceptual incongruence regarding subordinate participation, communication openness, and feedback to subordinates regarding performance; supervisors viewed these subjects more positively than their subordinates. Research has also shown differences between lesbian, gay, and bisexual workers and heterosexual workers regarding perceptual incongruence with their supervisors (Stavrou & Solea, 2020). There are also differences in perceptual incongruencies between workers and male and female team leaders, with team members perceiving incongruencies with male team leaders more than with female team leaders (Yang & Ming Li, 2018).

Perceptual incongruence can have negative individual, relational, and organizational effects. It may be related to such issues as relationship development between the supervisor and a subordinate (Jablin, 1984), lower intrinsic job satisfaction for the subordinates, a higher level of perceived conflict, and negative perceptions of the organizational climate (Schnake et al., 1990). By contrast, perceptual *congruence* has been shown to have a positive impact on subordinate job satisfaction and subordinate satisfaction with the communication relationship with the supervisor.

Semantic-information distance, or perceptual incongruence, is often considered a natural by-product of the supervisor–subordinate relationship. Because supervisors and subordinates differ with regard to so many variables and do not always communicate effectively, gaps in understanding and perception tend to occur. Sometimes, the differences in perceptions can be reflected in the language that is used, which leads to further misunderstandings. Deanna, the co-owner of a small business, illustrates this point:

> I am the co-owner of a retail, brick and mortar boutique. I recently had two seasonal employees, ages 21 (Maritsa) and 42 (Bethany). They referred to their relationship as "she is my work mom," or "she is my work daughter." Referring to their relationship in that way made the other employees, who were similar to their ages, and my co-owner and myself uncomfortable. It also created a hierarchy that did not exist.
>
> Why is Bethany referring to Maritsa as her daughter? Bethany isn't my mom and can't tell me what to do, though our similar age difference would imply that she can. It made my co-owner and me uncomfortable, as we are around the same age as Bethany. We did not think of the younger employees as our daughters. When there is that label attached to someone, they treat them differently. We did not want our younger employees to think they could talk to or treat us like their mothers—we were their bosses.

Although communication difficulties may arise between supervisors and subordinates because of differences between them, in some situations either party may deliberately communicate in a manner that distorts information or is strategically ambiguous.

No one likes to be the bearer of bad news. This precept is particularly true for the subordinate. **Upward distortion** is a term used to describe the hesitancy of subordinates to communicate negative news up the chain of command and their tendency to distort such news to place it in a more positive light (Dansereau & Markham, 1987).

There are a number of explanations for the occurrence of upward distortion. First, subordinates may think that if they communicate negative news to the supervisor, they will be held personally responsible for it. Whether they are the cause of the negative news or not, they may think that the boss will blame them. As a result, they are likely to distort the information. Second, if the negative news is related to the supervisor's performance in some way, it might be interpreted as criticism of the supervisor. Subordinates might present negative information in a positive manner because they are unwilling to criticize their supervisors openly. Finally, Jablin (1990b) noted that several variables may moderate the occurrence of upward distortion, including the subordinate's desire for promotion, need for security, level of trust in the supervisor, and level of motivation. The quality of the relationship between supervisor and subordinate is also related to the quality of information relayed upward, with those in higher-quality relationships reporting higher quality information being communicated (Sias, 2005).

Whereas subordinates might use upward distortion with their supervisors to manage either perceptions or their relationship, in some situations, supervisors may consciously use ambiguity in communicating with a subordinate, not to mislead but to promote positive outcomes. Eisenberg (1984) forwarded the concept of **strategic ambiguity** as a potentially productive communicative tool in organizations. Strategic ambiguity is a situation in which contextual cues are purposefully omitted from communication to "allow for multiple interpretations on the part of the receiver" (p. 230). For Eisenberg, clarity in communication is not always necessary for effectiveness. In fact, on some occasions, purposeful ambiguity will benefit the situation, leading to improved relationships and creative problem-solving. Strategic ambiguity, then, although potentially a contributor to misunderstandings in organizations, can be used to promote identification and the sense of a shared vision.

Although Eisenberg does not limit the use of strategic ambiguity in organizations, we think that it is particularly useful in connection with the relationship between supervisor and subordinate. In particular, given the power differential, it would seem that the supervisor would have more freedom to be strategically ambiguous than would a subordinate. At the same time, if the supervisor and the subordinate have a particularly close relationship, it is more than likely that strategic ambiguity could be employed by the subordinate and tolerated by the supervisor.

Upward distortion and strategic ambiguity are two very different communication tactics used for very different reasons. Both could contribute to the gap in understanding between supervisor and subordinate. As such, the ethics involved should be examined. Upward distortion is certainly the more ethically suspect of the two because it is a conscious effort to mislead another through misrepresentation of reality. Strategic ambiguity, if used appropriately, should be considered an ethical tactic because it seeks neither to mislead nor to cause damage to the recipient. If, however, it is used with the intention of harming the recipient or if it causes the recipient undue stress, then it should be considered unethical.

A Dyadic View of the Supervisor–Subordinate Relationship

Perhaps the most popular theory of the past 50 years regarding supervisor–subordinate relationships is the leader–member exchange theory. Originally called vertical dyad linkage theory (VDL) and proposed by Graen and his colleagues (e.g., Dansereau et al., 1975), this theory posited that leadership consists of a dyadic relationship and that "work roles are developed and negotiated over time through a series of exchanges, or 'interacts,' between leader and member" (Bauer & Green, 1996). VDL theory is now known as **leader–member exchange (LMX) theory**, a label that connotes the bidirectional nature of the supervisor–subordinate relationship. With its focus on individual relationships, LMX theory considers the supervisor to have many individual relationships with a heterogeneous group of subordinates.

LMX theory begins with the assumption that supervisors have a limited amount of time and resources. As a result, the supervisor cannot expend the same amount of energy on every subordinate. Therefore, distinct relationships will form with individual subordinates (Bauer & Green, 1996). The relationships can be placed on a continuum, ranging from leader–member exchange (now known as higher-quality LMX) relationships to supervisory exchange (now known as lower-quality LMX) relationships. As the name leader–member exchange theory emerged and replaced vertical dyad linkage as the preferred name for the theory, the terms *higher-quality LMX* and *lower-quality LMX* came to represent the different types of relationships, leaving the term *supervisory exchange* behind. Because LMX theory focuses on the potential for *mutual* support, liking, trust, and interaction, the worker is now seen as an active participant in the relationship rather than a passive one (Sias, 2014).

Higher-quality LMX relationships are characterized by increased levels of information exchange, mutual support, informal influence, trust, and greater input in decision-making. Conversely, lower-quality LMX relationships are primarily based in formal supervision, involve less support, less trust, and less attention to the subordinate from the supervisor (Mueller & Lee, 2002). While some subordinates may actually prefer to be involved in lower-quality LMX relationships because it makes it easier for them to leave work at work, there can be negative consequences. One of those negative consequences involves workplace accommodation. Westerman et al. (2017) found that that willingness to disclose health information was related to the strength of the LMX relationship; the lower the quality of the relationship, the less likely the subordinate was to disclose health information. The problem with this is that the lack of disclosure regarding health conditions means that the subordinate cannot receive the accommodations they need to be successful in their position and thereby maintain employment.

Subordinates in higher-quality LMX relationships often experience positive outcomes, such as lower turnover, higher satisfaction, and higher performance ratings, as opposed to their colleagues in lower-quality LMX relationships (Bauer & Green, 1996). Part-time workers can also experience higher-quality LMX relationships and can experience positive outcomes as well, such as effective assimilation and organizational identification. Supervisors, then, should not only concentrate on full-time workers but also cultivate relationships with current part-time workers to not only increase positive outcomes currently but also to possibly groom future full-time organizational members (Sollitto et al., 2016)

Subordinates in higher-quality LMX relationships tend to define the breadth of their jobs (i.e., what their job duties and responsibilities are) closer to or greater than their supervisor's expectations (Hsiung & Tsai, 2009). To extend that last finding, research has shown that subordinates who are in higher-quality LMX relationships with their supervisors who perceived requests to perform a duty as outside of their role expectations were less likely to perceive that request as unreasonable as compared to subordinates who are in lower-quality LMX relationships (Sias & Duncan, 2019). Interestingly, then, the quality of the supervisor–subordinate relationship does not only relate to particular outcomes for the individual for the subordinate, but it even is related to how messages are perceived in the relationship.

So what determines which type of relationship a subordinate will be in with a supervisor? Although it is difficult to determine, one study has examined the role of the initial interaction in the formation of LMX relationships. Dockery and Steiner (1990) found that two factors affected the development of LMX relationships during the first time the pair interacted in their official positions: *liking* by the leader and *perceived ability* of the subordinate by the leader. Liking was defined by Dockery and Steiner as "mutual affection the leader and member have for each other based primarily on interpersonal attraction" (p. 397), which includes demographic similarity and similarity in values. "Perceived ability" involves the extent to which the supervisor believes that the subordinate will be able to perform the assigned tasks with little or no difficulty. Other factors, such as trust, perceived similarity, and the level of centralized decision-making are linked to the formation of the various member exchange relationships (Bauer & Green, 1996; Krone, 1994). It does not appear, based on at least one research study (Lamude et al., 2004), that demographic characteristics such as subordinate job classification and biological sex are related to becoming involved in an LMX relationship.

Once a relationship has been established, energy must be exerted to maintain that relationship, particularly on the part of the subordinate (Lee & Jablin, 1995; Waldron, 1991). **Maintenance communication** is the term Waldron (1991) applied to the "messages and behaviors used to preserve an acceptable and lasting relational state" (p. 289). Waldron noted four tactics associated with maintenance communication and found that subordinates in higher-quality LMX relationships tended to use more informal interaction, conform to the role requirements and expectations of their supervisor, and engaged in explicit discussions of perceived relational unfairness than those subordinates in lower-quality LMX relationships.

Just as subordinates can vary their communicative techniques depending on the quality of the LMX relationship with their supervisor, supervisors can do the same. For example, Lamude et al. (2004) found that supervisors tended to use more prosocial techniques (e.g., immediate reward, self-esteem, responsibility to others, supervisor modeling, and supervisor feedback) with those in higher-quality LMX relationships, and autosocial techniques (e.g., punishment, guilt, legitimate supervisor authority) were less likely to be used with this group. Remember, though, that communication is not just about speaking, it also involves listening. Listening behaviors of the supervisor, often associated with prosocial techniques, are also related to LMX. When a supervisee feels listened to by a supervisor, they will have an overall perception of job satisfaction as well as fair treatment (Lloyd et al., 2017).

As can be seen from our discussion of relational maintenance, communication plays an integral role in the supervisor–subordinate relationship. Communication not only affects the relationship (as evidenced by maintenance communication), but communication is also affected by the relationship. In other words, how supervisors and subordinates communicate with each other is rooted in the type of relationship they have. One way to describe this is through the concept of leader–member conversational quality (LMCQ). LMCQ involves the *richness* of the conversation between the members of the LMX relationship. Supervisors and subordinates in higher-quality LMX relationships have a rich conversational quality, which entails *efficiency* (using fewer words to convey more meaning), *coordination* (interactions are fluid and meanings generated are similar), and *accuracy* (communicating and interpreting messages precisely; Jian et al., 2017). Interestingly, these richness characteristics are often the same ones we use when describing how we interact with a best friend or long-time partner.

Leader–member exchange theory offers valuable insight into the dyadic nature of the supervisor–subordinate relationship. Research in this area has moved past the one-to-many theory of leadership posited by both trait and behavior research. LMX theory demonstrates that each relationship is unique, that the relationship type affects important outcomes, and that communication plays a central role in the formation and maintenance of the relationship. The necessity of analyzing this important relationship in this way is exemplified by this brief story from Jaimee, a residence hall director at a large university:

> I think each supervisor needs to treat each of their employees differently and not take a cookie-cutter approach. I think I have seen every type of supervisor. Like, there's the supervisor who will say, "Oh you're really self-sufficient, so I can let you handle this all by yourself," but then the worker feels the disconnect of "well you think I am self-sufficient, are you really there to still support me?" And then there's the supervisor who emphasizes more challenge than support. They will say, "Okay, you only get to ask three questions. What are the top three that you are going to ask?" And worker thinks, "Well, then I maybe don't feel supported in all these other things."
>
> So, I think a part of it is the means of communication and also how we are communicating, whether that is tone or other things like that. I also think a lot of time supervisors don't always share what is going on in

their lives. I am not saying they have to do that, but sometimes that also gives more context to why an email wasn't responded to right away or why they only have time for three questions, or why a phone call wasn't returned in a timely manner.

As Jaimee pointed out, the supervisor–supervisee relationship is a complicated one, and while some supervisors attempt to manage those complications by treating all of their subordinates in the same way, LMX theory shows us that perhaps that is not a good choice.

In the next section of this chapter, we discuss issues relevant to communication between a supervisor and subordinate, using LMX theory as a backdrop.

Communication Between the Supervisor and Subordinate

As stated earlier in the chapter, supervisors spend one third to two thirds of their time communicating with their subordinates. There are obviously, then, many formal and informal communication activities that occur between them. To help familiarize you with the communication between supervisees and subordinates, in this section, we introduce a few of the activities that LMX theory highlights, as well as some that are prevalent in the organizational communication research.

Trust

LMX theory has shown us that supervisors and subordinates are in a dyadic relationship, one constructed through communication and constrained by communication. When you think about it, perhaps the cornerstone of most important relationships in our lives is trust. Trust, or that sense that you can believe in and rely on the other person, is an important ingredient in the supervisor–subordinate relationship. Both parties are vulnerable; trust helps to alleviate some of the vulnerability and provide for a mutually beneficial situation. That trust, though, is not always easily earned or automatically granted. Recall the example from earlier in the chapter with Brent, the pharmacy manager. He found himself in a position where his new supervisor threatened his job if he did not start to improve performance in areas they had not even discussed. You can imagine that this will lead Brent not to trust his supervisor, but it is also very possible that his supervisor has lost trust in Brent because of his lack of expected performance.

Even though LMX theory demonstrates that higher-quality LMX relationships between supervisors and subordinates are characterized by *mutual* trust, much of the research attention is focused on how subordinates come to trust their supervisors (Brower et al., 2009). Consider this brief story from Steve, an intern for a baseball team, who was hoping to be granted some control over the marketing activities of the baseball organization but was finding it hard to get his supervisor to trust him:

My supervisor had some very strict bosses, and she knew that backlash would come to her if anything was done improperly, so I understand that it was a leap of faith to trust a 20-year-old to act professionally on social media. It's not necessarily a stereotype that our generation has. It was just more that I had to show her I could do the job in a professional way that would engage with the audience and the target market. It was a gradual ramping up through the rest of the season.

As Steve's situation shows us, trust in a supervisor–subordinate relationship is complicated and often impacted by factors outside of the control of both parties. In organizations, our relationships with people, particularly with our supervisors, are complicated by myriad factors inside and outside of the organization. Since trust is a central feature of the supervisor–subordinate relationship, we should not be surprised that it is not something that just happens because we have an organizationally dictated relationship with another person.

Trust, however, has the potential to be built through communication and other behaviors by both parties. According to Whitener et al. (1998), managers can have a significant impact on building trust through "managerial trustworthy behavior" (p. 513). According to these researchers, trust has three facets (p. 513):

1. Expectation that the other will act benevolently

2. Willingness to be vulnerable and risk that the other will not act accordingly (i.e., will not take advantage of that vulnerability)

3. Some level of dependence on the other

We see these three facets of trust in the relationship that Steve and his supervisor had. It took a while, but after Steve communicated with his supervisor about his desire to have more of a role in the social media marketing for the team, his supervisor began to expect that he would act benevolently (i.e., with good intention), took the risk by turning over some control, and increased the level of dependence that each of them had on the other's success.

One way to build trust with a subordinate is to communicate concern for them. A particular element of communication that is closely associated with the demonstration of concern—immediacy—has been studied in the context of the supervisor–subordinate relationship. **Immediacy** is "any communication that indicates interpersonal warmth and closeness" (Koermer et al., 1993, p. 269), either conscious or not (Richmond & McCroskey, 2000). Immediacy can be expressed both verbally and nonverbally and, in both cases, may affect a subordinate's perception of their supervisor and, hence, their level of trust in that person. Supervisors' use of nonverbal immediacy, for example, can enhance perceptions of the supervisor by the subordinate (i.e., their credibility and interpersonal attractiveness), the subordinate's satisfaction with the supervisor, and communication with the supervisor. Supervisors' general use of immediacy has also been shown to reduce employee burnout (Kelly et al., 2014) and is positively related to the subordinate feeling a sense of emotional support from their supervisor (Jia et al., 2017).

How, then, is immediacy conveyed in this relationship? Again, while LMX theory points to the idea that both parties would display immediacy behaviors, the majority of the research has been focused on the immediacy behaviors of the supervisor. Supervisors can display immediacy nonverbally and verbally. Nonverbally, supervisors' use of positive vocal tones, smiles, and positive gestures have been demonstrated to have positive outcomes from the subordinate (Jia et al., 2017). Verbally, supervisors can commend their subordinates on their work, solicit input on task and social issues, and express confidence in the subordinate's ability to do the job (Koermer et al.,1993).

Feedback

Feedback is any communication between organizational members that implicitly or explicitly provides task guidance, personal evaluation, or other guidance. The important to this definition is the notion that feedback can involve both task elements (what needs to be done and how) and personal elements (social and psychological development), what Kim and Miller (1990) refer to as *work-oriented* and *altruism-oriented* elements, respectively. Often, feedback is conceived of just in terms of tasks, but given the climate of coaching in the workplace, personal feedback is also expected. Feedback is of particular interest because it is a prime mechanism for addressing misunderstandings. Also, as will be noted in the following sections, it can create them as well.

Feedback from a supervisor to a subordinate has been shown to have a positive impact on motivation, satisfaction, organizational commitment, and performance (Mikkelson et al., 2017). These outcomes will be affected positively, however, only if the feedback is provided in a manner that is considered acceptable by the subordinate. For example, supervisors who provided feedback via the phone rather than text were judged by supervisees as being more competent and trustworthy (Kingsley Westerman et al., 2018). Geddes and Linnehan (1996) conducted research that showed that positive feedback is less communicatively complex (i.e., simpler for the receiver to process) than negative feedback, which often involves balancing information on task, role, and ego. As a result, they suggested adding complexity to the positive feedback because "it is likely recipients will engage in more controlled processing of *guidance* rather than *praise*" (p. 339). In other words, for positive feedback to have longer lasting effects than momentary good feelings, it should be cast in a way that engages the subordinate in thoughts about how to improve performance (or attitude) even further. Positive feedback from supervisors has additional interesting outcomes, including the subordinate having a greater sense that their supervisor is trustworthy, operating with goodwill, and has an appropriate level of expertise (Kingsley Westerman et al., 2018).

Delivering negative feedback to supervisees is difficult. Supervisors regularly avoid communicating negative feedback or bad news to "manage employee emotions, minimize negativity, and preserve relationships" (Wagoner & Waldron, 1999, p. 193), and employees tend to avoid their supervisors when they know negative feedback is coming (Kingsley Westerman et al., 2018). In other words, just as subordinates may engage in upward distortion to reduce the likelihood of being blamed for bad news, supervisors may engage in downward distortion to protect themselves, their subordinates, and their relationships.

Negative feedback can be about many things, but it typically involves such matters as poor performance, denied requests, and broken rules. As managers communicate negative feedback to subordinates, they have many possible ways to approach the conversation. For example, Wagoner and Waldron (1999) in a study at UPS found that when managers had to convey negative feedback about broken rules to their subordinates, they did so by stressing the need to conform to group standards. In this way, the feedback was designed to evoke commitment to coworkers and the organization rather than the supervisor. This approach allowed the supervisor to act more as a channel of news than as a critic, thereby reducing the possibility that the subordinate would have negative feelings in return toward them. Young et al. (2017) actually found that supervisors who communicated negative feedback with empathy or concern for the feelings of the supervisee were able to create a situation in which the supervisee experienced increased positive feelings toward the supervisor.

When feedback flows from supervisee to supervisor, rather than the other way around, the research literature tends to focus on formal performance management systems. In other words, most research discusses this type of feedback very formally and as part of a larger system of evaluation for the supervisor and the subordinate. We will cover a different form of feedback from supervisee to supervisor in the next section when we discuss upward influence.

Upward Influence

Upward influence, or the tactics used by a subordinate to influence or persuade their supervisor in some way, is an issue that is confounded by a variety of variables other than the relationship itself, such as the sex of the participants, organizational hierarchy, the quality of the LMX relationship, and the capacity of the supervisor to exert influence upward (Dansereau & Markham, 1987; Schilit & Locke, 1982). This last variable is referred to as the Pelz effect (Pelz, 1952) and indicates that "subordinates would initiate more upward messages if they believed their superiors had upward influence" (Putnam & Cheney, 1992, p. 74). In the following discussion of research on upward influence, keep in mind that its use is more than a matter of an individual subordinate's comfort and skill level.

Subordinates will differ in their upward influence strategies based on whether they are in a higher-quality LMX or a lower-quality LMX relationship. For example, Krone (1991) posited three potential upward influence strategies:

- **Open persuasion.** An overt form of influence where the desired outcomes are fully disclosed. It is characterized by empathic listening, open argument for a proposed course of action, and logical reasoning.

- **Strategic persuasion.** An influence technique that uses either open influence or clearly stated outcomes. There is only partial openness in revealing the ends that are sought.

- **Manipulation.** A disguised attempt at upward influence.

The results of Krone's research indicated that people in higher-quality LMX relationships tended to use more open and strategic persuasion than did those in lower-quality LMX relationships.

One extension of this line of research showed that supervisors who reported being in higher-quality LMX relationships with their supervisees indicated that their supervisees used rational/logical upward influence tactics more often and negative tactics, such as ingratiation and assertiveness, less often than those in lower-quality LMX relationships (Geertshuis et al., 2015). The following story from Jim, a new faculty member at a regional university, shows that we can also consider *deception* to be a negative upward influence tactic that can be used by supervisees, especially those in lower-quality LMX relationships:

> Our college was beginning the search for a new dean. The institution normally searched externally but regularly offered locals the ability to apply. Being new, I did not know this; besides, I had no intention of ever entering administration. So, when an email addressed to the entire college arrived in my inbox and the opening paragraphs referred to the dean search process, I decided I had read enough and put it in the virtual trash bin.

> A few months later, as candidates began to emerge, I was with the interim dean of our college, a jovial historian who knew how to converse. He inquired as to why I had not put my name forward as a candidate. Not wishing to seem that I was uninterested, I used ignorance as my explanation, saying, "I did not know I was eligible to be considered." A semihonest response given that being ignorant is often the same thing as not knowing something. He responded with, "Well, it was made public by the committee months ago," he said, "Or was supposed to be." We both let it drop.

> Not more than a few days later, the chair of the search committee contacted me, complaining angrily that I had "told the dean they failed to announce local eligibility." The fib I had told reflected badly on him and his team. As it turns out, the email I never finished had included details (near the end—bad placement, I thought later) about how local persons could be part of the candidate pool. He sent me (without request) a new copy of the email and highlighted that language. I apologized as only a junior faculty early in his probation can, knowing I was fully responsible not only for being ignorant but for spreading harmful implications about a committee made up of people who all outranked me.

Jim clearly engaged in deception in order to attempt to exert upward influence. In this situation, he was attempting to influence a supervisor's impression of him. In choosing this particular upward influence tactic, he unintentionally created a misunderstanding with the chair of the search committee, one that made that person look bad in the eyes of the interim dean and Jim look bad for being ignorant about the qualifications for the position because of his own negligence. Perhaps if the relationship between Jim and the interim dean was a higher-quality LMX relationship, he would have chosen a more positive upward influence strategy.

As you can see, the communication choices that subordinates make when engaging in upward influence attempts are not only a matter of their personality traits but also related to the quality of the LMX relationship they have with their supervisor. Importantly, recall that the quality of the LMX relationship that exists between the supervisor and the subordinate is not predetermined in any way but is itself a product of the interaction between the two parties. The supervisor and subordinate co-construct a relationship through communication that then influences how communication may unfold between them in the future.

Expression of Upward Dissent

There are many times in everyday life when we disagree with what is happening around us. Depending on the situation, we will express our disagreement with the hope that we can somehow positively affect the situation. In our organizational lives, when we disagree with an organizational policy or managerial practice, we must weigh the pros and cons of expressing our disagreement to someone in or outside of the organization. Sometimes, we decide that the nature of the organization, its culture, or the behaviors of management make it impossible for us to express disagreement. This has been labeled the **hierarchical mum effect**, which is when there is "hierarchical constraint on upward information flow created by command structures" (Bisel et al., 2012, p. 135).

At other times, though, the hierarchical mum effect is not in place or is not strong enough for organizational members to constrain their expressions of disagreement. For example, imagine you are a server in a restaurant, and your boss enacts a policy of needing to find your own replacement if you have to miss a shift for any reason. Even though you are a great worker and rarely miss work, you are new to the area and do not know any of the other servers well enough to ask them to cover for you. You feel that the policy is unfair and decide that you need to express your opinion. To whom will you express it? How will you do it?

"Expressing disagreement or contradictory opinions about organizational practices, policies, and operations" is known as **organizational dissent** (Kassing, 1998, p. 183). Three forms of dissent have been identified by Croucher et al. (2013): (1) **upward dissent** (expressed to a supervisor), (2) **lateral dissent** (expressed to an organizational member on the same hierarchical level), and (3) **displaced dissent** (expressed to someone not in the organization, such as a friend or family member). Returning to the earlier example, you realize that while you could express your dissent about the new restaurant policy to your coworkers (lateral dissent) or your significant other (displaced dissent), you feel that the best way to affect change is to express it to your supervisor (upward dissent) since that is where the policy originated. The concern of this particular section of the chapter is with *upward dissent* as it involves interactions between the supervisor and subordinate.

Once an employee has decided to express dissent upward, they must decide how best to communicate that dissent. Research has shown that the medium the supervisee uses to express dissent is related to the quality of the LMX relationship. Members of lower-quality LMX relationships were more likely to engage in upward dissent through email, for example, while those in higher-quality relationships were more likely to express dissent face-to-face (Turnage & Goodbody, 2016). Once the medium of communication is chosen, the dissenter also must decide how to construct their message.

Five upward dissent strategies have been identified in the literature according to Kassing (2011). Direct factual appeal is when an employee expresses dissent to a supervisor using some form of physical evidence such as knowledge of policies in the organization, personal experience with the situation, or physical evidence relevant to the dissenting opinion. This strategy helps the dissenter manage the supervisor's perceptions of him by appearing grounded in fact, not personal opinion or emotional reaction to a situation. Solution presentation is when the employee expresses dissent but at the same time also presents a solution. Kassing indicated that this is the strategy that employees see as most competent in that it allows them to appear to be proactive and not *just* complaining. Garner (2016) supported this claim and showed that from both the perspective of the dissenter and the supervisor, this solution-oriented dissent was more likely to be effective than dissent that did not involve a solution. Circumvention is when an employee does not express the consent to a direct supervisor but instead expresses it to someone higher in the organizational structure. While this is often considered to be a risky strategy, it tends to be used when the employee does not feel that the supervisor will be sympathetic or willing to listen. Threatening resignation is a way for an employee to create a sense of urgency about the situation; either address the situation or the employee will quit. Kassing reported that, because of the inherent risk to their employment, workers considered this to be the least competent strategy for expressing dissent. Finally, repetition involves the expression of dissent at multiple points in time with the hope of eventually building up a level of acceptance to the dissenting opinion.

Many factors are related to the desire and ability to express upward dissent. One useful way to categorize the factors related to the potential for expressing upward dissent is *external factors*, *organizational factors*, and *relational factors*. External factors are ones that exist outside of the boundaries of the organization and may not be in direct control of the potential dissenter. Family values and organizational location (i.e., country) are two external factors that have been studied. For example, Buckner et al. (2018) demonstrated that if you were raised in a family that encouraged embracing similarities with others, then you were less likely to express upward dissent. Zeng and Chen (2020) showed that there are differences internationally regarding upward dissent, with supervisees from Finland being more likely to engage in upward dissent than supervisees from China. This latter finding is consistent with the literature that indicates upward dissent is a form of disrespect in Chinese organizations.

Organizational factors are those factors that are related to the organizational-level actions, such as socialization efforts or engaging in questionable practices and structuring of organizational positions as being either part time or full time. If an organization socializes its employees with regard to the who, what, when, where, and how of expressing upward dissent, then there is an association with the actual expression of dissent. Employees were also more likely to express dissent if they perceived their organization to be operating ethically and maintaining a positive reputation (Croucher et al., 2019). When employees feel the organization has broken their promised obligations to them, then they are more likely to express dissent to their supervisor, despite the fact that the manager is not the one responsible, but the faceless organization is (De Ruiter et al., 2016). Finally, Kassing et al. (2018) showed that full-time employees are more likely to use prosocial upward dissent tactics (e.g., rational or solution based), while part-time employees tend to go around their direct supervisors and threaten to quit their jobs.

Relational factors are those that are based in the communication relationship between the supervisee and the supervisor. There are many of these factors, as you can imagine, but a few from the recent research involve a supervisee's perception of trust in the supervisor, their perception of the emotional support of their supervisor, and their perception of their supervisor's value of their embodied activities. Payne (2014) examined how trust in the supervisor is related to the ways in which dissent is communicated in the organization. She found that as trust in the supervisor increases, so too does upward dissent. Zeng and Chen (2020) reported that managerial support was found to be positively related to upward dissent. Therefore, it can be extended that supervisees in higher-quality LMX relationships are likely to engage in upward dissent if needed. Finally, Bisel and Arterburn Adame (2019) found that expression of upward dissent regarding private moral concerns could be related to the supervisee's perception of the value the supervisor has on their embodied activities or their feeling that they need to "go with their gut."

As should be becoming clear, upward dissent is not a simple concept or an easy thing for a supervisee to do in an organization. As Garner (2013) argued, dissent is an interactional event and should be studied not through the perspective of just one of the participants but both. Garner added to this critique by contending that dissent has been viewed as a discrete event instead of as an interactional phenomenon that unfolds over a series of interactions. So to understand upward dissent, we should not just look at the penultimate expression of consent, but we should attempt to view the dissent as occurring over a series of interactions between the worker and the supervisor. He proposed that whenever we examine dissent, we should do so by looking at the *precipitating event* (what led to the consideration of upward dissent), the *initial conversation* (the interaction between the supervisee and supervisor in which the dissent is expressed), and the *residual communication* (the interactions that follow from the initial conversation, which can take place among myriad organizational members).

With residual communication, we come to understand that the upward dissent conversation does not represent the end of the situation (Garner, 2017) but perhaps could be looked at like the aftershocks following an earthquake or the fingerprints left behind after a person touches a surface. The initial conversation may be over, but the communication continues in the organization. For example, the supervisor does not just listen to the dissent but also responds in some way. This is an under-researched area, but Garner (2016) has shown that supervisors perceive that they are more likely to respond to dissent with reasons why they could not act on the dissent rather than reject the dissent. This type of response reduces a typical concern of dissenters that they will somehow face negative repercussions for dissenting.

In the final section of this chapter, we turn our attention to communication technology and the supervisor–subordinate relationship.

Communication Technology and the Supervisor–Subordinate Relationship

As the proliferation and use of communication technologies continue to advance in organizations to the benefit of workers and organizations alike, scholars and practitioners are also concerned with their unintended consequences. With each new technological advance comes challenges or downsides; this phenomenon is known as a **technological dualism**. For example, online banking through smartphone apps and websites has simplified customers' lives by giving them control over their money without having to step foot in the bank, go through the drive-up, or write a check. On the other hand, this technology also takes away human interaction, which can lead to frustration on the customer's part, as well as a decreased need for the number of customer service representatives in the banking industry. You can see how technological dualisms feed easily into the concept of misunderstandings and can serve as an important reminder for us that we should always be anticipating misunderstandings.

The supervisor–subordinate relationship is not immune to technological dualisms as they are produced through the communication technology used by the members of the dyad. In addition to communicating face-to-face, supervisors and subordinates use technology to interact formally and informally, both inside and outside of the boundaries of the organization. While the technology may facilitate connection and improved work outcomes for both parties, it may also lead to negative outcomes, such as concerns with privacy, loss of trust, and cognitive dissonance. To illustrate the technological dualisms found in the relationship, we highlight a few important communication technologies used by supervisors and subordinates: *smartphones*, *internal social media*, *personal social media*, and *remote work*.

Let's start with one of the most recognizable forms of communication technology—the smartphone. Research has shown us that when used in the supervisor–subordinate relationship, smartphones can lead to both positive and negative outcomes for the supervisees in particular. One line of research showed that discussing family demands and concerns with a supervisor after hours through smartphones can help build organizational identification for the supervisee and reduce negative effects (such as burnout) of using smart media after working hours (van Zoonen et al., 2020). On the other hand, there is the problem with **phubbing**, or phone snubbing, which occurs when someone is attending to their smartphone rather than focusing their communicative energy on their relational partner. When phubbing is done by the supervisor to the supervisee, it has been shown to be related to lower trust in the supervisor, lower job satisfaction, and decreased job performance. These outcomes lend some support to the saying that "employees leave managers not companies" (Roberts & David, 2019).

Internal social media (originally termed *enterprise social media*) is communication technology that allows members to communicate and collaborate internally and have their work available to other organizational members (Leonardi et al., 2013). The work and messages that are created using internal social media are visible to other organizational members and persist over time. The advantages are many for the supervisor and subordinate, as they can easily share documents, chat via text or video, and have a readily accessible accounting of work and communication that can be reviewed and serve as a basis for performance appraisal. Since much of modern organizational work is team based, the flow of information and communication between supervisors and subordinates is more widely accessible to others in the organization. In addition to serving task-based concerns, internal social media allows for the opportunity for a supervisee to speak up about something they disagree with, knowing that it will be seen not only by supervisors but also coworkers. The disagreement, or perhaps even dissent, can generate likes or additional comments by coworkers that lead to what is termed a spiral of voice. *Spiral of voice* (Madsen & Johansen, 2019) represents the momentum that a dissenting message can receive from the positive reactions and additional comments of support made by coworkers.

Personal social media is a broad term for electronic social networking systems that connect people to one another through the internet. One of the difficulties that subordinates in particular face is what to do when their supervisor sends them a friend request on Facebook. Consider the following story told to the authors of the complexities involved when supervisors and subordinates are connected via personal social media:

> Juliet was at her new job for less than a few months when her supervisor, Loraine, sent her a friend request on Facebook. She didn't know what do. She didn't really want to have her boss on social media because she wanted that to be her own personal space where she could be free to be herself, plus she liked to keep work and the rest of her life separate. But she knew

that if she didn't accept the request, her boss, who could be moody and vindictive, would take it out on her. So, she accepted the request.

Each time Juliet posted something personal, she felt sour about the fact that her boss was getting a view into her personal life. She tried not to post very much but then would get mad that she felt that pressure and posted anyway. Inevitably, her boss would make a comment at work the next day about whatever Juliet posted, making her feel that much more uncomfortable.

After a year of this, Juliet had enough. She unfriended Loraine, which was anxiety producing, but she felt better. A few days later, one of her coworkers stopped Juliet in the hallway and said, "Loraine just asked me if you unfriended me too? What is she talking about?" Juliet trusted this coworker and told her she just couldn't handle having her boss connected on her personal social media and left it at that.

The next day, Loraine stopped into Juliet's cubicle and said, "I saw you unfriended me on Facebook!" She didn't say anything else; she just stared at Juliet. Juliet didn't know what to do or say, so she stumbled around and said, "Oh, I'm so sorry, that must have been a mistake. You know how Facebook does that sometimes." Loraine seemed satisfied with that answer, turned around, went to her office, and within seconds, Juliet heard the all too familiar ding on her phone from Facebook notifying her that Loraine had sent her a friend request. Too concerned for what could happen if she didn't, Juliet hit "accept."

This scenario is one that plays out often in organizational life: What do you do when your supervisor sends you a friend request on social media? The research in this area is interesting and demonstrates the technological dualism present with personal social media.

Some supervisees (those in higher-quality LMX relationships, for example), may find friend requests from bosses reassuring, while others may find it uncomfortable, as they do not want to share personal information with people from work (Van Eck Peluchette et al., 2013). A few demographic factors play a role in how supervisees react to the request. Supervisees are more likely to accept the friend request from a female supervisor than from a male supervisor (Rothbard et al., 2020). Additionally, there does not appear to be a significant difference in acceptance of friend requests from supervisors among the generations—baby boomers, Generation X, and millennials. However, millennials were more likely to feel obligated to accept the request from their supervisor so as not to offend them (Karl et al., 2017). A possible explanation for this is that they are perhaps more likely to be concerned about the implications for their job security since they are most likely early in their careers, much as Juliet was.

When the members of this important dyad are connected on personal social media, there are important organizational implications. Cistulli and Snyder (2019) explored psychological contracts or the expectations of the supervisee regarding obligations the organization has to them and found that when the supervisee feels as though their privacy has been infringed upon in social media, they feel the psychological contract has been violated, and they trust the supervisor less. To manage this infringement, some supervisees, particularly millennials, set up privacy settings and restrict access to certain material for their supervisors (Karl et al., 2017). Not all outcomes are negative, though. A study of hotel managers and employees suggests that personal social media relationships can have a positive impact on the face-to-face workplace through building non-work-based connections (Yang, 2020).

Remote work or working via communication technology from a location other than the physical workplace is the final area we will discuss. The COVID-19 pandemic necessitated that many organizations move as many workers as possible to work remotely from home. Advancements in Internet speeds, video meeting platforms, collaboration software, and internal social media made it possible for work to be done safely, and many organizations will continue to offer virtual work options for their members. Remote work, though, does pose its challenges to the supervisor–subordinate relationship. In particular, it has been shown that there is a negative correlation between physical distance and relational quality between the supervisor and the subordinate (Brunelle, 2013). In other words, when the dyad is not physically co-present, the quality of their relationship is not as high as when they are. Perhaps one reason that the relational quality decreased during remote work is that remote workers have reported that they do not feel that their supervisor trusts their ability to do their work remotely and that they are being closely monitored (Parker et al., 2020). Brunelle (2013) did show, though, that if the supervisor adopts a transformational leadership style, emphasizing creativity and innovation, then the negative effects of the physical distance can be moderated.

Summary

In this chapter, we examined many aspects of communication and the supervisor–subordinate relationship, such as semantic-information distance, upward distortion, and upward expression of dissent. The relationship between a supervisor and a subordinate is crucial to the success of both parties, particularly given that the relationship is characterized by a gap in understanding between the parties regarding important organizational activities and outcomes. The relationship is a social construction best thought of as a dyad that can be characterized by varying levels of trust, support, and frequency of interaction.

The supervisor–subordinate relationship is undergoing significant changes in the modern workplace. As more organizations turn to remote work as a viable option, and communication technology continues to simultaneously create opportunities and misunderstandings, both supervisors and subordinates must reimagine how to perform this important relationship. Also, organizations that have adopted decentralized structures, participative decision-making, and project teams have experienced a shift from traditional hierarchical relationships between supervisor and subordinate to relationships characterized by blurred lines of authority, increased communication, and a more equal distribution of power. These changes demand new skills. Whereas authority and control were the tools of traditional supervisors, supervisors in the current atmosphere must be accomplished communicators, able to develop interpersonal relationships with each worker as LMX theory describes. Despite endeavors in this direction, however, misunderstandings will undoubtedly occur. Recognizing that there is an inherent gap in understanding between supervisor and subordinate should sensitize both parties to seize opportunities to construct learning and could enhance the possibility of success in the future.

Peer and Coworker Communication

LEARNING OBJECTIVES

1. Analyze the types of peer relationships in organizations
2. Identify the positive effects of peer relationships on individuals and organizations
3. Examine the crucial role played by technology in organizational peer relationships
4. Indicate how negative peer relationships affect individuals and the workplace
5. Identify the dialectical tensions relevant to coworker relationships

Communication with coworkers can create one of the strongest connections between you and your job and between you and the organization. As people feel more connected to one another, morale, organizational commitment, and job satisfaction significantly increase (e.g., Higgins, 2000; Simon et al., 2010). When people are committed to working together, there is a desire to like the people around you, simply because a pleasant work environment is easier to work in than an unpleasant one (Morrison & Nolan, 2007). Peer relationships can provide a source of intrinsic reward for the employee, buffer job-related stress, improve job performance, and reduce job dissatisfaction and turnover (Kram & Isabella, 1985; Shah et al., 2017). These personal relationships are also connected to innovation, resource sharing, and better problem-solving (Chang et al., 2016). Albrecht and Hall (1991) discovered that coworker relationships characterized by trust, credibility, influence, and relationship importance were directly related to supportiveness of one's new ideas for the organization. Thus it is in the organization's best interest to foster coworker relationships.

We begin this chapter by examining the nature of peer relationships in organizations. Next, we offer an overview of factors influencing the development of relationships in the workplace and the positive and negative consequences of work relationships, as well as the impact that technology has had on workplace relationships. Then we dive into the dark side of organizational peer relationships by exploring the misuse of peer support, as well as bullying. We conclude the chapter with an overview of how dialectical tensions can help us understand the benefits of and misunderstandings that occur in coworker relationships.

Organizational Peer Relationships

To begin our discussion of peer relationships in the workplace, we first need to distinguish between personal life and work relationships. A personal relationship, or friendship, develops in everyday life because two people choose to spend time with each other because of mutual emotional needs. An **organizational peer relationship** is a relationship that is a result of the organizational structure. One main difference between personal and organizational peer relationships is the voluntary or involuntary nature of each: "Friendship cannot be imposed on people; it is an ongoing human association voluntarily developed and privately negotiated" (Rawlins, 1992, p. 9). Friendships develop by choice, not by required association, which is how organizational peer relationships form.

Many organizational peer relationships that begin as task-based relationships stay at that level, but some do not. Instead, some may develop more personal dimensions. For example, two women are assigned to work on a particular project; the organizational structure has forced them to spend time together on a mutual task. This relationship may remain mostly task oriented, or it may develop more personal dimensions. The women may talk in a friendly manner about their hobbies while completing their organizational tasks, but the relationship always ends at the close of work hours. It is also possible that the women will begin talking about their personal lives while completing organizational tasks and decide to continue their relationship outside of the organizational structure, either through social media or interactions that take place outside of the work environment.

When a coworker relationship develops dimensions of a friendship, it is referred to as a **blended relationship**. A blended relationship begins as a required association and develops into something more complex and interrelated with other organizational relationships (Bridge & Baxter, 1992). A key feature to remember is that, unlike personal relationships that begin outside of the work environment, if the blended relationship deteriorates, the individuals are not able to dissolve their organizational peer relationship and will need to continue working together productively.

To better understand organizational peer relationships, consider the three primary forms offered by Kram and Isabella (1985): (1) information peer, (2) collegial peer, and (3) special peer. An **information peer** relationship is characterized by low levels of self-disclosure and trust. Individuals in such a relationship tend to focus on work-related issues and share little intimacy beyond polite conversation. **Collegial peers** share moderate levels of trust, self-disclosure, emotional support, and friendship. These friends share information beyond that of an acquaintance, but not as much information as a close friend. Conversation could range from work-related issues and difficulties to information about one's personal life. The third form, **special peer**, is a relationship that is characterized by high levels of emotional support, trust, self-disclosure, and intimacy. These individuals are able to share feedback about work, as well as personal issues, and the content and depth of discussions are almost limitless (Sias, 2005). Collegial and special peers are engaged in blended relationships. Another way to think about these relationships is to consider an informational peer as an acquaintance, a collegial peer as a friend, and a special peer as a best friend at work (Sallitto & Myers, 2015).

Figure 10.1 shows the three types of organizational peers in light of the task and personal dimensions that comprise them.

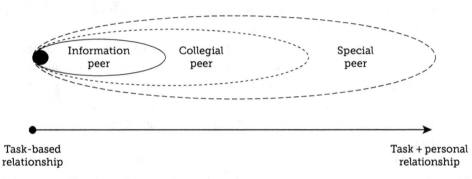

FIGURE 10.1 Organizational Peer Relationships

Consider the relationship to be like a rubber band anchored around a fixed point—that fixed point is the organization. The information peer is like the rubber band that is anchored by the organization but not stretched past the limits of the task itself. The collegial peer remains anchored but is stretched as the peers provide more emotional support for each other and increase their trust and self-disclosure. The special peer stretches even more as the peers increase their trust, time spent together outside of work, disclosure, and emotional involvement. As noted earlier, though, if a special peer or collegial peer relationship starts to deteriorate, the relationships cannot dissolve completely, as it is still anchored by the organizational task structure. In these instances, the rubber band, once stretched, returns to its previous shape, although the quality of the resulting relationship may not be as strong as it originally was.

To see how complicated it can be to manage coworker relationships, consider the following scenario that one of the authors witnessed:

> Sunshine Academy is a small elementary school that employs half-a-dozen employees. Because of its small size, the staff work closely together and have developed relationships outside of the work environment. The teachers and principal decided to celebrate the approaching end of the school year at a local restaurant one Friday night after work. Intertwined with the lightheartedness of the evening was discussion about the next school year; nothing negative was shared nor discussed. The principal was then shocked the following week to learn that he had received a negative performance evaluation from these same colleagues.

Simply put, the principal was hurt that his colleagues had hidden this news from him while the staff began to accuse one another of providing negative information in order to attempt to maintain their own friendship with him. The situation becomes more complex when all the relationships involved are added together; the principal has independent relationships with each of the staff members. Each of the staff members has relationships with one another and in various combinations with the principal. In addition to the number of relationships involved, some of these relationships were organizationally structured while others were more personal in nature. Many of the people in the relationships were involved in this conflict, which eventually escalated into the principal and half of the teachers resigning from their positions.

It is easy to imagine a variety of misunderstandings that can arise when professional and personal relationships merge. Before further discussing those challenges, we need to consider why organizational relationships may shift into something more personal. Reasons for this relationship shift can be categorized by workplace factors, such as proximity, shared projects, and work-related problems and personal factors such as similarity and personal needs. Often, organizational peers transition into more personal relationships because a person simply has more opportunities to interact with some people than others within the organizational setting. The research on **proxemics** (the distance between people) provides a strong indication that people develop friendships based on which individuals happen to share the same space. In an organization, individuals are more likely to develop relationships with those with whom they are in constant contact rather than with those they seldom see or hear. Sias and Cahill (1998) found that proximity is a major factor not only in forming relationships but also in increasing the closeness of the two partners. Therefore, simply placing individuals within the same physical space will increase the likelihood that they will develop a personal relationship. One reason the situation became more intense at Sunshine Academy was because there were so few employees in a relatively small space, so everyone was aware of activities and discussions that occurred outside the school.

If working closely with others increases the likelihood of relationship development, then it also makes sense that working closely together or sharing common work problems would be favorable for relationship development. Individuals with shared projects or individuals who perceive that they need to work together to successfully complete work tasks will engage in more communication, and this increased communication may motivate the development of a workplace friendship (Sias et al., 2020). Similarly, if an individual is having difficulty with their supervisor, conflict with another colleague, or experiencing work stress, they are more likely to seek out others whom they think will understand what they are going through; this task or emotional support can increase the likelihood of a relationship developing (Sias & Jablin, 1995; Sias et al., 2012).

There are also a number of personal factors that can increase the likelihood of organizational relationships morphing into something more personal. Perceptions of similarity, or how alike individuals perceive themselves to be, increase the likelihood that employees will develop more personal relationships with their coworkers. Research has shown that individuals are particularly drawn to other individuals with whom they feel they share similar attitudes, values, and interests (Anderson & Hunsaker, 1985). According to Morrison and Nolan (2007), organizational peers are likely to have similar educational backgrounds and perform similar tasks within their organization.

Relational balance also plays a role in relationships developing from organizational peer relationships to more personal ones. Relationships are identified as symmetrical when the two partners are equal in the relationship. In such a relationship, they participate equally in decision-making and share control over what they do together. Other relationships are complementary, meaning that one person's behavior complements the other person's behavior. For example, one may be dominant, whereas the other is submissive. Thus this second type of relationship is based on a maximization of differences between two people: one plays the "one-up position" and the other plays the "one-down position." Supervisor–subordinate relationships appear complementary, whereas coworker relationships appear symmetrical. In most relationships, however, the individuals shift in and out of these roles at various times.

The final factor in addressing why relationships evolve in organizations is personal needs. In any interpersonal relationship, both partners come to the relationship with the same psychological needs but at different levels of strength. Each partner is expressing three kinds of needs to some degree: (1) the need for affection, (2) the need for inclusion, and (3) the need to control others (Schutz, 1966). The need for affection can range from feeling liked by others to more intimate feelings. Most people need to feel included by others to feel like a full partner in a relationship. Some people, however, want to feel that they have a degree of control or influence over others in their relationships. This need may be met for some by offering organizational advice, being the go-to person for information, or being the more senior individual in the relationship who can guide the other partner.

Before closing our initial description of organizational peers, consider another type of coworker peer relationship that we often see portrayed in dramas and movies: the work spouse. While it appears that Owens coined the term in a 1987 article for the *Atlantic*, the term gained more widespread usage when Noah (2004) used it to describe the close relationship between President G. W. Bush and Secretary of State Condoleeza Rice. A work spouse is a special type of workplace friendship that occurs when individuals form a close emotional bond with extremely high levels of disclosure and support (McBride et al., 2015; McBride et al., 2020). Work spouses also share mutual trust, honesty, loyalty, and respect. French (2015) argued the importance of this relationship by stating that one party in the relationship will often consider leaving if the other leaves the organization. It is the exclusivity of this platonic relationship that seems to make it different from other workplace friendships (Whitman & Mandeville, 2019).

Not surprisingly, the conditions under which work spouse relationships develop are very similar to those of other close peer relationships: perceived similarities, compatibility, complimenting personal and work styles, and proximity. Work spouses, like many other coworker relationships, provide social support, motivation, and add an element of fun to work. Over one quarter of participants in one study identified their work spouse as someone they could use as a confidant for not only work but also personal issues (McBride & Bergen, 2015).

Organizational peer relationships are certainly complicated and bring about myriad misunderstandings; however, they do have significant benefits for the relational partners, as well as the organization.

Benefits of Peer Relationships

Given the amount of time people spend at work communicating with peers, it is not surprising that peer relationships, particularly those that move beyond task orientation, can provide a number of benefits to both of the individuals involved, as well as the organization. Remember that any relationship beyond the organizationally prescribed role is formed voluntarily; that is, friendship is a relationship that individuals choose to involve themselves in beyond the expected and anticipated working relationships. These relationships can provide many benefits to the individuals involved, such as social support, information exchange, and peer mentoring. For the organization, these relationships have the potential to increase overall productivity, job satisfaction, and organizational identification.

Benefits for Individuals

The first benefit of peer relationships is social support. Coworker friendships afford individuals an opportunity to know one another outside their organizationally prescribed roles and status (Sias & Cahill, 1998). Individuals can share workplace experiences and help one another make sense of them. Individuals can talk to their coworkers about organizational phenomena that friends outside the organization might not understand or be able to relate to. For example, medical students who formed relationships with their colleagues were better able to cope with the mental and physical demands of internships and learn more effectively, and these personal relationships diminished occupational stress and burnout (Mikkola et al., 2018). Metts et al. (1994) found that the advice and support received from coworkers are generally more effective and applicable than that received from outside sources. Additionally, individuals can usually talk to their coworkers without violating any confidentiality rules that would prevent them from discussing workplace issues with personal friends or family. These shared experiences, or social support, can provide valuable emotional, social, and task support to individuals and, in turn, benefit the organization by potentially reducing employee burnout and turnover.

A second benefit for individuals to peer relationships is information exchange. When Lincoln and Miller (1979) first studied workplace personal relationships, they argued that these relationships become systems for decision-making and transmittal of information. In other words, peer relationships at work can provide a network that supplies information and feedback people might not otherwise receive. Peers, particularly those with higher levels of trust and intimacy, can be valuable sources of important organizational information, as well as gossip (Rawlins, 1994). Employees in Sias's (2005) study reported receiving more accurate, timely, and useful information from their collegial and special peers than from their purely organizational peers.

A third benefit to individuals is mentoring. When Kram and Isabella (1985) looked for alternatives to the traditional mentorship relationships of supervisors and subordinates, they found the primary alternative was an employee's peers. Recall that collegial peers share both work and personal information, while special peers are similar to workplace best friends. In these types of coworker relationships, there are higher levels of trust and self-disclosure. If an individual is already seeking social support and information exchange from another in the organization, the progression to a mentoring relationship is logical. These peers are able to provide organizational insight, advice, and feedback and help one another improve performance and potential career progression. Individuals with a mentor tend to earn higher salaries, get more promotions, have a great sense of role clarity, and generally feel more competent at work (De Janasz et al., 2003). Mentoring relationships are particularly important for women and other minorities within the organization. In 2002, the Joint Leadership Council identified a lack of mentors and exclusion from information networks of communication (*information exchange*) as two of the top barriers for both women and people of color seeking upward organizational advancement.

Benefits for Organizations

Social support, information exchange, and mentoring opportunities are a few of the key benefits of positive peer relationships in organizations for the individuals participating in them. There are also benefits of these relationships for organizations. These benefits include increased worker productivity and overall organizational identification. Let's turn our attention now to the benefits of positive coworker relationships for organizations.

The first benefit is worker productivity. Research on power in the workplace suggests that coworker relationships can serve as a powerful form of control over an employee's behavior, particularly as related to their productivity. Gibson (1998) discovered this fact in an extensive study of blue-collar workers. At Industry International, an incentive plan that included every organizational worker provided the backbone of the company's success. Workers controlled one another's behaviors because income was dependent on the work of all; while this created high profitability and superior work levels, it also meant employees worked long hours, performed dangerous tasks, and had a highly competitive work environment. This is an excellent example of concertive control, which was discussed in Chapter 6.

Coworkers can also exert a great deal of influence over how their peers view organizational attitudes, behaviors, and policies. Kirby and Krone's (2002) research demonstrated that this coworker influence can determine whether an individual chooses to use family medical leave time, paternity leave, or flex time. An individual is less likely to use a benefit available to them if they feel that their coworkers will think less of them for doing so. This, in turn, affects their overall productivity. In similar studies, researchers found that women with the emotional social support of their coworkers were more likely to continue breastfeeding after maternity leave than those without perceived peer social support (Jantzer et al., 2018; Zhuang et al., 2019). Clearly, social support in the workplace can influence a wide variety of personal and professional decisions that employees make.

A second benefit for the organization of positive coworker relationships is **organizational identification**. Recall from Chapter 8 that organizational identification involves an individual's sense of connection with the organization and organizational members. Individuals who have multiple positive coworker relationships generally report being happier and more committed employees (Hugh Feeley et al., 2008). Research demonstrates that many organizations not only tolerate but also actively encourage positive coworker relationships because friendliness in the workplace not only increases one's personal sense of job satisfaction but also one's overall organizational identification (Berman et al., 2002). Individuals who are personally connected within the organization are less likely to leave because they are not only identified with the organization but also closely tied to their peer relationships. Friedman and Holtom (2002) also found that organizations that foster coworker networks are better able to lower their attrition rates for minority employees. This makes sense given our discussion earlier of peer mentoring.

There are definitely more benefits to individuals and organizations from positive coworker relationships than we have covered here, but these are the ones most noted in the research. Next, we discuss the roles technology plays in these peer relationships.

Technology and Peer Relationships

Technology presents both opportunities and challenges for coworker relationships and organizations. Consider the following, which was experienced by one of the authors:

> Jill, a server at a local campus bar, was hired in part because her friend, Kylie, put a good word in for her. When Kylie was put in charge of social media for the bar, she expected Jill to repost all of the status updates and tweets that she posted, such as advertising events or drink specials because she knew Jill had a large social network at a nearby university. Initially, Jill reposted everything, but after a concerned phone call from her grandma, who was worried that she was partying too much and paying too little attention to school because of all of the alcohol posts, Jill stopped reposting. Kylie became upset, and she felt that Jill wasn't supporting her or the organization, even after Kylie helped her get the job. Jill knows Kylie is in line to be the next assistant manager and worries that if she doesn't start posting the updates again or "unfriends" Kylie on social media, it may negatively impact her job. On the other hand, she doesn't want her family to worry about her when she knows they don't fully understand how social media can be used in modern workplaces.

While this example demonstrates the misuse of social support by friends in the workplace, the scenario is further complicated by the role of technology. Jill and Kylie were connected both professionally and personally through technology, and professional expectations clashed with personal concerns in this situation, and vice versa. The advertising needs of the organization, professional and personal expectations of Jill and Kylie regarding social media use, and concerns about future professional opportunities made this a situation fraught with misunderstandings.

As previously discussed, communication scholars have argued that proximity is important to the development of workplace relationships (Sias et al., 2003). With many companies today relying on telecommuting and remote work, it has been assumed that decreased face time would come at a significant cost in terms of human relationships. More recent research, though, suggests that as technology has become more social, it may be able to replace the need for physical proximity, particularly when employees have access to multiple forms of mediated communication, both internal and external to the organization. Additionally, as work practices like telecommuting and flextime become more widely available in organizations, employees' perception of time and space has been altered (Sias et al., 2012). In other words, employees are used to not working with their coworkers in the same space or having synchronous communication, and it is natural to assume that they would be equally comfortable with their friendship not being in the same space.

These mediated relationships may actually provide opportunities for relationships for employees who would not otherwise be able to interact; think about employees who work part time, who work exclusively from home, or use flextime. Robertson and Kee (2017) found that employee job satisfaction was positively associated with the amount of time that employees spent interacting with coworkers on Facebook. This was particularly true for part-time and contract workers. Other research has found that when employees perceive that they are "real" friends on Facebook with their coworkers, this leads to higher levels of commitment to their department or unit, and if the Facebook connection is to someone who has some type of power within the organization (even if the power is instrumental support like information) this can increase overall commitment and identification with the organization (Bartels et al., 2019). Because online disclosure and conversations allow for individuals to share a wider variety of their traits, talents, and interests, employees also get to know one another beyond their work identities, which can allow for greater workplace mentoring, networking, and career progression (e.g., Schmidt et al., 2016).

The concern of productivity and peer use of technology is highly debatable, with research on both sides of the fence. Pew Research Center (2016) data found that 77% of full-time workers reported using social media at work regardless of what their employer's social media policy was. Approximately 50% of employees believed that their employers did have a social media policy. The majority of these workers, though, did not feel that their social media use negatively impacted their productivity. Nduhura and Prieler (2017) found no evidence that social media use harmed productivity and in fact could potentially improve work conditions by improving employee moods and providing opportunities for stress relief and socialization. Other research, though, found that the relationship between social media and productivity depends on the social media being used. Facebook, without any organizational controls in place, was found to decrease project success, while LinkedIn use with or without controls increased project success (Vithayathil et al., 2020).

The benefits of technology are, however, mitigated by employees' perceptions of trust in upper level management. If employees worry that the technology is being monitored and information potentially used for performance evaluation or in a reward system, then the opportunities to use technology to develop or maintain peer relationships decrease (Awolusi, 2012). As individuals develop relationships at work and decide to "friend" request a colleague, it can cause a blurring of organizational and personal life boundaries that the individual had not intended. While professional networking sites such as LinkedIn are easier to manage when you have purely social friends, family, and work friends on a shared social site, it is difficult to post pictures and messages that are appropriate for all audiences; reflections about work or personal views can have a negative effect on your career (Skeels & Grudin, 2009; Yang & Wong, 2020). The constant connections to work and the blur between personal and professional can also cause additional stress, as coworkers may use social media connections to make requests for shift coverage, work favors, and other information outside of work hours.

To this point, we have emphasized the positive aspects of organizational peer relationships, but research in organizational communication has also attended to the more difficult aspects that can emerge as peers work together.

Dark Side of Peer Relationships

Lisa and Helen started working for a midsized company around the same time and quickly became friends; their children grew up together, and they frequently went out for drinks after work. When Dorothy was hired, she was quickly welcomed into their small social group. Over time, Lisa and Dorothy grew closer and were both eventually promoted into management positions in the company, while Helen stayed in her same role. According to Helen,

> Look I was happy, really really happy for both of them. But they started going to lunch and out for drinks without me. It was almost like I wasn't good enough anymore for them because I wasn't a manager. When I tried to ask them about it, Dorothy blew up, and then the next thing I knew I got a negative performance evaluation for absolutely no reason. I think it was because I questioned how they were acting and how they were treating me. I just don't get it. I didn't do anything, but honestly, I don't think I even want to go to work anymore.

While there are many benefits to peer relationships in the workplace, they are not without negative consequences, as demonstrated in Helen's example. These consequences can range from misuse of peer support to workplace bullying.

Misuse of Peer Support

While providing support to peers is often done for altruistic purposes, there are times in the workplace when support is misused—there is an alternative motivation for it that may lead to difficult circumstances. Berlin-Ray (1993) identified some of the potential misuses of peer support in the workplace. She contended that support can be misused in four ways: (1) as a commodity, (2) for information retrieval, (3) as a cause of codependency, and (4) against one's own interest.

First, support can be used as a commodity. In this case, support is given by one person who expects to be "owed" support at some future time. Such support may act as political currency, allowing the provider to dictate to recipients when the provider is ready to "cash in their chips." This exchange is often referred to as "social costs" or the cost of a relationship in terms of time and energy. Problems can arise if one member of the relationship feels that the other is receiving more or less commodity than they are (Morrison & Nolan, 2007).

Support can also be used as information retrieval, which is the support provided to make the other person feel she should give the supporter some information in return that is not ordinarily available to the supporter. People expect to be unique or special to their friends, which may lead to expectations of favoritism, special treatment, or inside information. For example, Paula invites Sarah for coffee and appears to be supportive while Sarah shares a work problem. Only later does Sarah realize that Paula has shared nothing about herself. In this instance, Paula obtained information she wanted, and Sarah may end up feeling used, which will damage the relationship. Rules about confidentiality in the workplace may negatively affect friendships because they place individuals who are used to disclosure between friends in awkward positions. Consequently, managing organizational information becomes more difficult.

Third, support can lead to codependency, which is a situation in which a coworker becomes dependent on the relationship to the extent that they are no longer able to act independently. Think back to complementary relationships where two coworkers are able to complete tasks by relying on each other's strengths to compensate for their own weaknesses. In a situation like this, one or both employees may miss out on a career opportunity because they have relied on a peer rather than learning the skills on their own. Similarly, individuals may report that their performance at work suffers because friendships mean more socializing and less productivity or that they can simply do less work because of the assistance that their friends provide.

Finally, giving support may work against the person providing it. The information-sharing nature of peer relationships may have one person sharing an opportunity within the organization that they are hoping for themselves with a peer, thereby lessening their own chances of success. For example, Paula tells Sarah about an opportunity

Paula was hoping to get herself. Because she feels obligated to Sarah, she tells her about it, even though she knows it will not be in her own best interest.

While peers can be logical and often much-needed sources of social support in organizations, even when the social support is not abused, it can lead to misunderstandings and be a downside to these organizational relationships. Friends are expected to listen, give advice, and generally be available to offer support whenever it is needed, not when it is convenient in the workday. Nor is social support always given equally in friendships. There will be times when one friend needs more support than the other, which can make it difficult if you are the friend providing support to balance the friendship and your own work demands (Methot et al., 2015; Toegel et al., 2013). Additionally, challenging or emotional conversations can be less restorative than traditional work breaks and make it difficult for employees to work on their core tasks (Pillemar & Rothbard, 2018).

Workplace Bullying

According to a survey conducted by Workplace Bullying Institute (2017), approximately 38% of U.S. employees reported having endured abuse in the workplace. Although the statistical reporting greatly varies by region, similar numbers are reported worldwide. For example, a study of Tasmania's public sector workers found that 23% reported workplace abuse (Easton, 2019). **Bullying** in the workplace is a communicative phenomenon whereby one employee repeatedly harasses and abuses another employee. Bullying behavior can take the form of verbal abuse, verbal or nonverbal threatening behaviors, intimidation, and workplace intimidation or sabotage (Lutgen-Sandvik et al., 2009). Abuse is not only occurring in face-to-face contexts, as 8 out of 10 U.S. employees reported being cyberbullied (Coyne et al., 2017). Cyberbullying is aggressive communication behaviors that occur through the use of information and communication technologies.

Key elements that help to identify bullying are as follows: the behaviors are persistent, there is escalation of the behaviors, there is power disparity, there is attributed intent, and there are adverse effects (Tracy et al., 2006). The acts occur repeatedly (persistence) and often become more intense (escalation) over a period of time. There is some degree of power disparity through formal roles, organizational resources, or informal social networks. In some cases, the power imbalance comes from the target being unable or unwilling to stand up to the bully. The target of the negative behavior views it as intentional and directed at them (attributed intent), and the behaviors have negative implications for the individual and the organization, such as lowered productivity, decreased morale, and increased absences (Cowan, 2012). Although studies have been inconclusive, it appears that work environments with high role conflict or workload, role ambiguity, and job insecurity increase the likelihood of bullying (Van den Brande et al., 2016).

Cyberbullying shares these same key elements but may have a stronger impact on victims for several reasons. First, information or pictures can be shared or viewed by a much wider audience, as cyberbullying is most common on email or social media platforms (Kowalski et al., 2018). This can lead to the perception of more frequent bullying because of the sheer volume. Instead of one person hearing the gossip or seeing a picture, information can be distributed to dozens with one click (Coyne et al., 2017). Cyberbullying is also particularly intrusive and can cross public-private boundaries, and the employee is not able to escape the bullying, even at home (Vranjes et al., 2017).

Helen's story from the beginning of this section is not unique in that the 2017 WBI survey found that while 70% of reported bullies are men, women bullies tend to target other females. Race also plays a factor in who is the target of bullying, as employees of color in the United States reported higher incidents of bullying than White employees, with Hispanic employees reporting the highest rates.

Bullying has a negative impact on both the individual targeted and the organization as a whole. Targets often report feelings of frustration, stress, alienation, and lowered self-esteem, as well as decreased levels of productivity, job satisfaction, organizational commitment, identification, and absenteeism (Nielsen & Einarsen, 2018). Bullying has also been associated with mental and physical conditions, such as anxiety, depression, post-traumatic stress disorder, headaches, heart disease, and, in some instances, even suicide (Nielsen & Einarsen, 2012; Verkuil et al., 2015). These negative impacts on individuals (and even those employees who witness the bullying incidents) also harm overall organizational job satisfaction and organizational identification. Lost productivity costs organizations tens to hundreds of thousands of dollars per year in addition to increased absenteeism and higher rates of turnover (Tye-Williams & Krone, 2015).

Salin's (2008) research on Finnish city administrators found that when anti-bullying policies do exist, the wording was often cut and pasted from other organizations, and the policies are more reactive in dealing with a bullying incident rather than proactive in attempting to prevent bullying from occurring. While there is a strong call for organizations to develop anti-bullying policies, many organizational representatives in Cowan's (2011) study reported that they felt that bullying fell under the umbrella terms of *conduct* and *ethics* and no further policies were necessary. Unless the bullying falls under existing antidiscrimination laws, little research exists to indicate how many workplaces have anti-bullying policies. There is also the question of the effectiveness of anti-bullying policies. One systematic review of anti-bullying policy research found that of the 12 different types of policies that had been studied, no policy had been found to have any effect on bullying, although policies were likely to increase employees' knowledge, attitudes, and self-perceptions about bullying (Nielsen & Einarsen, 2018). This seems to be similar to what happens in many public schools; the programs are not as effective at eliminating bullying as they are at making people more bully resilient.

Ironically, while peer relationships may lead to negative outcomes for individuals and organizations, those same peer relationships can provide a supportive network for dealing with behaviors such as bullying. Social support can moderate some of the indirect effects of workplace bullying, such as mental and physical discomfort and stress, help to prevent long-term health problems, and reduce the likelihood of individuals leaving the organization (Bao & Zhong, 2019; Fang et al., 2020; Quine, 2001). One study of nurses found, though, that a new employee's highest need for a strong peer network occurs within the first three months of transitioning from school to the job force, a time frame that may make it more difficult to have a strong peer network in place without direct organizational efforts to foster positive coworker relationships (Rush et al., 2014).

Next, we turn our attention to an emotionally intense workplace relationship: the workplace romance. Organizational communication research has explored the communication that occurs in this type of relationship, as well as how organizations attempt to manage them.

Romantic Relationships in the Workplace

Clearly, developing friendships at work can be beneficial, as well as detrimental, to both the individuals and the organization. When these friendships turn into romantic relationships, however, these consequences are heightened, and additional complications can develop. Despite the complications and risks, a 2017 SHRM survey found that 57% of employees reported having engaged in at least one romantic relationship at work.

A **workplace romance** is defined as a nonplatonic consensual relationship between two members of the organization that entails mutual sexual attraction and affection that has been communicated (e.g., Pierce & Aguinis, 2005; Pierce & Aguinis, 2009; Chory, 2019). The same-sex or opposite-sex relationship can include couples who are dating, living together, engaged, or married, as well as extramarital affairs, hookups, and friends with benefits. While the term, workplace romance, clearly covers a wide variety of relationships, they can be categorized by whom they are between. A *lateral romance* involves coworkers of equal status in the organization, while *hierarchical romances* involve coworkers occupying different levels, such as a supervisor and their subordinate. According to Powell (2001), hierarchical romances are more common but also much more problematic because of the power difference and the hostility that they can create. Organizations tend to be more concerned about hierarchical romances because of the real or perceived risks of favoritism, sexual harassment, and retaliation.

The workplace is an ideal environment for romances to begin. Coworkers have close and repeated contact, along with similar educational backgrounds, interests, and abilities (Chory & Hoke, 2020; Cowan & Horan, 2014). Just as task interdependence can lead to friendships developing it can also lead to more romantic relationships. Small group and interpersonal communication research suggest that working closely with another individual that you perceive to be capable and talented increases affinity. Add in similar interests and daily experiences and you have the perfect recipe for romance. Vault's (2017) study found that those who reported having an office romance identified that the relationship began at a happy hour or holiday event (17%) or because they had offices close to one another (18%).

Quinn (1977) first identified that romantic relationships in the workplace can be motivated by three primary reasons. He identified job motive (engaging in a romantic relationship for some sort of career advancement or reward), ego motive (the desire for excitement, adventure, and gratification), and love motive (interest in sincere affection, love, and long-term commitment). When Cowan and Horan (2014) reexamined motivations for workplace romance, they found the primary reasons to be ease of opportunity (proximity), similarity (attraction based on similarity), time (amount of time interacting), and hookups (similar to Quinn's notion of ego in that employees are looking for excitement and adventure in the workplace).

Like friendships, workplace romantic relationships have the potential to either benefit or harm the individuals involved. Romantic relationships can increase motivation and improve communication flow, job satisfaction, and performance (Chan-Serafin et al., 2016). However, they can also distract the couple from organizational responsibilities, as well as other organizational relationships (Hovick et al., 2003). For example, as Tracy and Logan's romantic relationship develops, they may exclude other team members' ideas or ignore aspects of their jobs that would require them to spend time apart. Furthermore, if the organization prohibits coworker romances, then Tracy and Logan may further distance themselves in an attempt to hide their relationship. In the absence of such a policy, the relationship will still be subject to the scrutiny and attention of coworkers and supervisors. If Tracy and Logan happen to be in a hierarchical relationship, coworkers are more likely to believe that the individual in the lower ranking organizational position has less than genuine motives for being in the relationship (Horan & Chory, 2011). In other words, coworkers are more likely to believe that the subordinate is only in the relationship for what they can get out of it professionally. This attention may be uncomfortable for both the couple and the individuals around them.

Deterioration of the romance can greatly strain the work environment. In daily life, we know that individuals often seek revenge after a breakup. Revenge in the workplace can involve charges of sexual harassment, negative performance reviews, or the creation of a hostile work environment. While the relationship once had the potential to increase job satisfaction and comfort, failed workplace romances can cause the individuals involved to feel insecure, unmotivated, unproductive, nervous, angry, or intimidated (Soloman & Williams, 1997). In addition, coworkers may feel caught in the middle of the breakup, resulting in the deterioration of additional relationships. Interestingly, research has found that coworkers and supervisors tend to evaluate claims of sexual harassment on the degree to which they consider the social-sexual behavior to be unethical in terms of organizational standards, participants' marital status, motivation for entering the relationship, or overall job performance (e.g., Brown & Allgeier, 1995; Pierce et al., 2004).

The Organizational Perspective on Workplace Romance

As with friendships, workplace romances have the potential to either benefit or harm the organization. These relationships are different, though, in that the potential for harm greatly increases if the relationship results in a breakup. In our daily lives, we are much more tolerant of ex-friends than we are of ex-lovers. Given the potential for complications, you would expect organizations to have firm and clear policies on dealing with workplace romance; however, a review of the literature finds that management has typically been given one of two pieces of advice: treat workplace romance as a purely private matter that is entirely unrelated to the organization or treat it as an organizational matter that is significantly related to the organization (Wilson, 2015). Regardless of their stance, historically, grounded in a classical perspective, organizations have banned organizational relationships with a strict no-fraternization policy. Boyd (2010) concluded that organizations that do ban organizational romances are motivated by one of several reasons, including *conflict of interest* (e.g., concern that a teacher might date a student), *grounds of productivity* (the notion that dating couples are likely to be distracted from work or distract their coworkers), *grounds of moral or religious stance* (e.g., concern about extramarital relationships or hookups that would be inconsistent with the company's beliefs), or fear of sexual harassment lawsuits. Organizations may also worry that romantic relationships will lead to perceptions of an unethical work environment, particularly after heightened awareness post-#MeToo (Von Bergen, 2020).

The Equal Employment Opportunity Commission (EEOC) defines sexual harassment as "unwelcome sexual advances, requests for sexual favors, and other verbal and physical conduct of a sexual nature." Quid pro quo sexual harassment literally translates into "this for that." This is a direct form of sexual harassment that involves someone offering a promotion, contract, or other employment condition or benefit in exchange for a sexual favor. For example, it would be quid pro quo harassment if a supervisor offered a desirable project to one of their employees in exchange for sex. **Hostile environment sexual harassment**, on the other hand, is the use of words and actions to make a work environment demeaning, intimidating, and abusive. Hostile environment harassment could include jokes, suggestive pictures, demeaning and inappropriate terms, gestures, touching, or crude and offensive language. Kellie, a sales associate in a retail store, described a particularly egregious series of behaviors by a coworker that should be considered hostile environment sexual harassment:

> Patrick was very inappropriate and manipulative and just took advantage of all of the women in the departments. He had a history of sleeping with people in the store outside of the department and just kind of pitting the girls against each other to try and keep every relationship on its own. Like he would tell me, "Oh you are my favorite employee," and literally walk away from me and tell another girl, "Oh Kellie is the worst." So that was very toxic, and it lasted for years, along with many other things. I finally had my last straw when I was bent over grabbing something in the back, and he pushed himself up on me, and I was like I cannot do this anymore. Like little touching here and there I feel like people can ignore and just think, oh he was just walking by me and happened to touch me, but then you

think about it and look back, and your like there was probably a hundred instances of him taking advantage of tight quarters or any situation; he would always use it to his advantage.

Kellie went on to say that after she finally summoned the nerve to report Patrick to human resources, their solution was to promote him and move him to another location.

Sexual harassment can occur between any members or nonmembers (e.g., a client or outside vendor) of the organization regardless of their organizational relationship or rank, although it is more common for quid pro quo harassment to occur between a supervisor and their subordinate. The victim can also be someone other than the actual target of the harassment; sexual harassment can be experienced by those affected by the offensive conduct, even if they were not the intended target. The EEOC has made it clear that as long as the conduct is unwanted, sexual harassment perpetrators and targets can be either men or women, and the harassment does not need to include individuals of the opposite sex. As with bullying, sexual harassment can occur face-to-face or virtually and has many of the same job performance, mental, and physical effects on its victims (Raj et al., 2020).

As the workplace has transformed, organizational management seems to have moved from a clear ban, to a "don't ask, don't tell" policy, to a surprising mixture of unclear and unresolved policies that are oftentimes not clearly communicated to employees. One of the most popular alternatives to no dating policies, however, is the *love contract*. This contract, signed at the onset of the relationship, identifies that the relationship is entered into voluntarily by both parties and typically outlines the company's policies on sexual harassment and retaliation. Realistically, individuals wanting to hide the relationship, such as those having affairs or coworkers engaging in spur-of-the-moment hookups are unlikely to contact the human resources department to initiate a love contract, and there is little research to suggest that they do much to protect individual employees. In fact, some human resources professionals worry that these contracts may encourage employees to try to hide the relationship because they were not able to or did not initiate the appropriate organizational paperwork ahead of time (Wilkie, 2013). Research does suggest that these policies seem to be designed more for the company to defend against potential sexual harassment suits, as evidence that it took steps to prevent possible abuse, than for employee protection (Von Bergen, 2020).

It is not surprising that more organizations are creating office romance policies given the personnel as well as legal problems such relationships can cause for the organization. In addition to the morale problems previously discussed, Hovick et al. (2003) found that workplace couples tend to exchange a great deal of personal information while on the company clock. Their study indicated that the average couple spoke face-to-face approximately five times, exchanged a little over four emails, and spoke on the phone several times in the course of an average workday. Practically speaking, this means that during an 8-hour workday, couples are emailing one another at least once every 2 hours. Obviously, time spent on personal issues is time not spent on organizational issues. As we know from our daily lives, sending the email is the least time-consuming part of the process; we must also think about and compose the email in addition to reading and digesting the email that we receive back. Therefore, the total time away from work-related duties is much greater than just the time involved in hitting the send button.

Regardless of whether the relationship is going well or not, coworkers may speculate about the nature of the relationship, leading to office gossip, increased scrutiny by coworkers and supervisors, and general awkwardness for both the individuals and their coworkers (Chan-Serafin et al., 2017 Horan & Chory, 2011). While being in a relationship can improve job performance, Riach and Wilson (2007) found that this can actually be because individuals in the relationship are working harder to counter negative coworker perceptions. Although millennials may have different relationship expectations (for example, waiting longer to get married or not getting married at all), one study that focused exclusively on millennials found few generational differences in their experiences of the positives and negatives of workplace romance (Chory & Hoke, 2019). Organizations that allow office romances to occur may face legal consequences. As previously discussed, sexual harassment charges are one possible legal consequence. Another possibility, though, is the potential for lawsuits based on preferential treatment. The *New York Times* reported on July 24, 2005, that the California Supreme Court ruled that "workers can sue when a colleague who is sleeping with the boss is shown repeated preferential treatment." Workers often are concerned that romantic relationships between supervisors and subordinates may result in unfair raises, unjust promotions, better assignments, and breaches in confidentiality. Coworkers are afraid that information they share with the colleague or boss may automatically be shared with the intimate partner. Edward Harold, a partner practicing employment litigation at Fisher & Phillips, LLP, identified other legal consequences outside of sexual harassment claims: "For example, if one party claims the relationship was not consensual, [they] can include claims of assault and battery, false imprisonment, and defamation" (Wilkie, 2015).

To conclude this chapter, we turn our attention to the dialectical tensions inherent in all of our organizational peer relationships (of all types) to help us understand some of the misunderstandings that occur in these complicated organizational relationships.

Dialectical Tensions and Coworker Relationships

Regardless of the importance of workplace relationships to both individuals and organizations, the potential for the relationship to become complicated does exist and is even likely. Imagine that you are close friends with someone in the organization who has access to all the job openings in the company before they are public knowledge. Your friend knows how much you would like to move into the social media department but does not share with you that there is going to be a job opening, and you miss out on this opportunity. You feel betrayed by your friend, but your friend insists that they were just following company policy and doing their job. Baxter and Braithewaite (2008) would argue that you are experiencing a dialectical tension, which is an opposing but inevitable and normal force that occurs in every relationship, including organizational peer relationships. Dialectical tensions are discursive struggles or contradictions that happen as individuals attempt to communicatively negotiate their relationship.

Bridge and Baxer (1992) identified five dialectical tensions that are prevalent in organizational peer relationships, including instrumentality-affection, impartiality-favoritism, autonomy-connection, openness-closedness, and judgment-acceptance.

Instrumentality-affection refers to the struggle over competing instrumental needs (information, interdependence, and cooperation to complete tasks) and genuine care and emotional needs. For example, you need your romantic partner's portion of the project in order to complete your tasks, but you are conflicted because you know that they are stressed by the project, and you do not want to add to that stress. The close physical proximity of coworkers can trigger this dialectic as well. We have all had coworkers that would rather talk than work, making it nearly impossible to get your work done. Such is the case for Ernest, a new factory worker:

> A worker who has been with the company for many years but has become jaded spends inordinate amounts of time leaning on walls and railings, complaining at length and in detail about what morons the managers are. The predicament this puts a new worker in is that respectful acknowledgment of position and seniority dictate paying attention to the coworker, while efficiency and productivity dictate getting some work done. In this factory, that was often the case, particularly with one worker whose activity was adjacent but not directly related to mine. Such proximity without barrier invites interaction, but the incongruous activities and efforts of the departments do not provide time for complaining.

Ernest was struggling as a new employee at this organization because of the instrumentality-affection dialectic. On one hand, he had a coworker who wanted emotional support, or at least someone to complain to, and on the other hand, Ernest was new and needed to concentrate on completing his tasks.

Impartiality-favoritism tensions exist because the organization creates standards for feedback and assistance based on a formal organizational role, but we tend to think about our friends as being unique and special individuals. Similarly, individuals in a close relationship often think of themselves as a special unit but also need to stand out as competent individuals who are able to perform their organizational roles, thus creating the *autonomy-connection* dialectic.

The *openness-closedness* dialectic is illustrated in the story of the social media opening recounted at the beginning of this section. This tension involves the expectation that friends share information and secrets with one another, while at the same time organizational roles often prescribe confidentiality or secrecy that can prove challenging. The feelings that an organizational member can experience while living with the dialectic of openness-closedness is evident in the story told to us by Carol, who was a receptionist in a manufacturing company:

> As a receptionist, I was neither a regular employee in production nor a true member of the front office. I felt like being all alone at the front desk kept me separated from other employees, so I did not always know about what was going on in production and was an outsider to that team. However, I also was not a part of management, so I was not privy to their knowledge either. I felt like I was stuck in the middle of the two parts of the company, where I had access to a lot of information and relationships but not to the same extent as other people. Sometimes, I knew more than I wanted, while other times, I didn't know enough. It made me feel uncomfortable and left out.

Carol found herself in a situation as a result of her formal role in the organization, where she knew most everyone in the organization; however, she was often not privy to the information that these peers were because of their different roles. As she said at the end of the interview, this tension made her feel uncomfortable and left out, which makes it difficult to be satisfied with and connected to the organization.

Finally, the *judgment-acceptance* dialectic is a product of peers expecting those close to them to affirm, accept, and provide social support, but organizational roles may at times require evaluation (e.g., feedback, reprimands, choosing one person over another for projects or promotions) or even additional stress. Take for example the situation described by Kevin, a contracted military cadet at his university:

> It's tough because being a cadet, you have a professional side where you have a very clear mission or task that you're supposed to accomplish, and you need to establish those professional roles. Then, a few hours later, you're with friends outside of that professional environment, and then the communication switches again. I think the switch is always hard because reestablishing who is doing what is always a tedious process that might take growing pains or getting used to, which may be negative, but I think once everyone gets into the swing of things, everybody is pretty good about adjusting to different peer leadership roles. One semester, or one month, you might have a lot of work that you're delegating to a lot of people, but the next month, all of a sudden, people are delegating tasks and projects to you. Everyone is pretty good about being respectful to different communication channels and getting stuff done in a timely fashion.

Kevin is describing the judgment-acceptance dialectic perfectly as he experiences leading his peers as a senior cadet and then being friends with them outside of the military context. As he indicates at the end, exerting communicative energy is necessary to not be paralyzed by this dialectical tension. In his case, effectively managing this tension may help strengthen the relationships he has with his junior cadets.

At the heart of organizational workplace relationships is the contradiction between the personal relationship and organizational roles, which can lead to tensions and misunderstandings. These tensions, much like misunderstandings, should be anticipated rather than avoided to be able to manage them through communication as effectively as possible.

Summary

Communication with peers at work can create a strong bond between the employee and the organization. When people feel more connected to each other, morale and organizational commitment increase significantly. Those outcomes can be adversely affected, though, when the misunderstandings that come with these relationships are not anticipated.

In this chapter, we discussed how organizational and personal relationships at work differ. We explored the reasons why more personal relationships are likely to develop at work, including proxemics, shared projects, similarity, relational balance, and personal needs. We examined the benefits of peer relationships for both individuals and organizations, as well as the role of technology in these relationships. We explored the darker side of personal work relationships, including the misuse of social support and bullying, such as cyberbullying, before turning our attention to romantic relationships. In addition to looking at the benefits of workplace romance, we also provided an overview of the negatives, including a discussion of sexual harassment. Finally, we looked at the dialectical tensions inherent in all workplace relationships.

Perhaps the most important thing to keep in mind from the chapter is that coworker relationships are anchored to the organizational structure. Friendships may develop from task-based relationships, but the organizational aspects of them still remain. If the relationship deteriorates, whether it is a workplace romance, a work spouse relationship, or a special peer, the organizational relationship still needs to remain.

As noted in the chapter, peer relationships have many benefits for both organizations and individuals, but at the same time, they bring with them the potential for misunderstandings. For organizational peers, competition for resources, differing personal goals, personality differences, and work-life balancing and blurring concerns could cause misunderstandings. For those in blended relationships, misunderstandings could arise when one person is promoted or moved in the organization, when something goes wrong in the personal relationship, or when other coworkers are unable to cope with the nature of their friendship. Individuals and organizations should recognize that coworker relationships have the potential for benefit as well as misunderstandings.

Organizational Teams

LEARNING OBJECTIVES

1. Describe an organizational team and what makes it effective

2. Outline the characteristics critical to the success of work teams

3. Describe the pros and cons of self-managed work teams

4. Evaluate factors that aid or challenge the effectiveness of virtual teams

5. Indicate how misunderstandings in the team environment may turn into conflict if not addressed

Teams are permanent fixtures in organizational life. Much of the work done in organizations is done by teams, committees, or some other sort of small group with tasks involving more than decision-making (Tripathy, 2018). Organizations attempt to develop small groups into organizational teams with a sharper focus to accomplish organizational projects. Why do organizations put so much energy into developing teams? The synergy and nonsummativity that come with an effective team enable the organization to respond to a dynamic organizational environment that demands constant innovation and change balanced with stability (McKinney et al., 2005). Specifically, research has shown that teams have many benefits, including increased productivity and employee empowerment (Shonk, 1992). Researchers have identified that teams are a unique opportunity for organizations to solve problems by bringing people of different skill sets, varying background experiences, and a range of functional experiences together (Dahlin et al., 2005).

While teams can help organizations accomplish tasks that individuals working alone could not, they can simultaneously create misunderstandings because of the complexity of interrelationships and demands on the communication system. Take for example the story told to us by Don, who is the coordinator of competitive sports and events for a university. This story demonstrates the opportunities and challenges of working in teams, even when the team members are dedicated and committed:

> Our department hosts an annual 5K race to raise money for multiple causes. This year we had gone with a new timing company, which

we have had to do for the second year in a row. Having a new timing company isn't an issue, we just need to make sure we are all on the same page during race day. My role is to serve as race director and to lead a team of five to six student staff members who plan the event fully. I also work with upper administration in the department on some of the large-scale requirements of the event, such as police support, university approval, budget, permits. This was my third year as race director, but the upper administration of the department has been working on this event since its creation 25 years ago. This year, the event had nearly 800 participants.

Around 4:00 p.m. the night prior to the race we learned that our course was partially flooded. Quickly, we were "on the clock." Immediately, we got on the phone with the city to seek approval for a different route but learned we couldn't get approval until (at the earliest) 5:00 a.m. to 8:00 a.m. (latest) on race day. My supervisor and I created two routes. One for if we get approval from the city and one for if we didn't. We felt confident about our options, reworked our volunteer assignments, and waited to hear from the city.

The day of the event, we got the word that we would be able to go with our Plan A, which is great. I began to notice that our timing company was asking a lot of questions about where to set up our race lines. Not thinking too much about it, my supervisor went with them to show them where to place the lines while another staff member created signage to notify runners of the change. While walking runners to the start line and pushing people out of the building, I realized that what my supervisor thought was the start line was not what I thought was the start line AND what was on the updated signage was also not the correct start line. Immediately, we removed the signage, notified our volunteers on bikes who lead our fastest runners through the course, and pushed the crowd in a different direction. While a miscommunication, it ultimately worked out since we trust all of our staff members and reminded ourselves to be adaptable with positive attitudes. Had this not been our team approach, I feel this could have been a big issue that could have jeopardized our event.

Communication was a big role in this problem. We were under pressure because of the last-minute changes and having to be flexible with getting approval from the city. Essentially, while Google Maps is detailed, it isn't detailed enough. While we had thought we were talking about the same start line, we weren't. But we were able to trust each other's decisions and have positive attitudes and handle the confusion in the moment.

I think what caused the problem in the first place was a combination of things. The night before we had printed multiple copies of what to post for each plan. I think the person who grabbed them just grabbed the wrong pile. We probably should have labeled them Plan B or Plan C instead of just saying "the stack closest to the copier." Additionally, on the day of the event, everyone has the mindset of "all hands on deck." Someone saw they weren't put up, asked which pile, and then just put them up. We didn't have a whole lot of communication for that process, and we didn't have it assigned directly for someone to do. We probably should have looking back!

Don's story demonstrates how even high-functioning teams can sometimes get in their own way. In this case, their core value of "adaptable with positive attitudes" allowed the team to manage a significant, unanticipated environmental change but that same value led team members to jump in and help without explicit instructions. The same value also led Don and his supervisor to assume that each of them had the same meaning for the "start line." This team and their experiences with the event provide an excellent example of why members need to anticipate that misunderstandings will occur in organizations. In doing so, this team was able to respond effectively to the misunderstandings, be successful in their tasks, and create the possibility of learning for the future.

Defining Organizational Teams

It is quite likely that you, as a newcomer to an organization, will be placed on more than one team at a time. One team might be allocated the task of developing a marketing plan to launch a new product or service and may be disbanded once the product is on the market. Another team might be a more permanent work team in a regional office. The result could be that you report to two different people at once.

Teams serve to link employees to the organization and can increase their loyalty. In fact, in one study, researchers found that employees identified more with their teams than with the larger organization (Barker & Tompkins, 1994). The implications for the organization are clear: Productive teams are critical not only to the success of the organization but also to the satisfaction of individuals.

As you can imagine, definitions of what constitutes a team abound. We offer the following definition of a **team**, which is a mild adaptation of one forwarded by Katzenbach and Smith (1993): *A team is a small group (three to nine) of interdependent people with complementary skills who are committed to a common purpose, performance goals, and approach for which they hold themselves mutually accountable.* Several important aspects of this definition make this a definition of not just any team but an *effective* one. First, a team must be larger than a dyad (otherwise, it is simply an interpersonal relationship), but not so large that direct communication among all members becomes impossible. Research seems to indicate that the breaking point for team effectiveness is 10 members. Second, the members of the team are interdependent, which means that the success or failure of one member is dependent on the success or failure of the others. If the members of a team are not interdependent, then the time and energy it takes to form and maintain the team are not necessary; work could instead be done independently. Third, members must be committed to each other and the goals, objectives, and processes of the team. Without this commitment, the team will be burdened by either unproductive or insubordinate members or conflict that does not allow the members to move forward in their tasks. This is not to imply, however, that conflict should be or will be avoided in a healthy team. As we discovered in previous chapters and will discuss further here, conflict on the appropriate levels and handled positively can be very constructive. Finally, the real strength of a team comes from the mutual accountability of the team members as they hold each other accountable for meeting and exceeding expectations. These expectations involve process concerns (e.g., communication, meeting deadlines, and attending meetings) and outcomes (e.g., quality of work and satisfaction).

Wageman (1997), as well as Sheard and Kakabadse (2002), identified features that differentiate a less effective team from one that is more effective:

1. **The team must have clearly defined goals and direction.** They have a sense of why the team exists; they understand their goal and know what direction their team needs to take.

2. **The basic work is designed to be done by a team.** There needs to be a clear reason that a team is completing the work as opposed to an individual. Projects suitable for teams should be large and/or complex projects that could not readily be completed by an individual.

3. **Resources are readily available.** Tools, appropriate meeting space, access to computing services, and other resources must be present if the team is to work in a timely, proactive, and effective fashion. Additionally, the team needs time to complete the group work process and produce the desired outcome.

4. **Team members need clearly defined roles and responsibilities.** All individuals on the team must be able to agree upon and understand the distribution of the tasks to complete the project.

5. **There must be a positive team dynamic.** Individuals on the team must have self-awareness regarding how their words and actions impact the rest of the team and need to establish and accept a working social system within their team.

6. **Team rewards are strongly associated with team effort.** A national car dealership wanted salespeople to work in teams to provide better coverage for their customers, but it continued to reward the individual salesperson for the number of cars sold. The reward system was in direct competition with the organizational goal. If a team is to work well together, there must be rewards for team efforts.

7. **The team, not the leader, has the authority to make decisions over basic work strategies.** If the team is to perform at a high level, it must feel it has the power to make decisions about how its work is done.

8. **The team establishes norms that promote strategic thinking.** To be innovative, the team must set norms that allow it to think ahead and define future actions instead of reacting to current conditions.

Clearly, successful teams must be able to have open dialogue. They need to recognize and be able to articulate their team's goal and feel that their members' individual fates are linked directly with the success of the team. This is a difficult concept to instill in the United States, where individualism is a strong value. The organization must create rewards based on the success of the team as a whole to establish successful teams.

We begin this chapter by outlining the characteristics of teams. Next, we discuss teams in the workplace, followed by descriptions of two types of workplace teams—self-managed work teams and virtual teams. We conclude by discussing effective teams and showing how misunderstandings and conflict affect team life.

Characteristics of Teams

Certain factors are inherent in any team. The way in which the team manages these characteristics is critical to its success. Relational communication, cohesiveness, diversity, resilience, satisfaction, stress, and stuckness are all characteristics explored in the following sections.

Relational Communication

In addition to completing tasks, teams can serve social, or relationship, goals. First, relationships are formed that help employees feel more connected to the team, and these personal relationships make the link between the employee and the organization stronger. Second, teams provide individuals an opportunity to receive social support. As discussed in Chapter 10, a supportive climate can influence not only personal but also professional decisions and help organizational members solve problems.

Third, the team can provide a chance for individuals to demonstrate leadership abilities. Working with a team gives employees a chance to step forward and organize tasks, as well as provide a vision for the future. If social support is present, teams can be a great environment for employees to showcase their knowledge and abilities beyond their traditional organizational roles.

Finally, teams provide a setting for new ideas to be tested before going public. Trying out ideas in the relative safety of one's team can give an indication of how ideas might be perceived by a larger audience. Individuals seem to be more accepting of feedback or failed ideas in this smaller setting than when an idea is launched in a larger more public arena.

As has been demonstrated throughout your textbook numerous times, we need interpersonal relationships to feel engaged and teams can give us a place to do so while also testing our ideas and abilities. At the same time, poor relationships can lead to dysfunctional teams. Sometimes the dysfunction is caused by one individual whose behavior is inconsistent. Stohl and Schell (1991) referred to this type of person as a farrago. Interactions with a farrago can result in confusion about responsibilities, tasks, decisions, procedures, and relationships, which in turn undermine the team experience because inconsistency is one of the most difficult behaviors to cope with; you never know what to expect from this team member. A relationship that is always negative is easier to deal with because we expect it, as opposed to a relationship that seems to switch from positive to negative without any reason.

The result of such dysfunctional relationships in the team can include the following: (1) decision-making procedures are compromised, (2) issues are defined according to the poor relationship or the weak member, (3) a great deal of energy is consumed trying to resolve issues, (4) confusing behaviors are exhibited in response to this conflict, (5) time and energy are consumed in mending the relationships, and, finally, (6) negative emotions are displayed toward the team as a whole (Keyton, 1999). Teams trying to solve relationship issues can spend a majority of their time and energy trying to resolve those issues and far less time and energy accomplishing the task.

Cohesiveness

Cohesiveness is the degree to which members feel connected to the team. The members' identification with the team and its goals is accomplished through "forging, maintenance, and alteration of linkages between persons and groups" (Scott et al., 1998, p. 304). The more these linkages are identified and reinforced, the greater team cohesiveness. For example, an individual might feel a link to a team because they believe in the task on which the team is working. That task could further the organizational goal or advance the success of the team itself. Another individual might feel connected to the team because of relationships formed there. If people are attracted to other team members as friends and colleagues, they will want to work for the team's success.

Jablin's (1984) work on organizational assimilation is consistent with team cohesiveness as well. He suggested that the "newcomer attempts to become an accepted, participating member of the organization by learning new attitudes and behaviors or modifying existing ones to be consistent with the organization's expectations" (p. 596). This happens on a smaller scale in organizational teams. Team members adapt to the norms of the team, learn new attitudes and behaviors, and increase team cohesiveness. When members are not able to forge these linkages with the team, cohesiveness is affected. Can a team function that is not cohesive? In some cases, yes, but it is much more difficult for team members to focus on the team goal. Cohesiveness in teams has been linked to many different positive outcomes, such as increased cooperation and decreased absenteeism (Sanders & Nauta, 2004).

Diversity

As the U.S. workforce continues to adapt to the changing demands of customers, increasing competition, and globalization, organizations are recognizing the need to use more diverse teams. Surface or demographic diversity refers to characteristics such as race, age, gender, sexuality, and nationality, while informational or deep-level diversity is the difference in education, ability, and experience (e.g., Kearnery et al., 2009; van Veelen & Ufkes, 2019).

Research from the past 50 years has yielded mixed results when examining the relationship between team diversity and performance (van Veelen &Ufkes, 2019). The research results depend on the work context, type of diversity, and performance outcomes measured. What is clearer, though, is *how* diversity leads to improved performance. Diverse teams mean a larger and more varied pool of information, ideas, and perspectives for the team to work with. This pool of ideas can serve as a springboard for ideas to be shared, debated, and integrated into organizational goals and tasks. This in turn can improve innovation, decision-making, problem-solving, and critical thinking (Cletus et al., 2018).

The challenge is that these positives seem to only happen when there is a strong enough sense of team identification (or sense of "we") to overcome any intergroup bias that may occur as a result of members interacting with people who are different than themselves. Research on homogenous teams (teams with members from similar backgrounds and perspectives) have found that these teams can also be creative, innovative, and highly effective at problem-solving with superior teamwork and outcomes because they don't have the barriers of difference to overcome (e.g., Cox & Blake, 1991; Hambrick et al., 1996; Horwitz & Horwitz, 2009). Following the similarity-attraction paradigm or social identity theory, we are drawn to and most comfortable with those individuals that we perceive to be most like us and will consequently work better in a team comprised of individuals we perceive to be like us (Lincoln & Miller, 1979).

Think about group projects that you have had to complete for school. One of the first questions we as teachers are asked is, "Who gets to pick the teams?" When given the choice, you usually want to pick either your friends or individuals with whom you think you identify. Because you perceive a higher degree of similarity, you don't feel as though you need to spend as much time getting to know one another and can more quickly move to the assigned project.

Homogenous teams can yield similar ideas because of their similar backgrounds and similar voices, which can make it easier to fall into **groupthink**. Groupthink is a flawed group process or decision resulting from the desire to maintain conformity. Because diverse teams already have differences in experiences and backgrounds, they may be more likely to share different ideas and stimulate debate and dissent. Think back again to that group project for class, only this time, the groups were assigned for you rather than self-selected. You are placed into a group of people you do not know as well, who have taken different classes than you, and have had completely different experiences. Thinking outside the box may come more naturally, and it may be easier to speak up because there are not the same assumptions. This all assumes, however, that the team experience is devoid of hostility, disrespect, and discrimination (Cletus et al., 2018).

Diverse team success also depends on the team's design, team climate, and the individuals who comprise the team (Guillaume et al., 2017). *Team design* refers to factors such as overall team characteristics and size, while *team climate* includes variables such as trust and psychological safety. *Individual differences*, as you probably guessed, include things like being open to working with people who are different and having a desire for more and different kinds of information.

Resilience

Teams work in complex environments often complicated by competition, instability, and rapid change. Resilience is the capacity of some teams to bounce back from this adversity (Masten, 2014; West et al., 2009). While research has found that resilience can represent a team's ability, capacity, outcome, or process, if the team is able to proactively avoid adversity to achieve its goals, that is more of a measure of team effectiveness than resiliency (Stoverink et al., 2020). At the same time, a team consisting of resilient individuals without a collective sense of team identity ("we") will not automatically equate to a resilient team. Think about it this way, just because you bring people together who have the knowledge and skills to be successful, it doesn't mean that they will successfully work together in a team. The same is true of resilience. Individuals may have the coping skills to be resilient, but those skills may not transfer to the team dynamic. Brittle work teams, those teams low in resilience, are much more susceptible to failure.

The difference between resilient and brittle teams is that resilient teams are more flexible and adaptable to change, similar to organizations (see Chapter 4). Resilient teams embrace diverse knowledge and experiences and have a psychologically and interpersonally safe environment for team members to take risks and share new ideas that allow them to adapt to ever-changing environments. Resilient teams also provide social support and communicatively manage conflict as it arises (Stoverink et al., 2020).

Satisfaction

Satisfaction is the degree of positive affect members of a team feel in being associated with a team (Robert & You, 2017). This can mean the team members feel accomplished for completing the team tasks and being recognized for their contributions. Higher levels of satisfaction increase job performance and the likelihood that individuals want to stay together as a team (de la Torre-Ruiz et al., 2014). Satisfaction and rewards are uniquely tied to each other. A team feels satisfied with its work to the degree that the work has been accepted and recognized. The rewards can be *internal*, such as meeting individual goals, or *external*, such as a promotion. Satisfaction can also refer to meeting relational needs.

Stress

Think back to that group project we just talked about. How did you feel when you first learned that you had a group project? Students often express that group projects stress them out because it is hard to find a time when everyone is available; they have to worry about their teammates completing their portion of the projects; they worry about relying on others for their grade. Working with others requires coordination and compromise. We experience **stress** because of our own desire to perform and the strain of negotiating with others. In organizations, we can also experience stress because we are constantly switching between individual roles and teams or more collaborative roles (Driskell et al., 2018).

As we attempt to communicatively manage these challenging relationships, conflict is a natural outcome. In several studies that looked at the use of teams in the medical setting, where multidisciplinary teams were necessary to provide high-quality patient care, the likelihood of conflict was high. The researchers concluded that one of the most beneficial strategies administrators could teach teams was how to effectively resolve conflict to prevent negative effects rather than trying to prevent it in the first place (García-Campayo et al., 2016).

Stuckness

Another characteristic of teams that can have a negative impact on the team's success is **stuckness**. Stuckness occurs when teams are unable to break a negative pattern of behavior, which causes them to make the same mistakes over and over again (Keyton, 2000). Sometimes the team sticks with what is comfortable rather than confronting opposing forces or beliefs within the team and finding connections between them. When the team is stuck, trying a new process, changing the environment or climate, or shifting resources can be helpful. A team may be very willing but unable to perform a task, or it may be quite able and unwilling to do so. Either way, the team is stuck in one position, unable to move forward.

Therefore, teams can be characterized by relational communication, the cohesiveness of the team, how resilient the team is, the degree to which members are satisfied with the actions of the team, how open the team is to outside opinions and information, how the team handles stress, and the team's degree of "stuckness." All these traits make each team unique, with its own history and behavior patterns. Examine the teams to which you belong and try to describe the characteristics that define them.

With that general description of the characteristics of teams, we now turn our attention to a more specific discussion of teams in the workplace.

Teams at Work

Although it is difficult to determine exactly what percentage of organizations are using teams today, researchers and practitioners alike agree that a vast number of organizations use them and that their use will only continue to grow. As a result, organizational members find themselves spending a considerable portion of their workdays working in teams (Reimer et al., 2017).

Because of the growing demands for flexibility and adaptability to rapidly changing environments, the prevalence of teams in organizations will only continue to grow. For more than 50 years, some organizational theorists have been arguing for making teams the basic work unit. This has been traced by one researcher back to the work of Eric Trist and his coal mine experiments in 1951 (Shonk, 1992). The call for such an organizational structure is still being heeded and repeated with even more strength by writers, such as Katzenbach and Smith (1993), who said, "We believe that teams—real teams, not just groups that management calls 'teams'—should be the basic unit of performance for most organizations regardless of size" (p. 15).

So what would a team-based organization look like? Team-based organizations can take on several appearances and follow a variety of processes, but they must make cultural shifts to support teams. Sherriton and Stern (1997) said that the following cultural shifts must occur:

- **From hierarchical to flat.** Organizations must decentralize their decision-making and power structures; in other words, power and authority must be distributed throughout the organization.

- **From fragmentation to cohesion.** Cultures that had previously segmented different factions of the organization from one another (e.g., management and workers, accounting and distribution) must now become comfortable with these groups being thrown together.

- **From independence to interdependence.** Individual organizational members will no longer work on projects in singular, isolated ways; their processes and products will be interlinked with other organizational and extra-organizational members.

- **From competition to cooperation.** Many organizations tend to breed competition among coworkers as a means of motivating them to work harder; however, a team-based culture must replace the ethic of competition with one of coopera- tion, as team members will need to rely on one another, build trust, and increase cohesiveness to have an effective and satisfied team.

- **From tried-and-true to risk-taking.** When individuals work in relative isolation from one another, they tend to go with what they know works best and works best for them; however, moving into the realm of teams means that diversity of thought, process, and execution increases and, therefore, so does the need to break out of old habits and take risks on new ideas, processes, and products.

Although this cultural shift will take time and necessarily cause misunderstandings, the move to teams as basic work units should increase performance. Teams tend to perform well for several reasons. First, they bring more skills and experiences to bear on the situation than a single individual. Second, because of the diversity of skills and experiences, teams are more flexible and responsive to change than individuals tend to be. Third, teams afford the members opportunities for close interpersonal relationships, which, as we described earlier, can significantly affect their quality of work and personal lives. Finally, teams offer the possibility of fun as interpersonal relationships are developed and hardships and successes bring social rewards (Katzenbach & Smith, 1993).

Types of Organizational Teams

Organizational teams can be of a variety of types, and those types can take different forms. There are four major types of organizational teams (Cohen & Bailey, 1997): (1) work teams, (2) parallel teams, (3) project teams, and (4) management teams. These types can take different forms (e.g., supervised, self-directed, virtual). Let's first turn to the four major types of organizational teams.

Although organizational teams can be classified in a number of different ways, researchers Cohen and Bailey (1997) provide a useful and manageable typology. **Work teams** are continuing units that are responsible for the production of goods or providing services, such as customer service. They are sometimes referred to as production or service teams. Members are relatively stable and full time. These teams have traditionally been directed by supervisors, but there is a movement toward self-management. Examples of this type of team are apparel manufacturing teams or sales teams.

Parallel teams tend to pull together people from different work units or departments to complete tasks that the organization is not otherwise prepared or equipped to perform well. Membership in these teams is a bit more flexible and short-lived than membership in work teams. These teams have limited authority and tend to be more advisory, making recommendations rather than final decisions. Parallel teams tend to be used for problem-solving and improvement activities. Typical examples of parallel teams include advisory teams and task forces.

The third type of team is a project team. **Project teams** produce one-time outputs and are time limited. Members tend to have specialized expertise, and each member of the team is recruited (and should be valued) for that expertise. An organization might use a project team to bring together experts from a variety of areas to combine their efforts in the development of a new product.

Management teams are created to "coordinate and provide direction to subunits under their jurisdiction, laterally interdependent subunits across key business processes" (p. 243). Often, as other types of teams are assembled that require different specialties, it is helpful to have teams of managers who have the ability to understand and direct their activities (diverse management perspectives to supervise diverse teams).

Finally, there is some research devoted to **action teams**, which are also sometimes called performing teams. Action teams are groups of independent experts who are brought together for complex, coordinated, and time-constrained events (Kozlowski & Bell, 2013). These team members also balance full-time independent organizational roles, but their roles on the action teams are vital. One prime example of an action team would be a surgical team.

Self-Managed Work Teams

Self-managed work teams, also known as self-directed or autonomous work teams, are gaining popularity in organizations. **Self-managed work teams** (SMWTs) have responsibility for their own work. They designate project management priorities, monitor their own performance, problem-solve, and in some cases even conduct their own performance evaluations instead of having a supervisor do these things (Oh, 2012). Every member of the SMWT takes responsibility for their own work, as well as that of the team. As workers become involved in SMWTs, they tend to lose their individual-task orientation and define their work roles in relation to how they can personally contribute to the mission and goals of the team (Manz & Sims, 1987).

SMWT members share power and authority (Eseryel et al., 2020; Magpili & Pazos, 2018). Oh's (2012) research found, though, that either designated informal or formal leaders do tend to emerge in the initial stages of formation of the SMWTs. This leadership can be instrumental in the success of the team. Additional factors that influence the SMWT's success include role fluidity (how easily members are able to assume more than one team role), individual team member self-management skills (the ability to self-structure one's tasks and workday), and openness to change and flexibility in general. SMWTs are also more successful when individual members have work experience both with the task and with teams, and, overall, the team is composed of diverse knowledge and experiences. SMWTs also need a supportive corporate climate that provides rewards for individual and team efforts.

Why would organizations use SMWTs instead of traditional teams? SMWTs are thought to increase employees' commitment to the organization because participation in decision-making should increase support for those decisions. In addition to increasing employee commitment, the use of SMWTs is related to the following important outcomes: competence, productivity, innovative problem-solving, increased job satisfaction, increased quality of workers' lives, increased flexibility, and increased customer satisfaction (Chansler et al., 2003; Kauffeld, 2006; Thomas et al., 2002).

Clearly, SMWTs offer many benefits; however, they are not to be used in every situation. Orsburn and Moran (2000) argued that SMWTs are inappropriate in two situations. First, SMWTs should not be used when interdependence is not required for the outcome. This is useful advice for organizations considering the development of any type of team but particularly SMWTs. Second, they should not be used in situations where challenging deeply held organizational assumptions would be detrimental. SMWTs are prime organizational contexts for generative learning, which involves questioning the way things have been done and the assumptions on which they are based. Sometimes organizations are not prepared for such challenges, and at other times, they are not stable enough to survive them. In these cases, SMWTs, which tend to challenge basic assumptions, should not be used.

By now you might be wondering, If SMWTs do not have a supervisor, what role does leadership play? Barry (1995) tells us that although a SMWT is a "bossless team," it still requires leadership. This leadership is needed in the areas of task-based processes, as well as in group development. A number of broad types of leadership roles and behaviors are needed in SMWTs (Barry, 1995, pp. 58–59):

- **Envisioning.** Creation of new and compelling visions, which involves generating ideas and defining goals.

- **Organizing.** Coordination of the many elements that are connected to the team's tasks, which involves attention to deadlines, efficiency, and structure.

- **Spanning.** Connection of the team's activities with the important constituents in the relevant environment, which includes networking, securing resources, and being politically aware.

- **Social.** Concern for the social and psychological needs of the team members, which includes interpreting and paraphrasing, using humor, and mediating conflicts.

These leadership roles and behaviors, which are enacted by various members within the SMWT, vary in importance, depending on the type of project. For example, when working on a problem-solving project, such as how to decrease harmful emissions from a manufacturing plant, the behaviors of organizing and spanning may be most relevant as the SMWT begins work. However, with a project-based SMWT, goals will need to be set at the outset, which requires envisioning.

Virtual Teams

As globalization, geographically disparate workforces, and the need to balance work-family lives have continued to define modern organizational life, organizations have relied on communication technologies to facilitate teamwork. A **virtual team** relies on technology to work across space, time, and organizational boundaries (Lipnack & Stamps, 1997). Virtual teams fall on a continuum of face-to-face teams that use technology, teams that are in the same building, or teams that have no face-to-face time at all (Liao, 2017). An SHRM survey found that of all the organizations polled, nearly half use virtual teams in some capacity (Minton-Eversole, 2012). **Global virtual teams**, also known as multinational, transnational, or multicultural teams, are those virtual teams that include members who are geographically dispersed and culturally diverse (Jimenez et al., 2017).

Global virtual teams provide organizations with several unique benefits over face-to-face teams. One of the biggest advantages discussed in business literature is the economic one because managers are able to use the best talent available regardless of location because cost isn't a factor (Jimenez et al., 2017). Similar to face-to-face teams, diversity on global virtual teams can improve problem-solving, creativity, and the idea pool while also increasing the resources available, and if the experience is positive, it will increase overall employee motivation and job satisfaction. The challenges for global virtual teams include pragmatic issues, such as time zone differences, which can make work-life balancing difficult, and the communication and cultural differences can cause conflict or miscommunication among team members.

Computer-mediated communication has changed the ways in which people communicate. **Polychronicity** is an individual's preference for multitasking and is made easier by electronic devices that are capable of making calls, sending messages or emails, accessing information via the cloud, or posting messages on social media. It is often said that in organizations, it is important to have the right people in the right positions, and Zhu and Smith (2019) found that this is particularly true of virtual teams. An individual's polychronic values (to what degree do they enjoy juggling multiple asynchronous and synchronous work activities at the same time) greatly impact their overall success and job satisfaction on virtual teams.

While juggling multiple project demands, virtual teams also require multicommunicating. **Multicommunciating** is defined as engaging in at least two interactions simultaneously with different interactional partners (Reinsch et al., 2008). An example of multicommunicating occurs during meetings or even class as you take notes on the content while also messaging another individual via text and carry on a completely separate conversation on email. From a task standpoint, this ability allows you to work with multiple clients or colleagues, on multiple projects, at the same time. This also allows you to prevent wasteful downtime; while you are waiting for a response on one chat conversation, you can be talking to a customer on the telephone or responding to a text from a second person.

The use of such technology does, of course, bring with it concerns. First is the need to ensure that all members are trained and comfortable with using the full range of technology that might be necessary for the team to function effectively and efficiently. Second, security is a major concern for virtual teams. As hackers, viruses, and data theft proliferate, virtual team processes, data, communication, and outcomes are all at risk. Finally, technology can just simply break or malfunction, and when teamwork is all done virtually, this can be detrimental to the team.

Challenges aside from technology also exist for virtual teams. According to the 2012 SHRM study mentioned earlier, members of virtual teams also experience difficulties related to building interpersonal relationships, bridging time differences, and equitably distributing work (Minton-Eversole, 2012). To address these challenges, organizations employing virtual teams and the members of the teams themselves can engage in certain behaviors and processes that can help enhance the possibility of the success of the virtual team. Gilson et al. (2015) summarized recent research in this area and noted that studies have revealed several ways in which success can be enhanced. In particular, they point to research that suggests the following: (1) team members and the organization should strive to make sure that team members feel connected and equal to each other so that cooperation can be enhanced; (2) virtual teams should develop goals early in their process to increase team cohesion and performance; (3) virtual teams should integrate communication behaviors that are predictable (when possible) and socially positive in nature; (4) geographically dispersed teams should spend time and energy on the central task goals to be accomplished; (5) the virtual team should ensure that processes and procedures are formally and informally structured so that all team members are oriented to them early and often.

Misunderstandings and Conflict in Organizational Teams

Recall the definition of a team that we presented at the beginning of this chapter: *A team is a small group (three to nine) of interdependent people with complementary skills who are committed to a common purpose, performance goals, and approach for which they hold themselves mutually accountable.* This definition points to several ways in which misunderstandings could arise (although the possibilities are indeed endless). We conclude this chapter with a discussion of misunderstandings in the team environment and show how they may turn into conflict if they are not anticipated and addressed.

The first area of misunderstandings in the team environment we will examine comes from the concept of team size. As the size of the team increases, so does the potential diversity of thought, values, background, personality, and so on, which can be productive but also a source of misunderstandings. As team members interact, they may find themselves in situations where a team member has divergent and perhaps seemingly irreconcilable differences regarding communication or task process. These differences, if not attended to in a constructive manner, can be harmful to the team as team members attempt to complete their tasks. Another potential misunderstanding that can arise from team size is that as team size increases, so, too, does the likelihood that cliques might form. The formation of cliques in work teams is potentially damaging to team cohesion and, subsequently, to satisfaction and performance.

The second area of misunderstandings stems from the concept of interdependence. A lack of understanding, appreciation, or commitment to the notion of interdependence leads to the team not taking advantage of the synergy and nonsummativity that are the prime benefits of teamwork. For example, consider this story from Eustace, a chemist at a chemical research and technology firm who works as part of a team, although not all members work on the same shift. Communication and lack of understanding or care for how the team members' activities affect the others are main concerns of his:

> We are supposed to update the next person on the remaining tasks to be done during the next shift. We finish and then prioritize lab requests that aren't complete, but we prioritize them by due date. Say, if I were working on something and I got to a certain point, I would communicate that to the team member who follows me on the next shift. The team member who follows me, though, does not come in early and is usually running late. I send out an email with the pass off and I include the chemists' supervisor as well as the chemist who is coming in, and I list the tasks and prioritize them in chronological order for what needs to be done.

> There is a bad habit where my coworkers like to pick and choose what they want to work on. Usually, the easiest stuff gets done first. It is more of what they feel like working on. Stuff that is more time-intensive will be pushed back because they don't want to do it. They will do a lot of smaller

tasks to make it seem like they did a lot throughout their shift, but really it wasn't that significant. Then the larger tasks get pushed onto the other team members.

This team did not understand or appreciate the concept of interdependence. The effects were many: project quality suffered, the organization lost time and resources because of the extra energy these team members had to expend to reprioritize their work, and the individuals certainly suffered as they dealt with the stress of having to complete larger or more difficult tasks that should have been completed by other team members.

The final area of misunderstandings that we will examine involves the acceptance of common goals. Perhaps the biggest complaint we hear from team members around the country is that they cannot handle that their team members are more interested in looking out for themselves than they are for accomplishing the goals of the team. What we are really talking about here are the power plays that individual members bring into the team environment. Oftentimes, members are more interested in pursuing their individual goals as a means of acquiring or wielding power than they are in subduing their personal goals to the goals of the collective. This inevitably leads to conflicts among team members and the complication of team decision-making processes and resource allocation. Consider this story from Walt, who works for a consumer packaged-goods company and is part of a cross-functional team:

> Due to a new regulation that impacted our products, we now had to label a particular product characteristic on the product packaging. In order to decide on the product characteristic, we had to survey our suppliers to understand the input characteristics. In order to develop the supplier survey, I engaged a cross-functional team. This included procurement, data management, supplier management, and quality. We worked for several months developing a supplier survey.
>
> Once completed, we thought there might be value in having an industry standard in order to minimize supplier confusion over seeing many different survey formats. So, I engaged with one of the leading trade groups that was open to developing the industry survey. The trade group engaged approximately 30 other trade group members. Over the course of several months, the trade group worked with its members to develop a suggested template. We were close to being done.
>
> Then a new player entered the discussions. The individual was an internal employee returning from leave. This new individual was in a senior leadership position and started the internal conversations again. The result: There was a new format that our company was going to use. While the substance was generally the same, the format and look were very different. The senior leader's impact was immediate, direct, and decisive. The

> new look and format required me to reengage discussions with the trade group. In so doing, the trade group revealed a schism, and the industry group consensus was lost.
>
> In the end, we have our internal form. But over the course of 6 months, the process of consensus building resulted in a considerable drain on the time resource and produced several different forms that at one point or another seemed to be final.

We feel Walt's pain here and the pain of the rest of the team who had their hard work, time, and energy wiped away because of the self-interest and power-wielding nature of a new member. This is a perfect example of how the extra energy and success that can be generated by a team can be destroyed when one member is more interested in individual goals rather than team goals.

One common complaint with teamwork is that not everyone is equally invested in the team's goals or objectives. **Social loafing** occurs when a group member has decreased motivation or puts in less effort than they would have working on the project as an individual (Awee et al., 2020; Ying et al., 2014). Social loafing can be caused by an individual's lack of genuine effort, or it can come about as a result of goal or role ambiguity, personality type, and comfort working within groups. Virtual team members are particularly susceptible to loafing as they often lack the face-to-face relationships that would increase organizational (and team) identification and are exposed to many electronic diversions. Consider the steps you would take after logging into your computer to write a paper. Maybe you check your social media, look for last night's sports scores, or do a little online shopping simultaneously while researching, organizing, and writing your report. Electronic loafing is known as cyberloafing. Gupta and Chakraborty (2020) found that cyberloafing is related to a decrease in team potency (the team's belief in their capabilities to complete their tasks) and an increase in team conflict.

Misunderstandings also come about when team members accept what they perceive to be common goals and processes in an effort to avoid conflict, a form of misunderstanding introduced earlier in the chapter as groupthink. Consider this example from Haley, a third-grade teacher:

> So a problem that I've had with my coworkers would be how to assess or test our students in the best way possible. We are having trouble coming to a decision because we don't want to hurt any feelings. Sometimes I know we don't agree on the best way to see what kids know because a lot of our instruction nowadays is based on group work and teamwork. So, while there are probably a lot of conflicting opinions on whether kids need to be assessed individually or if we can look at work they do in a group to see what they know, we don't always express that. The team I work with includes three people, including myself and two other third-grade

teachers. The problem is that we're all kind of easygoing personalities, so we don't like to really speak up about not agreeing.

The team of teachers that Haley is on, while concerned with the task they have to complete, is stuck in their team processes because they do not want to upset each other. When the group's efforts are spent maintaining their cohesiveness and justifying the decision they are making, the benefits of group input, such as diverse opinions, a checks and balance system, and idea testing, are greatly diminished.

As introduced in Chapter 1, and reinforced throughout this text, misunderstandings have the potential to turn into conflict if they are not anticipated and addressed appropriately. This may not be detrimental to the team, however, as conflict can have either negative or positive consequences for the individual, the team, and the organization.

Negative Consequences of Team Conflict

Much research has been done on the negative consequences of conflict. When team members have interpersonal problems and are angry with one another, they work less effectively; they produce suboptimal products, their cognitive functioning is inhibited (Humphrey et al., 2017). Resolving interpersonal conflict takes time and psychological energy. Much of the team's efforts are focused on resolving the conflict, thereby limiting productivity. Think about the last time you were in conflict with someone. You probably worried about how to resolve it. Your concentration on anything else was diminished. Consider the following story from Jeston about a work team he was on:

> As a team, we met various times with different members of the team and at different times. During these meetings, team members who weren't present were brought up in conversation and were then judged or gossiped about. Each member has their good and bad qualities, and over time, I think each member had been judged or gossiped about, some more than others. One member was judged more for their actions and physical manners than other members, viewed as a little different or strange, while another member was judged for their tone of voice and way of presenting themselves each time we met. This judging and gossiping had an impact on our team's success and ability to work together, as some team members did not want to work with others at all times because of this or got frustrated with one another over things that they did differently or their tone of voice.

Jetson's team suffered from unproductive gossiping and judging that had an impact both on the individual relationships and the team's ability to be successful. His team was unable to move past this conflict and could never agree on how to complete their tasks.

Even when a team thinks it has reached an agreement on resolving conflicts, it can be betrayed. One team with which the authors worked was directed by an administrator and two assistants who wanted to rebuild trust among the team members. Over the years, the finances of the team had come into question, and the administrators wanted to disclose fully the budget decision-making process and invite members' input. After a lengthy meeting in which the entire budget was explained and comments were invited, the team agreed on some guidelines that would not only balance the budget but also allow for an enrichment program for new projects. Three days after this discussion, the three administrators announced budget cuts that did not follow the guidelines to which they had agreed. This decision was never a part of the budget discussion; consequently, mistrust and anger on the part of the members quickly replaced a sense of accomplishment that the previous budget discussion had established.

The results of these actions may have a long-term effect on the team. Members will refer to this event in future years as an example of how particular individuals cannot be trusted. Trust can be lost quickly, and it can take years to gain it back: "In some organizations, disputes may have a long history, decisions and actions in the present being shaped by conflicts, grudges, or differences that others believe are long forgotten or settled" (Morgan, 1997, p. 170).

When you enter a new organization, typically you have no knowledge of the history of prior disputes, and therefore you should be careful not to fall into a dispute by accident. You do not want to step unknowingly on a land mine. Therefore, as a newcomer, you should avoid taking a position until you know more of the facts and information. Becoming involved in a conflict early in your career can affect other people's perceptions of you for your entire time at that organization. As much as individuals dislike conflict, there are some surprising positive consequences of conflict. If you find yourself enmeshed in a conflict, the best alternative is to attempt to turn it into a positive outcome.

Positive Consequences of Team Conflict

Despite the obvious negative consequences of conflict, there are many positive outcomes as well. Whereas affective conflict (conflict based on personal or emotional differences) often results in negative consequences, cognitive conflict (conflict based on differences in understandings regarding a task) can yield positive outcomes (e.g., Flores et al., 2018). Teams, as well as individuals, who experience conflict are able to make better decisions (Amason, 1996; Fiol, 1994; Schweiger et al., 1986). Conflict over tasks can help people identify and better understand the issues involved (Putnam, 1992). Opposing points of view, when expressed, can actually clarify issues and uncover problems that have been less obvious or unknown. Critiquing solutions helps a team avoid groupthink. Open discussions of opposing views about the task can be associated with completing tasks and using resources more effectively (Tjosvold et al., 1992). One team in conflict over a work schedule discovered additional criteria to be used in developing the schedule only after making the conflicting issues more obvious. Discussions aroused by conflict can lead to creative solutions.

Conflict can improve decision-making by encouraging individuals to use creative problem-solving. Conflict, and the resulting creative process, can help keep the work environment lively and interesting. Constructive conflict can stimulate thinking about otherwise mundane tasks or behaviors. At the same time, conflict can cause marginal employees who are not willing to be team oriented or use creative problem-solving and task resolution to decide to leave the organization, thus increasing the team's cohesiveness and effectiveness (Shell, 2003). This can also promote healthy change for individuals, as well as organizational growth (Darling & Brownlee, 1984). Part of this change and growth may come from management taking a critical look at the organization and its members and making strategic changes (Shell, 2003). All of this combined can serve as a motivational force for all levels of organizational members.

Summary

Organizational teams will continue to be a part of organizational life. As a future employee, your challenge is to understand how you can make a significant contribution to team activities and help the organization provide systems that will enhance the likelihood that the teams you serve on will be successful.

Most of you are used to being a part of a group that has a purpose, whether that is a family, a choir, a band, a student organization, a sports team, or a class-based project team. Despite our heavy participation in group activities throughout our lives, we find organizational teams challenging. As we have discussed, teams are a commonplace organizational form and will continue to be, and they are definitely contexts for misunderstandings to prevail. But with communicative energy, organizational teams can be invigorating, successful enterprises for both the individuals involved and the organization.

In this chapter, we defined teams in a way that centers communication and shows the interdependent nature of the individuals on the team. You were exposed to the elements that characterize a team and that require the attention of the team members. Different types of teams were discussed, with particular attention paid to the primary forms of teams in organizations today—SMWTs and virtual teams in particular. You could make the argument that we could eliminate those designations as team types because most teams are self-managed and much organizational work is done virtually, making the labels redundant. Finally, you were introduced to the myriad forms of misunderstandings that organizational teams can face but remember that anticipating misunderstandings and responding to them with the appropriate strategy determines the extent to which those misunderstandings lead to success or failure.

CHAPTER 12 Leaders and Leadership

LEARNING OBJECTIVES

1. Identify the communication activities of leaders
2. Outline the evolution of leadership theories
3. Describe the feminist perspectives on leadership
4. Identify different cultural approaches to leadership
5. Explain the importance of emotional intelligence for an organizational leader

This chapter is not just about the "official" leaders in the organization, such as the boss, the supervisor, and the CEO. It is about the characteristics, behaviors, attitudes, and values of leadership that can be exhibited by any organizational member, depending on the situation. Given the right set of circumstances, any organizational member can contribute to the success of the group by providing leadership when needed. As expressed by Raelin (2003),

> In the twenty-first-century organization we need to establish the experience of serving as a leader, not sequentially, but concurrently and collectively. In other words, leaders coexist at the same time and all together. In addition, we expect each member of a community to make a unique contribution to the growth of that community, both independently and interdependently with others. (p. xi)

Consider the following story, which exhibits an everyday instance of leadership told to use by a 20-year-old college student regarding her experience as the leader of an organization on campus.

> I think delegation skills are the most important thing a leader can have. One person can't do everything, especially when you are dealing with a large student organization. For example, I handle the email with the other organizations on campus that we need to coordinate with because I also do the scheduling, but another person handles the email to the students—that's my job, and that's her job. I know I hear

stories about last year's president where she did everything, but I also hear that there were a lot of problems with stuff not getting done. I don't think that's a good leader; that's just being too dependent on yourself and not trusting your executive team. This whole team got elected because they are good people, and I trust them to do a good job.

Now read this story from Donna about her experiences as a summer lifeguard at a local country club.

The head lifeguard was an ineffective leader who displayed many dysfunctional characteristic traits. He was inexperienced and didn't even know how to make spreadsheets in order to staff the rest of the lifeguards. However, instead of asking for help, he would just tell his co-head lifeguards to make the schedule. He was egotistical, arrogant at times, and very money motivated. He was incompetent and corrupt because he had the skills to ask for help and plan, but he didn't care about the job. He would lie to our boss, saying that every weekend was staffed but they weren't, and then other people would get into trouble. Leaders have bad days and are not always going to display the leadership skills everyone is expecting from them, but I think it is important for leaders and followers to have a strong connection and communication. It is important for a leader to show that they care about their people and to also lead by example.

Although these stories represent two very different organizational situations, scopes of leadership, and experiences, we put them side by side to demonstrate two things. First, leadership happens wherever and whenever it is needed. Second, leadership is about understanding and addressing the needs of organizational members and helping them move forward in meeting their personal and professional goals.

This chapter presents major issues related to organizational leadership and communication as they have developed over the years. We begin with a general overview of the nature of leadership and then move to a brief summary of how leadership theories have emerged and developed over the past century. We then look at diverse perspectives on leadership before concluding with a discussion of emotional labor and its relationship to misunderstandings.

Overview of Leadership

Leadership is a complex subject; in this section, we point to a few basic aspects that highlight its communicative and interactive aspects. The following is an important concept central to the notion of this way of viewing leadership: *Leadership is not a particular trait some people have, and others do not. It is a process that takes place in every human interaction.* Leadership, therefore, is interactional (it takes place through communication), contextual (different people contribute leadership in different circumstances), and a process (changing as the needs of the people and situation change—e.g., Fairhurst & Grant, 2010).

Leadership can happen in any setting with any combination of individuals. There is no age limit or required background. Leaders can emerge at any time and be anyone. How do we know a leader when we see one? One definition is the following: A **leader** *is a person who takes charge of the situation and influences the attitudes and actions of others.* Watching young children arguing over who will be the leader of a game or activity can be instructive. Often, one of them will finally say, "OK. You (pointing to one youngster) be a leader, and you (pointing to the other youngster) be a leader too. Now follow me." The person who acts to move the group forward, with or without the title of leader, will be the true leader in this setting. The person who sees a need or has a possible answer and is not afraid to give voice to her ideas will emerge as a leader. However, if the goal is only to get others to do what one wants, it may be a case of propaganda or persuasion, not leadership.

Based on research and as observed through practical experience, we can say that leadership demonstrates another element: *The leader influences the behavior of others to reach a common goal that benefits the group, not just an individual.* Warren Bennis, a well-known author on management, defined the difference between *leadership* and *management* by saying that the manager does things right, whereas the leader does the right thing (Bennis & Nanus, 1985). In other words, the manager may know all the policies and procedures to follow and perform them correctly, but the leader will know how to do the right thing, even if it is not spelled out in the policy manual. In their survey of 90 successful corporate and public leaders, Bennis and Nanus found that managers are problem-solvers who are efficient, whereas leaders are effective problem identifiers who focus on all available resources to move a group forward.

For example, a director in a company had an employee with an extended illness who ran out of sick days. Her colleagues in the office volunteered to give their sick days to her so she could recover fully before coming back to work. The employee manual did not have a provision on this, but it was the right thing to do. The director allowed the employee's colleagues to help her through this difficult time and cover her sick time by giving away their own. Later, it turned into a policy that this company adopted so others in crisis situations could benefit from the generosity of their colleagues. This leader demonstrated the elements of leadership described earlier and exemplifies what is called leadership as serving. The leader removed bureaucratic barriers in an attempt to ensure a successful and humane outcome for her employees—the essence of leadership as serving.

Numerous studies have attempted to identify what characteristics leaders possess, and the results are as varied as leaders themselves (Iordanoglou, 2018). Depending on the study, the results have included strong ethics, passion, clear vision, persistence in the face of adversity, willingness to take risks, creativity, the ability to accept feedback, self-confidence, and strong communication skills. One survey of 20,000 professions from 176 countries found that contemporary leaders need to be able to anticipate change, be willing to challenge and disrupt processes that threaten the success of their project, interpret various forms of data, engage in high levels of critical thinking and decision-making, communicate and gain buy-in from various constitutes, and constantly engage in learning (Schoemaker & Cecchini, 2015). Ideas about what makes a good leader are as varied as the models of leadership which we will discuss in the next section.

Development of Leadership Theories

Authors have developed theories of leadership to expand on the basic elements discussed earlier and to capture the complexities of the concept. First explored in the early 20th century, leadership theory has seen many changes over the last 100 years. Literally thousands of studies have been conducted and pages have been written about leadership in an attempt to help us understand how leadership emerges and what makes it effective. In this section of the chapter, we provide a brief outline of some of the major developments in theories of leadership.

Trait Approach to Leadership

Early research on leadership was primarily concerned with identifying traits that differentiated effective from ineffective leaders. **Traits** are characteristics, either psychological or physical, that affect behavior (House & Baetz, 1979). From this perspective, "leaders are born rather than made" (Bryman, 1996, p. 277). Trait research began around 1904 and continued for approximately 50 years (Owens, 1992). By midcentury, researchers realized that identifying a definitive set of traits as markers of effective leadership in all situations was probably impossible.

Although no definitive traits of leaders were identified that could be carried across all leadership situations, several traits were found with relative consistency across studies. These traits include extraversion, openness to new experiences, agreeableness, and being conscientious, as well as demonstrating intelligence, energy, and self-confidence (House & Baetz, 1979; Kovach, 2018).

Trait research continued through the mid-1900s, when researchers began to identify other factors in addition to individual personality traits that contribute to effective leadership. Ralph Stogdill (1974) reviewed over 3,000 books and articles that had been written in the 1940s, 1950s, and 1960s. One of his conclusions was, "Theorists no longer explain leadership solely in terms of the individual or the group. Rather it is believed that characteristics of the individual and demands of the situation interact in such a manner as to permit one, or perhaps a few, persons to rise to leadership status" (p. 23). Instead of focusing on the traits of a leader, researchers began to identify leader behaviors and the impact on group outcomes.

Situational Approach to Leadership

As trait research started to taper off in the mid-1900s, researchers began examining *behaviors* as markers of effective leadership. This work was pioneered by the Ohio

State Leadership Studies, beginning in 1954 (Owens, 1992). The results of these studies led to the notion of the "average leadership style"; that is, leaders were assumed to have a "typical" style that was used with all subordinates (Dockery & Steiner, 1990; Fairhurst & Chandler, 1989).

From these beginnings, a theory of leadership emerged that suggested shifts in leadership behavior depending on variables in the group setting. This approach was referred to as **situational leadership**. It assumes that the leader's behavior depends on a variety of circumstances in the specific situation. A number of early writers identified possible situational variables, including how followers interact, the relationship of the leader to the followers, the motivations of both, and the task itself (e.g., see the discussion of Blake and Mouton's Managerial Grid in Chapter 3).

One situational variable was identified by researchers as two distinct needs of a group: getting the *task* completed and developing strong *relationships* in the group. For example, some projects require a great deal of attention to accomplish the task, whereas others need strong relationships among the team members. If the leader spends all their time getting the task done without any attention to relationships, then the team members may not work well together for the next task, even if this task was accomplished. However, if the leader only focuses on relationships, everyone may feel good about the experience but not get the job done. A leader who does not focus on either tasks or relationships and basically leaves the group to their own devices is called a **laissez-faire leader**, as the following interview demonstrates. This interview was with Li, a 22-year-old female who works as an administrative assistant for a community college:

> I would say a big problem that the administrative assistants have encountered is communication between us and our boss. I think that we can collectively agree that the communication we receive from our boss hasn't been sufficient. Our boss never really trained us well, and we have been continuously trying to determine a way to tell her that our room reservation and scheduling training hasn't been enough for us to fully understand our daily duties. We have felt a lack of communication from our boss for some time now, so when we are in a situation where we don't exactly know how to do something, we usually lean on each other for that support rather than our boss. I think my boss would rather have it that way, to be honest. She can be standoffish at times.

Alternatively, the leader may try to control all aspects of the group. Micromanagement will not allow individuals to learn and grow in their jobs.

Hersey et al. (2001) extended the situational approach to leadership and coupled the task and relationship behaviors of leaders with what they termed the "readiness level" of the followers. They posited that leadership style should depend on the "extent to which a follower demonstrates the ability and willingness to accomplish a specific task" (p. 175). A follower's readiness level should not be considered a personal trait or characteristic but something that varies by task. Because readiness level varies based on the situation, so too should the extent to which the leader exhibits task and/or relationship behaviors. According to their Situational Leadership® Model, there are four basic follower readiness levels (R1, R2, R3, and R4) that determine which leadership style (S1, S2, S3, and S4) is most appropriate. The four leadership styles can be characterized by the extent to which they include task and relationship behaviors (Hersey et al., 2001, p. 174):

- **Style 1 (S1).** Characterized by above-average amounts of task behavior and below-average amounts of relationship behavior.

- **Style 2 (S2).** Characterized by above-average amounts of both task and relationship behaviors.

- **Style 3 (S3).** Characterized by above-average amounts of relationship behavior and below-average amounts of task behavior.

- **Style 4 (S4).** Characterized by below-average amounts of both relationship and task behaviors.

With these behaviors available, the leader must determine the extent of follower readiness for the particular situation at hand. There are four basic readiness levels (Hersey et al., 2001, pp. 177–178):

- **Readiness Level 1 (R1).** The follower is unable and unwilling to complete the task or is unable and insecure regarding the situation.

- **Readiness Level 2 (R2).** The follower is unable but willing to complete the task or is unable but confident that she can complete it.

- **Readiness Level 3 (R3).** The follower is able but unwilling to complete the task or is able but insecure that she can complete it.

- **Readiness Level 4 (R4).** The follower is both able and confident about completing the task.

With the readiness level of the follower determined, the leader must select the leadership style that best matches the particular readiness level. In a situation in which the follower is unable and unwilling (or insecure) regarding the task (R1), the leader should employ the telling style (S1). When using the telling style, the leader issues task guidance and direction by focusing on facts and consequences. This would be most effective because the follower will have no self-motivation or previous positive experience with completing this type of task. The selling style (S2) will be an appropriate style when the follower feels they can complete the task but is actually unable to (R2). This style of leadership will have the leader providing guidance but also emotional support by opening up dialogue to help bring the follower along and to allow for questions. The addition of emotional support will afford the extra motivation to keep the follower going when their abilities may cause frustration.

The participating style (S3), which involves encouragement and open communication, is useful in situations where the follower is able but unwilling or insecure regarding the task (R3). In this situation, the follower may have the necessary skills to complete the task, but they are usually newly developed and therefore confidence levels are not sufficiently high. With appropriate emotional support from the leader and opportunities for asking questions and seeking feedback, the follower will become more confident and able to complete the task. Finally, in situations where the follower is both able and confident with regard to the task (R4), the leader should choose the delegating style (S4). The follower knows how and wants to do the task, so the leader should let them do it. The follower's activities should still be monitored, but the leader should not micromanage the situation.

The most important contribution made by Hersey and Blanchard was the notion that leaders can change their style of interacting with followers, depending on the followers' ability and involvement in the task. We find this to be extremely beneficial to anyone who wants to emerge as a leader or be a successful leader. The leader should not treat all individuals as if they are driven by the same motivation or have the same level of skill or interest. The best leaders adapt to the traits of the group members and the particular situation (see Jacobson, 1981) for a useful instrument to measure one's ability to select the best leadership style given the needs of followers). In other words, a successful leader is one who tailors their communication about the task and organizational relationships to the specific needs of the individuals involved. This can be challenging for the leader, as they will need to have the flexible skills to change communication styles as the situation demands.

Charismatic Leadership

Since the early 1980s, the number of "new" leadership theories has exploded. The root of the contemporary theories that we will discuss next, such as transformational leadership, can be found in House's (1977) charismatic leadership theory. Further developing Weber's (1947) work on charismatic authority, House defined **charisma** as the effect a leader has on their followers. Charismatic leadership theory received some push back though because until recently the definition of charisma was thought to be too vague or abstract to be useful as a guiding theory. Antonakis et al., (2016) offered up a more precise definition by stating that charisma is an emotionally laden leadership style based on values, beliefs, and symbols and relies heavily on the transmission or signaling of information. Charisma, from this view, entails followers' identification with the leader, as well as the leader's ability to communicate emotional involvement with the organization's mission. The personal characteristics of a charismatic leader include having a strong presence, a desire to influence others, demonstrating self-confidence, and displaying a strong sense of one's own moral values (Northouse, 2001).

Charismatic leadership, though, is not only about personality traits but also specific behaviors (Northouse, 2001). Charismatic leaders must be strong role models for their followers, and their actions and behaviors must match at all times. Second, charismatic leaders must appear competent and able to handle any situation in front of their followers. These leaders must be able to communicate rhetorical visions and ideological goals with a strong moral overtone to their followers in a clear, concise, and passionate manner. They must be able to convey to their followers that they have high moral and performance standards for them. Finally, they must be able to provoke task-relevant motives, such as affiliation, power, or esteem in their followers.

Transactional and Transformational Leadership

In the mid-1980s, Bass (1985) expanded the notion of charismatic leadership into what is now known as *transformational leadership.* This leadership approach focused not only on what characteristics a leader needed to possess but also the attributes the followers needed from a leader. Much attention is paid by this theory to the role that follower perceptions of the leader play in the leadership process. In addition, communication and communication practices are foregrounded in the transformational leadership approach.

Bass (1985) began by arguing that there are two types of leaders: transactional leaders and transformational leaders. **Transactional leaders** hold designated authority positions and try to motivate followers with clear goals and defined expectations (Kovach, 2018). Transactional leaders are focused on *contingent rewards.* Followers have specific performance goals to meet and are either rewarded or punished based on their ability to either meet or not meet these goals. Transactional leaders can employ the *active management by exception* method in which they actively monitor the follower's progress and take corrective action when needed. On the other hand, the *passive management by exception* method involves waiting until deviances or problems occur. The leader offers little monitoring because they are waiting for problems to occur, at which point, they take punitive action. The essence of transactional leadership is the motivation of followers through a system of rewards and punishments that will be more or less monitored (Gardner & Cleavenger, 1998).

Transactional leadership, as previously mentioned, is an expanded version of charismatic leadership. Unlike transactional leadership, which is grounded in the more mundane task exchanges that occur between leaders and followers, **transformational leaders** appeal to the higher order needs of their followers (Kirkman et al., 2009; Wolfram & Mohr, 2009). Transformational leaders inspire their followers to go beyond the tasks or goals. They use motivational strategies, such as making the follower aware of how important their job is, stressing the need for personal growth, and helping their followers focus on the good for the entire organization (Kavach, 2018).

Transformational leadership involves several factors (Bass & Avolio, 1994). First, the leader must have *attributed charisma,* or the ability to gain trust, respect, and confidence from their followers. This leader must be able to demonstrate *idealized influence*, which is the perception of being a role model. If successful at demonstrating idealized influence, followers will often look up to or want to emulate (be like) the leader. Next, the transformational leader must be able to instill *inspirational motivation,* which is the ability to encourage followers to pursue a goal and persevere through difficult times. This aspect of the leadership model demands that leaders be able to draw on a wide emotional range to convey inspiration, commitment, or dedication to the organization's mission and goals. *Intellectual stimulation* is also necessary and requires a leader who is willing and able to consider every solution that is brought forward by followers. Finally, the transformational leader must be able to communicate *individualized consideration*, or concern for each of their followers.

Raelin (2003) wrote of the leaderful organization, which is an extension and modification of the transformational leader:

> Leaderful practice is unique compared to empowerment models . . . in that it does not merely present a consultative model wherein leaders in authority allow "followers" to participate in their leadership. Nor does it equate to stewardship approaches that see the leader step aside and allow others to take over when necessary. Instead, it offers a true mutual model that transforms leadership from an individual property into a new paradigm that redefines leadership as a collective practice. (p. 5)

Raelin (2003) provided the following example of this model of leadership: A vice president of a small company on the West Coast planned to resign because his family was planning a move to a city some 500 miles away. The president of the company scheduled a meeting of top management to talk about how to replace him. Prior to the meeting, a member of the leadership team started a campaign to keep "James," the vice president, because of the difficulty of replacing him and because he added a great deal to the success of the organization. She wanted others to think about alternatives to see if they could reach a consensus on what might keep James a part of the company. Some people came up with ways for his work to be done by audio and video technology. James also indicated that he would be willing to travel back to the company's location for critical meetings. By the time the meeting occurred to discuss how to replace James, everyone, including the president, believed that the topic of the meeting had shifted to how to work with James from a remote location. In this case, the president was not the only organizational leader. In fact, the management team member who worked for this solution contributed strong leadership to the group (p. 189). This solution demonstrates collective and collaborative action that results in a compassionate response to a problem. It goes beyond consulting with others and creates an environment in which employees feel empowered to take the lead in critical decision-making processes.

Relational Leading

Olivia, a member of the executive board on her college's campus activities board, told us the following story:

> One of my primary responsibilities was to find local musicians to perform on campus. I would contact them, make all the arrangements, and then it

was up to the social media person to do the promotion work. I had worked really hard at the beginning of the school year to survey the student body to find out what kind of bands they were interested in, and I had collected a lot of good data. The problem is that they wanted music that our activities board president didn't like, so she constantly went behind my back and made other arrangements. The college trusted us to spend the money in our budget wisely, and I felt responsible when few people showed up for the events that she planned, but there wasn't anything I could do because she was all friendly with the organization's advisor. I tried to remind her and the advisor of the survey results several times, but they also had a reason why we should just go with the bands that our president wanted. It was just a really odd and frustrating situation.

Olivia was frustrated because she did not feel as if she did the job that she was elected by her peers to do, and she was embarrassed by the bands that she was part of bringing to campus. She was also embarrassed for the bands when few people showed up. In reality, the activities board had collected the data that they needed to make informed decisions and, in all actuality, began the year on a positive note.

Olivia's president could have benefited from understanding and following a relational leadership model. Although many theories have alluded to the necessity of positive relationships between leaders and followers, this model advocates that relationships are central to an individual's success or failure as a leader (e.g., Drath, 2001; Murrell, 1997; Uhl-Bien, 2006). **Relational leadership** focuses on the process of relationships and how they can be used to make a difference for the common good (Komives et al., 1998; Nicholoson & Kurucz, 2019). In this model, leadership effectiveness depends on the leader's ability to create positive relationships with leaders (or employees) of all levels within the organization.

Relational leadership is defined by five principles: (1) inclusiveness, (2) empowerment, (3) ethics, (4) purposefulness, and (5) process (Early, 2020; Komives et al., 1998). *Inclusiveness* is the leader's commitment to diversity and appreciation of how multiple perspectives and experiences can positively shape an organization's goal or project. *Empowerment* is providing a sense of ownership, voice, and genuine participation to all organizational members. This also means that anyone in the organization can become a leader in the decision-making process depending on the topic, context, etc.

Ethics refers to values, morals, and a standard of conduct not only for oneself but also those around you. Relational leadership is intertwined with questions about ethics of right and wrong but also ethics about care because the model is grounded in the leader–follower relationship (Nicholson & Kurucz, 2019). In the example of Olivia's president, one could question the ethics driving the president's decision not to listen to Olivia's informed decisions. If she had open and ethical communication channels, she would have been able to accept the data and Olivia's suggestions regardless of her own personal interests. From an ethical perspective, we could also argue that this board president is showing little care about their executive board members as well as the student population in general by the sheer fact she is ignoring the survey results that showed what kind of events they were hoping for on campus. This leads us to the idea of *purposefulness*. A relational leader must be able to convey their own commitment to a common goal, as well as motivate others to accept and work toward that common goal. Again, this leadership model works for employees of all levels in the organization, not just those individuals with formal management titles. An employee who encourages their coworkers to share an idea and increase the company's bottom line is using the notion of purposefulness.

Finally, relational leadership relies heavily on a *process orientation* philosophy. As a communication and leadership principle, this means that leaders must constantly be aware of how groups operate, as well as how past group interactions influence future group interactions. Again, if we look back on the example of Olivia and her president, conceivably we could argue that the president's actions will make it difficult for not only Olivia but also other executive board members to work with her. At the same time, as few students attend the events, the college may decide to reduce the activities board budget, thus impacting future executive board decisions, as well as the larger student population.

Diverse Perspectives on Leadership

Feminist Perspectives

With the leaderful organization viewpoint on leadership, we begin to see a perspective on the topic that encourages leaders to empower followers to make decisions and act independently. Organizational members are encouraged to work for collective goals rather than focusing only on personal ones (Bass et al., 1996). Empowering the followers reinforces current thinking about the need for organizations to have a less hierarchical structure and be more flexible and team oriented. Some authors believe that this style of leadership is tied to the increase of female leaders in organizations:

> This concept of leadership can be readily associated, at least partially, with stereotypes of women and how they would be expected to behave as leaders . . . and may have triggered the growing interest in the study of the intersection of transformational leadership and gender. Furthermore, the massive entry of women into the workforce in the last half-century, followed by their movement to management roles, might have contributed to changes in the conceptualization of leadership, towards transformational leadership theory and empowerment of followers. (Kark & Gan, 2004, p. 161)

One leadership theory, executive leadership development, serves as a theoretical transition point that begins the turn toward feminist perspectives on leadership. **Executive leadership development** entails ongoing socialization processes that begin in childhood and continue throughout the organizational socialization and assimilation process (Avolio & Gibbons, 1988). Researchers who study executive leadership development (e.g., Bass, 1990; Burns, 1978; Gibbons, 1986; Kotter, 1982) argue that factors such as family, culture, and social factors influence the development of leadership capacity. Early family experiences, school, part-time jobs, religious involvement, and community activities influence leadership development (Parker, 2003). Tannen (1990) argued that women and men are socialized from early childhood to engage in distinctively different communication styles with different purposes, rules, and understandings of how to interpret interactions. These differences may lead to two different leadership models: one based on masculine instrumentality and the other on feminine collaboration. Whereas this can be useful to an organization, many feminist scholars argue that the feminine model has historically been rejected by male-dominated organizational structuring processes (i.e., Grossman & Chester, 1990; Helgesen, 1990). With the influx of women into positions of higher authority and leadership in organizations, it is possible that the feminine model is beginning to obtain credibility in leadership circles.

Several forms of feminism, including radical feminism, focus on the positive value of those qualities normally associated with female leaders: sensitivity, nurturing, and expressing emotions. They would argue that these characteristics and voices should not be marginalized in the organization but rather highlighted, welcomed, and, in some cases, used as a replacement for the traditional male perspective. We would like to begin this section by highlighting one feminist perspective on leadership—leadership as serving.

Leadership as serving (Fine & Buzzanell, 2000) means "doing things for others that enable them to do their jobs; serving means taking obstacles out of employees' way rather than putting them up" (Fine & Buzzanell, 2000, p. 131). According to Fine and Buzzanell, some suggest that this "softer" view of leadership actually can be more productive. Rather than have the leader be the person who solves problems, the leader becomes the person who facilitates others' ability to solve their own problems.

In describing leadership as serving, Fine and Buzzanell (2000) argued that this perspective on leadership revises the concept of serving by removing the domination intonations present in the term servant:

> In a different constellation of meanings, service is an honorable term that suggests providing gifts from the self and giving of oneself for the good of others in the service of some greater good. Using the Greek root word for service, *diakoneo*, which includes the office of helper and helped as agent, we invest serving or service with the accoutrements of both agent and agency to displace the harmful feminine characteristics. Those who serve are no longer servants or slaves bereft of the freedom to choose what they do. (p. 152)

According to Fine and Buzzanell (2000, p. 157), leaders who serve exhibit the following:

- **Hopefulness** for fundamental change
- **Strength** in the feminist vision

- **Watchfulness** lest service become servitude
- **Humbleness** in knowledge that the server is an instrument of change
- **Wonderment** at the passages of self, other, community, and principal growth

Leadership as serving involves a personally and professionally involved approach. A leader must be willing to think of other organizational members first and to remove bureaucratic barriers that stand in the way of their success. The serving approach can be quite trying and tiring for some who attempt it, but it offers the opportunity to inject the feminist ethic into a traditionally male-defined skill set.

Cultural Perspectives

While the concept of leadership is a global phenomenon, most of the leadership research has been conducted from a western perspective. While there are many claims that the leadership theories thus far discussed in this chapter apply across cultures, there are several studies that would indicate otherwise. We will briefly overview several of these studies before taking a closer look at several non-Western theories of leadership.

Research on leadership in Western cultures shows a preference for leaders who maximize performance, teamwork, morale, and employee satisfaction. Blunt and Jones (1996) examined leadership styles in East Asia and Africa and found very different leadership assumptions. In East Asia, leaders often have their roots and legitimacy in intra- and extra-organizational structural arrangements rather than needing to rely on attracting followers. Their leadership position is more secure in the organization as a result, and they can expect obedience and compliance from their followers. However, in return, followers can expect to be afforded respect and dignity. The leader–follower relationship is characterized largely by harmony.

In Africa, where culturally individual achievements are less desirable than interpersonal relationships the leader–follower relationship also looks different. Within the same age groups, there tends to be an egalitarian relationship, but a strong sense of hierarchy prevails between generations. Leaders give favor and in turn can expect to receive obedience from their followers (Blunt and Jones, 1996). Consensus is high, and as a result, decision-making is a slow process.

Shahin and Wright (2004) specifically looked at Bass's transactional and transformational leadership model in Egyptian culture. While charismatic leadership does exist in Egyptian culture, these researchers found that it looks very different than what Bass conceptualized in his model. In this culture, charismatic leadership has strong elements of authority (including unquestioning trust in decisions), and that obedience equated to dependence on the leader and high degrees of conformity rather than the more socialized charisma (i.e. developing and stimulating followers) in Bass's model. There was some applicability in terms of rewards and punishments though. Shahin and Wright (2004) found that both followers and management more favorably perceived benevolent leaders (those who offered direction, who were fair, offered rewards, and assigned tasks) over domineering leaders who constantly reminded everyone that they were in charge or made everyone obey.

Performance-Maintenance leadership theory was developed in Japan by Misumi (Ly, 2020). This theory identifies four types of leaders based on the extent to which they perform essential leadership functions. The P stands for planning and refers to leader activities, such as guiding and developing followers' work, as well as motivating subordinates to get the work done while M stands for maintenance and is the activities the leader does to promote group stability and social processes. The four types of leaders that emerged in this model are PM (this leader embodies both characteristics), P (this leader just demonstrates the planning function), M (this leader just demonstrates the maintenance function), and PM type (this leader does a little of both but neither fully). Ling and Fang (2003) extended this model for applicability in China by the addition of C which is character and entails morals.

Sinha created the nurturant task-oriented model of leadership to explain leadership in India (Ly, 2020). In this model, the ideal leader demonstrates both nurturance and task orientation. Nurturance is showing affection, care, and commitment to followers' growth and development while task orientation has to do with the task elements. In this leadership model, nurturance is contingent, or dependent on, the task accomplishment of the followers. The leader is a benevolent source of support if the followers respect, obey, work hard, and are productive. Otherwise, the leader removes or withholds their nurturance.

Warner and Grint (2006) developed the Tahdooahnippah leadership model based on their observation and understanding of the leadership practices of the Comanche. The Comanche have an oral culture, and the four predominant leadership styles reflect that cultural tradition in different ways. *The elder* uses tradition as their primary means of leadership enactment. Elders are designated by the tribe for the knowledge and lived experiences that they have, and elders use this as the basis of their leadership style. *Role models* use experience as their primary means of persuasion; they are community leaders who use their experiences to guide others. Role models depend on their actions to set standards for their followers over spoken or written word. Observation is critical for the *social scientist*. Social scientists rely upon observation and discussion of important community activities such as ceremonies to not only learn more about traditions and culture but also how to best share this information with others in the community. For example, in the Comanche community, social scientists are often responsible for taking on the task of language preservation or ensuring that other important cultural aspects are not lost from one generation to the next. Finally, *authors* are the only leaders in this particular community who rely heavily on the written word or narration. Authors often combine the traditions they are hearing about with their own experiences to create songs, plays, or other works of art that can teach and preserve culture for future generations. In the Tahdooahnippah model, no particular leadership style is better than another; instead, the appropriate leadership style is dependent on the situation and the needs of the community (followers).

Modaff (2014) developed a model of leadership based on several traditional principles and practices of the Lakota, as demonstrated in their Sun Dance ceremony. The Lakota Sun Dance is a sacred ceremony brought to them by White Buffalo Calf Woman to help save the people. The Lakota-based leadership model is grounded in (1) the Lakota value system and (2) following leadership trails rather than vision. The Lakota are guided by the underlying philosophy of mitakuye oyasin, or the idea that "we are all related." That philosophy means that leaders and all organizational members must treat each other as relatives worthy of assistance rather than as competitors for scarce resources and attention. Leaders and all organizational members should enact the four primary values of bravery, generosity, fortitude, and wisdom as they confront the challenges of organizational reality. Finally, but most importantly, the Lakota-based model asks that we value the past as much or more than the future such that the job of the leader is less to set forth a vision than to provide trails for the organizational members to follow as evidence for what has worked and from where to begin when facing new challenges. The trails do not constrain organizational members from making individual choices—they are not unyielding tracks—but they provide guidance based on the wisdom of the leader.

More recently, Brooks and Mutohar (2018) have worked on developing an Islamic model of leadership. In line with Islamic culture, this leadership model draws heavily on principles of tradition and faith. Their model details the five characteristics that Islamic leaders engage in to complete the day-to-day work of a leader in this culture. The first characteristic is *good counsel and sincere conduct*. Leaders should be knowledgeable and well-informed, seeking out information in a respectful manner. Second, leaders should allow for consultation and dissent. This is direct communication with one's followers. Third, leaders must have public interest in mind at all times; public interest refers to the common good of the followers, as well as the larger community. The fourth characteristic of this leadership model is encouraging right while discouraging wrong. In other words, this leadership model includes a strong code of ethics and high standards of behavior. Next leaders must be held to public accountability. This ensures that leaders are socially responsible and not abusing their authority or power. Finally, leaders engage in personal reflection.

In the final section of this chapter, we explore an aspect of leadership that is often underrepresented in the leadership literature—emotional intelligence.

Emotional Intelligence

While Jimmy was in high school, he worked for the same restaurant for three years. It was a "small-time, family-owned restaurant," managed by Nick who was a lot of fun to be around but did not always show the greatest leadership skills. Jimmy told us the following story about Nick:

He had a short temper and very little patience. There were a lot of high schoolers who worked in the kitchen, and I'm sure that is still true today. For most, it was their first or second job ever in their lives. If someone made a mistake or didn't have the time to do something, he would get frustrated. His frustration would cause him to get really quiet and have a grim look on his face. He would stop communicating and almost pout. Teamwork suffered.

Maybe Nick had the technical skills to manage the restaurant, but he was lacking a key leadership skill known as emotional intelligence. He did not realize, or maybe he did not care, that the way he showed his frustration had an impact on everyone on staff.

In 1990, Salovey and Mayer identified **emotional intelligence** (EQ) as a noncognitive aspect of intelligence that refers to one's ability to monitor their emotions and the emotions of people around them (Cherniss, 2000). EQ involves being able to recognize, understand, evaluate, and demonstrate a wide variety of emotions in oneself and the people around you. Daniel Goleman popularized the term in 1995 with his mainstream book titled *Emotional Intelligence*. Although numerous studies have discussed the domains of EQ in slightly different ways, generally, the areas identified include self-awareness, self-management, social awareness, and relationship maintenance.

Self-awareness and self-management are both intrapersonal forms of intelligence. *Self-awareness* is just that, having an awareness of your own emotions and the fact that your emotions have an impact on the people around you. If you snap at a coworker because you are stressed about a work project, self-awareness is recognizing that the coworker might take your emotional expression personally, even though it had nothing to do with them. *Self-management* is the process of being able to control your own emotions, as well as adapt your emotional response to the context. In the previous example, self-management would be tempering your stress and response so that you did not actually snap at your coworker or immediately apologizing if you did.

Social awareness and relationship maintenance are forms of interpersonal intelligence. Having empathy is one of the defining features of *social awareness*. Social awareness is being able to read the room and recognize the emotions that others are expressing. *Relationship maintenance* refers to networking, teamwork, and using cooperative skills to build and maintain relationships.

Numerous studies have found that EQ is a better predictor of career success than the traditional measure of intelligence (IQ). In fact, in longitudinal studies that have been conducted over 40-year periods, EQ is a 4 times better predictor (more important) than IQ in determining professional success (Cherniss, 2000). Think about it this way: It takes a certain level of IQ to finish school, but then it is EQ that takes over to help you land a job and progress through your career.

In terms of leadership, individuals with higher EQ, have better communication and performance and overall better relationships (Maamari & Majdalani, 2017. Higher levels of emotional intelligence were also associated with degrees of responsibility, warmth, and support, and leaders with increased EQ were more likely to be able to find creative or out-of-the-box rewards for their followers.

Emotional intelligence, then, may be one of the factors that either increase or decrease misunderstandings between a leader and their followers. If the leader or followers are unaware of the impact of their own emotions or are not able to regulate and adapt their emotional responses, the likelihood of misunderstandings is high.

Summary

Leadership is not about a specific person; it is a set of behaviors and attitudes relevant to a particular situation. As such, anyone in the organization could be a leader at any particular time, depending on the needs of the situation and the people involved.

Leadership theory has developed and changed over the past several decades as researchers and practitioners have come to realize that leadership is not only relevant to the "official leaders" of the organization. The theory began with trying to isolate the specific traits of good leaders, whereas more recent efforts articulate prescriptions for transforming the organization or serving its members. As leadership theory developed, the role of communication moved from one where the leader uses communication to articulate a vision to leadership being co-constructed through communication with the organizational members. Leadership theories abound, but attention to theories developed outside of Western culture is minimal. In this chapter, we have attempted to expose you to some of the cultural perspectives that you might not otherwise have been aware of and hope that you realize that what makes a good leader is in no way universal.

With the changes in how leadership is defined and practiced have come additional concerns for leaders throughout an organization. Leaders no longer have the luxury of just getting the job done; they must do so with an understanding of not only the task but also the emotional and relational complexities that are involved with organizational life.

Glossary

Action teams: groups of independent experts who are brought together for complex, coordinated, and time-constrained events

Activity coordination: interactions that involve negotiation of task roles within the organization (from communicative constitution of organizations)

Adaptive mechanism: communication mechanisms in place for the organizational system to exchange relevant information with its environment

Affective conflict: inconsistencies within interpersonal relationships

Agency: the individual makes choices over their actions (from structuration theory)

Anticipatory socialization: first phase of the assimilation process

Arbitrators: people who have the legal authority to make decisions for conflicting parties when a decision cannot be reached in other ways

Artifacts and creations: consists of the tangible, physical, or hearable things in the environment of the organization

Authority of leadership: ascribed to a communication based on the knowledge and ability of the person communicating the message, regardless of the position they occupy (from Chester Barnard)

Authority of position: ascribed to a communication based on the fact that it originates from a superior position in the organizational structure (from Chester Barnard)

Authority-compliance management style: high concern for production and low concern for people (from Managerial Grid)

Bargaining: a unique form of conflict management in that participants negotiate mutually shared rules and then cooperate within these rules to gain a competitive advantage over their opponent

Basic assumptions: represent the essence of organizational culture

Benevolent authoritative system: motivation is based partially on rewards and also on the potential for punishment (from Likert's System IV)

Blended relationship: begins as a required association and develops into something more complex and interrelated with other organizational relationships

Boundary: part of the system that separates it from its environment

Boundary spanner: people who exchange information with the environment

Bounded emotionality: bringing elements of nurturance, caring, community, supportiveness, and interrelatedness into the workforce, although for task effectiveness, the emotionality is bound by feeling rules that emphasize individual and relational needs alongside organizational limits

Bullying: communicative phenomenon whereby one employee repeatedly harasses and abuses another employee

Bureaucracy: idealized organizational structure based on a written rule for every contingency (from theory of bureaucracy)

BYOD policy: policy that requires employees to bring their own personal device into the workplace to serve as their organizational device

Centralization: when decisions are made at the top of the hierarchy (from administrative theory)

Charisma : the effect a leader has on their followers

Charismatic authority: based on personal trust in the character or skills of the person to whom authority is attributed (from theory of bureaucracy)

Closed systems: those that have no exchange of material with the environment

Cohesiveness: the degree to which members feel connected to the team

Collective socialization: involves putting a group of recruits through a common set of experiences together

Collegial peer: share moderate levels of trust, self-disclosure, emotional support, and friendship

Command: managers must begin implementing the plan (from administrative theory)

Concertive control: based on adherence to socially constructed norms and values developed by organizational members themselves as they attempt to structure their environment

Concrete ceiling: referring to the unique challenges faced by women and minorities of color

Conflict: competition between interdependent parties who perceive that they have incompatible needs, goals, desires, or ideas

Conflict management: implementing strategies to decrease the negative effects of conflict and creating an environment in which conflict can enhance the learning and effectiveness of individuals and the organization

Conflict resolution: reduction, elimination, or termination of conflict

Consultative system: workers are motivated through rewards, occasional punishment, and limited involvement in decision-making and goal setting (from Likert's System IV)

Contain strategy: minimize the negative impact of a misunderstanding

Contingency theory: there is no one best way to structure and manage organizations

Control: the comparison of the activities of the personnel to the plan of action (from Fayol's administrative theory)

Construct strategy: new interpretation of the misunderstanding so learning can occur; in particular, new attitudes, values, behaviors, or practices could emerge

Coordination: high-level manager must now work to harmonize all the activities to facilitate organizational success (from administrative theory)

Cope strategy: dealing with the present situation and allowing all affected members to express their concerns and have their problems addressed

Corporate social responsibility: context-specific organizational actions and policies that take into account stakeholders' expectations and the triple bottom line of economic, social, and environmental performance

Cost-per-hire: dollar amount attributed to hiring a new employee

Counterculture: a subculture whose basic understandings question and oppose the overall culture in some way

Country club management style: puts concern for people above concern for production (from Managerial Grid)

Cultural feminism: men and women have different values and assumptions

Culture-as-root- metaphor : organizational culture as something the organization is

Culture-as-variable : organizational culture is something the organization has

Custodial response to socialization: newcomer could accept the role as it is presented, without questioning the status quo

Deep acting: emotional display that stems from an internal state or the use of cognitive strategies to proactively adapt how one is feeling

Dialectical tension: opposing but inevitable and normal force that occurs in every relationship, including organizational peer relationships

Digital Taylorism: use of technology to monitor and restructure work to be more efficient

Discrimination: treatment or action based on a stereotype is invisible or ingrained into cultural practice, it becomes difficult to overcome

Discursive consciousness: activities and/or feelings are easily explained by individuals (from structuration theory)

Disguising conversations: jokes and self-disclosure to ease information from a source without being obvious

Disidentification: a purposely chosen, negotiated response by organizational members facing significant change and upheaval in their actual work lives

Disjunctive socialization: no role models are available or provided for the newcomer

Displaced dissent: dissent expressed to someone not in the organization, such as a friend or family member

Diversity: variety of personal and societal bases of identity, including age, country of origin, ethnicity, gender, mental or physical ability, political affiliation, race, religion, sexuality, socioeconomic status, and veteran status

Divestiture socialization: seeks to deny and strip away certain personal characteristics of a newcomer

Division of work: each worker should have a limited set of tasks to accomplish (from administrative theory)

Duality of structure: the macrolevel structure (organization) is both a medium and an outcome of microlevel social practices (interaction) (from structuration theory)

Dynamic homeostasis: a balance of energy exchange

Emotion regulation: the efforts to increase, maintain, or decrease one or more components of an emotion

Emotional intelligence: a noncognitive aspect of intelligence that refers to one's ability to monitor their emotions and the emotions of people around them

Emotional labor: the management of one's emotions to induce a desired reaction or response in another individual

Entropy: the tendency is for the system to become disorganized

Equifinality: the same final state may be reached from different initial conditions and in different ways

Equivocality: any input into a system carries with it some level of uncertainty

Esprit de corps: a strong organization is one that has loyal members who will strive to keep the organization together at the cost of their personal interests (from administrative theory)

Executive leadership development: entails ongoing socialization processes that begin in childhood and continue throughout the organizational socialization and assimilation process

Exploitative authoritative system: managers tend to motivate their workers through fear, threats, punishment, and occasional reward (from Likert's System IV)

Feedback: any communication between organizational members that implicitly or explicitly provides task guidance, personal evaluation, or other guidance

Fixed socialization: provides the newcomer with a precise timetable for when to expect progression to the target role

Formal organization: system of activities that are coordinated consciously by two or more people (from Chester Barnard)

Formal socialization: newcomers are segregated, in one form or another, from regular organizational members

Function creep: when technologies are used to gather data, either purposefully or not, outside of their original purpose

Gangplank: also known as Fayol's bridge, is what allows people on the same hierarchical level to communicate directly with each other (from administrative theory)

Gender: culturally defined set of behavioral, cultural, psychological, or social traits that society has associated with a particular sex

Gender expression: an individual's choices with regard to how they express themselves using gendered behaviors and appearance

Gender identity: one's psychological, or deeply felt, sense of gender, which may or may not align with one's sex

Gender transition: a continuum of options that allow an individual to modify how they present, or express, their gender identity

Glass ceiling: a metaphorical barrier that prevents minorities from advancing in an organization

Global virtual teams: also known as multinational, transnational, or multicultural teams, are those virtual teams that include members who are geographically dispersed and culturally diverse

Groupthink: flawed group process or decision resulting from the desire to maintain conformity

Hawthorne effect: observing people's behavior tends to alter their behavior

Hawthorne studies: series of studies that led to the development of the human relations approach

Hegemony: indicates the process by which one group actively supports the goals and aspirations of another, dominant group, even though those goals may not be in the subordinate group's best interest

Heroes: individuals that embody the values of the organizational culture

Hierarchal mum effect: hierarchical constraint on upward information flow created by command structures

Hierarchy: strict chain of command; in a hierarchy, every lower office should be under the strict control and supervision of a higher office (from theory of bureaucracy)

Home-to-work conflict: occurs when an employee's home activities and commitments interfere with work responsibilities

Hostile environment sexual harassment: the use of words and actions to make a work environment demeaning, intimidating, and abusive

Ideology: an integrated set of values, ideals, and understandings about a particular part of social reality that justifies certain commitments and actions

Immediacy: any communication that indicates interpersonal warmth and closeness

Impoverished management style: characterized as being laissez-faire—that is, hiring workers for particular jobs and then leaving them alone to do their work (from Managerial Grid)

Indirect questioning: getting another person to respond to hints and noninterrogative questions

Individual socialization: recruits are brought into the organization in relative isolation from one another and put through a unique set of experiences

Informal communication: communication that is not formally prescribed or task related

Informal cultural rules: prescriptions for what kind of behavior is required, discouraged, permitted, and preferred or not preferred in the organization

Informal organization: is indefinite, is structureless, and has no definite subdivisions of personnel (from Chester Barnard)

Informal socialization: processes do not segregate the newcomer in any special way or distinguish the newcomer's role specifically

Information peer: the relationship is characterized by low levels of self-disclosure and trust

Innovative response to socialization: newcomer makes substantive changes to the knowledge base or strategy associated with the role or redefines the purpose of role functions

Input : the open system imports some form of energy or material through its boundaries from the environment

Institutional positioning: presentation of the organization at the macrolevel or to those outside of the organization (from communicative constitution of organizations)

Interactive cultural elements: can only be observed in interactions between organizational members

Internal (enterprise) social media: communication technology that allows members to communicate and collaborate internally and have their work available to other organizational members

Interpersonal conflict: conflict that occurs between two or more people that may or may not have to do with organizational tasks or task-related feelings

Interrelated: the existence and proper functioning of one part is dependent on the existence and proper functioning of the other parts

Intersectionality: points where multiple aspects of a person's identity intersect, cross, or overlap

Investiture socialization: affirms the personal characteristics and identity that the newcomer brings to the organization

Knowledgeable agent: individuals know that their interactions are either helping to maintain or change the existing organizational structure (from structuration theory)

Laissez-faire leader: leader who does not focus on either tasks or relationships and basically leaves the group to their own devices

Lateral dissent: dissent expressed to an organizational member on the same hierarchical level

Leader : a person who takes charge of the situation and influences the attitudes and actions of others

Leader-member exchange theory: bidirectional nature of the supervisor–subordinate relationship

Leadership as serving: doing things for others that enable them to do their jobs, serving means taking obstacles out of employees' way rather than putting them up

Liberal feminism: within patriarchal structures, people are differentiated based on sex

Machine metaphor: organizations are viewed as if they are machines; managerial principles, modes of operation, treatment of workers, and communication in the organization are considered in light of this metaphor

Maintenance communication: messages and behaviors used to preserve an acceptable and lasting relational state

Maintenance function of communication: provide for the flow of information among the subsystems

Management teams: coordinate and provide direction to subunits under their jurisdiction, laterally interdependent subunits across key business processes

Mechanistic systems: appropriate for a stable environment, where there is little change, or the change is predictable

Mediation: balancing power between disputing individuals, full participation of the individuals involved in the conflict, flattened lines of communication that allow all voices to be heard, and a democratic decision-making process

Membership negotiation: series of interactions that lets the employee's status emerge in relation to the organization (from communicative constitution of organizations)

Message: use of a symbol or symbols (written, spoken, or nonverbal) that the recipient interprets as having been created intentionally

Metamorphosis: when the new employee actually begins to change some of their behaviors and expectations to meet the standards of the new environment and begins to alter the requirements of their role to match their needs, desires, and skills

Microagression: communicates a negative or derogatory message to an individual who occupies a minority status

Microassault: the use of explicit and intended verbal or nonverbal behaviors

Microinsult: frequently unconscious verbal or nonverbal communication that is insensitive or demeaning about a person's heritage or identity

Microinvalidation: unconscious communicative acts that exclude or negate the experiences of an individual of an oppressed group

Middle-of-the-road management style: medium concern for both people and production, is best characterized as a compromise or balance-seeking position (from Managerial Grid)

Misunderstandings: represent the inherently problematic nature of organizational life

Multicommunicating: engaging in at least two interactions simultaneously with different interactional partners

Negative entropy: state of survival and growth

Negative feedback: information that indicates to the subsystems that they should return to the status quo

Negotiation: a deliberative process in which the participants create knowledge about their situation

Nonsummativity: principle that the whole or total is greater than the sum of the individual parts

Open systems: those that attempt to maintain a balance as they import and export material to and from the environment

Organic systems: required in changing environments with unstable conditions

Organism metaphor: an organization is a living entity in an environment that can provide it with energy and to which it can return an output

Organizational anticipatory socialization: includes the information intentionally and unintentionally gathered as the job seeker interacts with potential employing organizations

Organizational assimilation: the process by which an individual becomes integrated into the culture of an organization

Organizational communication: the process of creating, exchanging, interpreting (correctly or incorrectly), and storing messages within a system of human interrelationships.

Organizational culture context elements: how organizational cultures are shaped by aspects that may be outside the direct control of the current organizational members

Organizational democracy: involves the encouragement of (1) self-reflection, (2) collective development, and (3) individual opportunity

Organizational dissent: expressing disagreement or contradictory opinions about organizational practices, policies, and operations

Organizational entry/encounter: the newcomer confronts the reality of his or her organizational role

Organizational identification: individuals identify with their collectives to the extent that they feel similar to other members, they feel a sense of belonging, and they consider themselves to be members

Organizational peer relationship: the relationship that is a result of the organizational structure

Organizational socialization: the process by which an individual acquires the social knowledge and skills necessary to assume an organizational role

Organizational subculture: may diverge only minimally from the values and practices of the organizational culture

Organizational culture: is a communicatively constructed, historically based system of assumptions, values, and interpretive frameworks that guide and constrain organizational members as they perform their organizational roles and confront the challenges of their environment.

Organizing: managers need to provide everything necessary to carry it out, including raw materials, tools, capital, and human resources (from administrative theory)

Outlaws: individuals who represent values or ideals that are counter to the espoused values of the organization

Output: the system returns some product to the environment

Parallel teams: pull together people from different work units or departments to complete tasks that the organization is not otherwise prepared or equipped to perform well

Participative system: genuine participation in decision-making and goal setting, free-flowing communication, full use of every worker's skills and creative energy, and a high level of responsibility and accountability for the goals of the organization (from Likert's System IV)

Permeable: a boundary is capable of having material pass through it, to and from the environment

Phubbing: phone snubbing

Piecework system : employees are paid a sum of money for producing a certain amount during an average day (from scientific management)

Planning: creating a plan of action for the future, determining the stages of the plan and the technology necessary to implement it (from administrative theory)

Polychronicity: an individual's preference for multi-tasking

Positive feedback: information that alerts the subsystems to move from status quo behavior to a specified state of behavior

Postmodern feminism: gender is a communicative and social construction

Practical consciousness: experiences, behaviors, and feelings are not as easily put into words (from structuration theory)

Project teams: produce one-time outputs and are time limited

Proxemics: physical distance between people

Radical feminism: alternative forms of organizing around feminist ideals are necessary to resolve inequalities

Random socialization: occurs when the sequence of steps leading to the target role is unknown, ambiguous, or continually changing

Rational authority: also known as rational-legal or legal authority; based on the rational application of rules or laws (from theory of bureaucracy)

Realistic recruitment: presents outsiders with all pertinent information without distortion

Recursivity: the continual production and production of the structure similar to the process nature of communication (from structuration theory)

Reflexive self-structuring: flow that allows the organization to come into being because it communicates decisions such as division of labor, rules, and policies (from communicative constitution of organizations)

Relational leadership: focuses on the process of relationships and how they can be used to make a difference for the common good

Relative openness: system has some ability to regulate permeability

Relevant environment: consists of those entities outside the system that are relevant to the survival of the system

Remote work: working via communication technology from a location other than the physical workplace

Remuneration: employees should be paid a fair price for their services (from administrative theory)

Requisite variety: complex inputs must be addressed with complex processes, and vice versa

Resilience: the capacity of some teams to bounce back from this adversity

Rituals: social actions in which a group's values and identity are publicly demonstrated or enacted in a stylized manner, within the context of a specific occasion or event

Scalar chain: chain of superiors ranging from the ultimate authority to the lowest ranks (from administrative theory)

Self-managed work teams: have responsibility for their own work

Semantic-information distance: supervisors and subordinates often have vastly different perceptions of and meanings for important behavioral and organizational activities

Sequential socialization: the degree to which the organization specifies a certain set of steps to be completed to advance to the target role

Serial socialization: uses an experienced organizational member, who occupies a similar role to the one the newcomer will occupy, to help "groom" the newcomer

Sexual harassment: unwelcome sexual advances, requests for sexual favors, and other verbal and physical conduct of a sexual nature

Signaling function: RJP signals or calls attention to important organizational characteristics and realities for the applicant

Site of domination: interests of the dominant group (typically owners and management) are elevated above the interests of subordinate groups

Situational leadership: shifts in leadership behavior depending on variables in the group setting

Social loafing: when a group member has decreased motivation or puts in less effort than they would have working on the project as an individual

Special peer: a relationship that is characterized by high levels of emotional support, trust, self-disclosure, and intimacy

Strategic ambiguity: contextual cues are purposefully omitted from communication to allow for multiple interpretations on the part of the receiver

Strategic misinterpretation: purposeful misunderstanding of the message because it benefits the listener in some way

Stuckness: occurs when teams are unable to break a negative pattern of behavior, which causes it them to make the same mistakes over and over again

Subordination of individual interests: the interest (e.g., demands, needs, wants, desires) of an individual employee or group of employees should not come before the interest of the entire organization (from administrative theory)

Substantive conflict: organizational members disagree on task or content issues

Subsystems: interrelated parts of the system that do the processing

Supersystem: larger system to which the focal system belongs

Surface acting: external state of emotion or public display of emotions

Symbolic elements of culture: those elements in the culture that stand for or represent cultural values

Symbols: the physical representations of the organization's culture

Synergy: the subsystems work in conjunction with one another and produce extra energy

System : a set of interrelated parts that turns inputs into outputs through processing

Systematic soldiering: behavior of deliberately working slowly to avoid expending more effort than deemed necessary (from scientific management)

Team: a small group (three to nine) of interdependent people with complementary skills who are committed to a common purpose, performance goals, and approach for which they hold themselves mutually accountable

Team management style: high concern for people and a high concern for production with no inherent conflict between them (from Managerial Grid)

Technological dualism: each new technological advance comes with challenges or downsides

Telepressure: when employees have a preoccupation and urge to frequently check and quickly respond to work-related messages after their normal working hours

Telework: working from locations other than a principal office one or more days per week

Testing: breaking a rule and then monitoring the target person's response for information

Theory X: represents the tenets of classical theory (from Douglas McGregor)

Theory Y: represents the tenets of human relations theory (from Douglas McGregor)

Third-party questioning: asking someone other than the primary information source

Throughput: the parts of the system (or subsystems) transform the material or energy in some fashion

Time and motion studies: determine the most efficient and effective means of accomplishing every aspect of every task (from scientific management)

Traditional authority: based on past customs and involves personal loyalty to the person in the leadership position (from theory of bureaucracy)

Traditional recruitment: the practice of "selling" the organization to the potential employee

Traits: characteristics, either psychological or physical, that affect behavior

Transactional leader: holds designated authority positions and try to motivate followers with clear goals and defined expectations

Transformation model: input-throughout-output

Transformational leader: appeals to the higher-order needs of their followers

Transgender: an umbrella term used to describe a wide spectrum of individuals whose gender identity or gender expression differs from the sex they were assigned at birth

Trust: the sense that you can believe in and rely on the other person

Turnover cost: refers to the amount of money that can be attributed to losing one employee and replacing that employee with another

Unintended consequence: while individuals can control their own responses, they cannot control how others in the organization will respond or react (from structuration theory)

Unity of command: each employee should receive orders from only one supervisor (from administrative theory)

Unity of direction: one head (i.e., one manager) shall administer a group of activities having the same purpose (from administrative theory)

Upward communication: communication that flows up the hierarchy

Upward dissent: dissent expressed to a supervisor

Upward distortion: the hesitancy of subordinates to communicate negative news up the chain of command and their tendency to distort such news to place it in a more positive light

Upward influence: tactics used by a subordinate to influence or persuade their supervisor in some way

Values: individual's or group's sense of what ought to be

Variable socialization: provide no real cues to the newcomer as to when to expect movement to the target role

Virtual teams: relies on technology to work across space, time, and organizational boundaries

Vocational anticipatory socialization: includes the information gathered during childhood and adolescence from a variety of sources, including parents, peers and friends, teachers/school, media, and part-time jobs

Work spouse: special type of workplace friendship that occurs when individuals form a close emotional bond with extremely high levels of disclosure and support

Work teams: continuing units that are responsible for the production of goods or providing services such as customer service

Work-family enrichment: the experiences and resources that individuals gain in one role (employment) will improve the quality of life that they experience in their other roles such as being a friend or family member

Workplace romance: nonplatonic consensual relationship between two members of the organization that entails mutual sexual attraction and affection that has been communicated

Work-to-home conflict: occurs when participation in work interferes with home roles or activities

Zone of indifference: marks the boundaries of what that person will consider doing without question, based on expectations developed upon entering the organization (from Chester Barnard)

References

Acker, J. (1990). Hierarchies, jobs, bodies: A theory of gendered organizations. *Gender & Society, 4*, 139–158.

Adkins, C. L., & Premeaux, S. F. (2019). A cybernetic model of work-life balance through time. *Human Resource Management Review, 29*(4), article 100680. https://doi.org/10.1016/j.hrmr.2019.01.001

Agovino, T. (2019, February 23). *To have and to hold.* All Things Work. https://www.shrm.org/hr-today/news/all-things-work/pages/to-have-and-to-hold.aspx

Aguinis, H., & Glavas, A. (2012). What we know and don't know about corporate social responsibility: A review and research agenda. *Journal of Management, 38*(4), 932–968. https://doi.org/10/1177/0149206311436079

Aktouf, O. (1992). Management and theories of organizations in the 1990s: Toward a critical radical humanism? *Academy of Management Review, 17*(3), 407–431.

Alavi, M., & Keen, P. G. W. (1989). Business teams in an information age. *The Information Society: An International Journal, 6*(4), 179–195.

Albrecht, T. L., & Hall, B. J. (1991). Facilitating talk about new ideas: The role of personal relationships in organizational innovation. *Communication Monographs, 58*, 273–288.

Alder, G. S., & Tompkins, P. K. (1997). Electronic performance monitoring: An organizational justice and concertive control perspective. *Management Communication Quarterly, 10*(3), 259–288.

Aley, M. R., & Levine, K. J. (2020). From whom do young adults actively seek career information? An ego-network analysis of vocational anticipatory socialization. *Communication Studies, 71*(2), 351–367. https://doi.org/10/1080/10510974.2020.1735464

Allen, B. J. (1995). "Diversity" and organizational communication. *Journal of Applied Communication Research, 23*, 143–155.

Allen, M. W., Coopman, S. J., Hart, J. L., & Walker, K. L. (2007). Workplace surveillance and managing privacy boundaries. *Management Communication Quarterly, 21*(2), 172–200.

Allen, T. D., Cho, E., & Meier, L. L. (2014). Work–family boundary dynamics. *Annual Review of Organizational Psychology and Organizational Behavior, 1*, 99–121. https://doi.org/10.1146/annurevorgpsych-031413-091330

Allen, T. D., Eby, L. T., Chao, G. T., & Bauer, T. N. (2017). Taking stock of two relational aspects of organizational life: Tracing the history and shaping the future of socialization and mentoring research. *Journal of Applied Psychology, 102*(3), 324–337. http://dx.doi.org/10.1037/ap10000086

Almaney, A. (1974). Communication and the systems theory of organization. *Journal of Business Communication, 12*(1), 35–43.

Alvesson, M. (1993). Cultural-ideological modes of management control: A theory and a case study of a professional service company. In S. A. Deetz (Ed.), *Communication Yearbook 16* (pp. 3–42). Routledge.

Alvesson, M. (2002). *Understanding organizational culture.* SAGE Publications.

Alvesson, M., & Deetz, S. (1996). Critical theory and postmodernism approaches to organizational studies. In S. R. Clegg, C. Hardy, & W. R. Nord, (Eds.), *Handbook of organization studies* (pp. 191–217). SAGE Publications.

Amason, A. C. (1996). Distinguishing the effects of functional and dysfunctional conflict on strategic decision making: Resolving a paradox for top management teams. *Academy of Management Journal, 39*, 123–148.

Amy, A. H. (2005). *Leaders as facilitators of organizational learning* [Unpublished doctoral dissertation]. Regent University.

Anderson, C. M., & Hunsaker, P. L. (1985). Why there's romancing at the office and why it's everybody's business. *Personnel, 62*(2), 57–63.

Angelou, M. (1997, January 22). *America's renaissance woman* [Interview]. Academy of Achievement. https://achievement.org/achiever/maya-angelou/#interview

Anteby, M., & Chan, C. (2018). A self-fulfilling cycle of coercive surveillance: Workers' invisibility practices and managerial justification. *Organization Science, 29*, 247–263. https://doi.org/10.1287/orsc.2017.1175

Antonakis, J., Bastardoz, N., Jacquart, P., & Shamir, B. (2016). Charisma: An ill-defined and ill-measured gift. *Annual Review of Organizational Psychology and Organizational Behavior, 3*(1), 293–319. https://doi.org/10.1146/annurev-orgpsych-041015-062305

Ashcraft, K. L. (2000). Empowering "professional" relationships: Organizational communication meets feminist practice. *Management Communication Quarterly, 13*(3), 347–392.

Ashcraft, K. L. (2014). Feminist theory. In L. Putnam & D. K. Mumby (Eds.), *The SAGE handbook of organizational communication* (pp. 127–150). SAGE Publications.

Ashforth, B. E., & Humphrey, R. H. (1993). Emotional labor in service roles: The influence of identity. *Academy of Management Review, 18*, 88–115.

Ashforth, B. E., Kreiner, G. E., & Fugate, M. (2000). All in a day's work: Boundaries and micro-role transitions. *Academy of Management Review, 25*(3), 472–491.

Altass, P., & Wiebe, S. (2017). Re-imagining education policy and practice in the digital era. *Journal of the Canadian Association for Curriculum Studies (JCACS), 15*(2), 48–63.

Avolio, B. J., & Gibbons, T. C. (1988). Developing transformation leaders: A life-span approach. In J. A. Conger & N. Kanungo (Eds.), *Charismatic leadership: The elusive factor in organizational effectiveness* (pp. 277–308). Jossey-Bass.

Awee, A., Hanim Mohsin, F., & Makhbul, Z. K. M. (2020). The factors why people exert less: The relationship between workplace envy and social loafing moderated by self-esteem. *International Journal of Management Studies, 27*(2), 27–46. https://doi.org/10/32890/ijms.27.2.2020.7523

Awolusi, F. (2012). The impacts of social networking sites on workplace productivity. *Journal of Technology, Management, and Applied Engineering, 28*(1), 2–6.

Bachrach, P., & Baratz, M. (1970). *Power and poverty.* Oxford University Press.

Bain, P., Watson, A., Mulvey, G., Taylor, P., & Gall, G. (2002). Taylorism, targets and the pursuit of quantity and quality by call centre management. *New Technology, Work and Employment, 17*(3), 170–185.

Banerjee, P., & Gupta, R. (2019). Talent attraction through online recruitment websites: Application of Web 2.0 technologies. *Australasian Journal of Information Systems, 23*, 1–32. https://doi.org/10/3127/ajis.v23i0.1762

Bao, Y., & Zhong, W. (2019). How stress hinders health among Chinese public sector employees: The mediating role of emotional exhaustion and the moderating role of perceived organizational support. *International Journal of Environmental Research and Public Health, 16*(22), 4408. https://doi.org/10.3390/ijerph16224408

Barker, J. R. (1998). Tightening the iron cage: Concertive control in self-managing teams. In J. Van Maanen (Ed.), *Qualitative studies of organizations* (pp. 126–158). SAGE Publications.

Barker, J. R., & Tompkins, P. K. (1994). Identification in the self-managing organization: Characteristics of target and tenure. *Human Communication Research, 21*(2), 223–240.

Barley, S. R. (1983). Semiotics and the study of occupational and organizational cultures. *Administrative Science Quarterly, 28*, 393–413.

Barnard, C. I. (1938). *The functions of the executive.* Harvard University Press.

Barnes, J. (2017). Climbing the stairs to leadership: Reflections on moving beyond the stained-glass ceiling. *Journal of Leadership Studies, 10*(4), 47–53. https://doi.org/10.1002/jls.21503

Barnett, G. A. (1997). Organizational communication systems: The traditional perspective. In G. A. Barnett & L. Thayer (Eds.), *Organization-communication: Emerging perspectives V: The renaissance of systems thinking* (pp. 1–46). Ablex.

Barry, D. (1995). Managing the bossless team: Lessons in distributed leadership. In *Self-managed, teams: A special report from Organizational Dynamics* (pp. 53–69). American Management Association.

Bartels, J., Pruyn, A., & de Jong, M. (2009). Employee identification before and after an internal merger: A longitudinal analysis. *Journal of Occupational and Organizational Psychology, 82*, 113–128.

Bartels, J., van Vuuren, M., & Ouwerkerk, J. W. (2019). My colleagues are my friends: The role of Facebook contacts in employee identification. *Management Communication Quarterly, 33*(3), 307–328. https://doi.org/10.1177/0893318919837944

Bass, B. M. (1985). *Leadership and performance beyond expectations.* Free Press.

Bass, B. M. (1990). *Bass & Stogdill's handbook of leadership: Theory, research & managerial applications.* Free Press.

Bass, B. M., & Avolio, B. J. (1994). Potential biases in leadership measures: How prototypes, leniency, and general satisfaction relate to ratings and rankings of transformational and transactional leadership constructs. *Educational and Psychological Measurement, 49*, 509–527.

Bass, B. M., Avolio, B. J., & Atwater, L. (1996). The transformational and transactional leadership of men and women. *Applied Psychology: An International Review, 45*, 5–34.

Bauer, T. A., & Green, S. G. (1996). Development of leader-member exchange: A longitudinal test. *Academy of Management Journal, 39*(6), 1538–1567.

Baur, J. E., Buckley, M. R., Bagdasarov, Z., & Dharmasiri, A. S. (2014). A historical approach to realistic job previews: An exploration of their origins, evolution, and recommendations for the future. *Journal of Management History, 20*, 200–223.

Baxter, L. A., & Braithwaite, D. O. (2008). Relational dialectics theory: Crafting meaning from competing discourses. In D. O. Braithwaite & L. A. Baxter (Eds.), *Engaging theories in interpersonal communication: Multiple perspectives* (pp. 349–361). SAGE Publications.

Bean, H., Lemon, L., & O'Connell, A. (2013). Organizational rhetoric, materiality, and the shape of organizational democracy. *Southern Communication Journal, 78*(3), 256–273. https://doi.org/10.1080/1041794X.2013.791717

Becker, C. B. (1997). The analysis of organizational culture as a thermodynamic process. In G. Barnett & L. Thayer (Eds.), *A turn of the wheel: The case for a renewal of systems inquiry in organizational communication research* (pp. 121–139). Ablex.

Becker, W. J., Belkin, L. Y., Conroy, S. A., & Tuskey, S. (2019). Killing me softly: Organizational e-mail monitoring expectations' impact on employee and significant other well-being. *Journal of Management.* https://doi.org/10.1177/0149206319890655

Belkin, L. Y., Becker, W. J., & Conroy, S. A. (2020). The invisible leash: The impact of organizational expectations for email monitoring after-hours on employee resources, well-being, and turnover intentions. *Group & Organization Management, 45*(5), 709–740. https://doi.org/10.1177/1059601120933143

Benedict, B. C. (2020). Examining the experiences of remaining employees after a coworker dismissal: Initial message characteristics, information seeking, uncertainty, and perceived social costs. *Management Communication Quarterly, 34*(4), 495–526. https://doi.org/10.1177/0893318920949327

Bennis, W, & Nanus, B. (1985). *Leaders: The strategies for taking charge.* AMACOM.

Berlin-Ray, E. (1993). When links become chains: Considering dysfunctions of supportive communication in the workplace. *Communication Monographs, 60*(1), 106–111.

Berman, E. M., West, J. P., & Richter, Jr., M. N. (2002). Workplace relations: Friendship patterns and consequences (according to managers). *Public Administrative Review, 62*, 217–23.

Bible, D., & Hill, K. L. (2007). Discrimination: Women in business. *Journal of Organizational Culture, Communication and Conflict, 11*(1), 65–76.

Bisel, R. S. (2010). A communicative ontology of organization? A description, history, and critique of CCO theories for organizational science. *Management Communication Quarterly, 24*, 124–131.

Bisel, R. S., & Arterburn Adame, E. (2019). Encouraging upward dissent in organizations: The role of deference to embodied expertise. *Management Communication Quarterly, 33*(2), 139–159. https://doi.org/10.1177/089331898811949

Bisel, R. S., Messersmith, A. S., & Kelley, K. M. (2012). Supervisor-subordinate communication: Hierarchical mum effect meets organizational learning. *Journal of Business Communication, 49*, 128–147.

Blake, R., & Mouton, J. S. (1964). *The managerial grid*. Gulf.

Blank, R., & Slipp, S. (2000). *From the outside in: Seven strategies for success when you're not a member of the dominant group in your workplace*. AMACOM.

Blumenfeld, S., Anderson, G., & Hooper, V. (2020). Covid-19 and employee surveillance. *New Zealand Journal of Employment Relations, 45*(2), 42–56.

Blunt, P., & Jones, M.L. (1997), Exploring the limits of Western leadership theory in East Asia and Africa, *Personnel Review, 26*(1/2), 6–23. https://doi.org/10.1108/00483489710157760

Boje, D. M. (1991). The storytelling organization: A study of story performance in an office-supply firm. *Administrative Science Quarterly, 36*(1), 106–126.

Boselovic, L. (2006, March 21). Gender stereotypes hold back investors. *Pittsburg Post-Gazette*. https://www.post-gazette.com/business/top50/2006/03/21/Gender-stereotypes-hold-back-investors/stories/200603210355

Bourdeau, S., Ollier-Malaterre, & Houlfort, N. (2019). Not all work-life policies are created equal: Career consequences of using enabling versus enclosing work life policies. *Academy of Management, 44*, 172–793. https://doi.org/10.5465/amr.2016.0429

Boyd, C. (2010). The debate over the prohibition of romance in the workplace. *Journal of Business Ethics, 97*, 325–338.

Breaugh, J. A., & Billings, R. S. (1988). The realistic job preview: Five key elements and their importance for research and practice. *Journal of Business and Psychology, 2*, 291–305.

Brewster, M. E., Velez, B. L., Mennicke, A., & Tebbe, E. (2014). Voices from beyond: A thematic content analysis of transgender employees' workplace experiences. *Psychology of Sexual Orientation and Gender Diversity, 1*(2), 159–169. https://doi.org/10.1037/sgd0000030

Bridge, K., & Baxter, L. A. (1992). Blended relationships: Friends as work associates. *Western Journal of Communication, 56*(3), 200–225.

Britton, D. (2004). *At work in the iron cage: The prison as gendered organization*. New York University Press.

Brooks, M. C., & Mutohar, A. (2018). Islamic school leadership: a conceptual framework. *Journal of Educational Administration and History, 50*(2), 1–15. https://doi.org/10.1080/00220620.2018.1426558

Brower, H. H., Lester, S. W., Korsgaard, M. A., & Dineen, B. R. (2009). A closer look at trust between managers and subordinates: Understanding the effects of both trusting and being trusted on subordinate outcomes. *Journal of Management, 35*(2), 327-347. https://doi.org/10.1177/0149206307312511

Brown, T. J., & Allgeier, E. R. (1995). Managers' perceptions of workplace romances: An interview study. *Journal of Business and Psychology, 10*(2), 169–176.

Bruck, C. S., & Allen, T. D. (2003). The relationship between big five personality traits, negative affectivity, type A behavior, and work-family conflict. *Journal of Vocational Behavior, 63*, 457–A72.

Brummans, B. H. J. M., Cooren, F., Robichaud, D., & Taylor, J. R. (2014). Approaches to the communicative constitution of organizations. In L. Putnam & D. Mumby (Eds.), *The SAGE handbook of organizational communication: Advances in theory, research, and method* (3rd ed., pp. 173–194). SAGE Publications.

Brunelle, E. (2013). Leadership and mobile working: The impact of distance on the superior-subordinate relationship and the moderating effects of leadership style. *International Journal of Business and Social Science, 4*(11), 1–14. https://doi.org/10.30845/ijbss

Bryman, A. (1996). Leadership in organizations. In S. R. Clegg, C. Hardy, & W. R. Nord (Eds.), *Handbook of organization studies* (pp. 276–292). SAGE Publications.

Buckley, M. R., Fedor, D. B., Carraher, S. M., Frink, D. D., & Marvin, D. (1997). The ethical imperative to provide recruits realistic job previews. *Journal of Managerial Issues, 9,* 468–484.

Buckner, M. M., Ledbetter, A. M., & Payne, H. J. (2018). Family communication patterns as predictors of organizational dissent: A replication study. *Communication Studies, 69*(3), 326–335. https://doi.org/10/1080/10510974/2018.1461668

Bullis, C. (1993). Organizational socialization research: Enabling, constraining, and shifting perspectives. *Communication Monographs, 60*(1), 10–17.

Bullis, C., & Bach, B. (1989). Socialization turning points: An examination of change in organizational identification. *Western Journal of Speech Communication, 53,* 273–293.

Bullis, C., & Stout, K. R. (2000). Organizational socialization: A feminist standpoint approach. In P. M. Buzzanell (Ed.), *Rethinking organizational and managerial communication from feminist perspectives* (pp. 47–75). SAGE Publications.

Burke, K. (1950). *A rhetoric of motives.* Prentice Hall.

Burns, J. M. (1978). *Leadership.* Harper & Row.

Burns, T, & Stalker, G. M. (1968). *The management of innovation.* Tavistock Publications.

Butler, J. A., & Modaff, D. P. (2008). When work is home: Agency, structure, and contradictions. *Management Communication Quarterly, 22*(2), 232–257.

Buzzanell, P. M. (1994). Gaming a voice: Feminist organizational communication theorizing. *Management Communication Quarterly, 7*(4), 339–383.

Buzzanell, P. M. (2020). Gender and feminist theory. In A. M. Nicotera (Ed.), *Origins and traditions of organizational communication* (pp. 250–269). Routledge.

Calas, M. B., & Smircich, L. (1996). From "the woman's" point of view: Feminist approaches to organization studies. In S. R. Clegg, C. Hardy, & W. R. Nord (Eds.), *Handbook of organization studies* (pp. 218–257). SAGE Publications.

CareerBuilder. (2018, August 9). *More than half of employers have found content on social media that caused them NOT to hire a candidate* [Newsroom press release]. http://press.careerbuilder.com/2018-08-09-More-Than-Half-of-Employers-Have-Found-Content-on-Social-Media-That-Caused-Them-NOT-to-Hire-a-Candidate-According-to-Recent-CareerBuilder-Survey

Chan-Serafin, S., Teo, L., Minbashian, A., Cheng, D., & Wang, L. (2017). The perils of dating your boss: The role of hierarchical workplace romance and sex on evaluators' career advancement decisions for lower status romance participants. *Journal of Social and Personal Relationships, 34*(3), 309–333. https://doi.org/10.1177/0265407516635285

Chang, H.-T., Chou, Y.-J., Liou, J.-W., & Tu, Y.-T. (2016). The effects of perfectionism on innovative behavior and job burnout: Team workplace friendship as a moderator. *Personality and Individual Differences, 96,* 260-265. http://dx.doi.org/10/1016/paid.2016.02.088

Chansler, P. A., Swamidass, P. M., & Cammann, C. (2003). Self-managing work teams: An empirical study of group cohesiveness in "natural work groups" at a Harley-Davidson Motor Company plant. *Small Group Research, 34*(1), 101–120.

Chehade, H. M., & EL Hajjar, S. T. (2016). An empirical study to examine the effect of realistic job preview on expectancies, personal goals and performance. *International Journal of Business and Management, 11*(2), 164–183. https://doi.org/10.5539/ijbm.v11n2p164

Cheney, G. (1983). On various and changing meanings of organizational membership: A field study of organizational identification. *Communication Monographs, 50,* 342–362.

Cheney, G. (1995). Democracy in the workplace: Theory and practice from the perspective of communication. *Journal of Applied Communication Research, 23,* 167–200.

Cheney, G., Christensen, L. T., & Dailey, S. (2014). Communicating identity and identification in and around organizations. In L. Putnam & D. K. Mumby (Eds.), *The SAGE handbook of organizational communication: Advances in theory, research, and methods* (3rd ed.,pp. 695–716). SAGE Publications.

Cheng, S. S., & Seeger, M. W. (2012). Cultural differences and communication issues in international mergers and acquisitions: A case study of BenQ debacle. *International Journal of Business and Social Science, 3,* 116–127.

Cherniss, C. (2000). Emotional intelligence: What it is and why it matters. http://www.tal-entsmart.com/media/uploads/pdfs/eq-what-it-is.pdf

Chesloff, J. D. (2010). Corporate social responsibility: A "cutting edge" policy for employers. *CSR Journal, 3*–5.

Chi, N. W., & Grandey, A. A. (2016). Emotional labor predicts service performance depending on activation and inhibition regulatory fit. *Journal of Management.* https://doi.org/10.1177/0149206316672530

Chory, R. M., & Gillen Hoke, H. (2020). Coworkers' perceptions of, and communication with, workplace romance participants: Proposing and testing a model. *International Journal of Business Communication.* https://doi.org/10.1177/2329488420908321

Chory, R. M., & Hoke, H. G. G. (2019). Young love at work: Perceived effects of workplace romance among Millennial generation organizational members. *Journal of Psychology, 153*(6), 575–598. https://doi.org/10.1080/00223980.2019.1581722

Christoforou, P. S., & Ashforth, B. (2015). Revisiting the debate on the relationship between display rules and performance: Considering the explicitness of display rules. *Journal of Applied Psychology, 100*(1), 249–261. https://doi.org/10.1037/a0026871

Cistulli, M. D., & Snyder, J. L. (2019). Privacy in social media friendships with direct supervisors: A psychological contract perspective. *International Journal of Business Communication, 39*, 1–17. https://doi.org/10.1177/2329488419856072

Cletus, H. E., Mahmood, N. A., Umar, A., & Ibrahim, A. D. (2018). Prospects and challenges of workplace diversity in modern day organizations: A critical review. *HOLISTICA—Journal of Business and Public Administration, 9*(2), 35–52. https://doi.org/10.2478/hjbpa-2018-0011

Cohen, S. G., & Bailey, D. E. (1997). What makes teams work: Group effectiveness research from the shop floor to the executive suite. *Journal of Management, 23*(3), 239–290.

Coca-Cola Company. (2021). *Sustainable business.* https://www.coca-colacompany.com/sustainable-business

Collins, D. (1998). *Organizational change: Sociological perspectives.* Routledge.

Comer, D. R., & Stites-Doe, S. (2006). Antecedents & consequences of faculty women's academic-parental role balancing. *Journal of Family Economic Issues, 27*, 495–512.

Conrad, C. (1983). Organizational power: Faces and symbolic forms. In L. Putnam & M. Pacanowsky (Eds.), *Communication and organizations: An interpretive approach* (pp. 173–194). SAGE Publications.

Conrad, C. (1990). *Strategic organizational communication: An integrated perspective* (2nd ed.). Holt, Rinehart & Winston.

Conrad, C., & Witte, K. (1994). Is emotional expression repression oppression? Myths of organizational affective regulations. In S. Deetz (Ed.), *Communication yearbook, 17* (pp. 417–428). SAGE Publications.

Constantine, M. G., Smith, L., Redington, R. M., & Owens, D. (2008). Racial microaggressions against black counseling and counseling psychology faculty: A central challenge in the multicultural counseling movement. *Journal of Counseling & Development, 86*, 348–355.

Cote, S. (2005). A social interaction model of the effects of emotion regulation on work strain. *Academy of Management Review, 30*(3), 509–530.

Cowan, R. L. (2011). "Yes, we have an anti-bullying policy, but … ": HR professionals' understandings and experiences with workplace bullying policy. *Communication Studies, 62*, 307–327.

Cowan, R. L. (2012). It's complicated: Defining workplace bullying from the human resource professional's perspective. *Management Communication Quarterly, 26*(3), 377–403.

Cowan, R. L., & Horan, S. M. (2014). Why are you dating him? Contemporary motives for workplace romance. *Qualitative Research Reports in Communication, 15*(1), 9–16. https://doi.org/10.1080/17459435.2014.955587

Cowan, R. L., & Horan, S. M. (2021). Understanding information and communication technology use in workplace romance escalation and de-escalation. *International Journal of Business Communication, 58*(1), 55–78. https://doi.org/10.1177/2329488417731860

Cox, T, & Blake, S. (1991). Managing cultural diversity: Implications for organizational competitiveness. *Academy of Management Executive, 5*(3), 45–56.

Coyne, I., Farley, S., Axtell, C., Sprigg, C., Best, L., & Kwok, O. (2017). Understanding the relationship between experiencing workplace cyberbullying, employee mental strain and job satisfaction: A disempowerment approach. *International Journal of Human Resource Management, 28*(7), 945–972. https://doi.org/10.1080/09585192.2015.1116454

Crenshaw, K. (1991). Mapping the margins: Intersectionality, identity politics, and violence against women of color. *Stanford Law Review, 43*(6), 1241–1299. https://doi.org/10.2307/1229039

Croucher, S. M., Kassing, J. W., & Diers-Lawson, A. R. (2013). Accuracy, coherence, and discrepancy in self- and other-reports: Moving toward an interactive perspective of organizational dissent. *Management Communication Quarterly, 27,* 425–442.

Croucher, S. M., Zeng, C., & Kassing, J. (2019). Learning to contradict and standing up for the company: An exploration of the relationship between organizational dissent, organizational assimilation, and organizational reputation. *International Journal of Business Communication, 56*(3), 349–367. https://doi.org/10.1177/2329488416633852

Curran, C. J. (2005). Organizational culture: The path to better organizations. *Journal of Nonprofit Management, 9*(1), 28–40.

Dahl, R. (1957). The concept of power. *Behavioral Science, 2,* 201–205.

Dahlin, K., Weingart, L., & Hinds, P. (2005). Team diversity and information use. *Academy of Management Journal, 48*(6), 1107–1123.

Daily, C. M., & Dalton, D. R. (1999). Cracks in the glass ceiling? *Directorship, 25*(3), 4–6.

Dailey, S. L. (2016). What happens before full-time employment? Internships as a mechanism of anticipatory socialization. *Western Journal of Communication, 80*(4), 453–480. https://doi.org/10.1080/10570314.2016.1159727

Dailey, S. L., Alabere, R. O., Michalski, J. E., & Brown, C. I. (2020). Sports experiences as anticipatory socialization: How does communication in sports help individuals with intellectual disabilities learn about and adapt to work? *Communication Quarterly, 68*(5), 499–519. https://doi.org/10.1080/01463373.2020.1821737

Dansereau, E, Graen, G., & Haga, W. J. (1975). A vertical dyad linkage approach to leadership within formal organizations. *Organizational Behavior and Human Performance, 13,* 46–78.

Dansereau, E, & Markham, S. E. (1987). Superior–subordinate communication: Multiple levels of analysis. In F. M. Jablin, L. L. Putnam, K. H. Roberts, & L. W. Porter (Eds.), *Handbook of organizational communication* (pp. 343–388). SAGE Publications.

Darling, J. R., & Brownlee, L. J. (1984). Conflict management in the academic institutions. *Texas Tech Journal of Education, 11,* 243–257.

Deal, T. E., & Kennedy, A. A. (1982). *Corporate cultures: The rites and rituals of corporate life.* Addison-Wesley.

Deetz, S. A. (1982). Critical interpretive research in organizational communication. *Western Journal of Speech Communication, 46,* 131–149.

Deetz, S. A. (1992). *Democracy in an age of corporate colonization.* State University of New York Press.

De Janasz, S. C., Sullivan, S. E., & Whiting, V. (2003). Mentor networks and career success: Lessons for turbulent times. *Academy of Management Executive, 17*(4), 78–91.

de la Torre-Ruiz, J. M., Ferrón-Vílchez, V., & Ortiz-de-Mandojana, N. (2014). Team decision making and individual satisfaction with the team. *Small Group Research, 45*(2), 198–216. https://doi.org/10.1177/1046496414525478

Delanoeije, J., Verbruggen, M., & Germeys, L. (2019). Boundary role transitions: A day-to-day approach to explain the effects of home-based telework on work-to-home conflict and home-to-work conflict. *Human Relations, 72*(12), 1843–1868. https://doi.org/10.1177/0018726718823071

Deloitte. (2021). *Life at Deloitte: Deloitte volunteer impact research.* https://www2.deloitte.com/us/en/pages/about-deloitte/articles/citizenship-deloitte-volunteer-impact-research.html

De Ruiter, M., Schalk, R., & Blomme, R. J. (2016). Manager responses to employee dissent about psychological contract breach: A dyadic process approach. *Management Communication Quarterly, 30*(2), 188–217. https://doi.org/10.1177/0893318915623238

DeSanctis, G., & Gallupe, B. (1987). A foundation for the study of group decision support systems. *Management Science, 17*(2), 1589–1609.

Dhanesh, G. S. (2015). Why corporate social responsibility? An analysis of drivers of CSR in India. *Management Communication Quarterly, 29*(1), 114–129. https://doi.org/10.1177/0893318914545496

Di Domenico, M., & Phillips, N. (2009). Sustaining the ivory tower: Oxbridge formal dining as organizational ritual. *Journal of Management Inquiry, 18*, 326–343.

Dockery, T. M., & Steiner, D. D. (1990). The role of the initial interaction in leader-member exchange. *Group and Organizational Studies, 15*(4), 395–413.

Donia, M. B. I. (2020). *Employees want genuine corporate social responsibility, not greenwashing.* Phys.org. https://phys.org/news/2020-01-employees-genuine-corporate-social-responsibility.html

Drath, W. (2001). *The deep blue sea: Rethinking the source of leadership.* Jossey-Bass and Center for Creative Leadership.

Driskell, T., Salas, E., & Driskell, J. E. (2018). Teams in extreme environments: Alternations in team development and teamwork. *Human Resource Management Review, 28*(4), 434–449. https://doi.org/10.1016/j.hrmr.2017.01.002

Driskill, G. W. C. (2019). *Organizational culture in action: A cultural analysis workbook* (3rd ed.). Routledge.

Drouin, M., O'Connor, K. W., Schmidt, G. B., & Miller, D. A. (2015). Facebook fired: Legal perspectives and young adults' opinions on the use of social media in hiring and firing decisions. *Computers in Human Behavior, 46*, 123–128. https://doi.org/10.1016/j.chb.2015.01.011

Early, S. L. (2020), Relational leadership reconsidered: The mentor–protégé connection. *Journal of Leadership Studies, 13*, 57–61. https://doi.org/10.1002/jls.21671

Earnest, D. R., Allen, D. G., & Landis, R. S. (2011). Mechanisms linking realistic job previews with turnover: A meta-analytic path analysis. *Personnel Psychology, 64*, 865–897. https://doi.org/10.1111/j.1744-6570.2011.01230.x

Easton, S. (2019). Workplace bullying remains high among Tasmanian public servants. *The Mandarin.* https://www.themandarin.com.au/103380-workplace-bullying-remains-high-among-tasmanian-public-servants/

Eisenberg, E. M. (1984). Ambiguity as a strategy in organizational communication. *Communication Monographs, 51*, 227–242.

Eisenberg, E. M., & Riley, P. (2001). Organizational culture. In F. M. Jablin & L. L. Putnam (Eds.), *The new handbook of organizational communication* (pp. 291–322). SAGE Publications.

Elias, N. M., Johnson, R. L., Oyando, D., & Ramirez, J. (2018). Improving transgender policy for a more equitable workplace. *Journal of Public Management & Social Policy, 24*(2), 53–81.

Eseryel, U. Y., Crowston, K., & Heckman, R. (2020). Functional and visionary leadership in self-managing virtual teams. *Group & Organization Management.* https://doi.org/10.1177/1059601120955034

Fairhurst, G. T., & Grant, D. (2010). The social construction of leadership: A sailing guide. *Management Communication Quarterly, 24*(2), 171–210.

Fairhurst, G. T., & Chandler, T. A. (1989). Social structure in leader-member interaction. *Communication Monographs, 56*(3), 215–239.

Fairweather, N. B. (1999). Surveillance in employment: The case of teleworking. *Journal of Business Ethics, 22*, 39–49.

Fang, L., Fang, C. L., & Fang, S. H. (2020). Student nurses' bullying social support and their health status during clinical practicum programmes. *International Journal of Nursing Practicum, 26*(12869). https://doi.org/10.1111/ijn.12869

Fayol, H. (1949). *General and industrial management.* Sir Isaac Pitman & Sons.

Feeney, M. K., & Stritch, J. M. (2019). Family-friendly policies, gender, and work-life balance in the public section. *Review of Public Personnel Administration, 39*(3), 422-448. https://doi.org/10.1177/0734371X17

Felstiner, W. L. F., Abel, R. L., & Sarat, A. (1980–1981). The emergence and transformation of disputes: Naming, blaming, and changing. *Law & Society Review, 15*, 631–654.

Ferguson, K. (1984). *The feminist case against bureaucracy.* Temple University Press.

Fernandez, R. M., & Campero, S. (2017). Gender sorting and the glass ceiling in high-tech firms. *ILR Review, 70*(1), 73–104. https://doi.org/10.1177/0019793916668875

Fialka, J. (1973, July 22). Can job enrichment undo fifty years of 'Taylorism'? *Daytona Beach Sunday News Journal*, p. 7E.

Fine, M. G., & Buzzanell, P. M. (2000). Walking the high wire. In P. Buzzanell (Ed.), *Rethinking organizational and managerial communication from a feminist perspective* (pp. 128–156). SAGE Publications.

Fineman, S. (Ed.). (1993). *Emotion in organizations.* SAGE Publications.

Fink, J. (2014). *In defense of snooping employers.* CWSL Scholarly Commons. https://scholarlycommons.law.cwsl.edu/cgi/viewcontent.cgi?article=1079&context=fs

Fiol, C. M. (1994). Consensus, diversity and learning organizations. *Organization Science, 5*, 403–420.

Flores, H. R., Jiang, X., Manz, C. C. (2018). Intra-team conflict: The moderating effect of emotional self-leadership. *International Journal of Conflict Management, 29*(3), 424-444. https://doi.org/10.1108/IJCMA-07-2017-0065

Follett, M. P. (2013). *Creative experience.* Martino Publishing (Original work published 1924).

Former, K. L., & Timmerman, C. E. (2009). Organizational newc(ust)omers: Applying organizational newcomer assimilation concepts to customer information seeking and service outcomes. *Management Communication Quarterly, 23*(2), 244–271.

Foss, S. K., Foss, K. A., & Trapp, R. (1985). *Contemporary perspectives on rhetoric.* Waveland Press.

Foucreault, A., Ollier-Malaterre, A., & Ménard, J. (2018). Organizational culture and work-life integration: A barrier to employees' respite? *International Journal of Human Resource Management, 29*(16), 2378–2398. https://doi.org/10.1080/09585192.2016.1262890

French, S. M. (2015). My confidant, my coworker: The interpersonal relationship of work spouses [Doctoral dissertation, University of Southern Mississippi]. The Aquila Digital Community.

Friedman, R. A., & Holtom, B. (2002). The effects of network groups on minority employee turnover intentions. *Human Resource Management, 41*, 405–421.

Frone, M. R. (2000). Work-family conflict and employee psychiatric disorders: The national comorbidity study. *Journal of Applied Psychology, 85*, 888–895.

Frone, M. R., Russell, M., & Cooper, M. L. (1997). Relation of work-family conflict to health outcomes: A four-year longitudinal study of employed parents. *Journal of Occupational and Organizational Psychology, 70*, 325–335.

Frost, P. J. (1987). Power, politics, and influence. In F M. Jablin, L. L. Putnam, K. H. Roberts, & L. W. Porter (Eds.), *Handbook of organizational communication: An interdisciplinary perspective* (pp. 503–548). SAGE Publications.

García-Campayo, J., Puebla-Guedea, M., Herrera-Mercadel, P., & Daudén, E. (2016). Burnout syndrome and demotivation among health care personnel. Managing stressful situations: The importance of teamwork. *Actas Dermo-Sifiliográficas (English Edition), 107*(5), 400–406. https://doi.org/10.1016/j.adengl.2016.03.003

Gardner, W. L., & Cleavenger, D. (1998). The impression management strategies associated with transformational leadership at the world-class level. *Management Communication Quarterly*, 12(1), 3–41.

Garner, J. T. (2013). Dissenters, managers, and coworkers: The process of co-constructing organizational dissent and dissent effectiveness. *Management Communication Quarterly*, *27*, 373–395.

Garner, J. T. (2016). Open doors and iron cages: Supervisors' responses to employee dissent. *International Journal of Business Communication*, 53(1), 27–54. https://doi.org/10.1177/2329488414525466

Garner, J. T. (2017). An examination of organizational dissent events and communication channels: Perspectives of a dissenter, supervisors, and coworkers. *Communication Reports*, *30*(1), 26–38. https://doi.org/10/1080/08934215.2015.1128454

Gautiè, J., Jaehrling, K., & Perez, C. (2020). Neo-Taylorism in the digital age: Workplace transformations in French and German retail warehouses. *Industrial Relations*, *75*(4), 774–795. https://doi.org/10/7202/107456ar

Geddes, D., & Linnehan, F. (1996). Exploring the dimensionality of positive and negative performance feedback. *Communication Quarterly*, *44*(3), 326–344.

Geertshuis, S. A., Morrison, R. L., & Cooper-Thomas, H. D. (2015). It's not what you say, it's the way that you say it: The mediating effect of upward influencing communications on the relationship between leader-member exchange and performance ratings. *International Journal of Business Communication*, *52*, 228–245.

Gephart, R. P, Jr. (2002). Introduction to the brave new workplace: Organizational behavior in the electronic age. *Journal of Organizational Behavior*, *23*, 327–344.

Gibbons, T. C. (1986). *Revisiting the question of born vs. made: Toward a theory of development of transformational leaders* [Unpublished doctoral dissertation]. Fielding Institute.

Gibson, M. K. (1998). *The mud, blood, and beer guys: A structurational analysis of organizational power, ideology and discourse in a blue collar work community* [Paper presentation]. National Communication Association, New York.

Gibson, M. K., & Papa, M. J. (2000). The mud, the blood, and the beer guys: Organizational osmosis in blue-collar work groups. *Journal of Applied Communication Research*, *28*(1), 68–88.

Giddens, A. (1979). *Central problems in social theory.* University of California Press.

Giddens, A. (1984). *The constitution of society: Outline of the theory of structuration.* University of California Press.

Gilson, L. L., Maynard, M. T., Jones Young, N. C., Vartiainen, M., & Hakonen, M. (2015). Virtual teams research: 10 years, 10 themes, and 10 opportunities. *Journal of Management*, *41*, 1313–1337.

Gomez, L. F. (2009). Time to socialize: Organizational socialization structures and temporality. *Journal of Business Communication*, *46*(2), 179–207.

Goodier, B. C., & Eisenberg, E. M. (2006). Seeking the spirit: Communication and the (re)development of a "spiritual" organization. *Communication Studies*, *57*(1), 47–65.

Gossett, L. M. (2002). Kept at arm's length: Questioning the organizational desirability of member identification. *Communication Monographs*, *69*(4), 385–404.

Grandey, A. A., Foo, S. C., Groth, M., & Goodwin, R. E. (2012). Free to be you and me: A climate of authenticity alleviates burnout from emotional labor. *Journal of Occupational Health Psychology*, *17*(1), 1–14. https://doi.org/10.1037/a0025102

Grandey, A. A., Houston, L., & Avery, D. R. (2017). Fake it to make it? Emotional labor reduces the racial disparity in service performance judgments. *Journal of Management*. https://doi.org/10.1177/0149206318757019

Grandey, A. A., & Sayre, G. M. (2019). Emotional labor: Regulating emotions for a wage. *Current Directions in Psychological Science*, *28*(2), 131–137. https://doi.org/10.1177/0963721418812771

Granlund, M., & Lukka, K. (2017). Investigating highly established research paradigms: Reviving contextuality in contingency theory based management accounting research. *Critical Perspectives on Accounting, 45*, 63–80. https://doi.org/10.1016/j.cpa.2016.11.003

Greenhaus, J., & Allen, T. D. (2011). Work-family balance: A review and extension of the literature. In J. Campbell Quick & L. E. Tetrick (Eds.), *Handbook of occupational health psychology* (pp. 265-283). APA.

Greenhaus, J., & Beutell, N. (1985). Sources of conflict between work and family roles. *Academy of Management Review, 10*(1), 76–88.

Greenhaus, J. H., & Powell, G. N. (2006). When work and family are allies: A theory of work-family enrichment. *Academy of Management Review, 31*, 72–92.

Greening, D. W., & Turban, D. B. (2000). Corporate social performance as a competitive advantage in attracting a quality workforce. *Business and Society, 39*, 254–280.

Griffeth, R. W., & Hom, P. W. (2001). *Retaining valued employees.* SAGE Publications.

Gross, J. (1999). Emotion and emotion regulation. In L. A. Pervin & O. P. John (Eds.), *Handbook of personality: Theory and research* (2nd ed., pp. 525–552). Guilford Press.

Grossman, H., & Chester, N. (1990). *The experience and meaning of work in women's lives.* Erlbaum.

Grzywacz, J. G., & Bass, B. L. (2003). Work, family, and mental health: Testing different models of work-family fit. *Journal of Marriage and Family, 65*, 248–261.

Guillaume, Y. R. F., Dawson, J. F., Otaye-Ebede, L., Woods, S. A., & West, M. A. (2017) Harnessing demographic differences in organizations: What moderates the effects of workplace diversity? *Journal of Organizational Behavior, 38*, 276–303. https://doi.org/10.1002/job.2040

Günsel, A., & Yamen, M. (2020). Digital Taylorism as an answer to the requirements of the new era. In B. Akkaya (Ed.), *Agile business leadership methods for industry 4.0* (pp. 103–119). Emerald Publishing.

Gupta, M., & Chakraborty, A. (2020). Impact of cyberloafing on team potency & team conflict at the workplace. *Indian Journal of Industrial Relations, 55*(4), 696–709.

Hafen, S. (2004). Organizational gossip: A revolving door of regulation and resistance. *Southern Communication Journal, 69*(3), 223–240.

Hambrick, D. C., Cho, T. S., & Chen, M. J. (1996). The influence of top management team heterogeneity on firms' competitive moves. *Administrative Science Quarterly, 41*, 659–684.

Han, K. S., & Garg, P. (2018). Workplace democracy and psychological capital: A paradigm shift in workplace. *Management Research Review, 1*(9), 1088–1116. https://doi.org/10.1108/MRR-11-2016-0267

Hassan, K., Varadan, M., & Zeisberger, C. (2020, January 13). How the VC pitch process is failing female entrepreneurs. *Harvard Business Review.* https://hbr.org/2020/01/how-the-vc-pitch-process-is-failing-female-entrepreneurs

Hatch, M. J. (1997). Irony and the social construction of contradiction in the humor of a management team. *Organization Science, 8*, 275–288.

Hawkins, B. (2013). Gendering the eye of the norm: Exploring gendered concertive control processes in two self-managing teams. *Gender, Work & Organization, 20*, 113–126.

Heilmann, S. G., Bell, J. E., & McDonald, G. K. (2009). Work-home conflict on military officer turnover intention. *Journal of Leadership and Organizational Studies, 16*(1), 185–196.

Helgesen, S. (1990). *The female advantage: Women's ways of leadership.* Doubleday.

Hersey, P., Blanchard, K. H., & Johnson, D. E. (2001). *Management of school behavior: Leading human resources* (8th ed.). Prentice Hall.

Hesse-Biber, S. N., & Carter, G. L. (2005). *Working women in America: Split streams.* Oxford University Press.

Hickson, D., Astley, W., Butler, R., & Wilson, D. (1981). Organization as power. In L. Cummings & B. Staw (Eds.), *Research in organizational behavior* (pp. 151–196). Aigai Press.

Higgins, M. C. (2000). The more, the merrier? Multiple developmental relationships and work satisfaction. *Journal of Management Development, 19,* 277–296.

Hochschild, A. R. (1983). *The managed heart.* University of California Press.

Hoelscher, C. S., Zanin, A. C., & Kramer, M. W. (2016). Identifying with values: Examining organizational culture in farmers markets. *Western Journal of Communication, 80*(4), 481–501. https://doi.org/10.1080/10570314.2016.1163613

Hoffman, M. F. (2002). "Do all things with counsel": Benedictine women and organizational democracy. *Communication Studies, 53*(3), 203–218.

Horan, S. M., & Chory, R. M. (2011). Understanding work/life blending: Credibility implications for those who date at work. *Communication Studies, 62*(5), 563-580. https://doi.org/10.1080/10510974.2011.582663

Horwitz, S. K., & Horwitz, I. B. (2009). The effects of team diversity on team outcomes: A meta-analytic review of team demography. *Journal of Management, 33*(6), 987–1015.

House, R. J. (1977). A 1976 theory of charismatic leadership. In J. G. Hunt & L. L. Larson (Eds.), *Leadership: The cutting edge* (pp. 189–207). Southern Illinois University Press.

House, R. J., & Baetz, M. L. (1979). Leadership: Some empirical generalizations and new research directions. *Research in Organizational Behavior, 1,* 341–423.

Hovick, S. R. A., Meyers, R. A., & Timmerman, C. E. (2003). E-mail communication in workplace romantic relationships. *Communication Studies, 54*(4), 468–482.

Hsiung, H., & Tsai, W. (2009). Job definition discrepancy between supervisors and subordinates: The antecedent role of LMX and outcomes. *Journal of Occupational and Organizational Psychology, 82,* 89–112.

Hu, X., Santuzzi, A. M., & Barber, L. K. (2019). Disconnecting to detach: The role of impaired recovery in negative consequences of workplace telepressure. *Journal of Work and Organizational Psychology, 35,* 9–15. https://doi.org/10.5093/jwop2019a2

Hugh Feeley, T., Hwang, J., & Barnett, G. A. (2008). Predicting employee turnover from friendship networks. *Journal of Applied Communication Research, 36*(1), 56–73.

Human Rights Campaign (2020). *LGBTQ equality at the Fortune 500.* https://www.hrc.org/resources/lgbt-equality-at-the-fortune-500

Humphrey, S. E., Aime, F., Chushenbery, L., Hill, A. D., & Fairchild, J. (2017). Team conflict dynamics: Implications of a dyadic view of conflict for team performance. *Organizational Behavior and Human Decision Processes, 142,* 58-70. https://doi.org/10.1016/j.obhdp.2017.08.002

Hurrell, S. A., Scholarios, D., & Richards, J. (2017). "The kids are alert:" Generation Y responses to employer use and monitoring of social networking sites. *New Technology, Work and Employment, 32*(1), 64–83. https://doi.org/10.1111/ntwe.12085

Iordanoglou, D. (2018). Future trends in leadership development practices and the crucial leadership skills. *Journal of Leadership, Accountability and Ethics, 15*(2). https://doi.org/10.33423/jlae.v15i2.648

Islam, G., & Zyphur, M. J. (2009). Rituals in organizations: A review and expansion of current theory. *Group & Organization Management, 34,* 114–139.

Jablin, F. M. (1979). Superior-subordinate communication: The state of the art. *Psychological Bulletin, 86*(6), 1201–1222.

Jablin, F. M. (1982). Organizational communication: An assimilation approach. In M. E. Roloff & C. R. Berger (Eds.), *Social cognition and communication* (pp. 255–286). SAGE Publications.

Jablin, F. M. (1984). Assimilating new members into organizations. In R. N. Bostrom (Ed.), *Communication yearbook, 8.* SAGE Publications.

Jablin, F. M. (1987). Organizational entry, assimilation, and exit. In M. F. Jablin, L. L. Putnam, K. H. Roberts, & L. W. Porter (Eds.), *Handbook of organizational communication: An interdisciplinary perspective* (pp. 679–740). SAGE Publications.

Jablin, F. M. (1990a). Organizational communication. In G. L. Dahnke & G. W. Clatterbuck (Eds.), *Human communication: Theory and research* (pp. 156–182). Wadsworth.

Jablin, F. M. (1990b). Task/work relationships: A life-span perspective. In S. R. Corman, S. P. Banks, C. R. Bantz, & M. E. Mayer (Eds.), *Foundations of organizational communication: A reader* (pp. 171–196). Longman.

Jablin, F. M. (2001). Organizational entry, assimilation, and disengagement/exit. In F. M. Jablin & L. L. Putnam (Eds.), *The new handbook of organizational communication* (pp. 732–818). SAGE Publications.

Jacobson, C. M. (1981). *The development and evaluation of a self-report instrument to measure leader effectiveness* [Unpublished doctoral dissertation]. Ohio University.

Jantzer, A. M., Anderson, J., & Kuehl, R. A. (2018). Breastfeeding support in the workplace: The relationships among breastfeeding support, work–life balance, and job satisfaction. *Journal of Human Lactation, 34*(2), 379–385. https://doi.org/10.1177/0890334417707956

Jeung, D. Y., Kim, C., & Chang, S. J. (2018). Emotional labor and burnout: A review of the literature. *Yonsei Medical Journal, 59*(2), 187–193. https://doi.org/10.3349/ymj.2018.59.2.187

Jia, M., Cheng, J., & Hale, C. (2017). Workplace emotion and communication: Supervisor nonverbal immediacy, employees' emotion experience, and their communication motives. *Management Communication Quarterly, 31*(1), 69–87. https://doi.org/10.1177/0893318916650519

Jian, G., & Dalisay, F. (2017). Conversation at work: The effects of leader-member conversational quality. *Communication Research, 44*(2), 177–197. https://doi.org/10.1177/009365021456924

Jian, G., Shi, X., & Dalisay, F. (2014). Leader-member conversational quality: Scale development and validation through three studies. *Management Communication Quarterly, 28,* 375–403.

Jimenez, A., Boehe, D. M., Taras, V., & Caprar, D. V. (2017). Working across boundaries: Current and future perspectives on global virtual teams. *Journal of International Management, 23*(4), 341–349. https://doi.org/10.1016/j.intman.2017.05.001

Jobvite. (2018). *2018 recruiter nation survey: The tipping point—the next chapter in recruiting.* https://www.jobvite.com/wp-content/uploads/2018/11/2018-Recruiter-Nation-Study.pdf

Judge, T. A., Ilies, R., & Scott, B. A. (2006). Work–family conflict and emotions: Effects at work and at home. *Personnel Psychology, 59,* 779–814.

Jung, T., Scott, T., Davies, H. T. O., Bower, P., Whalley, D., McNally, R., & Mannion, R. (2009, November/December). Instruments for exploring organizational culture: A review of the literature. *Public Administration Review, 69,* 1087–1096.

Kanter, R. (1977). *Men and women of the corporation.* Basic Books.

Kark, R., & Gan, R. (2004). The transformational leader: Who is (s)he? A feminist perspective. *Journal of Organizational Change, 17*(2), 160–176.

Karl, K. A., Allen, R. S., White, C. S., Van Eck Peluchette, J., & Allen, D. E. (2017). Would you accept a Facebook friend request from your boss? Examining generational differences. *International Journal of Virtual Communities and Social Networking, 9*(1), 17–33.

Kassing, J. W. (1998). Development and validation of the organizational dissent scale. *Management Communication Quarterly, 12,* 183–229.

Kassing, J. (2011). *Dissent in organizations.* Polity Press.

Kassing, J. W., Fanelli, S. A., Chakravarthy, L. (2018). Full- and part-time dissent: Examining the effect of employment status on dissent expression. *International Journal of Business Communication, 55*(4), 455–465. https://doi.org/10.1177/2329488415597518

Katz, D., & Kahn, R. L. (1978). *The social psychology of organizations* (2nd ed.). Wiley.

Katzenbach, J. R., & Smith, D. K. (1993). *The wisdom of teams.* Harvard Business School Press.

Kauffeld, S. (2006). Self-directed work group and team competence. *Journal of Occupational and Organizational Psychology, 79,* 1–21.

Kaur, T., & Dubey, R. K. (2020). Employee review websites as source of recruitment communication: The role of source credibility, realistic information, and specific information.

Journal of Electronic Commerce in Organizations, 18(3), 74–94. https://doi.org/10/4018/JECO.2020070105

Kearney, E., Gebert, D., & Voelpel, S. C. (2009). When and how diversity benefits teams: The importance of team members' need for cognition. *Academy of Management Journal, 52*(3), 581–598.

Kelly, S., & Kingsley Westerman, C. Y. (2014). Immediacy as an influence on supervisor-subordinate communication. *Communication Research Reports, 31*, 252–261.

Keyton, J. (1999). Analyzing interaction patterns in dysfunctional teams. *Small Group Research, 30*(4), 364–392.

Keyton, J. (2000). The relationship side of groups—Introduction. *Small Group Research, 31*(4), 387–396.

Keyton, J. (2005). *Communication and organizational culture.* SAGE Publications.

Keyton, J. (2014). Organizational culture: Creating meaning and influence. In L. Putnam & D. K. Mumby (Eds.), *The SAGE handbook of organizational communication: Advances in theory, research, and methods* (3rd ed., pp. 549–568). SAGE Publications.

Keyton, J. (2017). Communication in organizations. *Annual Review of Organizational Psychology and Organizational Behavior, 4*(1), 501–526. https://doi.org/10.1146/annurev-orgpsych-032516-113341

Kim, J., Henly, J. R., Golden, L. M., & Lambert, S. J. (2019). Workplace flexibility and worker wellbeing by gender. *Journal of Marriage and Family, 82*(3), 892-910. https://doi.org/10.1111/jomf.12633

Kim, S., & Lee Y. (2011). The complex attribution process of CSR motives. *Public Relations Review, 38*, 168–170. https://doi.org/10.1016/j.pubrev.2011.09.024

Kim, Y. Y., & Miller, K. (1990). The effects of attributions and feedback goals on the generation of supervisory feedback message strategies. *Management Communication Quarterly, 4*(1), 6–29.

King, D., & Griffin, M. (2019). Nonprofits as schools for democracy: The justifications for organizational democracy within nonprofit organizations. *Nonprofit and Voluntary Sector Quarterly, 48*(5), 910–930. https://doi.org/10/1177/0899764019837603

Kingsley Westerman, C. Y., Reno, K. M., & Heuett, K. B. (2018). Delivering feedback: Supervisors' source credibility and communication competence. *International Journal of Business Communication, 55*(4), 526–546. https://doi.org/10/1177/2329488415613338

Kirby, E. L., & Krone, K. J. (2000). "The policy exists but you can't really use it": Communication and the structuration of work–family policies. *Journal of Applied Communication Research, 30*(1), 50–77.

Kirby, E., & Krone, K. (2002). "The policy exists but you can't really use it": Communication and the structuration of work-family policies. *Journal of Applied Communication Research, 30*, 50–77.

Kirkman, B. L., Chen, G., Farh, J., Chen, Z. X., & Lowe, K. B. (2009). Individual power distance orientation and follower reactions to transformational leaders: A cross-level, cross-cultural examination. *Academy of Management Journal, 52*(4), 744–764.

Koermer, C., Goldstein, M., & Fortson, D. (1993). How supervisors communicatively convey immediacy to subordinates: An exploratory qualitative investigation. *Communication Quarterly, 41*(3), 269–281.

Kolmar, C. (2020, December 28). *What do employers look for in a background check?* Zippia: The Career Expert. https://www.zippia.com/advice/what-do-employers-look-for-in-a-background-check/

Komives, S. R., Lucas, N., & McMahon, T. R. (1998). *Exploring leadership: For college students who want to make a difference.* Jossey-Bass.

Kotter, J. P. (1982). *The general managers.* Free Press.

Kovach, M. (2018). An examination of leadership theories in business and sport achievement contexts. *Journal of Values-Based Leadership, 11*(2), article 14. http://dx.doi.org/10.22543/0733.62.1215

Kowalski, R. M., Toth, A., & Morgan, M. (2018) Bullying and cyberbullying in adulthood and the workplace, *Journal of Social Psychology, 1*(158), 64–81. https://doi.org/10.1080/0022 4545.2017.1302402

Kowtha, N. R. (2018). Organizational socialization of newcomers: The role of professional socialization. *International Journal of Training and Development, 22*(2), 87–106. https:// doi.org/10.1111/ijrd.12120

Kozlowski, S.W.J., & Bell, B. S. (2012). Work groups and teams in organizations. In I. Weiner, N. W. Schmitt, & S. Highhouse (Eds.), *Handbook of psychology: Industrial and organizational psychology* (2nd ed., pp. 412–469). John Wiley & Sons, Inc.

Kram, K. E., & Isabella, L. A. (1985). Mentoring alternatives: The role of peer relationships in career development. *Academy of Management Journal, 28*(1), 110–132.

Kramer, M. W. (2010). *Organizational socialization: Joining and leaving organizations.* Polity Press.

Kramer, M. W, & Miller, V. D. (2014). Socialization and assimilation: Theories, processes, and outcomes. In L. Putnam & D. K. Mumby (Eds.), *The SAGE handbook of organizational communication: Advances in theory, research, and methods* (3rd ed., pp. 525–547). SAGE Publications.

Kreps, G. L. (1990). *Organizational communication* (2nd ed.). Longman.

Krone, K. J. (1991). Effects of leader-member exchange on subordinates' upward influence attempts. *Communication Research Reports, 8,* 9–18.

Krone, K. J. (1994). Structuring constraints on perceptions of upward influence and supervisory relationships. *Southern Communication Journal, 59*(3), 215–226.

Kurtyka, J. (2005, December). A systems theory of business intelligence. *Information Management Magazine.* www.information-management.com/issues/20051201/1042317-l.html

Kusztal, I. L. (2002). Discourses in the use and emergence of organizational conflict. *Conflict Resolution Quarterly, 20*(2), 231–247.

Lamude, K. G., Scudder, J., Simmons, D., & Torres, P. (2004). Organizational newcomers: Temporary and regular employees, same-sex and mixed-sex superior–subordinate dyads, supervisor influence techniques, subordinates' communication satisfaction, and leader-member exchange. *Communication Research Reports, 21*(1), 60–67.

Landsberger, H. A. (1958). *Hawthorne revisited.* Cornell University Press.

Lang, I. H, & Van Lee, R. (2020, August 27). Institutional investors must help close the race and gender gaps in venture capital. *Harvard Business Review.* https://hbr.org/2020/08/institutional-investors-must-help-close-the-race-and-gender-gaps-in-venture-capital

Larson, G. S., & Tompkins, P. K. (2005). Ambivalence and resistance: A study of management in a concertive control system. *Communication Monographs, 72*(1), 1–21.

Lawrence, P. R., & Lorsch, J. W. (1969). *Developing organizations: Diagnosis and action.* Addison-Wesley.

Lee, J., & Jablin, F. M. (1995). Maintenance communication in superior–subordinate work relationships. *Human Communication Research, 22*(2), 220–257.

Lego (2021). *About us: Sustainability.* https://www.lego.com/en-us/aboutus/sustainability/

Leonardi, P. M., Huysman, M., & Steinfield, C. (2013). Enterprise social media: Definition, history, and prospects for the study of social technologies in organizations. *Journal of Computer-Mediated Communication, 19,* 1–19.

Liao, C. (2017). Leadership in virtual teams: A multilevel perspective. *Human Resource Management Review, 27*(4), 648–659. https://doi.org/10.1016/j.hrmr.2016.12.010.

Likert, R. (1961). *New patterns of management.* McGraw-Hill.

Lincoln, J. R., & Miller, J. (1979). Work and friendship ties in organizations: A comparative analysis of relational networks. *Administrative Science Quarterly, 24,* 181–199.

Ling, W. Q., & Fang, L. (2003). The Chinese leadership theory. In W.H. Mobley & P. W. Dorman (Eds.), *Advances in global leadership, 3,* 183–204.

Lipnack, J., & Stamps, J. (1997). *Virtual teams: Reaching across space, time, and organizations with technology.* Wiley.

Lloyd, K. J., Boer, D., Voelpel, S. C. (2017). From listening to leading: Toward an understanding of supervisor listening within the framework of leader-member exchange theory. *International Journal of Business Communication, 54*(4), 431–451. https://doi.org/10.1177/2329488415572778

Louis, M. R. (1980). Surprise and sense making: What newcomers experience in entering unfamiliar organizational settings. *Administrative Science Quarterly, 25*, 226–251.

Lui, J. (2020, February 20). *78% of job seekers lie during the hiring process—Here's what happened to 4 of them.* Work. https://www.cnbc.com/2020/02/19/how-many-job-seekers-lie-on-their-job-application.html

Lukes, S. (1974). *Power: A radical view.* Macmillan.

Lutgen-Sandvik, P, Namie, G., & Namie, R. (2009). Workplace bullying: Causes, consequences, and corrections. In P. Lutgen-Sandvik & B. D. Sypher (Eds.), *Destructive organizational communication: Processes, consequences, and constructive ways of organizing* (pp. 27–52). Rawson Associates.

Luthans, F., Rosenkrantz, S. A., & Hennessey, H. W. (1985). What do successful managers really do? An observation study of managerial activity. *Journal of Applied Behavioral Science, 21*, 255–270.

Ly, N-B. (2020). Cultural influences on leadership: Western-dominated leadership and non-western conceptualizations of leadership. *Sociology and Anthropology, 8*(1), 1–12. https://doi.org/10.13189/sa.2020.080101

Maamari, B. E., & Majdalani, J. F. (2017). Emotional intelligence, leadership style and organizational climate. *International Journal of Organizational Analysis, 25*(2), 327–345. https://doi.org/10.1108/IJOA-04-2016-1010

MacDonald Milam, J., & Guarriello Heath, R. (2014). Participative democracy and voice: Rethinking community collaboration beyond neutral structures. *Journal of Applied Communication Research, 42*(4), 366–386. http://dx.doi.org/10.1080/00909882.2014.911944

Madsen, V. T., & Johansen, W. (2019). A spiral of voice? When employees speak up on internal social media. *Journal of Communication Management, 23*(4), 331–374. https://doi.org/10.1108/jcom-02-2019-0050

Magpili, N. C., & Pazos, P. (2018). Self-managing team performance: A systematic review of multilevel input factors. *Small Group Research, 49*(1), 3–33. https://doi.org/10.1177/1046496417710500

Manz, C. C., & Sims, H. P., Jr. (1987). Leading workers to lead themselves: The external leadership of self-managing work teams. *Administrative Science Quarterly, 32*, 106–128.

Martin, J. (1992). *Cultures in organizations: Three perspectives.* Oxford University Press.

Martin, J. (2000). Hidden gendered assumptions in mainstream organizational theory and research. *Journal of Management Inquiry, 9*(2), 207–216.

Martin, J. (2002). *Organizational culture: Mapping the terrain.* SAGE Publications.

Masten, A. S. (2014). Global perspectives on resilience in children and youth. *Child Development, 85*, 6–20. https://doi.org/10.1007/s10567-013-0150-2

Mayer, A. M. (1995). *Feminism-in-practice: Implications for feminist theory* [Paper presentation]. Annual conference of the International Communication Association in Albuquerque, New Mexico, United States.

McBride, M. C., & Bergen, K. M. (2015). Work spouses: Defining and understanding a "new" relationship. *Communication Studies, 66*, 1–22.

McBride, M. C., Thorson, A. R., & Mason Bergen, K. (2020). An examination of individually performed and (co)managed facework: Unique communication within the work-spouse relationship. *Communication Studies, 71*(4), 489–510. https://doi.org/10.1080/10510974.2020.1749866

McDonald, J. (2015). Organizational communication meets queer theory: Theorizing relations of "difference" differently. *Communication Theory, 25*(3), 310–329. https://doi.org/10.1111/comt.12060

McDonald's (2021). *Your right to know.* https://www.mcdonalds.com/gb/en-gb/help/faq/19263-what-is-mcdonalds-corporate-social-responsibility-csr-policy.html

McGregor, D. ([I960] 1985). *The human side of enterprise* (2nd ed.). McGraw-Hill.

McKinney, E. H., Jr., Barker, J. R., Davis, K. J., & Smith, D. (2005). How swift-starting action teams get off the ground. *Management Communication Quarterly, 19*(2), 198–237.

McPhee, R. D. (2015). Agency and the four flows. *Management Communication Quarterly, 29*(3), 487–492. https://doi.org/10.1177/0893318915584826

McPhee, R. D., & Iverson, J. (2009). Agents of constitution in communidad. In L. L Putnam & A. M. Nicotera (Eds.), *Building theories of organization: The constitutive role of communication* (pp. 49–87). Routledge.

McPhee, R. D., & Zaug, P. (2000). The communicative constitution of organizations: A framework for explanation. *Electronic Journal of Communication, 10*, 1–16.

McWilliams, A., Rupp, D. E., Stahl, G. K., Siegel, D. S., & Waldman, D. A. (2019). New developments in the study of corporate social responsibility. In A. McWilliams, D. E. Rupp, D. S. Diegel, G. K. Stahl, & D. A. Waldman (Eds.), *The Oxford handbook of corporate social responsibility* (pp. 3–16). Oxford University Press.

Meiners, E. B. (2004). Time pressure: An unexamined issue in organizational newcomers' role development. *Communication Research Reports, 21*(3), 243–251.

Methot, J. R., & LePine, J. A. (2016). Too close for comfort? Investigating the nature and functioning of work and non-work boundary segmentation preferences. *Journal of Business and Psychology, 31*(1), 103–123. https://doi.org/10.1007/s10869-015-9402-0

Methot, J. R., LePine, J. A., Podsakoff, N. P., & Christian, J. S. (2015). Are workplace friendships a mixed blessing? Exploring tradeoffs of multiplex relationships and their associations with job performance. *Personnel Psychology, 69*, 311–355. https://doi.org/10.1111/peps.12109

Metts, S., Geist, P, & Gray, J. L. (1994). The role of relationship characteristics in the provision and effectiveness of supportive messages among nursing professionals. In B. R. Burleson, T. L Albrecht, & I. G. Sarason (Eds.), *Communication of social support: Messages, interactions, relationships, and community* (pp. 229–245). SAGE Publications.

Mikkelson, A. C., Hesse, C., & Sloan, D. (2017). Relational communication messages and employee outcomes in supervisor/employee relationships. *Communication Reports, 30*(3), 142–156. https://doi.org/10.1080/08934215.2017.1300677

Mikkola, L., Suutala, E., & Parviainen, H. (2018). Social support in the workplace for physicians in specialization training. *Medical Education Online, 23*(1), 1–11. https://doi.org/10.1080/10872981.2018.1435114

Miles, R. E. (1965). Human relations or human resources? *Harvard Business Review, 43*, 148–163.

Miller, V. D. (1996, Spring–Summer). An experimental study of newcomers' information seeking behaviors during organizational entry. *Communication Studies, 47*, 1–24.

Miller, V. D., & Jablin, F. M. (1991). Newcomers' information-seeking behaviors during organizational entry: Influence, tactics, and a model of the process. *Academy of Management Review, 16*, 92–120.

Millward, L. J., Haslam, S. A., & Postmes, T. (2007). Putting employees in their place: The impact of hot desking on organizational and team identification. *Organization Science, 18*(4), 547–559.

Minton-Eversole, T. (2012, July 19). *Virtual teams used most by global organizations, survey says.* SHRM. http://www.shrm.org/hrdisciplines/orgempdev/articles/pages/virtualteamsusedmostbyglobalorganizations,surveysays.aspx

Mitchelson, J. K. (2009). Seeking that perfect balance: Perfectionism and work-family conflict. *Journal of Occupational and Organizational Psychology, 82*, 349–367.

Mizell, Jr., L. R., & Gips, M. A. (2020, December 10). *Do organizations rely on background checks too much?* Talent Acquisition. https://www.shrm.org/resourcesandtools/hr-topics/talent-acquisition/pages/do-organizations-rely-on-background-checks-too-much.aspx

Modaff, D. P. (2014). Leadership trails: Lessons from the Lakota Sun Dance. *Journal of Values Based Leadership*, *7*(1), article 3. https://scholar.valpo.edu/jvbl/vol7/iss1/3

Moore, M., & Jones, J. (2001). Cracking the concrete ceiling: Inquiry into the aspirations, values, motives, and actions of African American female 1890 cooperative extension administrators. *Journal of Extension*, *39*(6). http://www.joe.org/joe/2001december/rbl.html

Morgan, G. (1997). *Images of organization* (2nd ed.). SAGE Publications.

Morgan, J. M., Reynolds, C. M., Nelson, T. J., Johanningmeier, A. R., Griffin, M., & Andrade, P. (2004). Tales from the fields: Sources of employee identification in agribusiness. *Management Communication Quarterly*, *17*(3), 360–395.

Morgan, S. (1994). Personalizing personnel decisions in feminist organizational theory and practice. *Human Relations*, *47*, 665–684.

Morris, J. A., & Feldman, D. C. (1996). The dimensions, antecedents, and consequences of emotional labor. *Academy of Management Review*, *21*(4), 986–1010.

Morrison, R. L., & Nolan, T. (2007). Too much of a good thing? Difficulties with workplace friendships. *University of Aukland Business Review*, *9*(2), 33–41.

Moss, D. (2018). *The top 10 management skills you need: A Q & A with James Manktelow and Julian Birkinshaw.* SHRM. https://www.shrm.org/hr-today/news/hr-magazine/book-blog/pages/the-top-10-management-skills-you-need.aspx

Mueller, B. H., & Lee, J. (2002). Leader-member exchange and organizational communication satisfaction in multiple contexts. *Journal of Business Communication*, *39*(2), 220–244. https://doi.org/10.1177/0021943602039002904

Mumby, D. K. (1987). The political function of narrative in organizations. *Communication Monographs*, *54*(2), 113–127.

Mumby, D. K. (1988). *Communication and power in organizations: Discourse, ideology, and domination.* Ablex.

Mumby, D. K. (2000). Common ground from the critical perspective: Overcoming binary oppositions. In S. Corman & M. Poole (Eds.), *Perspectives on organizational communication* (pp. 68–86). Guilford Press.

Mumby, D. (2014). Critical theory and postmodernism. In L. L. Putnam & D. K. Mumby (Eds.), *The SAGE handbook of organizational communication: Advances in theory, research, and methods* (3rd ed., pp. 101–125). SAGE Publications.

Mumby, D., & Stohl, C. (1996). Disciplining organizational communication studies. *Management Communication Quarterly*, *10*(4), 50–73.

Murray, N. E. (2008). *Corporate social responsibility is the number one criteria for job hunters today.* http://normmurray.org/

Murrell, K. L. (1997). Emergent theories of leadership for the next century: Towards relational concepts. *Organizational Development Journal*, *15*(3), 35–42.

Nadal, K. L. (2008). Preventing racial, ethnic, gender, sexual minority, disability, and religious microaggressions: Recommendations for promoting positive mental health. *Prevention in Counseling Psychology: Theory, Research, Practice and Training*, *2*(1), 22–27.

Natalie, E. J., Papa, M. J., & Graham, E. E. (1994). Feminist philosophy and the transformation of organizational communication. In B. Kovacic (Ed.), *New approaches to organizational communication.* State University of New York Press.

Nduhura, D., & Prieler, M. (2017). When I chat online, I feel relaxed and work better: Exploring the use of social media in the public sector workplace in Rwanda. *Telecommunications Policy*, *41*(7–8), 708–716. https://doi.org/10.1016/j.telpol.2017.05.008.

Newport, F. (2017, May 10). *Email outside of working hours not a burden to US workers.* Gallup News. https://news.gallup.com/

Nicholson, J., & Kurucz, E. (2019). Relational leadership for sustainability: Building an ethical framework from the moral theory of 'ethics of care': JBE. *Journal of Business Ethics*, *156*(1), 25–43. http://dx.doi.org/10.1007/s10551-017-3593-4

Nicotera, A. M. (2020). Organizing the study of organizational communication. In A. M. Nicotera (Ed.), *Origins and traditions of organizational communication* (pp. 3–21). Routledge.

Nielsen, M. B., & Einarsen, S. (2012). Outcomes of exposure to workplace bullying: A meta-analytic review. *Work & Stress*, *26*(4), 309–332. https://doi.org/10.1080/02678373.2012.734709

Nielsen, M. B., & Einarsen, S.V. (2018). What we know, what we do not know, and what we should and could have known about workplace bullying: An overview of the literature and agenda for future research. *Aggression and Violent Behavior*, *42*, 71–83. https://doi.org/10.1016/j.avb.2018.06.007

Nifadkar, S. S. (2020). Filling in the "blank slate": Examining newcomers' schemas of supervisors during organizational socialization. *Journal of Management*, *46*(5), 666–693. https://doi.org/10.1177/0149206317707288

Noah, T. (2004). Prexy sks wrk wf: Condoleezza Rice's promotion creates a void. *Slate*. http://www.slate.com/id/2109876

Noe, J. M. (1995). *A communication rules perspective of emotional expression: An ethnography of impression management in an emergency medical services facility* [Unpublished doctoral dissertation]. University of Kansas, Lawrence.

Nordbäck, E. S., Myers, K. K., & McPhee, R. D. (2017). Workplace flexibility and communication flows: A structurational view. *Journal of Applied Communication Research*, *45*(4), 397–412. https://doi.org/10.1080/00909882.2017.1355560

Northouse, P. G. (2001). *Leadership: Theory and practice* (2nd ed.). SAGE Publications.

O'Connor, A., Paskewitz, E. A., Jorgenson, D. A., & Rick, J. M. (2016). How changes in work structure influence employees' perceptions of CSR: Millionaire managers and locked-out laborers. *Journal of Applied Communication Research*, *44*(1), 40–59. https://doi.org/10.1080/00909882.2015.1116706

Oh, S. H. (2012). Leadership emergence in autonomous work teams: Who is more willing to lead? *Social Behavior and Personality: An International Journal*, *40*(9), 1451–1464. https://doi.org/10.2224/sbp.2012.40.9.1451

Orsburn, J. D., & Moran, L. (2000). *The new self-directed work teams* (2nd ed.). McGraw-Hill.

Orton, J. D., & Weick, K. E. (1990). Loosely coupled systems: A reconceptualization. *Academy of Management Review*, *15*(2), 203–223.

Owens, D. (1987). Work marriage. *The Atlantic*, *259*(2), 22.

Owens, J. (1992). A reappraisal of leadership theory and training. In K. L. Hutchinson (Ed.), *Readings in organizational communication* (pp. 252–265). Wm. C. Brown.

Pacanowsky, M. E., & O'Donnell-Trujillo, N. (1990). Communication and organizational cultures. In S. R. Corman, S. P. Banks, C. R. Bantz, & M. E. Mayer (Eds.), *Foundations of organizational communication: A reader* (pp. 142–153). Longman.

Padavic, I., & Reskin, B. (2002). *Women and men at work* (2nd ed.). Pine Forge Press.

Papa, M. J., Auwal, M. A., & Singhal, A. (1997). Organizing for social change within concertive control systems: Member identification, empowerment, and the masking of discipline. *Communication Monographs*, *64*(3), 219–249.

Parker, P. S. (2003). *Learning leadership: Communication, resistance, and African-American women's executive leadership development* [Unpublished doctoral dissertation]. University of Texas, Austin.

Parker, L. D. (1984). Control in organizational life: The contribution of Mary Parker Follett. *Academy of Management Review*, *9*(4), 736–745.

Parker, S. K., Knight, C., & Keller, A. (2020, July 30). Remote managers are having trust issues. *Harvard Business Review*. https://hbr.org/2020/07/remote-managers-are-having-trust-issues.

Payne, H. J. (2014). Examining the relationship between trust in supervisor-employee relationships and workplace dissent expression. *Communication Research Reports, 31,* 131–140.

Payscale. (2019, May 7). *Racial wage gap for men.* https://www.payscale.com/data/racial-wage-gap-for-men

Pelz, D. (1952). Influence: A key to effective leadership. *Personnel, 29,* 209–217.

Pepper, G. L., & Larson, G. S. (2006). Cultural identity tensions in a post-acquisition organization. *Journal of Applied Communication Research, 34*(1), 49–71.

Peters, T. J., & Waterman, R. H., Jr. (1982). *In search of excellence: Lessons from America's best-run companies.* Warner Books.

Pew Research Center. (2016). *Social media and the workplace.* https://www.pewresearch.org/internet/2016/06/22/social-media-and-the-workplace/

Phillips, J. M. (1998). Effects of realistic job previews on multiple organizational outcomes: A meta-analysis. *Academy of Management Journal, 41*(6), 673–690.

Pierce, C. A., & Aguinis, H. (2005). Legal standards, ethical standards, and responses to social-sexual conduct at work. *Journal of Organizational Behavior, 26*(6), 727–732.

Pierce, C. A., & Aguinis, H. (2009). Moving beyond a legal-centric approach to managing workplace romances: Organizationally sensible recommendations for HR leaders. *Human Resource Management, 48*(3), 447–464.

Pierce, C. A., Broberg, B. J., McClure, J. R., & Aguinis, H. (2004). Responding to sexual harassment complaints: Effects of a dissolved workplace romance on decision-making standards. *Organizational Behavior and Human Decision Processes, 95*(1), 66–82.

Pillemar, J., & Rothbard, N. P. (2018). Friends without benefits: Understanding the dark sides of workplace friendships. *Academy of Management Review, 43*(4), 1–26. https://doi.org/10.5465/amr.2016.0309

Pizer, M. K., & Härtel, C. E. (2005). For better or for worse: Organizational culture and emotions. In C. Härtel, W. Zerbe, & N. Ashkanasy (Eds.), *Emotions in organizational behavior* (pp. 335–354). Earlbaum.

Plecher, H. (2020, November 4). *Distribution of the workforce across economic sectors in the United States from 2010 to 2020.* Statista. https://www.statista.com/statistics/270072/distribution-of-the-workforce-across-economic-sectors-in-the-united-states/

Ploeger, N. A., & Bisei, R. S. (2013). The role of identification in giving sense to unethical organizational behavior: Defending the organization. *Management Communication Quarterly, 27,* 155–183.

Poole, M. S. (1997). A turn of the wheel: The case for a renewal of systems inquiry in organizational communication research. In G. A. Barnett & L. Thayer (Eds.), *Organization—Communication: Emerging perspectives V: The renaissance of systems thinking* (pp. 47–63). Ablex.

Poole, M. S. (2014). Systems theory. In L. L. Putnam & D. K. Mumby (Eds.), *The SAGE handbook of organizational communication: Advances in theory, research, and methods* (3rd ed., pp. 75–100). SAGE Publications.

Popescu Ljungholm, D. (2017). Democratic forms of workplace governance. *Analysis and Metaphysics, 16,* 110–116. https://doi.org/10.22381/AM1620176

Powell, G. N. (2001). Workplace romances between senior-level executives and lower-level employees: An issue of work disruption and gender. *Human Relations, 2001*(54), 1519–1544. https://doi.org/10.1177/00187267015411005

Pruijt, H. (2000). Repainting, modifying, smashing Taylorism. *Journal of Organizational Change Management, 13*(5), 439–451.

Putnam, L. L. (1986). Contradictions and paradoxes in organization. In L. Thayer (Ed.), *Organizational communication: Emerging perspectives* (pp. 151–167). Ablex.

Putnam, L. L. (1992). Rethinking the nature of groups in organizations. In R. S. Cathcart & L. A. Samovar (Eds.), *Small group communication: A reader* (6th ed., pp. 57–66). Wm. C. Brown.

Putnam, L. L., & Cheney, G. (1992). Organizational communication: Historical developments and future directions. In K. L. Hutchinson (Ed.), *Readings in organizational communication* (pp. 70–89). Wm. C. Brown.

Putnam, L. L., & Poole, M. S. (1987). Conflict and negotiation. In M. F. Jablin, L. L. Putnam, K. H. Roberts, & L. W. Porter (Eds.), *Handbook of organizational communication: An interdisciplinary perspective* (pp. 549–599). SAGE Publications.

Quine, L. (2001). Workplace bullying in nurses. *Journal of Health Psychology, 6*(1), 73–84.

Quinn, R. E. (1977). Coping with Cupid: The formation, impact, and management of romantic relationships in organizations. *Administrative Science Quarterly, 22*(1), 30–45.

Raelin, J. A. (2003). *Creating leaderful organizations: How to bring out leadership in everyone.* Berrett-Koehler.

Rafaeli, A., & Sutton, R. I. (1989). The expression of emotion in organizational life. *Research in Organizational Behavior, 11*, 1–42.

Rafaeli, A., & Worline, M. (2000). Symbols in organizational culture. In N. M. Ashkanasy, C. P. M. Wilderom, & M. F. Peterson (Eds.), *Handbook of organizational culture & climate* (pp. 71–84). SAGE Publications.

Rahim, M. A. (2001). Managing organizational conflict: Challenges for organization development and change. In R. T. Golembiewski (Ed.), *Handbook of organizational behavior* (2nd ed., pp. 365–387). Marcel Dekker.

Rahim, M. A., Garrett, J. E., & Buntzman, G. F. (1992). Ethics of managing interpersonal conflict in organizations. *Journal of Business Ethics, 11*, 87–96.

Raj, A., Johns, N. E., & Jose, R. (2020). Gender parity at work and its association with workplace sexual harassment. *Workplace Health & Safety, 68*(6), 279–292. https://doi.org/10.1177/2165079919900793

Rawlins, W. K. (1992). *Friendship matters: Communication, dialectics, and the life course.* Aldine de Gruyter.

Rawlins, W. K. (1994). Being there and growing apart: Sustaining friendships through adulthood. In D. J. Canary & L. Stafford (Eds.), *Communication and social support* (pp. 275–294). Academic Press.

Redding, W. C., & Tompkins, P. K. (1988). Organizational communication: Past and present tenses. In G. M. Goldhaber & G. A. Barnett (Eds.), *Handbook of organizational communication* (pp. 5–33). Ablex.

Reimer, R., Russell, T., & Roland, C. (2017). Groups and teams in organizations. In C. Scott & L. Lewis (Eds.), *The international encyclopedia of organizational communication* (pp. 1–23). Wiley.

Reinsch, N. L., Turner, J. W., & Tinsley, C. H. (2008). Multi-communicating; A practice whose time has come? *Academy of Management Review, 33*, 391–403.

Resnick, C. A., & Paz Galupo, M. (2019) Assessing experiences with LGBT microaggressions in the workplace: Development and validation of the microaggression experiences at work scale. *Journal of Homosexuality, 66*(10), 1380–1403. https://doi.org/10.1080/00918369.2018.1542207

Riach, K. and Wilson, F. (2007), Don't screw the crew: Exploring the rules of engagement in organizational romance. *British Journal of Management, 18*, 79–92. https://doi.org/10.1111/j.1467-8551.2006.00503.x

Ribarsky, E., & Hammonds, J. (2019). Gossiping for the good of it? Examining the link between gossip and organizational socialization. *Kentucky Journal of Communication, 38*(1), 28–42.

Richmond, V. P., & McCroskey, J. C. (2000). The impact of supervisor and subordinate immediacy on relational and organizational outcomes. *Communication Monographs, 67*(1), 85–95.

Ridgway O'Brien, K., & Hebl, M. R. (2015). Great expectations in academia: Realistic job previews on jobs and work-family balance. *Gender in Management, 30*, 457–478.

Robert, L.P., Jr & You, S. (2018), Are you satisfied yet? Shared leadership, individual trust, autonomy, and satisfaction in virtual teams. *Journal of the Association for Information Science and Technology, 69*, 503–513. https://doi.org/10.1002/asi.23983

Roberts, J. A., & David, M. E. (2019). Boss phubbing, trust, job satisfaction and employee performance. *Journal of Individual Differences, 155*, 1–8. https://doi.org/10.1016/j.paid.2019.109702

Robertson, B. W., & Kee, K. F. (2017). Social media at work: The roles of job satisfaction, employment status, and Facebook use with co-workers. *Computers in Human Behavior, 17*, 191–196. https://doi.org/10.1016/j.chb.2016.12.080.

Roethlisberger, F. J., & Dickson, W. J. (1939). *Management and the worker.* Harvard University Press.

Ross-Smith, A., & Kornberger, M. (2004). Gendered rationality? A genealogical exploration of the philosophical and sociological conceptions of rationality, masculinity, and organization. *Gender, Work, and Organization, 11*(3), 280–305.

Rothbard, N. P., & Ollier-Malaterre, A. (2015). Boundary management. In T. D. Allen & L. T. Eby (Eds.), *Oxford handbook of work and family* (pp. 109–124). Oxford University Press.

Rothbard, N.P., Ramarajan, L., Ollier-Malaterre, A., & Sai-Lai Lee, S. (2020). OMG! My boss just friended me: How evaluations of colleagues' disclosure, gender, and rank shape personal/professional boundary blurring online. *Academy of Management Journal.* https://doi.org/10.5465/amj.2018.0755

Ruggs, E. N., Martinez, L. R., Hebl, M. R., & Law, C. L. (2015). Workplace "trans"-actions: How organizations, coworkers, and individual openness influence perceived gender identity discrimination. *Psychology of Sexual Orientation and Gender Diversity, 2*(4), 404–412. https://doi.org/10.1037/sgd0000112

Ruggs, E. N., Walker, S. S., Blanchard, A., & Gur, S. (2016). Online exclusion: Biases that may arise when using social media in talent acquisition. In R. Landers, G. Schmidt (Eds.), *Social media in employee selection and recruitment* (pp. 1–14). Springer.

Rush, K. L., Adamack, A., Gordon, J., Lilly, M., & Janke, R. (2014). Best practices of formal new graduate nurse transition programs: An integrative review. *International Journal of Nursing Studies, 50*, 345–356.

Russell, R. (1997). Workplace democracy and organizational communication. *Communication Studies, 48*(4), 279–284.

Sackmann, S. (1991). *Cultural knowledge in organizations: Exploring the collective mind.* SAGE Publications.

Sager, K. L. (2008). An exploratory study of the relationships between Theory X/Y assumptions and superior communicator style. *Management Communication Quarterly, 22*(2), 288–312.

Saks, A. M., & Ashforth, B. E. (1997). Organizational socialization: Making sense of the past and present as a prologue for the future. *Journal of Vocational Behavior, 51*, 234–279.

Salin, D. (2008). The prevention of workplace bullying as a question of human resource management: Measure adopted and underlying organizational factors. *Scandinavian Journal of Management, 24*, 221–231.

Sallitto, M., & Myers, S. A., (2015). Peer coworker relationships: Influences on the expression of lateral dissent. *Communication Reports, 28*(1), 36–47. https://doi.org/10/1080/08934215.2014.925569

Sanders, K., & Nauta, A. (2004). Social cohesiveness and absenteeism: The relationship between characteristics of employees and short-term absenteeism within an organization. *Small Group Research, 35*(6), 724–741.

Sandor Herrygers, K., & Bieland, S. M. B. (2017). Work socialization through part-time work: Cultivating self-efficacy and engagement through care. *Journal of Applied Communication Research, 45*(5), 557–575. https://doi.org/10.1080/00909882.2017.1382712

Santuzzi, A. M., & Barber, L. K. (2018). Workplace telepressure and worker well-being: The intervening role of psychological detachment. *Occupational Health Science, 2*, 337–363. https://doi.org/10.1007/s41542-018-0022-8

Sawyer, K., & Thoroughgood, C. (2017). Gender non-conformity and the modern workplace: New frontiers in understanding and promoting gender identity expression at work. *Organizational Dynamics, 46*(1), 1–8. https://doi.org/10.1016/j.orgdyn.2017.01.001

Schein, E. H. (1985). *Organizational culture and leadership.* Jossey-Bass.

Schein, E. H. (1990). Organizational culture. *American Psychologist, 45*(2), 109–119.

Schilit, W. K., & Locke, E. A. (1982). A study of upward influence in organizations. *Administrative Science Quarterly, 27*(2), 304–316. https://doi.org/10.2307/2392305

Schilt, K., & Connell, C. (2007). Do workplace gender transitions make gender trouble? *Gender, Work, and Organization, 14*(6), 596–618.

Schmidt, G. B., Lelchook, A. M., & Martin, J. E. (2016). The relationship between social media co-worker connections and work-related attitudes. *Computers in Human Behavior, 55*(A), 439–445. https://doi.org/10.1016/j.chb.2015.09.045

Schnake, M. E., Dumler, M. P., Cochran, D. S., & Barnett, T. R. (1990). Effects of differences in superior and subordinate perceptions of supervisors' communication practices. *Journal of Business Communication, 27*(1), 37–50.

Schoemaker, P. J. H., & Cecchini, M. (2015). The six skills of strategic leaders. *Accounting Today.*

Schutz, W. C. (1966). *The interpersonal underworld: A three dimensional theory of interpersonal behavior.* Science and Behavior Books.

Schwartz, M. S., & Carroll, A. B. (2003). Corporate social responsibility: A three-domain approach. *Business Ethics Quarterly, 13*(4), 503–530.

Schweiger, D., Sandberg, W., & Ragan, J. W. (1986). Group approaches for improving strategic decision making: A comparative analysis of dialectical inquiry, devil's advocacy, and consensus approaches to strategic decision making. *Academy of Management Journal, 19*, 51–71.

Scott, C. R., Corman, S. R., & Cheney, G. (1998). Development of a structurational model of identification in the organization. *Communication Theory, 8*(3), 298–336.

Scott, C., & Myers, K. K. (2005). The socialization of emotion: Learning emotion management at the fire station. *Journal of Applied Communication, 33*(1), 67–92.

Scott, C. R., & Stephens, K. K. (2009). It depends on who you're talking to ... : Predictors and outcomes of situated measures of organizational identification. *Western Journal of Communication, 73*(4), 370–394.

Shah, N. P., Parker, A., & Waldstrom, C. (2017). Examining the overlap: Individual performance benefits of multiplex relationships. *Management Communication Quarterly, 31*(1), 5–38. https://doi.org/10.1177/0893318916647528

Shahin, A. I. and Wright, P. L. (2004), Leadership in the context of culture: An Egyptian perspective. *Leadership & Organization Development Journal, 25*(6), 499–511. https://doi.org/10.1108/01437730410556743

Shell, R. L. (2003). *Management of professionals* (2nd ed.). Marcel Dekker.

Sherriton, J., & Stern, J. L. (1997). *Corporate culture/team culture.* AMACOM.

Shibly, S. A. (2019). Mapping the holistic impact of realistic job preview—pre-recruitment phase, post-recruitment phase and marketing spillover effect. *Journal of Organizational Psychology, 19*(1), 70–78. https://doi.org/10/33423/jop.v19i1.1091

Shonk, J. H. (1992). *Team-based organizations.* Business One Irwin.

Shuler, S., & Sypher, B. D. (2000). Seeking emotional labor: When managing the heart enhances the work experience. *Management Communication Quarterly, 14*, 751–789.

Sias, P. M. (2005). Workplace relationship quality and employee information experiences. *Communication Studies, 56*(4), 375–395.

Sias, P. M. (2014). Workplace relationships. In L. Putnam & D. K. Mumby (Eds.), *The SAGE handbook of organizational communication: Advances in theory, research, and methods* (3rd ed., pp. 375–400). SAGE Publications.

Sias, P. M., & Duncan, K. L. (2019). "I know it's not your job but ... ": Extra-role tasks, commu-nication, and leader-member exchange relationships. *Communication Quarterly, 67*(4), 355–382. https://doi.org/10/1080/01463373.2019.1596142

Sias, P. M., & Cahill, D. J. (1998). From coworkers to friends: The development of peer friend-ships in the workplace. *Western Journal of Communication, 62*(3), 273–299.

Sias, P. M., & Jablin, F. (1995). Differential superior–subordinate relations, perceptions of fairness, and coworker communication. *Human Communication Research, 22*(1), 5–38. https://doi.org/10/1111/j.1468-2958.tb00360.x

Sias, P. M., Pedersen, H., Gallagher, E. B., & Kopaneva, I. (2012). Workplace friendship in the electronically connected organization. *Human Communication Research, 38*, 253–279.

Sias, P. M., & Shin, Y. (2020). Workplace relationships. In A. M. Nicotera (Ed.), *Origins and tra-ditions of organizational communication: A comprehensive introduction to the field* (pp. 187–206). Routledge.

Sias, P. M., Smith, G., & Avdeyeva, T. (2003). Sex and sex-composition differences and similar-ities in peer workplace friendship development, *Communication Studies, 54*, 322–340.

Sias, P. M., Tsetsi, E., Woo, N., & Smith, A. D. (2020). With a little help from my friends: Per-ceived task interdependence, coworker communication, and workplace friendship. *Communication Studies, 71*(4), 528–549. https://doi.org/10.1080/10510974.2020.1749863

Simon, L. S., Judge, T. A., & Halvorsen-Ganepola, D. K. (2010). In good company? A multi-study, multi-level investigation of the effects of coworker relationships on employee wellbeing. *Journal of Vocational Behavior, 76*(3), 534–346. https://doi.org/10.1016/j.jvb.2010.01.006.

Skeels, M. M., & Grudin, J. (2009). When social networks cross boundaries: A case study of workplace use of Facebook and LinkedIn. In *Proceedings of the ACM 2009 international conference on supporting group work* (pp. 95–104). ACM.

Smircich, L. (1983). Concepts of culture and organizational analysis. *Administrative Science Quarterly, 28*, 339–358.

Smith, R. C., & Eisenberg, E. (1987). Conflict at Disneyland: A root-metaphor analysis. *Com-munication Monographs, 54*, 367–380.

Smith, A. C. T., & Stewart, B. (2011). Organizational rituals: Features, functions, and mecha-nisms. *International Journal of Management Reviews, 13*, 113–133.

Snyder, J. L., & Cometto, K. M. (2009). Employee perceptions of e-mail monitoring from a boundary management perspective. *Communication Studies, 60*(5), 476–492.

Sobering, K. (2019). Watercooler democracy: Rumors and transparency in a cooperative workplace. *Work and Occupations, 46*(4), 411–440. https://doi.org/10/1177/0730888419860176

Society for Human Resources Management (SHRM). (2017). *2017 Talent acquisition benchmarking report.* https://www.shrm.org/hr-today/trends-and-forecasting/research-and-surveys/Documents/2017-Talent-Acquisition-Benchmarking.pdf

Sollitto, M., Martin, M. M., Dusic, S., Gibbons, K. E., & Wagenhouser, A. (2016). Assessing supervisor-subordinate relationship involving part-time employees. *International Journal of Business Communication, 53*(1), 74–96. https://doi.org/10.11772329488414525462

Soloman, D. H., & Williams, M. L. M. (1997). Perceptions of social-sexual communication at work: The effects of message, situation, and observer characteristics on judgments of sexual harassment. *Journal of Applied Communication, 25*, 196–216.

Song, M., & Meier, K. J. (2020). Walking the walk: Does perceptual congruence between managers and employees promote employee job satisfaction? *Review of Public Person-nel Administration.* https://doi.org/10/1177/0734371X20966646

Sonnenfeld, J. (1983). Academic learning, worker learning, and the Hawthorne Studies. *Social Forces, 61*(3), 904–909.

Stark, L., Stanhaus, A., Anthony, D. L. "I don't want someone to watch me while I'm working": Gendered views of facial recognition technology in workplace surveillance. *Journal of the Association for Information Science and Technology, 71*(9), 1074–1088. https://doi.org/10.1002/asi.24342

Stavrou, E., & Solea, E. (2020). In the eye of the beholder: Employee sexual orientation, perceived supervisory support for life beyond work and job satisfaction. *Human Resource Management Journal, 31*(1), 225-241. https://doi.org/10.1111/1748-8583.12293

Staw, B. M., Sutton R. I., & Pelled, L. H. (1994). Employee positive emotion and favorable outcomes at the workplace. *Organizational Science, 5,* 51–71.

Stogdill, R. M. (1974). *Handbook of leadership: A survey of theory and research.* Free Press.

Stohl, C., & Redding, W. C. (1987). Messages and message exchange processes. In F. E. Jablin, L. L. Putnam, K. H. Roberts, & L. W. Porter (Eds.), *Handbook of organizational communication: An interdisciplinary perspective* (pp. 451–502). SAGE Publications.

Stohl, C., & Schell, S. E. (1991). A communication-based model of a small-group dysfunction. *Management Communication Quarterly, 5,* 90–110.

Stoverink, A. C., Kirkman, B. L., Mistry, S., & Rosen, B. (2020). Bouncing back together: Toward a theoretical model of work team resilience. *Academy of Management, 45*(2), 395–422. https://doi.org/10/5465/amr.2017.0005

Sue, D. W. (2010). *Microaggressions in everyday life: Race, gender, and sexual orientation.* Wiley.

Sue, D. W., Capodilupo, C. M., Torino, G. C., Bucceri, J. M., Holder, A. M., Nadal, K. L., & Esquilin, M. (2007). Racial microaggressions in everyday life: Implications for clinical practice. *American Psychologist, 62*(4), 271–286.

Tannen, D. (1990). *You just don't understand: Men and women in conversation.* William Morrow.

Taylor, F. W. ([1911] 1998). *The principles of scientific management.* Dover Publications.

Taylor, J. R. (2001). The "rational" organization reconsidered: An exploration of some of the implications of self-organizing. *Communication Theory, 11*(2), 137–177.

Taylor, P., & Bain, P. (1999). "An assembly line in the head": Work and employee relations in the call centre. *Industrial Relations Journal, 30*(2), 101–117.

Therkelsen, D. J., & Fiebich, C. L. (2003). The supervisor: The linchpin of employee relations. *Journal of Communication Management, 8*(2), 120–129. https://doi.org/10.1108/13632540410807592

Thomas, P., Pinto, J. K., Parente, D. H., & Urch Druskat, V. (2002). Adaptation to self-managing work teams. *Small Group Research, 33*(1), 3–31. https://doi.org/10/2224/sbp.2012.40.9.1451

Thompson, C. A., Beauvais, L. L., Lyness, K. S. (1999). When work-family benefits are not enough: The influence of work-family culture on benefit utilization, organizational attachment, and work-family conflict. *Journal of Vocational Behavior, 54*(3), 392-415. https://doi.org/10.1006/jvbe.1998.1681

Thoroughgood, C. N., Sawyer, K. B., & Webster, J. R. (2017). What lies beneath: How paranoid cognition explains the relations between transgender employees' perceptions of discrimination at work and their job attitudes and wellbeing. *Journal of Vocational Behavior, 103*(Part A), 99–112. https://doi.org/10.1016/j.jvb.2017.07.009

Tjosvold, D., Dann, V., & Wong, C. (1992). Managing conflict between departments to serve customers. *Human Relations, 45*(10), 325–337.

Toegel, G., Kilduff, M., & Anand, N. (2013). Emotion helping by managers: An emergent understanding of discrepant role expectations and outcomes. *Academy of Management Journal 56,* 334–357. https://doi.org/10.5465/amj.2010.0512

Tomczak, D. L., Lanzo, L. A., & Aguinis, H. (2018). Evidence-based recommendations for employee performance monitoring. *Business Horizons, 61*(2), 251–259. https://doi.org/10.1016/j.bushor.2017.11.006

Tompkins, P. K., & Cheney, G. (1985). Communication and unobtrusive control in contemporary organizations. In R. D. McPhee & P. K. Tompkins (Eds.), *Organizational communication: Traditional themes and new directions* (pp. 179–210). SAGE Publications.

Tom's. (2021). *Impact.* https://www.toms.com/us/impact.html

Tracy, S., Lutgen-Sandvik, P., & Alberts, J. (2006). Nightmares, demons, and slaves: Exploring the painful metaphors of workplace bullying. *Management Communication Quarterly, 20,* 148–185.

Trethewey, A. (1999). Isn't it ironic: Using irony to explore the contradictions of organizational life. *Western Journal of Communication, 63,* 140–167.

Trice, H. M., & Beyer, J. M. (1984). Studying organizational cultures through rites and rituals. *Academy of Management Review, 9*(4), 653–669.

Trice, H. M., & Beyer, J. M. (1993). *The cultures of work organizations.* Prentice Hall.

Tripathy, M. (2018). Building quality teamwork to achieve excellence in business organizations. *International Research Journal of Management, IT & Social Sciences, 5*(3), 1-7. https://sloap.org/journals/index.php/irjmis/article/view/159

Turnage, A. K., & Goodboy, A. K. (2016). E-mail and face-to-face organizational dissent as a function of leader-member exchange status. *International Journal of Business Communication, 53*(3), 271–285. https://doi.org/10.1177/2329488414525456

Tye-Williams, S., & Krone, K. J. (2015). Chaos, reports, and quests: Narrative agency and co-workers in stories of workplace bullying. *Management Communication Quarterly, 29*(1), 3–27.

Uhl-Bien, M. (2006). Relational leadership theory: Exploring the social processes of leadership and organizing. *The Leadership Quarterly, 17*(6), 654–675.

Urwick, L., & Brech, E. F. L. (1949). *The making of scientific management.* Management Publications Trust.

Van den Brande, W., Baillien, E., De Witte, H., Vander Elst, T., & Godderis, L. (2016). The role of work stressors, coping strategies and coping resources in the process of workplace bullying: A systematic review and development of a comprehensive model. *Aggressive and Violent Behavior, 29,* 61–71. https://doi.org/10.1016/j.avb.2016.06.004.

Van Eck Peluchette, J., Karl, K., & Fertig, J. (2013). A Facebook 'friend' request from the boss: Too close for comfort? *Business Horizons, 56,* 291–300. https://dx.doi.org/10.1016//j.bushor.2013.01.013

Van Maanen, J., & Kunda, G. (1989). Real feelings: Emotional expression and organizational culture. In L. L. Cummings & B. M. Staw (Eds.), *Research in organizational behavior* (pp. 388–416). JAI Press.

Van Maanen, J. V., & Schein, E. H. (1979). Toward a theory of organizational socialization. *Research in Organizational Behavior, 1,* 209–264.

Van Slyke, E. J. (1999). *Listening to conflict: Finding constructive solutions to workplace disputes.* AMACOM.

van Veelen, R., & Ufkes, E. G. (2019). Teaming up or down? A multisource study on the role of team identification and learning in the team diversity–performance link. *Group & Organization Management, 44*(1), 38–71. https://doi.org/10.1177/1059601117750532

Vangelisti, A. L. (1988). Adolescent socialization into the workplace: A synthesis and critique of current literature. *Youth and Society, 19*(4), 460–484.

van Zoonen, W., Sivunen, A., & Rice, R. E. (2020). Boundary communication How smartphone use after hours is associated with work-life conflict and organizational identification. *Journal of Applied Communication Research, 48*(3), 372–392. https://doi.org/10.1080/00909882.2020.1755050

Vault (2017, February 13). Work is for lovers: Vault's 2017 office romance survey. https://www.vault.com/blogs/workplace-issues/work-is-for-lovers-vaults-2017-office-romance-survey-results

Vithayathil, J., Dadgar, M., & Kalu Osiri, J. (2020). Does social media use at work lower productivity? *International Journal Information Technology and Management, 19*(1), 47–67. https://doi.org/10.1504/IJITM.2020.104504

Verkuil, B., Atasayi, S., & Molendijk, M. L. (2015). Workplace bullying and mental health: A meta-analysis on cross-sectional and longitudinal data. *PLoS ONE, 10*(8), e0135225. https://doi.org/10.1371/journal.pone.0135225

Versey, H. (2015). Managing work and family: Do control strategies help? *Developmental Psychology, 51*(11), 1672–1681. https://doi.org/10.1037/a0039607

Von Bergen, C. W. (2020). Love contracts in the workplace. *Journal of Organizational Psychology, 20*(4), 141–149.

von Bertalanffy, L. (1968). *General system theory: Foundations, developments, applications.* George Braziller.

Vranjes, I., Baillien, E., Vandebosch, H., Erreygers, S., & De Witte, H. (2017). The dark side of working online: Towards a definition and an emotion reaction model of workplace cyberbullying. *Computers in Human Behavior, 69*, 324–334. https://doi.org/10.1016/j.chb.2016.12.055

Wageman, R. (1997). Critical success factors for creating superb self-managing teams. *Organizational Dynamics, 26*, 49–60.

Wagoner, R., & Waldron, V. R. (1999). How supervisors convey routine bad news: Facework at UPS. *Southern Communication Journal, 64*(3), 193–210.

Waldron, V. R. (1991). Achieving communication goals in superior–subordinate relationships: The multi-functionality of upward maintenance tactics. *Communication Monographs, 58*(3), 289–306.

Waldron, V. R. (2000). Relational experiences and emotion at work. In S. Fineman (Ed.), *Emotions in organizations* (2nd ed., pp. 64–82). SAGE Publications.

Wang, K. L., Groth, M. (2014). Buffering the negative effects of employee surface acting: The moderating role of employee–customer relationship strength and personalized services. *Journal of Applied Psychology, 99*(2), 341–350. https://doi.org/10.1037/a0034428

Wanous, J. P. (1992). *Organizational entry: Recruitment, selection, orientation, and socialization of newcomers* (2nd ed.). Addison-Wesley.

Warner, L. S., & Grint, K. (2006). American Indian ways of leading and knowing. *Leadership, 2*(2), 225–244. https://doi.org/10.1177/1742715006062936

Weber, M. (1947). *The theory of social and economic organization.* Translated by A. M. Henderson & T. Parsons, T. Parsons (Ed.). Free Press.

Weick, K. E. (1976). Educational organizations as loosely coupled systems. *Administrative Science Quarterly, 21*, 1–19.

Weick, K. E. (1979). *The social psychology of organizing* (2nd ed). Addison-Wesley.

Weitz, J. (1956). Job expectancy and survival. *Journal of Applied Psychology, 40*, 245–247.

West, B. J., Patera, J. L, & Carsten, M. K. (2009). Team level positivity: Investigating positive psychological capacities and team level outcomes. *Journal of Organizational Behavior, 30*, 249–267. https://doi.org/10.1002/job.593

Westerman, C. Y. K., Currie-Mueller, J. L., Motto, J. S., & Curti, L. C. (2017). How supervisor relationships and protection rules affect employees' attempts to manage health information at work. *Health Communication, 32*(12), 1520–1528. https://dx.doi.org/10.1080/10410 236.2016.1234538

Wharton, A. (1999). The psychosocial consequences of emotional labor. *Annals of the American Academy of Political and Social Science, 561*, 158–176.

Whitener, E. M., Brodt, S. E., Korsgaard, M. A., & Werner, J. M. (1998). Managers as initiators of trust: An exchange relationship framework for understanding managerial trustworthy behavior. *Academy of Management Review, 23*(3), 513–530.

Whitman, M. V., & Mandeville, A. (2019). Blurring the lines: Exploring the work spouse phenomenon. *Journal of Management Inquiry.* https://doi.org/10.1177/1056492619882095

Wilkie, D. (2015, June 1). *Has the telecommuting bubble burst?* SHRM. http://www.shrm.org/publications/hrmagazine/editorialcontent/2015/0615/pages/0615-telecommuting.aspx

Williams, P., Ashill, N., Naumann, E. (2016). Toward a contingency theory of CRM adoption. *Journal of Strategic Marketing, 25*(5–6), 454–474. https://doi.org/10.1080/09652 54X.2016.1149211

Wilson, F. (2015). Romantic relationships at work. *International Journal of Management Reviews, 17,* 1–19. https://doi.org/10.1111/ijmr.12034

Wiseman, V., & Poitras, J. (2002). Mediation within a hierarchical structure: How can it be done successfully. *Conflict Resolution Quarterly, 20*(1), 51–65.

Wolfram, H., & Mohr, G. (2009). Transformational leadership, team goal fulfillment, and follower work satisfaction: The moderating effects of deep-level similarity in leadership dyads. *Journal of Leadership & Organizational Studies, 15*(3), 260–274.

Woodward, J. (1965). *Industrial organization: Theory and practice.* Oxford University Press.

Workplace Bullying Institute (2017). 2017 WBI U.S. workplace bullying survey. https://workplacebullying.org/download/2017-wbi/

Wright, B. M., & Barker, J. R. (2000). Assessing concertive control in the team environment. *Journal of Occupational and Organizational Psychology, 73,* 345–361.

Yang, F. X. (2020). Subordinate-supervisor friendship in cyberspace: A typological and comparative analysis of hotel employees. *Cornell Hospitality Quarterly, 61*(3), 271–286. https://doi.org/10.1177/1938965519894246

Yang, F.X., & Wong, I.A. (2020). How do cyberspace friendships transition to favorable workplace outcomes? The self-team joint influence. *International Journal of Hospitality Management, 85*(7), 102363. https://doi.org/10.1016/j.ijhm.2019.102363.

Yang, I., & Ming Li, L. (2018). 'It is not fair that you do not know we have problems': Perceptual distance and consequences of male leaders' conflict avoidance behaviours. *European Management Journal, 36*(1), 105–116. https://doi.org/10.1016/j.emj.2017.03.013

Yeginsu, C. (2018). If workers slack off, the wristband will know. (And Amazon has a patent for it.). *The New York Times.* https://www.nytimes.com/2018/02/01/technology/amazon-wristband-tracking-privacy.html

Ying, X., Li, H., Jiang, S., Peng, F., & Lin, Z. (2014). Group laziness: The effect of social loafing on group performance. *Social Behavior and Personality: An International Journal, 42,* 465–471.

Young, S. F., Richard, E. M., Moukarzel, R. G., Steelman, L. A., Gentry, W. A. (2017). How empathic concern helps leaders in providing negative feedback: A two-study examination. *Journal of Occupational and Organizational Psychology, 90*(4), 535–558. https://doi.org/10.1111/joop.12184

Yu, W., Chavez, R., Feng, M., Wong, C. Y., & Fynes, B. (2020). Green human resource management and environmental cooperation: An ability-motivation-opportunity and contingency perspective. *International Journal of Production Economics, 219,* 224–235. https://doi.org/10/1016/j.ijpe.2019.06.013

Zeng, C., & Chen, H. (2020). An exploration of the relationships between organizational dissent, employee burnout, and work-family balance: A cross-cultural comparison between China and Finland. *Communication Studies, 71*(4), 633–648. https://doi.org/10.1080/10510974.2020.1749864

Zerella, S., von Treuer, K., Albrecht, S. L., (2017). The influence of office layout features on employee perception of organizational culture. *Journal of Environmental Psychology, 54,* 1–10. http://dx.doi.org/10/1016/j.jenvp.2017.08.004

Zhu, Y., & Smith, S. A. (2019). Information and communication technology support for contextualization, polychronic values, and job satisfaction: Evidence from virtual teams. *International Journal of Business Communication.* https://doi.org/10.1177/2329488419832075

Zhuang, J., Bresnahan, M. J., Yan, X., Zhu, Y., Goldbort, J., & Bogdan-Lovis, E. (2019). Keep doing the good work: Impact of coworker and community support on continuation of breastfeeding. *Health Communication, 34*(11), 1270–1278. https://doi.org/10.1080/10410236.2018.1476802

Index